Cognitive
Orientation
and
Behavior

Hans and Shulamith Kreitler, an internationally
renowned professional husband-and-wife
team, collaborate on all their experimental and
theoretical research work and follow similar
academic careers. Currently professor and
associate professor of psychology, respectively,
at Tel Aviv University, where Hans Kreitler
founded and chaired the Department of
Psychology, the Kreitlers draw on European
and Israeli backgrounds of academic study.
Dr. Hans Kreitler studied with Karl and
Charlotte Bühler at the University of Vienna,
with Martin Buber and Bonaventura at the
Hebrew University in Jerusalem, receiving his
Ph.D. at Graz University. Dr. Shulamith
Kreitler was an undergraduate at Bar Ilan
University near Tel Aviv, and then a graduate
student of Richard Meili at Bern University,
where she received her Ph.D. summa cum
laude.

Recently, the Kreitlers completed a one-year
visiting professorship at Harvard University,
and earlier they spent a year doing research
and teaching at the Educational Testing
Service (Princeton), at Princeton University,
and at Yale University. They have published
numerous articles as well as four books, the
most recent of which is *Psychology of the Arts*.

COGNITIVE ORIENTATION AND BEHAVIOR

Hans Kreitler
Shulamith Kreitler

Tel Aviv University

SPRINGER PUBLISHING COMPANY
NEW YORK

To Ron, who grew together with this book

Springer Publishing Company, Inc.
200 Park Avenue South
New York, N.Y. 10003

76 77 78 79 80 / 10 9 8 7 6 5 4 3 2 1

Designed by Patrick Vitacco

Library of Congress Cataloging in Publication Data
Kreitler, Hans.

Cognitive orientation and behavior.

Bibliography: p.
Includes index.
1. Cognition.   2. Orientation (Psychology)   3. Psy-
chology.   I. Kreitler, Shulamith, joint author.
II. Title [DNLM: 1. Behavior.   2. Cognition.
3. Psychological theory. BF121 K915c]
BF311.K696   153.4   76-20597
ISBN 0-8261-2050-4

Printed in the United States of America

PREFACE

The term "cognitive orientation" (CO) designates a new theory of human molar behavior presented in this book. The core of this theory is the already well-substantiated hypothesis that the cognitive system, and in particular the orientative aspect of cognitive contents as well as their various forms of interplay, determine the direction of human molar behavior. Therefore the theory embedding this hypothesis must not merely give a detailed account of the processes occurring between stimulating input and behavioral output, but also has to demonstrate that information about crucial orientative contents yields reliable prediction of behavior, and that experimentally induced change of orientative contents induces a change of behavior in the expected direction. Moreover, in order to qualify as a theory (as distinct from a model), cognitive orientation has to present some reasonable hypotheses about the interaction of cognitive and noncognitive processes.

These are, to say the least, formidable requirements. The attempt to meet them even to a modest degree is difficult for any psychological theory, but in particular for a cognitive theory of behavior. Despite the recent renaissance and flourishing of cognitive psychology, most psychologists accept a cognitive approach, if at all, as useful only for the study of perception, attention, memory, and thinking; they are not yet inclined to consider the possibility that cognitive processes and their specific contents could be a major determinant of human molar behavior. Even we, the authors, had to await the results of many empirical studies and the development of a theoretical framework before being fully convinced that cognitive content is really the key issue in explaining, predicting, and changing the direction of human molar behavior.

Indeed, 16 years ago, when we made our first faltering steps toward a cognitive interpretation of some schizophrenic symptoms, we hardly expected that this line of research would eventually lead us to regard sense data, drives, and emotions merely as inputs to the cognitive system, which, owing to its own laws, determines what action(s) should be undertaken with regard to these inputs. In fact, we were truly puzzled by our own observations that the content of certain beliefs held by schizophrenics seemed to predispose some of their pathological behaviors. Therefore, when first publishing these findings, we devoted to their presentation only about 7 minutes of a 15-minute lecture at the International Congress of Psychology in Bonn, 1960. What prevented us from recognizing the significance of our data was the traditional contention that innate reflexes, conditioned responses, drives, emotions, social stresses, acquired inhibitions, and other behavioral habits are the sole determinants of human behavior, whereas cognition can only be considered as their derivative, as a secondary process, merely reflecting some of the underlying psychodynamic processes. Of course, we also had some arguments in favor of the assumption that cognition has an impact upon behavior, but we knew no answer to the decisive question: How can cognition be attributed even a minimal degree of functional independence without thereby ignoring or even renouncing all that is known about the determining power of internal stimulation, reflexes, conditioning, and Freud's primary process? Thus we decided, partly relieved and partly regretful, to put our data aside and to do some other work.

A year later, however, at a mental health convention in Paris, East European psychologists, who usually avoided conversations with Israeli colleagues, went out of their way to tell us how impressed they were by these very findings, which we ourselves found so utterly incongruent with the major theories of human behavior and our own physio-psychological reasoning. They obstinately refrained from telling us in a straightforward manner why our findings aroused their interest but indicated instead that their own research work centered on Pavlov's orienting reflex and its theoretical implications. This was telling enough. Remembering that Sokolov and others showed the orienting reflex to be the first reaction to every new or significant stimulus, we were struck by the sudden insight that the orienting reflex not only leads to the cognitive act of orienting but is itself elicited by the cognitive act of recognizing a stimulus as being new or significant. Hence there is no gap between the "higher" mental processes of cognition and the "lower" physiological processes like the orienting reflex and Sokolov's defensive responses, since the former are involved in the elicitation of the latter. While trying to verbalize this sudden eruption of understanding we recalled that the very Karl Buehler who coined for this kind of insight the phrase "Aha Erlebnis" regarded "oriented reference movements" as the most important characteristic of living organisms and as the phylogenetic and ontogenetic cradle of human knowledge and thinking. And Buehler was only one of the many philosophers and psychologists who upheld this ancient belief, notwithstanding the lack of an empirically supported theory explaining coherently how human behavior is guided by cognition.

When discussing all this in a sidewalk coffee house near the Sorbonne we did not know whether our intuitive insight about the basic function of cognition would withstand the test of a more rigorous analysis of the orienting reflex. But we thought it worthwhile to return to our discarded data, deciding to study the impact of cognition on normal and abnormal behavior. In doing so we found our interpretation of the orienting reflex well in line with all the available physiological data. Step by step we recognized the progressively unfolding stages of orientative input elaboration, culminating in the formation of a belief matrix that, by virtue of its cognitive content, fulfills a guiding function in regard to output behavior. Yet the four content variables we found to be predisposing human molar behavior did not yield reliable behavior predictions unless they were considered as a link in the chain of behavior evocation. Therefore we had to study the whole chain, including intent formation and programming of output behavior. Moreover, proper treatment of content variables required a method for evaluating their meaning. However, the already available methods in psychology and psycholinguistics seemed to us insufficiently developed. Therefore we also had to venture into the experimental study of meaning. Eventually meaning turned into a central concept in our theory of cognitive orientation, while its evaluation proved to be necessary for designing successful experiments in behavior prediction and modification.

Thus, the theory developed and matured rather slowly in the characteristic hothouse of field work, laboratory studies, lectures in Tel Aviv University and several American universities, and discussions with colleagues, graduate students, and undergraduates. The major force in its development was the constant interplay between theory and experiments, the unremitting effort to bring the two into accord, that is, to incorporate into the theory the findings of the latest experiment and to design the next experiment in accordance with the latest theoretical insights and formulations.

All in all, and despite its diversity, the theory of cognitive orientation is now coherent enough to be summarized in one flow chart (Fig. 6.2). Yet adequate understanding of this flow chart requires not only detailed information about the different concepts and processes outlined therein, but also familiarity with our concept of meaning and its relation to orientation on the reflex level and above. Indeed, without some understanding of meaning the concept of cognition remains vague; likewise, without understanding the cognitive implications of the orienting reflex the whole field of cognition seems precariously unrelated to other domains of psychophysiological inquiry and suspended uncomfortably in mid-air. Therefore we discuss meaning first (Chapter 2); then the orienting response together with our hypotheses with regard to primary input elaboration of simple responses (Chapter 3); later the nature and content of beliefs, which are the major units of cognitive content on the molar level (Chapter 4); and only afterwards (Chapters 5 and 6) the chain and processes involved in evocation and guidance of human molar behavior. This slow progression to the dynamic core of the CO theory may be tedious, but it is indispensable for adequate comprehension. It derives from the necessity of constructing the major building blocks used in the theory while simultaneously constructing the theory itself. In other words, it reflects the fact that we were paving the road on which we walked while we were walking on it. Indeed, the speed of our progression justifies the term "walking" rather than riding or driving.

Of course, not every step in this progression is of equal importance. Some sections in Part One of this book can be skipped without thereby losing track of the major ideas. Readers who are not particularly interested in the problem of meaning may skip the section "Conventional Approaches to Meaning" in Chapter 2; readers who are willing to accept our interpretation of the orienting response without delving into the supporting evidence may skip the section "Nature of the Orienting Reflex" in Chapter 3; and those who are unwilling to follow the evidence supporting our distinction between the program scheme and the operational program may skip the section "Theories of Programming and Guidance of Action" in Chapter 6.

Part Two of this book (Chapters 7–14) presents experimental studies of two types. The first type includes studies of behavior prediction and behavior change (Chapters 7–10) in many different domains, demonstrating the broad applicability of the CO theory. The second type includes studies intended to elucidate and explore some of the most basic parts of the CO theory (e.g., Chapters 11 and 13) as well as some of its implications, e.g., for the problem of the attitude-behavior gap (Chapter 12), and further developments, e.g., in the domain of abnormal behavior (Chapter 10). The presentation of so many studies is designed not only to lend massive support to the theory and to show how to work with it (for the latter see in particular Chapter 7, the section "Common Background Characteristics" and Chapter 13), but also to initiate a new approach to different domains of human activity and their psychological analysis. The chapters of Part Two are independent of each other and therefore can be selected by the reader according to interest. In particular, it should be noted that the nine studies reported in Chapters 7 and 8 are similar in design as well as in major methodological features (see Chapter 7, "Common Background Characteristics") and may be read or skipped in any order. Wherever necessary, cross-references to other chapters are given. However, reading chapters of Part Two before having read Part One is likely to lead to unfortunate misunderstandings.

It goes without saying that many of the studies presented here are the result of collaboration with associates and students, as will be indicated in footnotes at the appropriate places (see also "Collaborators in the Experimental Studies"). Yet in all cases we scrutinized data and statistical analysis and often used different statistical methods for recalculating. Therefore we take full responsibility for the soundness of the data and their elaboration as well as for design, even in regard to those studies carried out as theses under our supervision.

A preface provides the authors with the most pleasant opportunity of thanking those who have helped them. First and foremost among these was our late friend Bernhard Springer. He was so enthusiastic about our conception of orientation as a basic striving of human beings that he contracted this book for Springer Publishing Company well before the first word was written. In doing so he encouraged us to more theoretical and empirical work and to an unusual but, as we hope, adequate form of its presentation. We thus express our belated thanks. Many thanks are also due to Bernhard's wife and successor Professor Ursula Springer, first of all for her readiness to honor the contract and accept the manuscript without any questions asked (although we delivered it nearly five years after the agreed deadline), but also for her skillful efforts in supervising its publication. Our special gratitude is due to Mrs. Luba Elblinger, M.D., who once again volunteered to prepare the indexes for our book. We also want to thank Mr. Shimon Abramovici, Mrs. Sophie Oron-Grossman, and Mr. Dan Zakay for their devoted help in various studies.

Last but not least, we would like in particular to thank Professor Edward Zigler of Yale University, whose encouragement, trust, and help were of such great value to us during various stages of our work.

It is by now a well-established tradition to add to the list of acknowledgments the name of at least one foundation that supported the work presented. At this point we are in real trouble: the foundation we have to thank for its generous support has no officially registered name, in fact no name at all. It does not require writing up long proposals, and its grants have no provision for overhead payments to universities. Its ability to help is limited but never lacking. For those who want to obtain its support we can identify it as the Foundation of Enthusiastic Volunteers. It automatically starts to operate whenever a researcher suggests to his co-workers and students a new and promising idea, but it rapidly suspends its operation when the adventure of formulating an important question and searching for its most revealing answers degenerates into doing what can be done without the daily risk of failure. Therefore we hope that this foundation will go on supporting all those who use the theory and methods of cognitive orientation for widening the horizons of psychological knowledge.

CONTENTS

ILLUSTRATIONS

COLLABORATORS IN THE EXPERIMENTAL STUDIES

Mr. David Azikri

Mrs. Tirza Boaz

Mr. Nehemya Geva

Mrs. Talma Lobel

Mrs. Miriam Nehari

Mr. Anton Shahar

Miss Rivka Zemet

Mrs. Irit Zeltzer

Professor Edward Zigler

PART ONE

The Theory

The Cognitive Revolution

THE REVOLUTIONARY COMEBACK OF COGNITION

For about thirty years cognition was condescendingly identified with philosophically inclined armchair psychology and therefore ignored or avoided by most psychologists. Now, twenty-five years after its rediscovery as a legitimate and promising subject matter for psychological research, the number of studies in this domain has grown so enormously that it seems justified to speak of a cognitive revolution. Detailed description and explanation of why and how this revolution took place must be left to future historians of psychology. Yet it is already evident that after the heroic period of grandiose theory building, earmarked by Hull's behavioristic model and Freud's psychoanalytic system, the experimental search for data confirming these theories and their almost universal claims led to growing dissatisfaction with theories and schools in general and with these theories or schools in particular. Moreover, the limitations of the conception of an organism controlled solely by its drives or the environment became so obvious that a new concept for explaining form and direction of behavior had to be looked for.

It is remarkable that the cognitive revolution has occurred in the most diverse fields of psychology at almost the same time. Behavioristic psychologists, who for years have constructed learning theories on the skeleton of the S-R model, stumbled on latent learning or exploratory behavior; more often than not, while walking the tightrope of mediating processes, they have landed in the domain of cognition. The study of defense mechanisms has led many psychoanalysts from an exclusive preoccupation with primary processes to ego-psychology and the processes of cognitive control. Experimental psychologists dealing with perception were compelled by the accumulated evidence to concede that the fate of an

3

input is determined largely by central control and feedback processes (Pribram, 1971, chap. 5) and that "perception cannot be identified with an activity of the sensory cortex" (Teuber, quoted by Hebb, 1968, p. 468). The orienting reflex has turned the special attention of reflexologists toward the centrally monitored meaning assigned to a stimulus, while biochemically biased researchers had to concentrate on attitudes, goals, and values in order to understand better the well-known fact that the effect of a drug does not depend solely on its chemical properties. The discovery of the genetic code has persuaded physiologists and psychologists that processes such as communication of information and elaboration of information may help to characterize better and elucidate phenomena hitherto explained as automatisms. Last, but not least, the availability of the computer has not only stimulated the construction of models about information-processing organisms but has also made possible the testing of hypotheses about cognitive processes that prior to computer simulation were hardly accessible even to introspection.

In the history of science there are few parallels to the concentric development that zeroed in on the study of cognitive processes, and it would be erroneous to view this development as the outcome of the work of any single investigator or school. Take, for example, the studies of Piaget, which in recent years have triggered a flood of replications and modifications. Most of these studies were published and available at least thirty years ago. Yet only the contemporary insight that cognitive processes can and should be investigated has pushed Piaget's work into the focus of developmental theorizing and experimentation. The same goes for the work of those social psychologists who more than a generation ago concentrated on the study of attitudes. Their findings and failures could be newly evaluated only after it became clear that the understanding of interpersonal relations no less than of personality functioning and of physiological processes depended on principles of communication and information, and even on specific mental contents.

MODELS IN COGNITIVE PSYCHOLOGY

The term "cognitive" is being used so widely that one might wonder whether there is anything in psychology that is not cognitive. The traditional physiologically oriented explanations of psychological phemomena have been replaced almost everywhere by psychologically oriented explanations of physical phenomena. The conception of a reflex-directed psyche has been pushed aside in favor of a cognitively functioning body. "The popular current word is an 'information-processing point of view' rather than a stimulus-response conditioning viewpoint" (Bower, 1967a,

p. 112). Nonetheless, the greatest bulk of the work in the cognitive domain has remained piecemeal. The most characteristic property of this domain is the production of a great many specific models lacking integration into a broader theoretical framework. Even if their progenitors have preferred to baptize them as theories, most cognitive models of behavior refer to partial systems. Examples of such models would include the various theories of balance and cognitive dissonance (Abelson et al., 1968), models of communication and attitude change (Hovland, Janis, & Kelley, 1953; Osgood & Tannenbaum, 1955), of risk taking (Kogan & Wallach, 1964) and decision making (Kyburg & Smokler, 1964; Luce & Raiffa, 1957), of cognitive control (Gardner, Holzman, Klein, Linton, & Spence, 1959; Klein, 1970), cognitive structure (Crockett, 1965; Schroder, Driver, & Streufert, 1967), cognitive functioning (Newell & Simon, 1972; Norman, 1970; Reitman, 1965), and many others (e.g., Harvey, 1963; Kelly, 1955; Lazarus, 1966; Rotter, Chance, & Phares, 1972). All these are based on well-established empirical findings and have been confirmed to varying degrees in the prediction of specific behaviors. As a matter of fact, there is hardly a domain of human behavior for whose better understanding and prediction cognitive models have not been set up. This fact certainly demonstrates the fundamental utility of cognitive models of behavior, at least relative to other variables common in psychology. But it does not imply that the psychologist is able to predict everyday behavior with any degree of certainty. The major difficulty consists in the narrowness of these models. Essentially most of them apply only to those rare situations in everyday human behavior which are dominated by a single variable.

A naive observer might suggest that the complexity of human situations requires the simultaneous application of a number of different models, each of which refers to different variables. Yet there can be little doubt that the attempt to combine various models based on an array of divergent theoretical assumptions is doomed to failure. Let us illustrate by means of a concrete example. A university professor has made the relatively uncommon decision to devote half a year of his sabbatical to reviewing his somewhat outdated stock of knowledge through intensive reading. Yet, shortly before his vacation is to start, he gets an unexpected invitation from a most prestigious university to give a series of lectures during his vacation. Would he devote his sabbatical to learning or to teaching? In order to predict, or even to explain a posteriori the professor's choice, one should apply models relevant for variables of risk taking, cognitive dissonance, achievement motivation, scanning and evaluation of information, problem solving, and motivated trains of thought —to mention only a few.

The problems attendant upon such a procedure are enormous. To begin with, there are no theoretically formulated or empirically tested guidelines for spotting the variables relevant for the prediction of behavior. Therefore there is no way to establish whether we have not overlooked the major variables in the situation. Again, no studies exist of the manner in which different tests affect each other and distort one another's results. Finally, the main instrument for integrating the different findings is missing. How are we to combine the results derived from one model with those derived from another? What rule or mechanism or set-up regulates this combination? Indeed, what Janet T. Spence (1967, pp. vii–viii) wrote about theories of learning is no less true of theories in cognition during the last decade—"a period of intensive data collection and theoretically, of the development of 'miniature systems' based on relatively limited types of experimental phenomena." In both cases it has become all too evident that there is no passage from the mini-model to the normal-sized model adequate for explaining behavior.

In contrast, only a few models exist designed to be applicable to a wide range of behaviors and levels of action. Among these the best known is the theory developed by Miller, Galanter, and Pribram (1960). However, despite the fact that this theory of plans is regarded as an important contribution to psychological research, fifteen years after its publication no empirical studies demonstrate how the model may be used in predicting or manipulating behavior. As a matter of fact, no serious use has been made even of the theory's interpretative potential.

One can only conclude that the theory itself is to blame for this state of affairs. Its originators have indeed shown very persuasively that the operation of feedback mechanisms on all levels of behavior and a hierarchy of plans that direct action are necessary assumptions for explaining regular and regulated behavioral flow. Yet they have left unanswered most of those questions which are crucial for the theory's application. For example, they have not explained how the TOTE (Test-Operation-Test-Exit) unit, which represents the feedback principle, operates; how the "image," which in the first test stage is matched against the newly formed representation, is retrieved; how the results of the test trigger those processes of which the "operation" consists; what the nature of the "operation" is on different levels; or how that kind of "congruity" which makes "exit" possible is attained. Moreover, the theory does not dwell at all on the functional relation between the "images," which represent the sum total of knowledge in the individual's possession, and the set of instructions whose hierarchy constitutes the plan that controls behavior. Again, questions about the formation of new plans or the integration of existing plans are answered through a regressus ad infinitum.

Miller et al. suggest that there exist plans for the formation of plans, and also, apparently, plans for the plans for formation of plans, etc. But the most crucial weakness is the fact that no directions about the use of the model in a concrete situation, say, in the framework of an experiment, are given. Even if a complete repertory of the plans of an individual or a group were available, it would not be possible to predict which plan has the best chance to attain the state of performance in a given situation.

Yet all these criticisms do not detract from the essential contribution of this theory to the development of a cognitive model of human behavior. Miller et al. have shown that a theory of plans may explain how a behavioral intention is translated into manifest action. Also, they have demonstrated that interaction between cognitive components and other components is best described in terms of information-processing models. Nonetheless, it is evident that the theory of plans neither can nor was intended to represent a general model of human behavior.

Thus one major problem of cognitive psychology is that there exist, on the one hand, many miniature models which make possible predictions about the direction or intensity of specific forms of behavior but do so only within a very narrowly circumscribed domain, while on the other hand there are more general theories that apply to all or most forms of behavior but that have not been subjected to experimental confirmation and are overburdened with too many unspecified generalities to make such application and testing possible.

IMPLIED FUNCTION OF COGNITION

Another crucial problem of cognitive psychology is the role of cognitive processes. Thanks to the powerful tradition of organismic theories, the fashionable courting of observable behaviors coupled with hard-core explanations, and a certain modicum of success in physiological research, most psychologists have been led to believe that the physiological properties of the organism are the basic and ultimate determinants of behavior, at least of molecular behavior. The most powerful tools for the analysis of behavior, which have turned into the basic building blocks of psychological theories, include the following concepts: reflexes and their transposition into conditioned responses through classical conditioning; motor action and changes in its relative frequency through operant or instrumental conditioning; and drives—their primary manifestation and innate vicissitudes in the sense of Freud, their reduction in the sense of Hull, and the push they exert toward a goal in the sense of Lewin or Tolman. To erect on these fundaments a cognitive structure suitable to the analysis and manipulation of molar behavior requires either a deus-ex-machina solution to the bothersome psychophysical problem or a serious, possibly original, answer to the traditional questions: What is the root of cognitive processes? Where do they come from? How have they originated?

In order to circumvent this uncomfortable problem, psychologists at large have hit upon the solution of placing cognition in a secondary role, assigning to it only mediating functions, and treating it theoretically as a manifestation of behavior but not as its determinant. It is remarkable that this solution is equally supported by trends as divergent as psychoanalysis and behaviorism. In practice, however—that is, in their experiments, or psychotherapeutic work—most psychologists use cognitive manifestations as independent variables, and attribute to them the behavioral changes observed in the dependent variables. They do so without explicitly declaring what the function of cognition is. In this way, the use of an implicit assumption regarding the function of cognition prevents some cognitive psychologists from identifying their dilemma, others from adequately analyzing their data, and most of them from recognizing the content, nature, and implications of this well-hidden assumption. If made explicit, this assumption could serve as the common denominator of contemporary cognitive research. The implied assumption is that *cognitive contents and processes steer molar behavior.*

A few examples out of the great many available may serve to illustrate our claim. A case in point is the theory of cognitive dissonance and its ramifications. It is remarkable that the proponents of this theory have never postulated that cognitive contents shape behavior. Rather, they adhere to some variant of the assumption that a need for consistency or for the reduction of dissonance is a derivative or manifestation of the common homeostatic tendency (Abelson et al., 1968, sec. III, A. & C.). More concretely, they usually assume that their experimental instructions generate cognitive dissonance, which, due to the individual's homeostatic striving toward consistency, functions as a motive that influences output behavior like other homeostatic motives or, at least, as an aversive state to be avoided. The striving for consistency as such is conceived as a cognitive process, although its underlying determinant is the purely physiological tendency toward homeostasis. Yet the typical experiments in this domain do not indicate any concern with physiological processes. On the contrary, their properly controlled independent variables are almost invariably expectancies, judgments, and evaluations of the subjects, generated or manipulated through direct statements or indirect hints made by the experimenter. Variables such as justification for commitment (Brehm & Cohen, 1962), perceived freedom of choice

(Brehm, 1966), or anticipated severity of future deprivation (Zimbardo, 1969) fit very well the usual conception of cognitive elements or processes. Indeed, how else can such variables be characterized? One can hardly think of a more fitting title than "cognitive" to identify them. Thus, regardless of theoretical denials and protestations to the contrary, the consistency experiments themselves clearly demonstrate how various cognitive inputs and elements affect behavioral outputs.

Our second example concerns the theory of achievement motivation as developed by McClelland (McClelland, Atkinson, Clark, & Lowell, 1953), Atkinson and Feather (1966), and their followers (Birney, Burdick, & Teevan, 1969; Heckhausen, 1967; Weiner, 1970). This theory is not in general regarded as belonging to cognitive psychology. The achievement motive itself is defined by McClelland et al. (1953, p. 28) as a change in the affective situation elicited by certain stimuli, and by Atkinson (1964, p. 214) as an affective disposition, the "capacity to experience pride in accomplishment." However, many experiments have shown that the impact of this motive on behavior depends on the strength of the expectancy that a specific instrumental action will lead to the goal, on the incentive value of the goal (Atkinson, 1964), or on the anticipation of future goals (Raynor, 1970). These expectancies and evaluations are purely cognitive variables. Indeed, it seems that a greater part of variance in performance depends on these cognitive factors than on the absolute strength of the motive. Moreover, the essentially cognitive character of the achievement motive itself becomes evident in the rationale underlying its method of measurement. A response is regarded as reflecting the achievement motive if it contains some reference to competition with a standard of excellence (McClelland et al., 1953, chap. 4). Here again we find an inconsistency between the investigators' declared theory, which is noncognitive, and their experimental practice, which reveals consideration of the pervasive role of cognitive elements.

Similar developments have taken place in other research domains, like that of risk taking or decision making. Here too cognitive processes are often used in the role of independent variables without being presented or labeled as cognitive. Yet instead of elaborating these cases we shall bring a third example to illustrate a different aspect of the puzzling fate of cognition in psychology.

Many psychologists who do not assume explicitly that cognitive contents influence behavior stick with amazing tenacity to experimental paradigms based on this implicit assumption. This applies to the many investigators who uphold the concept of attitude and study the structure, contents, and effects of attitudes notwithstanding the repeated proofs that attitudes as commonly conceived and measured were shown in most studies (e.g., Wicker, 1969) to be unrelated to behavior. Correspondingly, changes in attitudes were found to be unrelated to changes in behavior (Festinger, 1964; Fothergill, 1968). Is it not surprising that the concept of attitude has neither been abandoned nor drastically changed in view of all this evidence? This paradoxical situation can be interpreted as belying the secret belief many investigators probably find· hard either to renounce or to face: that cognition determines behavior. Secret beliefs, right or wrong, are a poor guide for the scientist. In Chapters 4 and 12 we will show how an explicitly cognitive theory may solve the puzzle of the low or absent correlations between attitudes and behavior.

These three examples—of dissonance theory, achievement theory, and attitude research—amply demonstrate that psychologists tend to avoid direct confrontation with the hidden assumption about the role of cognition that their work implies. Indeed, there are some good reasons for this. To treat cognitive processes and elements as indicators for those forces which presumably shape behavior does not yet contradict the leading theories of personality, motivation, and behavior. But to postulate that cognition has the steering qualities of a motive, and may function even as the sum-total of all motives, engenders serious theoretical problems. First and foremost it would require a clarification of the relationship between cognitive processes, on the one hand, and drives, emotions, reflexes, and conditioned responses, on the other hand, the latter having traditionally been conceived as diametrically opposed to the "higher" processes. The complexity of these relations is more often than not even exaggerated, since it is disregarded that the modern concept of the organism as a unitary system in no way implies that cognition plays the same role for and within each of the subsystems of molar and submolar behavior. Yet if we were to assign to cognition a primary directive function with regard to behavior there would be no way to circumvent the necessity of formulating hypotheses about the onset of cognitive processes, about the stage in which they first appear, about their dynamic functions on the different levels of behavior, and about the interactions between them and other subsystems in the organism. It hardly needs mentioning that a basic precondition for such a clarification would be a workable definition of cognition.

To recapitulate, the problem does not reside in acknowledging the importance of cognitive processes per se. As we have mentioned, since the early sixties it has become increasingly fashionable to set cognition into the very limelight of psychological practice. The flood of introductory texts dealing with cognition unleashed in the early seventies is but a humble symptom of this fashion. The problem resides rather in acknowledging the primary function of cognition in steering behavior. Indeed, there have been tentative attempts in this direction too, the most notable of which are Kelly's (1955) theory and more recently some new developments within the context of attribution theory (Weiner, 1972). Yet while Kelly was outspoken enough in this matter his theory was too general; in contrast, attribution theory contains some highly specific formulations but it is not, or has not yet become, sufficiently outspoken with regard to the role of cognition.

EXPLICATION OF THE IMPLIED

Our theory of cognitive orientation and the experiments supporting it, which will be presented in this book, promise to overcome the above discussed dilemmas and shortcomings of cognitive approaches to the analysis and prediction of human behavior. However, the theory was not explicitly developed to serve this purpose. Rather it resulted from a synthesis of three different but interrelated lines of research. One was the attempt to study the relation of specific behaviors and meaning-related beliefs. Starting with a still unstructured inquiry into the belief matrix of schizophrenics with regard to their pathological behaviors, we later explored the relations between the belief matrices and relevant behaviors in the case of achievement, choice of defense mechanisms, tolerance of pain, intolerance of ambiguity, curiosity, coming late, abstaining from smoking, etc. (see the studies in Part II, especially Chapters 7–11), applying step by step the experimental and theoretical knowledge acquired in course of the last most recently completed study (as well as insights derived from the other two concomitantly pursued lines of research). Our second research endeavor was devoted to the systematization and quantification of "meaning," in order to make possible comparing the meaning of a particular behavior with the meaning of a particular belief or set of beliefs (Chapter 2). Our third line of research was mainly but not exclusively theoretical. It consisted in studying from a cognitive point of view the elicitation and sequence of innate responses above the level of spinal reflexes, orienting responses, and conditioned responses (Chapter 3), the function of these responses in the evocation of molar behavior, as well as the sequence of events between the evocation of molar behavior and actual performance (Chapters 4–6), including the structure and function of important elements in this sequence (Chapter 13).

The theory resulting from these research enterprises does not focus on the hitherto traditional subject matters of cognitive psychology—as attention, perception, organization of memory, retrieval strategies, the formal operations of thinking, and so on—but outlines the role of cognition in regard to behavior. The theory deals in particular with the contribution of cognitive contents to the controlling and steering of molar behavior. Yet there are enough indications to show that it may be useful also for understanding cognitive functioning as such. All in all the theory sets a conceptual framework for the analysis of the sequence of cognitive processes and elements intervening between input and output and provides methods for behavior prediction and, to a certain extent, for behavior change.

The core of our theory is the concept of *cognitive orientation*. We use this term in three different veins. First, it characterizes the basic striving of humans to attain, preserve, and widen external and internal orientation on a cognitive level. Second, it designates a particular matrix of beliefs that predisposes the formation of specific behavioral intents. Third, it is the name of our theory and as such includes much more than is indicated by its surface meaning.

It goes without saying that a theory with such a wide scope cannot be other than fairly complex. Nonetheless it could be summed up in one or two paragraphs designed to function as a sort of preview of the first part of this book. Indeed, we have already done this several times. However, as we thus discovered, any gain in orientation on the part of the reader is heavily outweighed by unfortunate misunderstandings, partly due to the impossibility of explaining in the course of a short summary why and how we had to redefine such hitherto vague concepts as meaning, cognition, and orientation. Yet most misunderstandings result from biases rooted in traditional approaches to psychology that are difficult to change without the weight of theory and data. Therefore we prefer another method of previewing, which, on the one hand, is less revealing than a summary and hence less likely to arouse erroneous preconceptions, but, on the other hand, places the authors under a greater obligation since it entails an implied promise. The method consists in presenting two hypotheses, which the theory and experiments discussed in this book are expected to confirm, to outline the context in which they make sense, and to indicate their contribution to the understanding of structures and processes steering molar behavior.

The two hypotheses are:

1. Human behavior above the level of spinal reflexes is controlled and directed by cognitive orientation, its contents and/or processes.

2. Knowledge about specific cognitive orientations, their content, strength, and mode of functioning, makes possible predicting the ensuing molar behavior—its form, direction, and intensity—given sufficient information about the stimulus situation (input), about the available

programs for output behavior, as well as about innate capacity and acquired skills required for performance of the program. As a corollary to this hypothesis it is expected that induced changes of cognitive orientation result in predictable changes of behavior.

As we have already mentioned, and as the two hypotheses make evident, the theory of cognitive orientation focuses on the hitherto neglected relation of cognitive-contents variables to behavior. It deals with cognitive processes insofar as they play a direct or indirect role in steering behavior, but does not in any way restrict the range of behaviors for which it is relevant.

The cognitive revolution succeeded in convincing most psychologists that cognitive processes are a legitimate, possible, and worthwhile subject matter for systematic research. As a further step, the theory of cognitive orientation attempts to convince psychologists that cognition, if duly defined and understood, is decisively involved in all kinds of human behavior and thus constitutes the core domain of psychological inquiry. Trying this step does not mean revolutionizing the revolution, since even its success would only constitute the fulfillment of a promise implicitly given by all kinds and branches of cognitive psychology.

Cognition, Information, and Meaning

DEFINITIONS OF COGNITION

Although many psychologists deal with cognition and even more use the term, only a few have bothered to define it. Does this mean that the term is unambiguous and stands in little need of clarification? The handful of available definitions testifies to the contrary. In the opening pages of a book remarkable for its contributions to the elucidation of cognitive functioning, Neisser (1967, p. 4) presents a definition that is typical of many others: "The term 'cognitive' refers to all the processes by which the sensory input is transferred, reduced, elaborated, stored, recovered and used." The limitations of this definition are immediately obvious. Since it is commonly held that physiological mechanisms must be involved in such processes as the reduction, elaboration, retrieval, transfer, and storage of input, and particularly in the latter two processes, it follows that many physiological processes should be regarded as cognitive. Again, Neisser's definition implies that the term "cognitive" applies equally well to Tolman's "cognitive map" and to Hull's drive reduction, oscillations, and other intervening variables that play a part in transforming the sensory input into an output.

A somewhat more precise definition was suggested by Kagan and Kogan (1970, p. 1275): "The term 'cognitive' has typically referred to mental activities in the sense of both product and process. . . . Cognitive process is a superordinate term, subsuming the more familiar titles of imagery, perception, free association, thought, mediation, proliferation of hypotheses, reasoning, reflection, and problem solving. All verbal behavior must be a product of cognitive processes, as are dreams and intelligence test performances. But, skeletal muscle movement or visceral reactions are not necessarily linked to cognition." The main advantage of this definition is its unassuming character. The loose formulation indicates that the listed processes should be regarded merely as examples of a common classification. One gets the impression that the definition was designed to be neither precise nor comprehensive. For instance, the question of whether perception as a cognitive process includes "sensing" (Hebb, 1969) as one of its stages is already too definite to be answered by means of this definition.

Of course, the emphasized unclarity of the definition may reflect the implicit assumption that setting limits prematurely might be detrimental to the future development of cognitive psychology. This may be so. Yet not every definition need be limiting; indeed, the most productive ones create a domain and contribute to its structuralization. Such a definition of cognition could be based, for example, on outlining a necessary although not sufficient criterion of cognitive processes reflecting a property common to these processes or a functional unit characteristic of them. To the best of our knowledge, a definition of this kind has not yet been suggested within the framework of cognitive psychology. The failure to do so reflects the difficult problems facing cognitive psychology, some of which have been mentioned in Chapter 1. But the absence of such a definition makes itself felt in the most varied respects—in the old-fashioned behavioristic treatment of linguistic phenomena no less than in the exclusion of many phenomena from the domain of cognition.

INFORMATION THEORY AND COGNITION

It might seem that information theory constitutes a natural candidate for providing the tools necessary for defining cognition. Indeed, the extensive use of concepts and ideas borrowed from information theory and system analysis has been one of the outstanding features of the cognitive revolution from its very beginning. As a matter of fact, one of its main triggers may well have been the opportunity which information theory presumably offered to perform computer simulation of the cognitive "black box" processes and to subject its contents to quantification by using information theory formulae. To many it seemed that information theory was a ready-made tool for the description and analysis of behavior patterns (Frick, 1959). Thus psychologists have found it convenient to avoid the ambiguity and possible circularity of the term "stimulus" by using instead "input." Likewise, they have replaced "reaction" with "output," thus circumventing the behavioristic constraints placed on "reaction" or "response." In fact, concepts like feedback, loop, format, channel capacity, and noise are as common in cognitive psychology as is the recent habit to present cognitive models in the form of flow charts, even when no simulation is intended.

Scanning definitions of cognition reveals that many of the processes making up the very common omnibus definitions are rooted in information theory. Again, analyzing much of the actual work done by cognitive psychologists shows that the bulk of it is devoted to the nature and vicissitudes of information. If so, we may well ask whether it would not be useful and justified to define cognition as the information processing system in the organism.

We have mentioned arguments in favor of this definition. There are much heavier arguments against it. Some derive from the nature of information theory per se, some from its limitations when applied to psychology, and some from its inadequacy for the domain of cognition.

Defining cognition as an information processing system would imply acceptance of the concept "information" as it is defined and measured in the framework of information theory. The oft-quoted definition is based on identifying information as "that which removes or reduces uncertainty" (Attneave, 1959, p. 1), and on equating the uncertainty of an event with the logarithm of the number of possible alternatives or outcomes, each weighted with the probability of its occurrence.

As a matter of fact, even outside the special domain of communication engineering, many situations allow for a univocal determination of existing or perceived alternatives and of their objective, sometimes also subjective, probabilities. This is particularly true of laboratory settings and game situations. In these contexts information concepts have been applied with success. However, the specification of alternatives and their probabilities is only one of the many facets of cognitive functioning. Yet, probably because it lent itself easily to measurement, this facet became so prominent in cognitive psychology that psychologists tended to overlook the importance of other facets.

An impressive example of the attempt to set up information as a central concept in psychology is the hypothesis that anxiety, as a basic human state, is produced by uncertainty and hence can be reduced by excluding alternatives (Berlyne, 1965). Nonetheless, the conscious threat as well as the subconscious threat that have been identified as the causes of fear and of anxiety, respectively, cannot be adequately interpreted in terms of uncertainty, which is characteristic of open alternatives—as is well known to every dinner guest who is uncertain about the dessert, expecting either his beloved strawberry shortcake or his adored peach Melba. Normally fear and anxiety do not stem from the mere existence of open alternatives but from what some of these alternatives imply. This is evident when one considers, for instance, the following pair of alternatives: "either dessert will be served or burglars will interrupt the dinner party." Conversely, even very precise information does not necessarily—through its precision and adequacy—stabilize the system and reduce fear and anxiety, as is psychologically evident from the information "Tomorrow you will be executed." This demonstrates that the core concepts of information theory, namely, the number of alternatives, their respective probabilities, and their eventual reduction to bits of information, have far less psychological relevance than their actual meanings.

The psychological absurdity of applying measures of information theory without due consideration of actual meanings can best be demonstrated through some examples. If two messages, say, "My friend deserted from his military unit" and "My friend got killed in action," have the same objective and subjective probabilities, their equivalence in terms of transmitted bits of information is misleading. It disregards the different impacts that the two messages have on my behavior. Again, my behavior in the two cases may be equally likely, yet still very different. Even in a case as simple as, for instance, "His name is Tristan Cohen," it is extraordinarily difficult, if not impossible, to calculate the information content of the message. Moreover, the approximation of the probability of such a name combination would still not help in explaining why this name makes me laugh while an equally unlikely combination, say Dorothy Handamura, leaves me indifferent. How absurd this method is for evaluating and comparing human information becomes glaringly evident when we try to estimate the informational or so-called surprise value of the statement "Yesterday on Fifth Avenue I ran into my friend John." To attempt to specify and count the set of alternatives reduced by this statement would be—to say the least—hazardous. To take another example: if I do not know where my friend spends his vacation, getting his postcard from Switzerland may give me real information. Yet since neither before getting his postcard nor afterwards did I consider where at all or where else he could have been, it would be nonsensical to take all the vacation resorts known to me as a baseline for calculating the information value of the postcard I luckily got.

Indeed, the danger inherent in blindly identifying information with meaning has not gone unnoticed. Many writers, like Bar-Hillel (1955), have made a special point of explaining that semantic information is not the same thing as statistical frequency of inputs and probabilistic relations between signals. As early as 1953, G. Miller called attention to the fact that "information" measures only the amount of information and hence cannot be synonymous with "meaning," since "the amount does not specify the content, value, truthfulness, exclusiveness, history or purpose of the information" (G. Miller, 1953, p. 3). Some, like Cherry (1957, p. 9), reserve for "information" at least the grammatical level of communication, excluding the semantical and pragmatical levels. Others, in contrast, have been very strict in separating the two concepts and in banishing information from the domain of meaning. We shall mention two examples. Garner (1962) attempted to distinguish between meaning as a structure, that is, the totality of the relations between events or elements in a system such as a language, and meaning as signification, that is, the particular specifying relations for any single event or element, such as that between a word and an object or the same word in another language. While information theory is applicable only to meaning as structure, meaning as signification requires qualitative evaluation. James G. Miller points out that information must be transmitted so that meaning may be communicated. But while information reflects "the degree of freedom that exists in a given situation to choose among signals, symbols, messages or patterns to be transmitted" (Miller, 1965, p. 193), "meaning is the significance of information to a system which processes it; it constitutes a change in that system's processes elicited by the information, often resulting from associations made to it on previous experience with it" (pp. 193–194).

Again, emphasizing the limitations of information theory does not imply an outright rejection of its use in psychology or even in cognition. In any informational process in which transmitted contents are less important than quantities, analysis in terms of information theory or in accordance with models based on information theory can be and has been applied with some scientific benefit. However, if we consider situations in which the existence of different alternatives can only be perceived by virtue of their different meanings, it becomes highly doubtful that cognition would be properly defined by calling it an information processing system. It would be more logical and psychologically more beneficial to reserve the term "information" and that which it implies for a general characterization and analysis of communication systems as such, including the human organism. Cognition, then, could be defined as the meaning processing subsystem or, more precisely, as the subsystem that processes meaning of a particular kind. The restriction indicated by the term "particular kind" is absolutely necessary. Yet the explanation of this restricting qualification can only be given in the last section of this chapter. For the time being it may suffice to point out that even the information conveyed by a thermostat has meaning within its respective system, but that this meaning is obviously of a kind different from the meanings relevant for cognition.

It goes without saying that to define cognition as the term designating a subsystem that processes a particular kind of meaning only makes sense if we can specify the kind of meaning and offer a method for its measurement.

Having worked our way through to such a definition and developed a suitable method for measuring meaning, we could present a very short outline of our results and proceed to define cognition as the subsystem that processes meaning of the described kind. This would suffice if our concern were simply to define cognitive processes in such a manner that their distinction from and relation to other psychological and physiological processes could be clearly perceived. As we define and use it, however, meaning is not only essential for a proper understanding of cognitive processes as such, it also constitutes a key concept in our theory of cognitive orientation and in the empirical research deriving from this theory and confirming it. Neither the different stages and processes involved in evoking and directing behavior nor even the design of experiments and the construction of our questionnaires can be adequately understood without some familiarity with the major features of our meaning concept. Hence a more detailed discussion of meaning must precede our presentation of the theory of cognitive orientation.

CONVENTIONAL APPROACHES TO MEANING

The importance a psychologically valid definition of meaning and an allied method of measurement would have for cognitive psychology can hardly be overrated. Notwithstanding which branch of cognitive psychology we choose to concentrate on, we shall find that what uniquely characterizes the cognitive aspect of this domain of research is the endeavor to understand how meanings are attained, coded, processed, combined, stored, retrieved, and used. Nonetheless the term "meaning" itself is rarely used in the context of research on such topics. Moreover, there seems to be a rather general tendency to shy away from dealing directly with meaning or clarifying its role in domains other than language proper. For a long time meaning was banned even from the linguistic field, as Neisser (1967, p. 275) aptly remarked—"not even psycholinguistics can ignore meaning indefinitely, however difficult it may be to treat." Indeed, the same remark applies to all cognitive psychology.

The tendency to avoid a confrontation with meaning is closely related to a similar tendency to ignore specific contents, which is characteristic of cognitive psychology no less than of other fields of psychology. For decades psychologists were interested almost exclusively in the processes of behavior rather than in the contents that codetermine behavior and in large part constitute its nature and effects. Reasoning that scientific laws should be primarily concerned not with the single event or case but with classes of phenomena, psychologists like other scientists have striven to understand structures, generalized relations, interactions, and functions between processes—doing so, however, at the expense of forming a solid basis for generalization. They have plunged into the study of learning processes without adequately considering types of learned material, into the analysis of memory functions without first establishing whether storage and retrieval are actually independent of contents, and into research on attitudes or beliefs without analyzing their expressed contents.

Twenty years ago McClelland (1955) claimed that reentering the domain of mental contents requires a theoretically fruitful and empirically valid set of categories for analyzing contents. Now it appears evident that such a set of categories constitutes or derives from what we would call "meaning." We may, of course, classify objects or events without direct reference to their meaning. But if we wish to consider these phenomena as psychologically relevant inputs, we must be able to determine what the specific input means to the individual(s) in question. Otherwise our analysis will yield poor predictions.

Scientists, however, are opportunistic, as Sir Frederick Bartlett has noted; they mostly try to do the possible and avoid the impossible. As long as no valid and reliable instrument existed for measuring meaning, meaning could not become an active factor in psychology. Now, developing such an instrument is not just a matter of cutting through the incredible jungle of definitions that have overgrown the term "meaning" since the pre-Socratic period and succeeded in completely obscuring its nature. An adequate method for measuring meaning should meet the following requirements: first, it should be *sensitive* to differences in the measured phenomenon, so that it can differentiate meanings at least to the degree to which they are differentiated on the level of ordinary language; second, it should make possible *comparisons*, so that the similarity between the meanings of the same sign or word for at least two individuals or for one individual on two occasions can be determined; third, it should have *generality*, in the sense that it should be applicable to a reasonably wide range of meaning phenomena and meaning users; and fourth, it should have *validity*, which, in the absence of a commonly accepted definition of meaning, implies that the technique should not utilize an index currently used to tap constructs other than meaning, and that its theoretical assumptions should at least not violate the loose conception of meaning implicit in its present uses in psychology. Although these requirements cannot be viewed as pedantic, the common techniques available in psychology for measuring meaning do not live up to them (S. Kreitler & Kreitler, 1968). We shall illustrate the point by referring to the main methods of measuring meaning.

The Semantic Differential (Osgood, Suci, & Tannenbaum, 1958; Snider & Osgood, 1969) undoubtedly figures as the most prominent of the various measurement techniques of meaning. It consists in asking the individual to locate a certain word or concept along any number of 7-point scales defined by pairs of bipolar adjectives, and yields the profile of the word in terms of these scales or in terms of the three major factors of evaluation, activity, and potency. The main shortcomings of this widely used method are inadequate sensitivity and validity. Osgood et al. (1958, pp. 322–323) clearly admit that the method yields similar profiles for denotatively distinct concepts and dissimilar profiles in cases of probable referential agreement. Yet they prefer to explain this relative insensitivity of the technique as due to the representational process, which is assumed to be capable only of gross differentiations. No less dubious are the theoretical assumptions designed to turn the Semantic Differential into a method reflecting the representational mediation processes that presumably constitute meaning. It is assumed that the quality of the mediation processes is indexed by factors extracted from correlation matrices between the scales described above. The use of adjectives to specify the scales has been justified by the finding that synaesthetic adjectives occur spontaneously in meaning communications of certain stimuli (Osgood et al., 1958, 20–25). Yet this finding at best supports the conclusion that a sample of heterogeneous common adjectives is capable of yielding dimensions "*representative* of the major ways in which meanings differ" (p. 19). The conclusion becomes untenable when the sample of adjectives is further restricted to bipolar adjectives only. This restriction excludes all possibilities for differentiating meanings through means other than adjectives and particularly pairs of contrasting adjectives. Likewise, there seems to be no particular reason to index the intensity of the mediation processes by the extremity of the checked scale position. Hull's concept of habit family hierarchy, which underlies Osgood's model of meaning, would lead us rather to index intensity by the frequency or probability of occurrence of the mediating responses. This procedure could also take account of meaning dimensions inexpressible in terms of bipolar scales.

The second class of meaning measures includes a variety of associative indices (e.g., Deese, 1962; Glaze, 1928; Hull, 1933; Marshall & Cofer, 1963; Noble, 1952). Mostly they reflect the view that meaning consists in the linguistic responses evoked by words acting as stimuli. These indices share with the Semantic Differential not merely complete reliance on verbal responses, but also inadequate sensitivity and validity. Too many studies support Jung's (1966) conclusion that factors alien to meaning, such as the subject's personality and set or the administration procedure, codetermine responses in word-association tests to an extent that seriously undermines the validity of such indices as measures of meaning. Moreover, verbal associations may be related to meaning, derive from it, or reflect it in a variety of ways that differ from each other crucially insofar as meaning is concerned. Yet there is no way within the association method itself to disentangle these various relations between meaning and the verbal response. In the absence of this possibility we cannot determine whether a specific index measures "meaningfulness" (Noble, 1952), associative meaning (Deese, 1962), common semantic contexts (Terwilliger, 1968), etc.

A class of methods partly related to the associative indices (Deese, 1965; McNeill, 1966; Perfetti, 1967) is based on the conception that meaning is a structure or bundle of bipolar semantic features, such as human-nonhuman, male-female, beginning-ending, and the like. This concept bears a strong similarity to componential analysis and forms the core of the semantic theory incorporated into transformational-generative grammar (Katz & Fodor, 1965; Katz, 1972). Methods for identifying semantic features include associations (Deese, 1965), free recall of learned material (Mandler, 1968), word sorting on the basis of similarity (Miller, 1969, 1972; Fillenbaum & Rapaport, 1971), and free postulation followed by empirical testing of deductions (Osgood, 1968; Quillian, 1968). The main problem with semantic features is that their nature and number are completely unspecified, indeed arbitrary. How many semantic features are assumed or postulated clearly depends on imagination (Bollinger, 1965), or required sensitivity of differentiation. Since, however, there is no underlying principle, an infinite number of sets of semantic features may be assumed, depending on the theory of the investigator, the context and the content of the words to be differentiated, the method of extraction, and so on. Indeed, a comparison of sets of features listed, for example, for verbs by Leech (1970), Miller (1972), and Osgood (1968) suggests the essential lack of comparability of the various systems, and hence, of words thus coded. Lastly, the assumed explicit or implicit bipolarity of semantic features is tempting, first, because it highlights the similarity between the semantic level and the phonological domain, which is characterized by binary distinctive features, and second, because it lends itself to easy integration into the prominent concept of markedness (Greenberg, 1966). Nonetheless, there is no reason to expect that the relevant aspects of meaning are all reducible to bipolarity.

Three further kinds of meaning measures should be mentioned, not simply because of their traditional standing in psychology but mainly because they may undergo revival. GSR recordings (Bingham, 1943; Jones & Wechsler, 1928; Mason, 1941; Smith, 1922) are an example of one type of measures, mostly autonomic, designed to tap mainly the emotional aspect of meaning. Yet GSR recordings are too gross to differentiate meanings sufficiently. Further, their validity is doubtful in view of the great number of variables other than meaning that affect them (Montague & Coles, 1966). The best case to be made for GSR responses as a measure of meaning is that they reflect a certain aspect of emotional meaning, probably novelty or complexity (Lynn, 1966).

The recording of action potentials in the striate musculature or even of gross muscular movements represents another type of measures, based on the view that meaning is an overt or implicit natural or conditioned response to a stimulus (Jacobson, 1932; Max, 1937; Watson, 1919). Since these indices are not always present when meaning is operative, their generality is seriously deficient. Even in the studies that support muscular contractions as measures of meaning (Jacobson, 1931, 1932) it is reported that no action potentials occurred while the subjects listened to the instructions of the experiments. This indicates that meaning was apprehended without the accompaniment of action potentials—unless it is assumed that the instructions were meaningless. Again, these measures are deficient in sensitivity and comparability (Thorson, 1925). Last but not least, their validity can hardly be upheld in view of the many demonstrations that muscular movements and potentials reflect degrees of arousal due to motivation, conflict, and difficulty (Duffy, 1962, pp. 52–59; Humphrey, 1963, pp. 185–216) rather than differences in meanings.

The last type of measures we shall mention is based on the identification of meaning with sensory or fantasy images in general or introspectively reported kinaesthetic sensations in particular (Clarke, 1911; Jacobson, 1911; Okabe, 1910; Pillsbury, 1908; Pyle, 1909; Shimberg, 1924; Titchener, 1909). Again it is all too evident that these measures are limited in generality to certain types of people or contexts (Binet, 1903; Ogden, 1911) and to certain stimuli (Humphrey, 1963, pp. 278–283). They also lack sensitivity and comparability (examples in Okabe, 1910; Shimberg, 1924) and their validity is at best obscure (Brown, 1958, pp. 82–93).

MEASURING MEANING MEANINGFULLY

The main source of the weakness of available methods for measuring meaning is a too narrow coverage of meaning. Each method is certainly based on some index relevant to meaning. But in view of the complexity of meaning, a method reflecting only the action tendencies evoked by meaning stimuli, or only the connotative meaning factors of evaluation, potency, and activity necessarily runs the risk of failing to be valid and sufficiently sensitive to differences in meaning. Indeed, limited validity and sensitivity are the shortcomings common to all the methods mentioned.

The conclusion that meaning is a highly complex phenomenon played a major role in the set of assumptions about meaning that guided us in devising a new method for measuring meaning. An additional assumption was that the complex structure of meaning must be flexible enough to allow, at the very least, for influences of context and bonding with other meaning structures. Further, we assumed that meanings are acquired through learning, particularly in interpersonal contexts, and that with time they undergo increasing differentiation and delimitation.

The experimental method we used (for a detailed description see Kreitler, 1965; S. Kreitler & Kreitler, 1968) corresponded to these assumptions. The conclusion that meaning is amenable to learning and communication has led us to structure an experimental task that consists of asking the subjects to communicate to some hypothetical "other" the meaning of various presented signs and symbols, as clearly and comprehensively as possible. The hypothetical partner was described as being ignorant of the meaning of the stimuli but as capable of understanding communications in verbal form—spoken or written, in drawings, acting, and the like. Since not all facets of meaning may be expressible directly in speech, the subjects were encouraged to use whatever media of expression they wanted or felt necessary—speaking, writing, drawing, pantomime acting, verbal descriptions of drawings, dancing, and so on.

On the other hand, assuming that meaning is characterized by structural complexity and flexibility helped us to devise the procedure for analyzing the subjects' responses. We concluded that the responses would include references to various aspects of meaning, and strove to uncover these aspects by posing the following questions in regard to each response: What conceptual means did the subject use in his or her communication? To which aspect(s) of the referent does the response relate? Which implied question(s) about the referent does the response answer? These questions reflect our concentration on the conceptual contents of the responses regardless of their objective correctness and the specific expressive media used in the communication. The questions mentioned above yielded an easy tool for identifying units within each response of a subject and for labeling these units. Common denominators of these labels made it possible to classify the response units into categories. Insofar as each of the categories serves as a superordinate

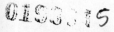

label for an infinite number of responses reflecting a definite general mode of classifying phenomena or of relating to phenomena, we refer to the categories as dimensions. Correspondingly, the response units themselves we call meaning values.

DIMENSIONS OF MEANING

The set of dimensions we present here is based on a most varied and rich research material (Kreitler, 1965; S. Kreitler & Kreitler, 1968; Kreitler & Kreitler, 1977), which was designed to provide as wide and comprehensive a coverage of meaning as possible. The dimensions were derived from and tested on the responses of a few hundred subjects who have participated in various studies on meaning. The subjects ranged in age from 2 years to well beyond 80 years. They included men and women, normal individuals and hospitalized schizophrenics, highly educated people and people who could hardly sign their names, subjects from different cultural communities—Western and Middle Eastern— and representatives of the most varied professions—mechanics, artists, farmers, professors, and . . . toddlers. No less general and heterogeneous were the stimuli used to elicit meaning communications—words of the most varied types of content and form, word combinations, phrases and sentences, pictures, drawings, geometrical figures, and more. Finally, since so many investigators have distinguished between the more interpersonally shared and the more personal-subjective meaning—called by Piaget (1948) socialized and egocentric meaning, by Goldstein and Scheerer (1941) abstract and concrete, by Ogden and Richards (1949) symbolic and emotive, to name just a few—we attempted to widen the range of dimensions obtained by using three types of instructions. One type, designed to elicit mainly lexical, interpersonally shared meaning, required the subject to communicate the most generally accepted meaning, so that the majority of people knowing the sign and its meaning would agree with the response. Another type, designed to elicit mainly personal-symbolic meaning, required the subject to communicate the most truly personal meaning each sign had for him or her, disregarding the meaning that most people would be likely to assign to the stimulus. The third type of instruction merely stressed the requirement to communicate meaning, without further specification.

The following set (differing in many important respects from our prior publications) represents all the dimensions that appeared in any of the subject groups in response to any of the stimuli—henceforth called "referents"—in the context of any type of instruction. Each meaning dimension will be exemplified by one or more meaning values.

1. *Contextual allocation and classification* of the referent: the superordinate concept or system of items or relations to which the referent belongs, or the concept or abstract superordinate structure of which it forms a part, e.g., "God"—belongs to religion; "eye"—is a part of the body; "to walk"—this is a verb.

2. *Range of inclusion* of the referent: the items or parts that constitute the referent or members of the class it designates, e.g., "art"—this is painting, music, dance, etc.; "body"—head, shoulders, feet, etc.; "boy" —Johnny, Bob, Freddy, etc.

3. *Function, purpose, or role* of the referent: stated either directly in terms of the uses to which the referent may be and is usually put, or, more indirectly, in terms of the usual activity (or activities) that the referent does or may be used for and that suggests its function, e.g., "bottle"—you can drink from it; "to eat"—you do it in order to have an excuse for going on a diet; "watch"—it shows the time.

4. *Action(s) and potentialities for action* of the referent: actions that the referent does, could do, or which others do with it or to it, and that are not intended to represent the referent's function or role, e.g., "man" —moves, breathes, consumes, reproduces, and kills.

5. *Manner of occurrence or operation* of the referent: the stages, processes, acts, instruments, means, organs, etc. involved in the occurrence or operation of the referent, i.e., which make it possible or of which its operation consists, e.g., "to walk"—first you lift one leg, then you place it, etc.; "democracy"—lists of candidates or party programs are published, then all grown-up citizens may vote for them by placing their ballots in specially constructed boxes or by pushing certain buttons on machines, etc.; "persevering"—describes how a person works.

6. *Antecedents and causes* of the referent's existence, occurrence, or operation: the necessary and/or sufficient conditions for the referent's existence, occurrence, or operation, or the circumstances under which it occurs, e.g., "anger"—thinking of your opponent's success; "but"—the impossibility of avoiding the dispensable reservation.

7. *Consequences and results* of the referent's existence, occurrence, or operation: consequences, results, effects, etc. that derive directly or indirectly from the referent's existence, occurrence, or operation or at least take place after the referent's occurrence, but do not imply the referent's function or purpose, e.g., "and"—a long sentence; "love"—parting, pregnancy.

8. *Domain of application* of the referent: the items (people, objects, events, etc.) to which the referent usually is or can be applied, the items with which it interacts in some sense or which are affected through it,

e.g., "beautiful"—it applies to women and the weather; "eating"—you can eat meat, fruit, etc.

9. *What the referent consists of*: the material out of which the referent is made or parts and components of which it consists, e.g., "sea"—it consists of oxygen and hydrogen atoms; "love"—it is sympathy, understanding, and sexual attraction.

10. *Structure* of the referent: the interrelations of the subparts, the organization and complexity of the material or the system variables on the molar level or at any submolar level, e.g., "personality"—the ego on top, the id below, the superego clinging around, highly complex but not sufficiently so.

11. *State and possible changes in state* of the referent: the actual, potential, or possible state of the referent at any point in time, and changes that could occur in this state under specified or unspecified conditions, e.g., "God"—exists; "water"—evaporates in heat, freezes in cold, but cannot be broken.

12. *Weight and mass* of the referent: the weight may be expressed in measured units or as an estimate of heaviness; similarly, the mass may be expressed in measured units but also in terms of other estimates of the quantity of inertia the object possesses, etc., e.g., "rock"—it is heavy, it weighs twenty pounds.

13. *Dimensionality and dimensions* of the referent: indication of the size of the referent, and of the number and/or measures of its dimensions, and so on, e.g., "this cube"—a three-dimensional body, four inches high, with angles of ninety degrees.

14. *Quantity* of the referent: the quantity or degree of occurrence may be expressed in measured units or as an estimate, e.g., "world"—there is only one of its kind and some people think it is too much.

15. *Location* of the referent: the usual place, address, or domain in which the referent exists or occurs, relative to other objects or to a fixed reference system.

16. *Temporal qualities* of the referent: the time at which the referent exists or existed, the frequency, duration, timeliness, durability, etc. of its occurrence, its age, etc., e.g., "sadness"—it has always existed.

17. *Possession and belongingness* of the referent: indication of the referent's actual or potential possessions, to whom or to what the referent belongs or may belong, literally or figuratively, who usually deals with it, possesses it, etc.

18. *Development* of the referent: the ontogenetic or phylogenetic development of the referent or of any of its subparts in the past, its historical forerunners, personal history, origins, manner in which it was

made or shaped to take its present form, and its expected or possible development in the future, e.g., "psychologist"—a person who after graduating from high school studied at a university, etc.; "buying"—the modern version of exchange, to be replaced in the future by just taking what you need.

19. *Sensations the referent has or evokes*: sensory qualities that characterize the referent (i.e., sensations it evokes) or that it has itself; the sensations may be subdivided as referring to *form and shape, color, nature of surface* (e.g., transparent, decorated), *sound, taste, odor, tactile-kinaesthetic qualities, temperature,* and *internal stimulation* as pain, etc.

20. *Feelings and emotions the referent has or evokes*: emotional responses that the reference has or that it evokes in others, e.g., "monster" —it frightens people and probably enjoys it; "bright"—I love a thing which is bright.

21. *Judgments, opinions, and values the referent has or evokes*: indication of the referent's attitudes and the attitudes it evokes in others, including evaluation and judgments of importance, e.g., "law"—most of it is bad or unjust, and the rest is superfluous or unenforced.

The method that made possible the derivation of the dimensions has been shown to be adequate for measuring meaning in any context of psychological study or practice. Since its nature and applications have been fully described elsewhere (S. Kreitler & Kreitler, 1968; Kreitler & Kreitler, 1977), it should suffice to mention here that the method has a high scoring reliability, is extremely sensitive to differences among meanings, makes possible reading back the referent from the meaning response, enables comparisons of meanings on various levels, and is characterized by a high degree of generality. This generality is evident not only in the applicability of the method to a wide range of meaning phenomena induced spontaneously or through some kind of experimental instruction, but also in the fact that our conception and method unite in one framework disparate definitions, concepts, and findings concerning meaning. For example, the dimension of the referent's function, purpose, and role was emphasized by Goldstein and Scheerer (1941) and by Rapaport (1945, pp. 149, 403), the dimensions of contextual allocation and of sensation appear in Kaplan (1952), the dimension of feelings and emotions was highlighted by Fromm (1951, pp. 12, 17–18), Smith (1922), and Spiegel (1959), the referent's manner of occurrence lies at the core of the operational definitions acclaimed by positivists such as Bridgeman (1927), while emphasis on consequences of the referent's occurrence or operation is characteristic of those who in the tradition of Peirce (1931–35, 1958) and Pavlov identify meaning with the response evoked by the stimulus.

These 21 meaning dimensions—and others of the same type that could probably be added—are, as already suggested by their labels, classifying conceptualizations, at least in the sense assigned to "concept" in the studies of Bruner, Goodnow, and Austin (1956) and others (Bourne, 1966). However, in view of other definitions of "concept" (Staats, 1961), we do not urge identifying the meaning dimensions as concepts. There can nonetheless be little doubt that the dimensions represent basic kinds of categorization. Indeed, they seem to be so basic that at least some of them may be innate or at least have some primitive counterparts in the neonate. In any case, it is learning and culture that institute the meaning dimensions as basic. Thus, certain dimensions may become so dominant that they may serve to characterize a culture. In this manner the meaning dimensions may come to represent the major classes of information available in a culture and made accessible to its members. Consequently, a full set of meaning values along all the meaning dimensions concerning a certain stimulus may serve as a summative inventory of information—or if one prefers, knowledge—available at the time about that stimulus.

One other feature common to meaning dimensions and concepts is that both may be used without awareness on the part of the users. As in the case of meaning values too, this lack of awareness is characteristic, but not unavoidable or necessary. A person may be made to become aware of meaning dimensions he applies. Experiments with children (Kreitler & Kreitler, 1977; Kreitler, Ensenberg, & Kreitler, 1976) showed that becoming aware of a meaning dimension leads not merely to a more frequent use of this dimension but also to an increase in the number, precision, and veridicality of meaning values pertaining to this dimension. Yet explicit training is not the only means for increasing awareness of meaning dimensions. Science provides a framework for the constant clarification and delineation of meaning dimensions implied in commonly used meaning values, for the analysis and operationalization of these dimensions, and for the generation and definition of new dimensions.

Essentially the meaning dimensions presented here define a semantic space, in a manner not unlike that described by Osgood et al. (1958). But whereas Osgood et al. strove to define a set of orthogonal dimensions, our dimensions are interrelated in various senses. Indeed, whereas Osgood et al. used the orthogonality of the extracted meaning factors as a practical criterion for the identification of the dimensions, we used a content analysis procedure for defining the dimensions and regard correlations between dimensions as a major characteristic and fruitful property of our system. Analysis of communications of meaning given in regard to different kinds of stimuli by various groups of subjects shows several types of relations among dimensions: relations reflected in rank-orderings of the dimensions in terms of their frequency, relevance, etc.; relations of joint occurrence (facilitation) and inverse occurrence (inhibition); relations based on sharing the same referent; and so on.

Each meaning dimension defines a domain of contents, information, images, etc. of a certain type. Thus, one meaning dimension may include, at least theoretically, everything about "the referent's manner of occurrence or operation" that you always wanted to know but were (or were not) afraid to ask. The labels of the meaning dimensions sufficiently discriminate the domains of meaning subsumed under them, but do not make possible the degree of differentiation within each dimension that is required in order both to compare meaning values of the same dimension and to describe developmental phenomena. A higher degree of differentiation may be obtained, however, by introducing subsections within each meaning dimension that represent more specific or specialized types of contents. For example, the meaning dimension "the referent's function, purpose, or role" can profitably be subdivided into such sections as the referent's function, purpose, or role in the life of individuals, the referent's function, purpose, or role for society at large, and so on; whereas the dimension "contextual allocation" subdivides, for example, into allocation within some concrete system, allocation within some supraordinate class, and allocation within the syntactic-grammatical domain. The requirements of a specific behavioral context may of course dictate the nature and number of these potential subdivisions. If, for instance, we are involved in communicating meanings that focus on sensory qualities, it may be useful to deal with several specific subcategories within this domain rather than pooling them all together under one label.

The possibility of subdividing each meaning dimension indicates the hierarchical structure of the dimensions. This is, however, only one aspect of the hierarchization characteristic of meaning—although one that is largely overlooked. Another aspect, more often noted (Bever & Rosenbaum, 1970; Mandler, 1967; Collins & Quillian, 1972a, 1972b), consists in the continuum of generality-specificity in each of the subsections of a meaning dimension. What we have in mind is a sequence such as the following concerning a definite color: (1) a sensory quality, (2) a visual quality, (3) a color, and (4) a specific hue; or a sequence such as the following concerning the meaning of the preposition "on": (1) a preposition, (2) a preposition that expresses a locational quality, (3) a preposition that expresses a locational quality with respect to relations between two objects, etc.

It may be assumed that switches in meaning value from one degree of generality to another are not infrequent. The task of "keep[ing] the organism matched to its field of purposeful activity" (MacKay, 1968, p. 205) often requires changing the level of specificity of the relevant meaning values so as to render them significant for the individual and adequate for coping with the signal or problem. For example, Abramovici (1973) showed that when people are required to judge whether a combination of words is acceptable or anomalous, they rely in their judgments on increasingly higher degrees of specificity in the meaning values if lower degrees of specificity prove to be inadequate.

VALUE-REFERENT RELATIONS
AND THE MODES OF MEANING

We started with the conception that meaning must be a learnable process, structurally complex and flexible. The findings yielded by the method shaped in correspondence with these assumptions confirm them but also reach beyond them. They show that communicating meaning consists of stating one or more particular specifications about the referent. When pooled, these specifications allow for grouping in terms of categories, similar to some general modes of classifying phenomena defined by Aristotle, if not earlier. Accordingly, while the process of communicating meaning is reducible to the specification of one or more particular values along one or more dimensions, meaning itself emerges as *a pattern of values along these dimensions*.

By the nature of things, a definition is a summary statement that stands in need of explication. We will explicate our definition by pointing out some of the major properties of the system of structured contents we call meaning.

Meaning is always focused on a referent. There are no restrictions on the referent's nature or extent. It may range from an object, a word, an abstraction, or an event to a process, an activity, a sentence, a theme, or a whole present, past, or future situation, period, and so on.

The two main elements of our definition of meaning are meaning values and meaning dimensions. The actual meaning, however, consists of meaning values and not dimensions. When verbalized, meaning values are usually formulated as propositions. However, they need not be sentences, and need not be verbally expressed or expressible. They may take any preverbal or averbal form, and may range from very low-level generalizations, even mere perceptual discriminations, to the most encompassing degrees of abstractness. Indeed, meaning is totally independent of the means and media of its conception and expression. Further, meaning values need not be conscious or even directly accessible to consciousness. An individual need not be aware of meaning—that is, of meaning values—and certainly not of the underlying dimensions, in order to operate adequately with meanings and in line with them. Indeed, there is every reason to assume that communicating or expressing meanings and acting in accordance with meanings are mediated through completely distinct mechanisms. Again, meaning values differ greatly in veridicality. Yet the veridicality of a meaning value, in the sense of its being shared by many people or at least not contradicted by the meaning values held by others, does not in any way affect the classification or status of the meaning value. It may only affect behavior.

Irrespective of veridicality, meaning values refer to some kind of referent. The reference may be positive, in the sense of an *assertion* (e.g., "yoga"—it is an Indian discipline) or negative, in the sense of a *denial* (e.g., "yoga"—it is not a religion). Further, the reference of two meaning values to a referent may be *conjunctive* (either or both of them may be related to the referent, e.g., "and"—it is a conjunction, connects sentences) or *disjunctive* (either but not both of the meaning values is related to the referent, e.g., "animal"—it is either awake or asleep). These formal distinctions, however, play a lesser role in shaping meaning than do more basic relations between a meaning value and a referent. These relations may be of different kinds; the major types we have thus far identified are the following:

1. *The attributive relation*, which consists in specifying certain attributes that are assigned the role of qualities of the referent. When, for example, one asserts of a referent such as "meaning" that it is an important but unclear concept, that it is used by muddle-headed scientists, that it belongs to psychology, and plays havoc in many domains, etc.—one is using in an attributive manner these various meaning values, which belong to such diverse meaning dimensions as "contextual allocation," "the referent's possession and belongingness," "judgment and beliefs the referent has or evokes," etc.

The two main forms of the attributive relation are the *substance-quality relation*, which is based on assigning to the referent the role of a substance and to the meaning values the role of properties of the substance (e.g., sensory, locational, temporal qualities), and the *actional relation*, which is based on assigning to the referent the role of "doer" that causes, brings about, produces, effects, etc. certain actions or effects stated in the meaning values (e.g., describing what the referent does, consequences of its actions, etc.).

2. *The comparative relation*, which consists in stating meaning values related to the referent through the intermediation of another meaning value or stimulus. The four major forms of the comparative relation are: the relation of *similarity*, which includes identity or synonymy, equivalence, match, and similarity in some specified or unspecified sense (e.g., "moon"—it is like the earth; "justice"—similar to truth, both do not exist); the relation of *dissimilarity*, which includes difference, mismatch, contradiction, contrast, reversal, inversion, and antonymy (e.g., "day"— the contrast of night); the relation of *complementariness*, which includes also reciprocity (e.g., "husband"—has a wife, "wife" has a husband; "parent"—has a child, "child"—has a parent); and the *relational* relation, which consists in a comparison with some other meaning value or stimulus that explicitly or implicitly serves as a standard (e.g., "intelligent"—wiser than the average person).

3. *The exemplifying-illustrative relation*, which consists in stating meaning values of the most diverse meaning dimensions in the form of examples. The most frequent forms of the exemplifying-illustrative relation are an *exemplifying instance*, which presents the meaning value through an object, a phenomenon, an event, an animal, or a person (e.g., "evil"—war); an *exemplifying situation*, which presents the meaning value through a situation, a sort of picture that is richer than an exemplifying instance, may include some activity and has duration, but lacks dynamism and development (e.g., "motherhood"—a woman with a baby in her arms); an *exemplifying scene*, which presents the meaning value through an unfolding situation or story, structured in a sceno-dramatic manner.

4. *The metaphoric-symbolic relation*, which consists in stating meaning values that do not belong strictly to the referent's conventional spheres of connotation or denotation but are related to the referent or to one of its aspects in a mediated double-attributive bond. The three major forms of the metaphoric-symbolic relation are the following: the relation of *interpretation*, which consists in presenting a general interpretation of the referent or of any one of its aspects, stated in terms of abstractions (e.g., "happiness"—that which can never be found in the found); the relation of *metaphor*, which consists in presenting an image illustrating the referent or any one of its aspects whereby the illustrative function is mediated through an interpretation (e.g., "life"—a colored kerchief that blazes for a second and disappears in the hand of a magician); the relation of *symbol*, which consists in presenting a metaphoric image that illustrates at least two contrasting aspects of the referent and resolves this contrast at the level of the image (e.g., "wisdom"—a

"sunny" eye or an "eye'y" sun, the drawing of an eye with rays issuing from its iris, for wisdom is both absorption from the outside, and irradiation from the inside).

TABLE 2.1
The System of Meaning

I. DIMENSIONS OF MEANING	II. FORM OF RELATION BETWEEN
1. Contextual allocation	MEANING VALUE AND REFERENT
2. Range of inclusion	1. Assertion (positive)
3. Function, purpose, or role	2. Denial (negative)
4. Action(s) and potentialities for action	3. Conjunctive
5. Manner of occurrence or operation	4. Disjunctive
6. Antecedents and causes	III. TYPES OF RELATION BETWEEN
7. Consequences and results	MEANING VALUE AND REFERENT
8. Domain of application	1. Attributive
9. Material(s) of which it consists	a. Substance-quality
10. Structure	b. Actional
11. State and possible changes in it	2. Comparative
12. Weight and mass	a. Similarity, including identity
13. Dimensionality and dimensions	b. Dissimilarity, including contrast
14. Quantity	c. Complementariness
15. Location	d. Relational
16. Temporal qualities	3. Exemplifying-illustrative
17. Possession and belongingness	a. Exemplifying instance
18. Development	b. Exemplifying situation
19. Sensations it has or evokes	c. Exemplifying scene
20. Feelings and emotions it has or evokes	4. Metaphoric-symbolic
21. Judgments, opinions, and values it has or evokes	a. Interpretation
	b. Metaphor
	c. Symbol
	IV. MODES OF MEANING
	1. Lexical (interpersonally shared) meaning (1 and 2 under *Types*)
	2. Symbolic (personal-subjective) meaning (3 and 4 under *Types*)

Empirical findings and theoretical considerations show that these four kinds of relations between meaning values and referents fall into two groups: (1) the attributive and comparative relations, and (2) the illustrative-exemplifying and the metaphoric-symbolic relations. Relations of the first group are used mainly in conveying interpersonally shared, lexical meanings, and those of the second group in conveying personal-subjective symbolic meanings. This finding gives major support for our suggested distinction between the two *modes of meaning*: the lexical and the symbolic. Another finding that supports this distinction shows that in conveying lexical meanings one usually uses several meaning values, which, when presented additively, irrespective of order, together reflect the meaning, whereas in conveying symbolic meanings one may also use several meaning values but each meaning value often suffices to serve as an autonomous expression of the meaning, other values being either further elaborations or independent presentations. Moreover, in the symbolic mode there is an interaction among meaning values, meaning dimensions, and relations of values to referent. This interaction produces a continuum reflecting not only content characteristics of responses but also the sequence of responses of individuals engaged in conveying symbolic meanings (Kreitler, 1965). A continuum of this kind is completely missing in the lexical mode. Finally, as would be expected, the process of decoding is subject to more errors in the symbolic than in the lexical mode.

PROPERTIES OF THE MEANING SYSTEM

Having discussed meaning from the viewpoint of dimensions and of value-referent relations, we turn now to several major properties of the system of meaning as a whole.

First, meaning is a *regressive* system. The meaning of each and any stimulus is couched in terms of the system. The meaning of these terms may again be expressed in terms of the same system, etc. The regression seems to be unlimited.

Second, meaning is a *generative-developing* system. The generative aspect is evident in the fact that the basic process which has made possible the derivation of the present list of meaning dimensions may be used to generate further dimensions if necessary. The practical implication is that the following basic question, which we have used for deriving and defining the dimensions, may be posed with regard to meaning communication in any context: "To which aspect of the stimulus or the referent does the response relate?" If the answer to this question cannot be fitted into the existing set of dimensions, a new subsection or dimension is called for.

The developing aspect of meaning is evident in the fact that the system of meaning is constantly open to changes through the addition of new dimensions or deletion of existing dimensions, prompted by the need to accommodate new information, insights, and practical requirements. The same is true of the meaning of any specific stimulus. It too is not a stable structure but a system in flux, constantly undergoing changes—additions and deletions of dimensions and values.

Third, meaning is a *stimulus-focused* system. This implies that it is not an abstract descriptive set of concepts but a dynamic system whose qualities become manifest when it is set in operation. A necessary condition for making the system operative is to focus it on a stimulus.

Fourth, meaning is a *multidimensional* system. This applies to the system as a whole and often, apart from extreme cases, also to the meanings of single stimuli. The essential multidimensionality of meaning accounts for possible intersections and overlappings between meaning values of specific stimuli. Thus, on the one hand, it is responsible for the potential ambiguity or vagueness of meanings but, on the other hand, it contributes towards the possibility of interpersonal communication by increasing the probability of shared meaning values in the meanings of different individuals and by making meanings rich enough to fit flexibly into a diversity of contexts, interpersonal and other.

Fifth, meaning is a *selectional* system. By this statement we wish to highlight the fact that the meaning dimensions themselves reflect only a selection of the total infinite number of conceivably possible meaning dimensions. The same goes for the meaning of any specific stimulus. Potentially it could reflect the whole system of meaning. In practice it never does, but represents only a selection out of the total possible set. The selection proceeds in terms of at least three factors. One is the nature of the stimulus. A dimension such as "sensations the referent has or evokes" is more likely to be used with concrete referents than with abstract referents. An examination of the meaning dimensions that recur with very high frequency in the responses of different individuals to the same stimulus suggests that the higher position of these dimensions in the frequency hierarchy may be partly due to their more pronounced criteriality. Since, however, this hierarchical position changes across cultural communities, there is no doubt that it also reflects convention, conceptual clichés, and verbal habits shared by members of a culture. A second selectional factor is the individual's personality tendencies. It is evident that certain individuals tend to prefer certain meaning dimensions. For example, a study of twelve-year-olds showed that, in regard to concrete objects, highly talented and creative children prefer to use the dimensions "sensations the referent has or evokes," "what the referent consists of," and "the referent's range of inclusion," in contrast to normal children, who prefer the dimension "the referent's function, purpose, or role," and subnormal children, who prefer "the referent's location." These personal preferences are only minimally conscious and voluntary. Essentially they seem to reflect learned tendencies and cognitive modes of operation acquired directly or derived from other cognitive and emotional habits. Finally, the third factor of selection is the behavioral situation in which and for the sake of which the system of meaning is put into action. It is clear that if an individual has to decide quickly whether some stimulus may be dangerous for him, he has little use for the dimension "the referent's development." When, however, one is immersed in experiencing a work of art, the referent's past and future development are of an importance at least equal to the referent's action and potentialities for action. In contrast to the first two factors of selection, which produce relatively stable meaning structures, this third factor reveals the dynamic aspect of the system of meaning. It may cause a complete restructuring and reversal of the meaning structures, bringing to the fore meaning values that have long been hidden in the background. The dynamic quality is indeed so essential that its effects may override the selectional impact of the stimulus and of personality.

The preceding discussion suggests the need for a new definition of the meaning of a particular stimulus. The meaning of a stimulus should be defined as the pattern of meaning values that have occurred in response to that stimulus in all possible, or at least in all major, behavioral situations. Accordingly, the meaning we get by measuring under particular circumstances should be regarded as bound to those circumstances and as a better or poorer approximation to the total meaning of the stimulus.

Sixth, the system of meaning operates in accordance with the principle of *successive contextual embedding*. The term "successive" is used in a logical and not a temporal sense; the various embeddings may occur sequentially or concomitantly. This principle applies both to the various modes of integration of smaller units of meaning into larger units of meaning and to the opposite set of processes of disengagement of a smaller particular unit of meaning out of a larger unit of meaning. This principle reflects the hypothesis that in both cases the meaning of a particular unit undergoes what is essentially a process of increased specialization, and that increased specialization is a product of interactions between systems of meaning. An example for integration of meanings is provided by a verbal phrase such as "boys ran." The meaning unit of "boy" has to be embedded within the context of the meaning of the plural and to be brought into interaction with the meaning of "ran" before the meaning of the whole unit emerges. As a result of this process, the meaning of "boy" may be regarded as having undergone specification and differentiation. These processes may consist either in selecting specific meaning values to replace the former more general ones, or in adding new meaning values along previous or additional meaning dimensions. The same is true for the complementary process of abstracting a unit such as "a flower" out of an image of a landscape. Focusing on the single unit implies specifying and differentiating its meaning beyond the primary statement "it is a part of the landscape" until it is disengaged from its entanglements in the situation.

The seventh and last property is that meaning is a *multipurpose* and *multinatured* system. Some of the possible functions of the system of meaning are obvious. The dimensions of meaning may serve as guidelines for the assimilation and absorption of information and knowledge, as coding categories for acquired information, as rules for search in long-term memory, as strategies for cue search in the course of identification in perception, and even as transformational rules, which, when applied to the Chomskian base string viewed as a nucleus of meaning, may account for the generation of various surface meanings and thus complement syntactic transformations as another aspect of the same process.

However, it is important to note that there seem to be shifts in the nature of meaning that parallel changes in function. Until now we have referred to meaning predominantly as a system, sticking to the common definitions of system as any entity, conceptual or physical, which consists of independent parts (Ackoff, 1960), or as a "distribution of the members in a dimensional domain" (Angyal, 1941, p. 153). This conception emphasizes the structure of meaning. If, however, we concentrate on contents in meaning, it might seem appropriate to refer to meaning as a set of representations. In this case the representation has to be conceived of as distinct from actions, emotions, perceptual or physiological responses, and the like, which may all be reflected in the representation without becoming identical with it. Alternately, if we put meaning to use in the domain of perception, meaning dimensions appear as categories and meaning values play the role of cues. An allied conception would turn the dimensions into rules controlling search, scanning, coding, retrieval, and so on. Finally, on a higher level of abstraction, meaning may be regarded as a function of several variables, each of which designates a universe of values. The complete set of variables includes all the dimensions described, but if a dimension is not used with regard to a certain referent, it is assigned a value of zero. This conception does justice to the fact that the labels of the referents change concomitantly with greater or smaller changes in the elements and structure of the meaning. It also reflects the selectional quality of stimulus-centered meanings, which are never more than approximations of the whole system of meaning.

COGNITION AND MEANING

As we have shown earlier, information should not be identified with meaning. The two concepts are distinct on the level of theory and of measurement techniques. At best, information and meaning—when stretched to their extremes—intersect to a marginal degree or bear tangential relations to each other. Cognition, however, is involved mainly with meaning and only minimally with information. Indeed, cognition does not start with the cancellation of alternatives; it first makes its appearance at the point where the meaning of incoming signals has to be established so that information may be used for reducing uncertainty. Accordingly, we have suggested defining as cognitive those processes which are involved in producing and processing a particular kind of meaning— the very kind of meaning defined and described above. In this context, production of meaning refers to the process(es) whereby representations, that is, neuronally coded stimuli, are turned into meaningful representations. Processing refers to the modification, elaboration, and further development of meaning as required within the framework of activities such as the storage and retrieval of meanings, testing the similarity, matching, or mismatching of meanings, bringing about combinations, separations, and other interactions of meanings, providing for an ever-increasing expansion of meaning coupled with an intensified differentiation of meaning values, and maintaining the almost constant process of coding and recoding that goes on in the "central conceptual system."

These remarks imply that cognition is the "meaning-processing subsystem." If we distinguish between action or matter-energy subsystems and communication or information-processing subsystems in living organisms (Hunt, 1971; J. G. Miller, 1965a, 1965b; Pribram, 1960), then our definition places the "meaning-processing subsystem" at the center of the information-processing subsystems.

Emphasizing the adequacy of the dimensions and values of meaning for the cognitive subsystem does not imply the adequacy of these same values and dimensions for other subsystems or functional levels in the living organism. Within the context of a level on which our meaning dimensions and values are not applicable, a certain stimulus or pattern may be described as devoid of the particular meaning we are discussing. Yet even within a subsystem for which our meaning dimensions were shown to be adequate, it would be possible to designate a certain signal input as meaningless. A stimulus or pattern would be meaningless as long as not even one value along any of the dimensions relevant for that level has been established. Since the measurement of meaning is based on the number of meaning values assigned to a referent, the quantitative expression for such an extreme case would be: 21 dimensions $= 0$ values. (Our example also demonstrates the possibility of expressing the production of meaning in quantitative terms.) In principle it would indeed be correct to denote as meaningless an incoming signal, a representation of some external or internal stimulus object, for which it has not been possible to determine by means of meaning values what it represents, what the stimulus object causing the representation is. In reality, however, the very perception of a signal requires in the very least the prior determination of at least one value along any one dimension, which would make possible in some sense the decision "similar/ dissimilar." Without such a decision it would be senseless to talk of a change in the stimulus situation. In other words, perception necessitates a minimal degree of meaningfulness. Further, in the reality of perceptual dynamics, meaning production implies production of more meaning. Accordingly, total meaninglessness is a hypothetical limit, not unlike infinity. Similarly, in view of the infinite and infinitely expanding number of possible meaning values, also total meaningfulness is a hypothetical limit, which may be approximated but never fully realized.

To a reader with only a little experience in philosophical semantics, the term "meaningless representation" may sound like a clumsy tautology. He may argue that if A is a representation, for instance a representation of B, then B is the meaning of A. Without this meaning A itself could not be called a representation, for a representation without meaning is no representation at all. This argument may be tenable in a metaphysical sense but it does not hold true on what Cherry (1957, p. 224) calls "the pragmatic level," the level of actual communication and understanding. I may well know that a certain signal represents something, but unless I also know what it represents it is for me meaningless in a psychological sense. On the level of cognitive processes all inputs are signal inputs representing some external or internal stimulus object or pattern. Therefore, the basic difference between these representations —between a meaningful and a meaningless representation—is a difference in the degree of meaning characterizing the representation. In the ideal limiting case this distinction is reducible to a difference between the infinitely meaningful and the infinitely meaningless.

Another possible argument against our definition of cognition is the claim that it is too comprehensive. It is obvious that the meaning dimensions make it possible to establish meaning values for any imaginable signal whatsoever. If so, it could be argued that the suggested definition is relevant not only for cognitive processes but for processes on all distinguishable levels, physiological no less than psychological. The argument is valid if and only if a person attempts to interpret processes on other levels as if they reflected a communication designed for him as a human being. In such a case, however, the meaning values of these processes would be the meaning values corresponding to his interpretation. Yet this interpretation is a cognitive act. If, however, an attempt is made to determine the meaning for the involved cells, or nerve fibers, or tissues, or organs, etc., then it usually becomes necessary to devise another set of values, perhaps along dimensions somehow differently defined. In comparative psychology the presumed meaning of certain signals for certain animals is still interpreted as if the receivers were human beings. A similar tendency can be detected in alchemy and in medieval physics. Yet the natural scientists have made considerable progress toward the solution of this problem by determining wherever possible the meaning values and dimensions adequate for the specific level with which they were dealing. From a philosophical viewpoint the problem remains unsolved even here. Nonetheless, for the purposes of scientific classification our meaning dimensions—if adequately understood and applied—should suffice to distinguish between cognitive and noncognitive processes.

The most important feature of our definition of cognitive processes, however, is that it implies the necessity of considering content variables. As mentioned earlier ("Conventional Approaches to Meaning"), the tendency of psychologists to avoid confrontation with meaning is not unrelated to their shying away from contents. No matter how hard we try to formalize meaning, in the last count it will always refer to specific contents. This core of specific contents is an irreducible element of meaning. When cognition is regarded as a subsystem that processes meaning of a certain kind, models of this subsystem must contain data and descriptions of how the meaning of an input is initially established and how the meaning is modified within the subsystem itself. This seemingly trivial statement is nevertheless necessary, for in models of problem solving, concept formation, planning, and the like, these aspects have been too frequently overlooked, with detrimental effects for the resulting research. Indeed, in studies of perception, pattern recognition, and short-term memory the problem of the production or attainment of meaning is often raised. Yet rarely, if ever, is an attempt made in the framework of cognitive models or otherwise to deal with such questions as: What happens to meaning after its initial determination? How is it modified? Through which meanings stored in memory does it undergo modifications? Which principles govern the combination of other interactions between different meanings, or images, or other cognitive units? It should not come as a surprise that no essential progress has been made in the elaboration and solution of these problems since the heyday of associationists, Freud, and gestalt psychologists of Wertheimer's generation. Yet the operations described by Piaget (Inhelder & Piaget, 1958), the factors of intelligence presented by Meili (1966), as well as conceptualizations developed by Hebb (1968) and by Bruner (1957) provide enough hypotheses to stimulate and make possible the study of how meaning is elaborated, to what degree the different hypothesized processes are content-bound, and what happens to a specific contents in the course of its processing. Indeed, Bruner's (1957) observation that the strategies applied in the formation of a concept depend to a certain extent on the connotative meaning of that concept—for example, on whether the formation of the concept eliminates a certain danger—provides sufficient evidence for the possibility and necessity of such studies.

Consideration of meaning and the use of content variables are even more important when an attempt is made, as in the present book, to study the effect of cognitive processes on other forms of behavior. If we assume that cognitive processes exist and that they function as a subsystem, then their impact on other subsystems can only be conceived of as the output of the cognitive subsystem. Similarly, the impact of other systems on the cognitive subsystem can be conceptualized only in terms of an input. In line with their cognitive bias, psychologists differ somewhat in what they would identify as cognitive output. A decision, a behavioral intention, a specific idea or insight, the solution of a problem, an image, a plan, and a signal for action have all been mentioned as examples of cognitive output. The feature common to all these and other possible suggestions, the feature that turns them all into cognitive products, is their dependence on meaning. Therefore, the primary tasks of a cognitive theory of behavior should be, first, to investigate how the meaning of the cognitive output is created, as well as which processes and components contribute to its shaping and formation; and second, to determine how and to what extent this meaning affects and modifies the functioning and functions of other subsystems in the human organism.

The Lowest Level
of Cognitive Functioning

TOWARD THE SUBMOLAR LEVEL

Since the conquest of the psychological scene by behaviorism and allied trends it has been fashionable to explore how far up one may get in the hierarchy of increasingly complex behaviors by using only the simplest responses as the primary building blocks. A complementary problem will probably haunt cognitively oriented psychologists. They should explore how far down the hierarchy of increasingly simple behaviors one may detect the first signs of the operation of cognitive processes. Indeed, denoting the behavioral level at which cognition sets in is a requisite of any definition of cognition. When we identify cognition as the meaning-processing subsystem it is incumbent upon us not only to demonstrate the behaviors affected by cognitive processes but also to point out which behaviors are not affected by processes involved in the production and processing of the type of meaning described in Chapter 2. In other words, we must answer the question: Where should the boundary between the cognitive and the noncognitive in human behavior be traced?

The majority of studies on the relation between cognitive variables and variables of other behaviors deal with what is generally called molar behavior. Hence the temptation to postulate that the impact of cognition is relevant only or mainly for performance on the level of molar behavior. This ready conclusion is unsatisfactory. Since the study of behavior reveals a continuum of increasingly complex acts on increasingly complex levels of neural organization, one is at a loss to determine where molar behavior starts and submolar behavior ends. Even if we could easily agree in placing the segmental reflexes at the submolar level, locating the intersegmental reflexes is already controversial, and even more so is locating the suprasegmental reflexes, particularly the various postural and cortical-postural reflexes. Nor does the usual application of the term "molar" indicate whether a conditioned response or, for that matter, a series of conditioned responses belongs to the molar or submolar level. On the other hand, a characteristic molar act, such as lighting a cigarette, may indeed be a voluntary and conscious behavior, yet still contain some conditioned and even unconditioned responses. Do these mar its molar character?

There is another argument against willfully restricting the involvement of cognition to the molar level. Such a decision would obviate the need to pinpoint the behavioral level at which cognitive processes first become relevant, thus robbing every cognitive theory of the chance to become a comprehensive theory of behavior and exposing it to the harsh and justified criticism that it is unrelated to basic psychological processes. Further, it would stimulate superfluous metaphysical speculations about the presumed relations of mind and body. Lastly, it would leave cognition theoretically hovering in the air, like a roof without a house beneath it.

At first glance it might appear that the "test-operate-test-exit" (TOTE) unit, which was suggested by Miller, Galanter, and Pribram (1960) as a functional unit designed to succeed the reflex arc, includes an implicit answer to our question. TOTE means an initial test performed in order to check for an incongruity between an input and some internal standard, an operation designed to reduce or eliminate the incongruity if such is found, another test undertaken to check the result of the former operation, and output in case congruity is attained, or another operation if no congruity is established. Yet, since by explicit declaration of its progenitors (pp. 27–28), this basic feedback unit is equally applicable to energy flow, information flow, and control, it cannot be treated as specific only to cognitive processes. Even the incorporation of the "bias" stage into the newer version of the TOTE, expanded in order to account also for the feedforward phenomenon (Pribram, 1971, p. 94), does not turn it into a characteristically cognitive unit. Testing the strength of an input against the threshold potentials should not be viewed as a cognitive act, no more so than incongruity as a generic instigator can be regarded as a cognitive product or stimulus. Indeed, the very generality of the TOTE conception, which renders it useful for processes as varied as the physiological and the cognitive, is based on the failure to elaborate the elemental feedback loop in terms of specific inputs, tests, processes, and behavioral complexes that require more than the chaining of one TOTE unit to another or the embedding of one within the other. Thus, the TOTE unit cannot suffice as an adequate description of the basic cognitive unit, nor does it provide any cues for discovering the lowest level at which cognition exerts its impact on behavior.

Yet is is interesting to note that the answer we give to the question of where cognition sets in also takes issue with the mechanistic conception of the reflex arc. Here, however, the similarity between our answer and that suggested by Miller et al. (1960) ends. Another observation, interesting historically, is that the very same Pavlov whose work on conditioning furnished enough material to legitimize the behavioristic attempt to banish cognition from its role in human psychology also paved the way for a new view of cognition. Indeed, it is a tribute to his exceptional open-mindedness that he did not reject observational evidence that contained suggestions threatening to undermine the main edifice of his physiological theory of behavior. We refer of course to his most important discovery—the orienting response.

NATURE OF THE ORIENTING REFLEX

It is our thesis that cognitive processes are already instrumental on a level below that of conditioned responses. Practically this implies that the orienting reflex is the product of a cognitive act (Kreitler & Kreitler, 1970). Which properties of the orienting reflex serve as a basis for our claim?

Since there exist excellent reviews and summaries of the mass of research in this domain (Berlyne, 1960; Lynn, 1966; Sokolov, 1963; Voronin, Leontiev, Luria, Sokolov, & Vinogradova, 1958), it should suffice to point out those aspects of the orienting response that highlight the largely overlooked role of cognition in producing this response.

The orienting reflex is a matrix of specific somatic, autonomic, electroencephalographic, and sensory responses. In spite of the fact that these responses do not always occur together, the orienting reflex should be viewed as a holistic response of the organism (Anokhin, 1958), shaped, directed, and integrated cortically (Sokolov, 1963, p. 15). It can be discriminated from both defensive and adaptive reactions (Lynn, 1966, p. 10) as well as from arousal per se, with which it shares various features (Johnson, 1968; Mackworth, 1969). By and large, it is independent of the nature, source, and modality of the stimulus (Maltzman & Raskin, 1965; Sokolov, 1963, p. 154ff.). The antecedents of the orienting response are novelty, change, surprisingness, incongruity, complexity, and indistinctness of stimuli. It has been suggested that the common denominator of these qualities is personal uncertainty and conflict (Berlyne, 1960, pp. 243–246), novelty and special significance of the stimulus (Lynn, 1966, p. 13), or merely any minimally significant change in stimulation (Maltzman & Mandell, 1968). The orienting response disappears upon repeated presentation of the stimulus and may be followed by a defensive or adaptive response, conditioned or unconditioned. It reappears, however, when some change occurs in the strength or quality or content of the previously habituated stimulus. The process of habituation is slowed down or even arrested when cortical functions are reduced, as in the state of sleep (Johnson, 1968; Johnson & Lubin, 1967), brain damage or pathology (Lynn, 1966, p. 30), mental retardation, and sometimes also in psychosis (ibid., p. 91). Finally, the orienting reflex has been spotted in animals as low on the evolutionary scale as frogs, tortoises, fish, and birds. Comparative studies have shown that the orienting response is more pronounced, particularly in its somatic components, and habituates more quickly in phylogenetically more developed animals. As a matter of fact, it seems to be a rather recent development phylogentically and appears in its most structured and comprehensive form in primates. In more highly developed animals the response occurs sooner after birth than in the lowly developed. In human newborns, some elements of the response already occur in the first two or three days after birth, but its stability is still low and habituation relatively slow (Graham & Jackson, 1970; Jeffrey, 1968).

Less clearly determined than these facts is the conclusion that there are two types or stages of the orienting response. The findings of Bykov (1958), Kvasov and Korovina (1958), Pribram (1971), Sokolov (1963), and others (Biriukov, 1958; Dolin, Zborovskaya, & Zamakhovev, 1958; Lagutina, 1958) indicate that two phases may be distinguished in the orienting response. The first, the actual "what-is-it?" reflex, appears immediately following stimulation, consists of certain motor and autonomic changes, and makes for optimal sensory reception of the stimulus. It seems to be largely subcortically integrated since it is difficult to extinguish, it is stereotypical in its manifestations, and it occurs even in decorticate animals. The second stage is the exploratory reaction proper. As such, it is directed toward the source of stimulation and consists of a chain of natural and conditioned orientation reflexes, visceral and motor in nature, that "represents a general reaction of the central nervous system to the perception of the stimuli" (Kvasov & Korovina, 1958, pp. 185–186). It is aimed at investigating "the object in detail" (Sokolov, 1963, p. 11) and assessing its biological value (Bykov, 1958, p. 28). The exploratory reaction seems to be of more recent phylogenetic origin than the "what-is-it?" reflex and is directed mainly cortically. The two phases of orienting probably coincide with the orienting stages identified by Pribram (1971): (1) alerting, searching, and sampling; and (2) registration in awareness and memory of the events sampled (occurring later and influenced by the cortex and the amygdala). However, our distinction between the two phases does not coincide with the distinction drawn by Sokolov (1963) and others (Gastaut, 1957; Sharpless & Jasper, 1956) between the generalized and the localized orientation reactions, the latter being faster, briefer, and more resistant to habituation than the former, which it displaces in the course of habituation.

FUNCTIONS OF THE ORIENTING REFLEX

As is well known, Pavlov (1927) called the orienting response the "what-is-it?" reflex and proclaimed enthusiastically that it lay at the origin of science and culture. Later investigators were less openly enthusiastic but not more modest in the functions they ascribed to the orienting response. The functions differ somewhat among investigators but usually remain focused on the role played by the orienting response in the acquisition of information and in conditioning. Thus, Mackworth (1968, p. 313) emphasizes the role of the orienting response in "preparing the organism for fight or flight, once the nature of the unknown stimulus has become clear." Following Sokolov, Jeffrey (1968) highlights the fact that the orienting response sharpens attention and focuses it on a certain cue or some salient feature of that cue, although habituation may cause a hitherto less salient cue to be focused, until a schema is established "that may be used to explain higher problem solving behavior" (p. 323). Anokhin (1958), who has worked in this domain since the early thirties, mentioned in particular two roles. One, which has become a commonplace with Russian researchers, is facilitation of conditioning or the linking of the relevant cortical representations of the analyzers by increasing the excitation level of the cortex up to a degree optimal for the unification of representations. The other role, however, has remained largely overlooked. It is the role of "afferent feedback, which we long ago came to regard as the determining factor in the evaluation by the organism of the results of completed reflexive action" (p. 5). It implies that the orienting response can never be terminated in its process. Starting from Anokhin's linking function, Zaporozhets (1958) develops the notion that the orienting response produces the initial discriminations among stimuli and the clarification of their interconnections, which are necessary for forming that kind of image or program of what to do that is indispensable for any voluntary action. Another link between the orienting response and voluntary behavior is highlighted by Razran (1971), following Gershuni, who identifies this response as an indication of liminal consciousness.

Most central is the role of the orienting response as a necessary condition for the formation of a conditioning response (Lynn, 1966, p. 77ff.; Sokolov, 1963, p. 247ff.). This unanimously accepted conclusion is in no way invalidated by those marginal observations that showed the occasional establishment of conditioning in drowsy adults possibly without preceding orienting (Paramanova, 1958; Vinogradova, 1958). It is precisely the abnormalities of such conditioning—the invariability of response, its short latency and duration, its instability, its alien character for the subject, and so on—that prove the indispensability of orienting for normal conditioning. More precisely, the first stage in the formation of a conditioned response consists of the appearance or reappearance of the orienting response. But the actual formation of the conditioned reflex coincides with the weakening and disappearance of the orienting response. The same holds true whenever a hitherto unconditioned stimulus acquires a signal function. In human subjects this can be achieved by a verbal instruction to react to a well-known stimulus in an unaccustomed manner. If the stimulus has previously been habituated, the orienting response to it is restored if it turns into a conditioned stimulus. Also, the orienting response to a conditioned stimulus is larger, stronger, and faster than to the same stimulus as a neutral stimulus. In the conditioning situation even the neutral stimuli, namely, those stimuli from which the signal stimulus has to be discriminated, turn into signals for nonreaction and hence produce orienting responses. The orienting response is extinguished when a balanced and steady conditioned response sets in. But any change in the conditioning procedures or the conditioned stimulus brings back the orienting response until the response to the changed situation has again become stabilized. Thus, the orienting response prevents a too fast development of rigid, overspecialized connections under changing conditions that require constant adaptations (Vinogradova, 1958).

The orienting response, however, should not be regarded as merely a stage in the acquisition of a conditioned response but as an indication for every situation requiring clarification. If different well-conditioned stimuli that no longer elicit orienting responses have to be discriminated from each other, orienting responses reappear. The more difficult the discrimination—for example, the closer the frequency of the sound stimuli to be discriminated to each other or to an absolute threshold—the more persistent is the orienting reaction (Sokolov, 1963, p. 173ff.). When the discrimination proceeds satisfactorily, the orienting reflex disappears.

Yet this difficulty in discrimination should not be viewed as merely physical in nature or as caused mainly by physical conditions such as intensity of stimulus or duration of background illumination. It may derive as well from lack of clarity about the meaning of the new stimulus or of the stimulus situation. Notably, a meaningful word evokes a stable orienting response, whereas a word devoid of any particular significance for the individual does not evoke the response (Sokolov, 1958, p. 151). Further, magnitude, that is, strength and duration of orienting, appears to be a function of the relative meaningfulness and difficulty of the stimulus. To accommodate these findings, Sokolov has developed the concept of a neuronal model of a stimulus, which is a certain cell system for recording the information concerning the properties of a repetitively presented stimulus. The term suggests that the nervous system is presumed to produce an exact model of the qualities of external objects impinging on the sense organs. When a stimulus does not match the previously established neuronal model, an orienting response is elicited. The strength of the orienting response is assumed to be proportional to the degree of discrepancy between the stimulus and the model. Sokolov's theory is thus based on a two-stage model. The first stage is designed to determine whether an orienting response is necessary, and the second involves sending excitatory or inhibitory signals to evoke or suppress the orienting response. The main elements of the model are a mechanism for perception, a device for producing models of external stimuli, a mechanism for comparing afferent stimulation with the model, some center for controlling the orienting reflex, and another one for activating a conditioned response. This theory has been somewhat expanded and developed in neurological terms by Douglas and Pribram (1966) and Pribram (1967).

Sokolov (1969) is very explicit in his claim that since nervous impulses "anticipate the meaning of a stimulus" (p. 683) that "is either changed or suddenly omitted, afferent impulses no longer agree with the extrapolated meaning of the signal" (p. 683). This situation triggers the orienting response. Accordingly, "the orienting reflex is a regulator which corrects an extrapolation, influencing the way new information is secured, selected, transmitted, and handled" (p. 683), and "represents a system of active 'questions' addressed to an object" (p. 685). The question is posed if the neuronal model, which Sokolov also calls "hypothesis" (p. 686), differs from the meaning of the input, and is "intended to eliminate the lack of clarity in a particular situation by securing additional information about it or by changing the way in which information is handled" (p. 689). It terminates if clarity has been attained, or, in the information theoretical terms preferred by Sokolov, when the probability of one of the hypotheses has become significantly higher than that of the others and the entropy of the system is decreased below the threshold value.

It should, however, be emphasized that the evocation of an orienting response is not due merely to the physical features of the stimulus but to the informational content of these features. Convincing evidence concerning this point was adduced by Luria and Vinogradova (1959). They instructed subjects to press a button whenever the experimenter said a certain word, for instance, "violin." The conditioned words evoked no orienting response; nonconditioned words did. But the orienting response of the subjects was stronger when the experimenter said a word different from the original in acoustic features but similar in meaning, as for instance "conductor," than when he said a word similar in sound but different in meaning, as "violent."

THE COGNITIVE ANTECEDENTS
OF THE ORIENTING REFLEX

In summing up the main conclusions about the orienting response that are supported by available research findings, we find it misleading to conceive of this reflex simply as a reaction evoked by a new or unfamiliar stimulus. Rather, the experimental findings support the conclusion that an orienting response occurs as a reaction to uncertainty about the meaning of a stimulus as such or about its meaning in a given situation. Uncertainty refers here to the state of a person who does not know whether to react at all, or how to react. By the same token, it would be misleading to interpret Sokolov's neuronal model theory in purely mechanistic terms. Studies of semantic generalization, including Luria's and Vinogradova's (1959) experiment mentioned above, have repeatedly demonstrated that the same neuronal model can be used selectively, for instance, once in order to match acoustic characteristics and again in order to match meaning characteristics of a stimulus. Further, it has been shown that at least in children various stimulus dimensions contribute unequally to the elicitation of an orienting response. Color changes produce stronger orienting reflexes than size, while changes in number of elements and spatial orientation of the visual array generate weaker orienting (Lewis, 1970). Also, changes in some values of stimulus dimensions cause stronger orienting than changes in other values along the same dimensions. For example, the addition of color to an achromatic picture results in greater orienting responses than the subtraction of color from an initially chromatic picture. Likewise, the change of a straight line to a curved line produces stronger orienting than the change of a curved line to a straight line (Dodd & Lewis, 1969). This high selectivity in the matching process is obviously determined by the nature of the signal or the structure of its meaning, by innate peculiarities of the perceptual system, and last but not least by the set of the subject, which reflects experimental instructions, the manner in which the subject interprets the whole situation, and so on.

Moreover, a purely mechanistic interpretation of the process whereby an orienting response is evoked would require the immediate availability of a tremendous amount of neuronal models, all of which have to be matched against afferent stimulation so as to make possible the evocation either of an orienting response or of some conditioned or unconditioned response. This requirement cannot be satisfied by the limited storage capacity of short-term memory. Hence, the neuronal models necessary for matching have to be retrieved from long-term memory, which alone holds enough information to make possible identifying the input and determining its actual significance.

Further, since it was shown (Johnson, 1968) that a conditioned stimulus does not elicit an orienting response minutes and sometimes even hours after the occurrence of conditioning, it is evident that the neuronal model of the conditioned stimulus has to be preserved for hours in an active state of availability. In the meantime, however, other stimuli are perceived and undergo a process of neural modeling. Thus, when the original conditioned stimulus recurs, it has to be matched against a considerable number of neuronal models. But—and this remarkable fact is unexplained by the neuronal model theory—the scanning of so many neuronal models and their unavoidable mismatch with the conditioned stimulus do not elicit orienting responses before the previously established conditioned response recurs.

In discussing neuronal models as the neural embodiment of hypotheses that the individual holds about stimulations and their significance, Sokolov clearly indicates the cognitive character of the evocation of an orienting response and the need for retrieval from long-term memory. In other words, the process of matching the input to the neuronal model may pass as purely automatic. But to bring about this matching by producing at the right moment the right neuronal models presented from the required angle of selectivity necessitates a complex act of retrieval of meaning patterns and their translation—possibly even transformation—into neuronal models. Hence, the very determination whether a stimulus is so new or relevant that an orienting response is required presupposes a complex cognitive act.

There exist many different models of memory functioning that can be used to explain this process. Essentially they reflect one of two main theoretical approaches to the problem of pattern recognition or stimulus identification. One approach is that of template matching, namely matching the input against a basic model or standard stored in memory (Arbib, 1972). Although the very process of matching input and template may be envisaged as purely automatic, two further processes, indispensable in order to make template matching possible, may not be. These are the processes involved in setting up the crieterion or criteria of similarity between input and template, and the processes involved in preparing the input for matching with the template. The latter, which consist mainly of "cleaning up" the input and of normalizing it, constitute a special state of "preprocessing" that has to be inserted between the input and the template. Neisser (1967, p. 64) aptly notes that this stage implies the functioning of internal information processes in adjusting the input. Hence, models of this type are cognitive.

The key issue of the second approach is "feature analysis," which accords special importance to checking the presence or absence of certain characteristics or attributes in the input. We may mention, for instance, the formal models for recognition proposed by Kintsch (1967), the concepts of search set and the two-way buffer zone geared for handling both sensory inputs and material retrieved from long-term memory (Shiffrin, 1970), and Norman's (1968) memory model, which consists of a multidimensional framework of nodes or "addresses" produced through intersections of trends of associations, chains of related meanings, or similar features. According to this latter model, for example, sensory inputs are first subjected to an initial feature analysis and then forwarded to their appropriate "address." If the "address" proves to be empty, the input is treated as new or at least as new in a certain aspect, and is therefore subjected to further elaboration for the purpose of recognition and elicitation of response.

All these and other feature analysis models that may account for the initial determination of the novelty of an input anchor recognition in three stages of operations, which they either explicate in detail or leave tacitly implied. The first stage, mentioned by relatively few investigators, is devoted to general alerting and sampling (Pribram, 1971), to increasing the inflow of information from the environment as a whole with a minimum of prior filtering (Berlyne, 1960, p. 95), and is characterized by the operation of preliminary preattentive processes (Neisser, 1967). The second stage, which is often viewed as amalgamated with the first, consists of multileveled hierarchical extraction and analysis of specific features, ranging from primary sensory analysis, through the detection of relatively simple features, up to the identification of complex features presumably by high-level analyzers like those suggested by Selfridge

(1959) or Sutherland (1969). The extraction of each feature involves a rearrangement of the information available following the previous steps of analysis, and consists sometimes of rendering this information more specific or more general and sometimes of relating to each other features that were first analyzed separately. The third and final stage usually consists of some process of synthesis or reconstruction. It may be—to mention just a few possibilities—an "active synthesizing process" (Lindsay & Norman, 1972) that proceeds through analysis-by-synthesis (Neisser, 1966) or some other generation-recognition model (Tulving & Thomson, 1973), combining information from the features and from memory to construct and test several hypotheses in parallel; it may be a process of resynthesis that combines digital information "read off" from several different levels of transformation (Corcoran, 1971); or it may be a process of converting the features into an overall statement, which is then matched against stored statements about known patterns (Sutherland, 1969). The details of the process understandably depend on the conception held about the structure and contents of memory. It should be noted that all of these and similar models of recognition make use of a set of basic processes that are generally called cognitive. Major among these are feature analysis, scanning of memory, search of memory, retrieval, matching of input with some sort of stored representation, and so on. The main point to be stressed is that the operation of all of these processes must be assumed to precede the elicitation of the orienting response (Kreitler & Kreitler, 1970).

Moreover, all of these models require the selection of certain features, or markers, or characteristics, or prompters, or criteria, as guides for memory search and matching the input with the information stored in memory in some form. Yet the variety of labels attached to these features or indicators cannot conceal their essential nature. All of them are in fact values that can be easily classified in one or more of our meaning dimensions.

Finally, common to all of the recognition models is the structuring of the process of recognition in terms of two or three stages, which necessarily occur in sequence even though each of them may be characterized by parallel processing. Each of the stages makes possible a progressively more complete analysis and consequent identification of the incoming stimulation pattern. It is, however, notable that not all stages are requisite for the elicitation of all acts of behavior. For some acts even the first stage suffices. Neisser (1967) aptly notes that the first stage alone elicits movements of head and eyes in line with redirections of attention and to a certain extent controls guided routine movements. Another important characteristic of the models of stages is that attention and hence also selection are progressively more evident in the latter than in the primary stages of the process. This does not of course preclude the operation of selection at the very start of the process. Indeed, the fact that one specific input and not another entered the system is evidence of selection. But that particular type of selection underlying the mechanism of attention, or focal attention, requires for operation a certain amount of previous information, which may be assumed to be retrieved from long-term memory, extracted from preceding analysis of the input and shaped in the form of expectations, hypotheses, and so on. These processes, however, demand some minimum amount of time. Hence the delay in the full deployment of attention. In other words, attention may be a hierarchical system of cognitively directed mechanisms on different levels, of which those mentioned by Gibson (1966)—organ adjustments, selective attention, and conceptual attention—may be only three representative examples.

A COGNITIVE MODEL
OF PRIMARY INPUT ELABORATION

By combining the features common to most models of input identification with our theory of meaning (Chapter 2), we are in a position to suggest a cognitive model that accounts satisfactorily for the primary elaboration of inputs and the ensuing behavioral acts, including orienting responses. For due understanding of this model it is useful to outline in general terms the sequence of events before delving into a more detailed discussion of the cognitive processes involved. First, the representation of every fresh input to the system is checked against the representation of the immediately preceding stimuli, which have been preserved in short-term memory as a kind of neuronal model. The neurological as well as the psychological systems are keyed to react in particular to changes. Accordingly, the check consists only in registering match or mismatch. If, according to the match-mismatch criterion, mismatch is registered, a rudimentary process of signal identification sets in. This process continues until one of the following three conditions is met:

1. the input is identified as a signal for a defensive or an adaptive reflex or for a conditioned response;

2. the input is identified as a signal for molar action and hence stands in need of more elaborate clarification of its meaning than is warranted by meaning processes on this level;

3. the input is so well known that it is at once labeled and, due to set, identified as irrelevant to the present situation; it is then referred either to the stage of "programming" for storage in memory, or for directed forgetting. If neither occurs, it is simply ignored and fades away.

These three conditions can also be viewed as consecutive steps in a hierarchical process of signal search and signal identification. They are tested for sequentially, so that if condition 1 applies, condition 2 is not checked, whereas if condition 2 applies, condition 3 is not checked. If none of the relevant signals is detected, that is, if none of these conditions is met, an orienting response is elicited. The neuronal, sensory, motor, and autonomic components of the orienting response facilitate the acquisition and absorption of more information about the input and the whole stimulus situation. Concomitantly with the relatively slowly unfolding orienting response a further stage of simple input identification begins, which, however, is no longer restricted to determining only signal aspects. The orienting response terminates when, owing to the new information, the input is identified either in the sense of conditions 1, 2, or 3, or as satisfying other conditions necessary for the elicitation of molar behavior (see Chapter 4).

This sequence of events is guided by a simple cognitive process of input identification that we call *meaning action*. In contrast to meaning generation, which will be discussed in the next chapter, meaning action is limited in regard to both the meaning dimensions employed and the meaning values retrieved. It is the most rudimentary manifestation of the operation of the meaning system. When successful, meaning action leads to the establishment of what we call *initial meaning*. Results of meaning action are not full-fledged concepts but simple denotations or labels with few, if any, connotations. We therefore designate these products of meaning action *denocepts*. Hence, initial meaning consists of denocepts.

In principle, meaning action starts with every fresh input and hence is virtually continuous. However, in comparing the input and the hitherto dominant neuronal model merely the "comparative" type of relation (Chapter 2, p. 33) is used for determining whether input and neuronal model are alike (match) or critically different (mismatch). In the latter case, that is, when mismatch and therefore change of stimulation is registered, meaning action proper sets in, gradually gaining in range. In this stage of signal identification only the meaning dimensions "sensory qualities" and "contextual allocation" are employed for input analysis. This assumption reflects the essentially selective nature of the system of meaning (Chapter 2). Regardless of whether it is assumed that this analysis leads to template matching or results in the abstraction of independent features, the outcome, that is, initial meaning, must be coded in terms of meaning values in order to make possible a reaction adequate to the meaning of the input. The great number of cognitive models attempting to account for memory search, scanning, identification procedures, and retrieval strategies, as well as the considerable contradictions among them, demonstrate that none of them has proved to be sufficiently successful to warrant final adoption. For our present purpose it suffices to point out that, of all hitherto mentioned input characteristics, encoding in terms of meaning values along meaning dimensions seems to have the best chance of explaining recognition, notwithstanding the exact details of the identification process.

In case this stage of meaning action (that is, encoding and searching in terms of values of the two meaning dimensions) does not lead to the establishment of initial meaning (that is, identifying the input as a signal according to one of the three conditions discussed above), an orienting response is elicited preparing the organism for better discrimination and evaluation. Concomitantly with the orienting response, meaning action proceeds by bringing into play more meaning dimensions. Besides "contextual allocation" and "sensory qualities" the dimensions most likely to be employed in this stage are: the referent's action and potentialities for action; the referent's temporal qualities; and judgments, opinions, and values the referent has or evokes (particularly those it evokes). This set of dimensions is, as it were, preselected for situations of the prescribed type as the set most likely to yield the necessary information quickly and reliably in an adequate form. The preselection may reflect innate predispositions or categories as well as inferences reached on the basis of previous experience, and even more personal biases. However, we do not have to assume that in each case all of the meaning dimensions mentioned come into play, nor that there is any predetermined fixed order in which the dimensions are applied in the course of meaning action.

The orienting response and the meaning action continue either until initial meaning is stabilized (that is, the input is sufficiently identified for triggering off one of the signals required by any of the three conditions discussed above) or until orienting response and meaning action no longer furnish new information that might enable the establishment of initial meaning. In the latter case molar processes for identification of more complex inputs and stimulus situations are set into action. Thus meaning action gradually develops into meaning generation. The orienting response disappears but may be replaced by exploratory behavior.

Figure 3.1 shows clearly that the main part of meaning action, namely input recognition beyond the initial stage of signal identification, takes place concomitantly with the orienting response. This assumed concomitance between the orienting response and the progressively widening range of meaning has important implications. It provides better understanding of some hitherto rather obscure features of the orienting response and is well in line with its temporal development as observed

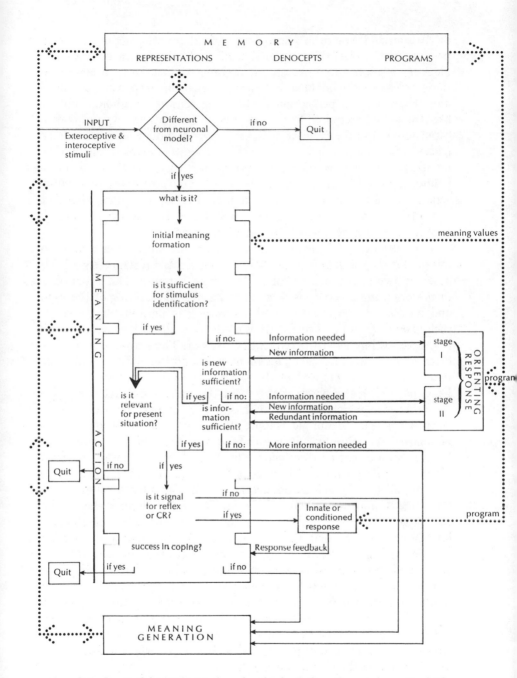

FIGURE 3.1 Input elaboration on the submolar level through meaning action. The outputs terminating this stage are innate and conditioned responses and/or transfer to meaning generation. The dotted lines represent connections with memory.

by Russian and American researchers. Considering the nonmotoric components of the orienting response, such as slowing down of heart rate, blocking of alpha rhythms, etc., it becomes difficult not to agree with those researchers who believe that the orienting response does much more than sharpen perception by lowering sensory thresholds, and the like. Indeed it is required by psycho-physiological parsimony and logic to hypothesize that the facilitating activities of the orienting response serve perceptual input mechanisms as well as cognitive elaboration of these inputs. In other words, the orienting response, triggered off by the initial failure of meaning action, facilitates the further unfolding of meaning action but disappears owing to the results of meaning action. Therefore, instead of concomitance we may assume a functional relationship between meaning action and the orienting response.

As mentioned, this hypothesis is well in line with observations and interpretations of many researchers in the field. Pribram (e.g., 1971) observed two forms or stages of the orienting response. The initial phase of the orienting response is devoted to an overall scanning of the input and its context. In our terms, this scanning is presumably guided by such general meaning dimensions as contextual allocation, sensory qualities, and possibly what the referent consists of. The scanning is not only external but also internal. The findings about the diffuse, undifferentiated, whole characteristic of the initial stage of perception (Flavell & Draguns, 1957), the observations about the meaningful, relatively large segments into which an image is fragmented under conditions of the "stopped image" technique (Hebb, 1963), the demonstration that the familiarity of a stimulus affects recognition in terms of a memory image but not the perceptual threshold (Hochberg, 1968; Robinson, Brown, & Hayes, 1964), and the conclusions of Neisser (1967) about preattentive control—all these provide evidence supporting our suggestion about the first stage. Following Pribram (1971, pp. 286–287), we may assume that this stage is characterized neurally by the enhancement of collateral inhibition (i.e., of one nerve by another)—due mainly to sensory-specific intrinsic mechanisms—which accentuates the difference between active and less active sites so as to make possible a sharper differentiation of incoming stimuli from their background. It is evident that certain unconditioned responses such as defensive reflexes and certain conditioned responses such as focusing attention on a particular part of the perceptual field, reactions to motion, motor acts that prevent collision with objects, and so on, may be released at this early stage before full identification of the object is available.

The next major phase of orienting seems to be much more focused. It appears to involve an effort to construct meaning values along more specific meaning dimensions, referring to the referent's actions and potentialities for action, sensory qualities and judgments it has or evokes, and so on. It may be recalled that Sokolov characterized it as the phase of conditioned orienting, implying that its form depends to a certain extent on stimuli from the former stage that act as conditioned stimuli. Further, Pribram emphasizes that the main process of this phase is "registration," i.e., the active mapping, encoding, and organizing of experience along the temporal dimension, which depends upon internal rehearsal and affects familiarization with the novel aspects of the input. When completed, registration brings about inhibition of collateral inhibition through the mediation of the fronto-temporal cortex and results directly in the habituation of the orienting response. Accordingly, in terms of our suggested theory, this second phase of orienting seems to be devoted to an extension of meaning action beyond the generalized groupings of the first phase, and to its proper unfolding. The cortical control of this phase and its relatively recent phylogenetic origin support our conclusion. The results of this extended meaning action are crucial for determining the habituation of orienting and its replacement by another act on some level.

Incidentally, it is to be noted that this second phase is characterized by the evocation of the autonomic indicators of orienting. Since some of these autonomic components such as the GSR and increase in muscular tonus are common to the matrix of orienting responses and the arousal system, the claim has been raised that orienting and arousal are the same process (Mackworth, 1969). This claim is unjustified (Graham & Jackson, 1970; Sokolov, 1963). Yet, a certain measure of plausibility should perhaps be accorded to Kvasov's (1958) claim that the autonomic responses are guarding reactions to the not completely identified stimulus, so that they represent in a certain sense the "what's-to-be-done?" reflex, analogous to Pavlov's "what-is-it?" reflex. Indeed, other findings (Boiko, 1958; Sokolov, 1963) also point to the gradual transition from orienting to subsequent conditioned or unconditioned responses. The transition is often manifested by the gradual omission of one or another reaction of orienting, and by the use of one or another component of orienting within the pattern of the new response elicited in the wake of orienting. This demonstrates that behavioral acts may be tentatively prepared and sometimes even evoked before meaning action is fully completed. It also shows that meaning action and the activation of behavioral systems may operate, at least partly, in parallel. Most important, it highlights the progressive, gradual character of meaning action and the correspondingly gradual habituation of the orienting response as it passes from the habituation of the generalized (tonic) orienting response through the habituation of the localized (phasic) orienting response, and the return of these responses before full habituation is attained.

Conceptualized in this manner, meaning action is an integral part of perception, although sometimes perceptual analysis may require more meaning than can be furnished by meaning action alone (Chapter 4). The process of perception proceeds step by step as more meaning values, as well as meaning values from more meaning dimensions, are brought to bear on the task of input identification. Hence there is no justification for separating the early input analysis in terms of physical characteristics, such as tone of voice, from a later analysis in terms of meaning, as claimed by Broadbent (1958) in contrast to Treisman (1969). Evocation and exploitation of meaning values is required for all stages of perception. In this respect Broadbent's (1958) early filter model does not differ basically from Treisman's (1969) model of attention, as has been acknowledged by Broadbent (1972) himself, but for a different reason. Even unattended sensory information undergoes an analysis in terms of meaning, as is evidenced by the findings of many experiments (Moray, 1969a; Norman, 1969). Nonetheless there is no need to assume, as Deutsch and Deutsch (1963) do, that every input is first fully analyzed and identified, and that only later is a selection met on the basis of the different "importance" weights of the inputs. For, as we have seen, the output of meaning action, even in an initial stage, may already imply the need for increased attention to the input, no less than it may imply that attention can be suspended temporarily—which may lead to the "attenuation" of the signal in the sense suggested by Treisman—or that attention can be withdrawn permanently—which may lead to expelling the input actively or passively from the system. Accordingly, placing meaning action at the very core of perception implies two things. First, it implies that attention is not random but rather a loop-structured process in which the outcomes of earlier stages of meaning action determine the course and contents of later stages. Hence, a solution to the riddle of how we know what to attend to before we have identified the stimulus (Norman, 1969): the knowledge derives from information included in previously established meaning values. As mentioned, some meaning values imply, connote, or elicit other meaning values. Second, the placement of meaning action at the core of perception implies that there is no one particular stage or fixed point, "channel," "switch," or whatever, at which the selection of what to attend to is established. There simply could not be such a stage, because the selection depends on the already established meaning values, and what they imply reflects their unique contents. Sometimes one meaning value may suffice for determining selection, sometimes a dozen or more are required. Further, the selection necessary for the guidance of attention is a continuous process that changes—is increased or decreased—according to the currently proceeding outputs of meaning action.

In postulating that a cognitive process, namely the elementary input identification through meaning action, precedes any other response, we in no way suggest that an elaborate decision-making process is necessary for the elicitation of unconditioned reflexes above the level of spinal reflexes, for the triggering of conditioned responses, or for the reappearance of orienting reactions. On the lowest level, we would rather propose the operation of a multiple-choice procedure guided by innate or acquired associations between specific inputs and particular responses. In other words, we assume that each reaction pertaining to any one of the three conditions that mediate the cessation of meaning action is bound to specific meaning values. Thus, there would be particular meaning values bound to specific unconditioned responses, particular meaning values that act as signals for conditioned responses, other meaning values that are identified as requiring transfer of the input to the molar level—for example, meaning values bound to an instinctual act—and still others that would signify the lack of need for any action whatsoever. Accordingly, the occurrence of the relevant meaning values would activate the particular response, while the absence of such meaning values would automatically act as a signal for the elicitation of an orienting response.

However, the fact that the cognitive system is operative at this lowest level, even though only in a rudimentary sense, demonstrates the existence of a framework adequate for the absorption of more complex cognitive contents and geared to making possible the operation of these contents in determining behavior on more complex levels or even in determining simple behaviors in more complex organisms. The latter is most notable, for it exemplifies a well-known paradoxical principle in the economics of behavior: whereas in simpler organisms a simple act may be controlled by relatively simple processes, in more complex organisms the same apparently simple act is controlled by higher-level processes. For instance, whereas in relatively simple organisms the establishment of conditioning may not involve cognitive processes beyond those necessary for identifying the input and holding its conception constant over repeated trials, in human adults the establishment of conditioning depends on the operation of high-level symbolic-semantic contents (Razran, 1935, 1965), on evaluations of the whole situation, on one's own norms, purposes, and self-conceptions, and so on (Dykman, 1965; Kimble, 1967; Spence, 1963). Yet, as we have said, the scaffolding for the involvement of cognitive contents in the determination of behavior is already available at the lowest behavioral level.

COGNITIVE AND MOTIVATIONAL IMPLICATIONS

Owing to the functional unity of a highly structured living organism, each process relates to a multitude of other processes, and, in principle, affects all processes in the organism viewed as a system. Consequently, the discovery of even a minor phenomenon makes it incumbent upon the scientist to reevaluate existing conceptions and draw new conclusions, which may sometimes range far afield of the immediate level characteristic of the hitherto unknown phenomenon. This is all the more true if the relevant phenomenon is as basic and central as the orienting response. Thus Sokolov's (1963, p. 11) statement that "the orienting reflex is the first response of the body to any type of stimulation" is obviously meant to be more than a mere description. It should rather be read and understood as a programmatic declaration, similar to Pavlov's earlier but ideologically less cautious exclamation about the orienting response as the core of all knowledge and culture.

Research focusing on the orienting response has many important implications for the different domains of psychology, physiology, anthropology, and even philosophy. We shall discuss only those which are directly related to our own hypotheses. The occurrence of an orienting response as the very first reaction in response to each relatively new stimulus demonstrates that there exists no purely mechanical or physical linkage between stimulus and response on that level of behavior on which defensive, adaptive, and conditioned reflexes take place. Moreover, the very existence of the orienting response sets in doubt any purely mechanistic concept of association or bond. Before an orienting response, or for that matter any other response, can be elicited the organism must in the very least decide whether the input is new or familiar. A decision of this kind requires selective matching, selective retrieval, and the establishment of meaning, either the meaning of the known stimulus representation or the minimal meaning of similarity or dissimilarity along at least one meaning dimension. It is only after the input's initial meaning has been established that a reaction to the input other than meaning action can take place.

Without allusion to the orienting response, Eccles (1966, p. 322) assumed that "the brain events evoked by sensory information from the retina are interpreted so that they give a valid picture of the external world . . . in which I can effectively move." It is obvious that the findings about the orienting response provide empirical proof in support of interpretations of this type. Also, they make it possible to establish with greater precision—as we have done earlier—which processes one has to postulate in order to account for input processing on the psychological level.

Meaning action is to our mind the most important among these postulated processes. Meaning action occurs whenever a change in the stimulus situation is represented, that is, registered. Yet it would be erroneous to consider meaning action as separate from occurrence of the reflex itself on this level. All evidence runs against conceiving of meaning action as merely a phase of perception, which when completed is followed by an unconditioned or a conditioned reflex. An attempt to combine or to couple through chaining a cognitive model of perception with a mechanistic model of reaction cannot be brought in accord with the results of research on the orienting response. As mentioned above, the autonomic components of the orienting response are not elicited merely through the output of meaning action. They directly contribute to meaning action; in fact they enable the very continuation of meaning action and influence its course.

The recent revision of the outdated model of the reflex suggested by Sherrington is due precisely to rich neurological evidence that all of the organism's input mechanisms are directly controlled by the central nervous system. That is, "output fibers, efferents, regulate the organism's receptor and therefore sensory functions, as well as [its] movements" (Pribram, 1971, pp. 85–86). In other words, the organism revises its perceptions and actions as it goes along, actions and perceptions being inextricably interwined through a multitude of feedback and feedforward loops. The same conclusions are valid to no less degree with regard to conditioned responses. Moreover, they become even clearer when we examine unconditioned and conditioned reactions from the standpoint of the performance mechanism rather than from the standpoint of antecedents and manner of elicitation. Using the terminology of Miller et al. (1960), one may speak of innate or learned plans for unconditioned and conditioned responses, respectively. We, however, prefer the term "behavioral programs" (Chapter 6). It is evident that the choice of the behavioral program is determined by the initial meaning that results as output of meaning action. It is less evident, though nonetheless equally true, that meaning action—either the continuation of the former meaning action or a newly started meaning action—affects the course of the sequence of phases and of the responses chained to one another so as to constitute a well-organized behavioral act.

Our outspoken emphasis on the role of meaning action might overshadow the fact that we in no way urge the identity of our type of cognitively relevant meaning with any relevant kind of meaning or with meaning as such. To take an example from a closely allied behavioral domain: numerous studies show that verbal instructions may affect autonomous behavior (e.g., Nisbett & Valins, 1971; Schachter, 1964, 1967; Valins & Nisbett, 1971). This demonstrates that autonomous processes may be controlled through the kind of meaning dimensions and meaning values that we set up as criteria for cognitive processes. But these findings in no way exclude the possibility that the physiological regulation of these processes occurs through a kind of meaning that perhaps cannot be adequately expressed by means of our meaning dimensions. Hence, it cannot be grasped as cognitive. Moreover, as long as the nature of the "neuronal code" or of any autonomically relevant meanings remains unclear, any attempt at translating our meaning dimensions into neurological or any other physiologically significant meaning dimensions is premature. For translation requires in the very least control of two languages; it is, however, greatly benefited by awareness of the rules that bridge the gap separating the two languages. So far both languages are only very partially deciphered, one barely at all, and the bridging rules are still a mystery.

The major conclusion warranted by this discussion is that reactions or actions above the level of spinal reflexes but below the level of molar behavior are determined, or at least codetermined, by cognitive processes, namely, by meaning action. Accordingly, cognitive processes do not set in at the point where conditioned and unconditioned reflexes end, but rather at the point where conditioned and unconditioned reflexes begin, provided that the descriptive term "begin" is taken to signify not the elicitation of the performance program but the preceding indispensable clarification of representations of stimuli and the choice of adequate reactions. This conclusion implies not merely a lowering of the presumed line of partition between the so-called higher (cognitive) forms of behavior and the lower (noncognitive) forms. In fact, it suggests total removal of the partition as well as awareness of the primary nature of cognitive processes at large.

One important implication of this conclusion is that common "motivational" variables such as reinforcement, frustration, or incentives as such can no longer be assigned the role of steering behavior or determining reactions. All they do is provide stimuli that may become effective through meaning action and only through it. Many studies—too numerous to be cited—demonstrate that a stimulus object cannot turn into a reinforcer merely through the physiological processes to which it gives rise but only through its cognitive elaboration, that is, through the products of meaning action to which it is subjected. Jeffrey (1968, p. 332) has expressed the same idea more operationally by stressing that "a virtue of what is typically called reinforcement is the strength of the OR [orienting response] associated with it." Hebb (1955) reached this conclusion long before the publication of convincing findings about vicarious conditioning (Berger, 1962), learning through modeling (Bandura, 1969), and secondary reinforcement (Longstreth, 1971). Indeed, the assumption that cognitions such as anticipation of reinforcing consequences or information about reward and outcome of performance are the main factors in reinforcement has prevailed in incentive theories of reinforcement and perceptual-cognitive theories of learning (Tolman, 1932) for many years. Yet these were mostly regarded as specialized or restricted theories. It is our contention that meaning action is the factor that explains the effects of reinforcement. Thus, it serves as the common denominator underlying the most varied reinforcers—sensory stimuli, consummatory responses, prepotent responses, intracranial stimulation, and so on—and binding together different theories of reinforcement— sensory stimulation hypotheses, drive reduction hypotheses, incentive hypotheses, and the like. The crucial role of meaning action has probably been overlooked by many since it is all too often masked by the high correlation that exists on the submolar level between certain stimulus objects and specific reactions. It is only when experimental conditions are made less artificial and abstract so as to allow for a range of stimulus interpretations beyond a fixed value superimposed by the experimenter or, alternatively, when those experimental subjects who respond idiosyncratically even under highly artificial conditions are not ignored or removed from the sample—only then does the spurious perfect correlation of 1.00 drop to a lower level. It is then that one may attain or join Hebb's (1955) insight that motivation too cannot be understood separately from cognition.

This insight, however, raises the problem whether there could be a theory of motivation that corresponds to the basic tenets and findings of cognitive psychology. For understandable reasons all too many cognitive psychologists still shy away from this problem. The basic theoretical approaches that dominate the psychological scene do not favor assigning to cognition a more prominent role in motivation. The psychoanalytic theory, for example, postulates that behavior is determined mainly through the primary drives and developmentally conditioned drive components. The role of cognitive processes is restricted to discovering opportunities for drive satisfaction and, in case such opportunities cannot be spotted, to initiating appropriate modifications in the goals of the drives. In principle, the framework of classical psychoanalysis is sufficiently broad to allow for assigning to cognition a more prominent role than Freud and his closest allies gave to it. But such an attempt would run counter to the authentic spirit of psychoanalysis. Therefore it should not be surprising that even cognitively oriented psychologists who operate within the framework of psychoanalysis do not proceed beyond ascribing to cognitive processes a regulative function with regard to behavior. Klein (1970, p. 103), for example, declares: "Working from the psychoanalytic assumption that thought originates in the enforced postponement of drive satisfaction . . . I found it useful to consider cognitive attitudes as contributing to drive activity in a secondary way, not necessarily defensive, by modulating, facilitating, or inhibiting the effects of a temporarily active drive upon behavior." In other words, the main role of cognition is to make possible a delay in drive satisfaction (p. 195). Similarly, other cognitive theories (Gardner, 1964; Holt, 1967; Rapaport, 1967) also demonstrate how difficult it is for psychoanalytically biased psychologists to accord to cognition even some restricted measure of functional autonomy. Yet it is glaringly evident that a phenomenon such as the orienting reflex cannot at all be integrated within the structure of psychoanalysis. For it proves that sublimation, for example sublimation of repressed sexual needs, could neither be the only source nor the major source of curiosity and the desire for knowledge.

This conclusion also contradicts the spirit of behavioristically oriented theories of motivation. It would be superfluous to mention the point were it not that a compromise seems to be easier in the case of behaviorism than psychoanalysis. Evidence for the essential flexibility of behaviorism or neobehaviorism in this matter is provided, for example, by Tolman's (1951) early postulation of exploration as a primary need, by Berlyne's (1960, 1965) introduction to curiosity as a drive aroused by novel, surprising, and complex stimuli and reduced by the "accrual of information" (1960, p. 252ff.), which further strengthens exploration, no less than by Fowler's (1965) more conservative assumptions about curiosity as an incentive-motivational construct.

It has recently become fashionable among psychologists of various disciplines to discuss the human tendency to seek out, absorb, and acquire information. The best empirical foundation for such a tendency has been provided by Jones (1966). In an ingeniously designed series of experiments, Jones exposed human subjects to both sensory deprivation and information deprivation. His findings clearly support the postulation of an information drive. Jones was able to show that information-seeking behavior evidences all those features which in the sense of Hull or Freud would serve as sufficient criteria for assuming the existence of an information drive. Like hunger and thirst this drive is subject to the principles of homeostasis and drive summation. It is elicited by lack of information and is reinforced by information but not by mere stimulation, that is, by signals with little or no informational value. Moreover, some hints suggest that this information drive is at least partly innate.

The adequacy of such theories is a much more relevant problem in our context than the question of whether they are still faithful to the behavioristic credo. It is by no means evident that these various hypotheses or theories attain the goal for which they have been formed. Exploratory drive, perceptual drive, epistemological needs, information drive, the anticipatory consummatory response to change, and the like have been postulated in order to justify the existence of those cognitive processes which until now behaviorists have overlooked on the level of conditioned reflexes and have either ignored or only insufficiently explained on the level of molar behavior. This would undoubtedly be a positive contribution if the postulation of these drives were accompanied by the attempt to investigate the impact of cognitive processes on other functions. Yet such an attempt has hardly been made. As a matter of fact, the S-R bond is still grasped in a purely mechanistic sense. Now as before, reinforcement, frustration, generalization, and the like are rarely if ever considered in terms of their cognitive aspects. Indeed, one gets the impression that the acquisition of information is restricted merely to the function of serving as reinforcement for epistemological drives of different kinds. Evidently, cognition is not yet grasped as a basic process that affects all other processes of perception and response, but rather as a type of behavior similar to other behaviors, such as sleeping or eating, that is, as merely one process among many, devoid of any special status theoretically or practically.

Again, it is doubtful whether the anchoring of cognitive processes in some kind of drive concept designed to serve as their motive does not raise more problems that it solves. With regard to hunger and sex it is relatively easy to specify which behaviors bring about or initiate drive reduction and reinforcement. In the case of perceptual curiosity, exploratory behavior, and information seeking this is hardly possible at all. Berlyne's (1965, pp. 247ff.) suggestion in this matter is that stimuli characterized by novelty, complexity, and other collative variables increase uncertainty. In this context uncertainty means that the present situation may be followed by any of a number of mutually exclusive events, each with its own probability. Thus, a conflict arises among the various incompatible tendencies of response corresponding to the envisaged possibilities. Conflict, however, is characterized by an increase in drive or arousal. The reduction of perceptual curiosity and of uncertainty, apparently through enhanced perception, contributes toward the solution of this conflict and may thus provide reinforcement. On the other hand, Jones (1966) insists that it is the information itself, that is, the intake of information or its contribution to the solving of a conflict, that acts as reinforcement. Maltzman and Raskin (1965) produce a further complication. They argue that "an OR interpretation of curiosity and exploratory behavior does not require the assumption of any sort of drive or drive reduction as a basis for reinforcement. In this respect we differ from Berlyne . . ." (p. 13). Nonetheless, they claim that paying attention (p. 11) or elicitation of the orienting response are in themselves reinforcing (p. 15). Thus, we have here reinforcement without drive or drive reduction. The position adopted by Maltzman and Raskin is highly instructive. It demonstrates the confusion attendant upon coping with cognitive processes in terms of concepts from another domain without first redefining them. These concepts might have served well the analysis of eating and mating behaviors and preparatory manipulations, but they seem oddly out of place, nonrelevant, and unproductive in the new domain of cognition.

Regardless of whether perceptual-exploratory-informational drives may be useful or misleading in the motivational analysis of molar behavior, there is no doubt that they are inadequate for the motivational analysis of the orienting response. If one were to assume that the various components of the orienting reaction are designed to make possible the reduction of an exploratory or information drive, habituation would appear to be a manifestation of relative satiation. Accordingly, it might be expected that a different but new stimulus occurring only a short time after habituation would elicit no orienting response or only a very weak one. This is clearly not the case. The phenomenon of information satiation indeed exists (Jones, 1966). But it is equally true that stimuli which are sufficiently new or complex elicit orienting responses even when they occur sequentially in a long series.

A much more adequate and parsimonious suggestion was made by Hebb (1955). Hebb claims that each sensory event has two distinct yet interrelated functions. One is the arousal or vigilance function and the other is the cue function. Summing up physiological data available at the time and still uncontradicted today, Hebb argues that incoming sensory input is processed not only through the major sensory routes to the adequate sensory projection areas in the cortex, but also through other routes to the nonspecific projection system that may be called the "arousal system." In this manner it mobilizes energy stored in the organism and makes it available for action on any level. Yet this freed energy is undirected. At the same time, the input is also dealt with as a cue.

This means that it elicits cognitive processes whose feedback may generate further arousal and whose products direct the released energy. Thus, the immediate drive value of cognitive processes is no less important than their channelizing function. It is to be noted that this theory is based on the implicit hypothesis that the conceptual nervous system not only has the capacity to elaborate stimuli cognitively but also tends to deal with incoming stimuli as cues. This means that a tendency exists to determine what the incoming stimuli signalize. The common denominators of the various motivational drive theories suggest that drive should be defined as some kind of initiator of energy mobilization or action in the direction of rewarding and/or drive-reducing consummatory behavior. In contrast, by the term "tendency" we refer only to the innate inclination to use a certain ability whenever possible and appropriate. As hypothetical constructs tendencies are superordinate to more specific hypothetical constructs, as, for instance, drives and motives. Cannon's (1932) homeostasis, Helson's (1959) adaptation level, Freud's (1933) repetition principle, and Allport's (1937) functional autonomy are examples of laws that govern such tendencies.

Hebb's theory provides the physio-psychological basis for our concept of signal input developed in Chapter 2 and thus also for the motivational determinants of meaning action and the orienting response. Meaning action and the orienting responses that sometimes result are not produced, at least not primarily, by curiosity and exploration drives, but serve the basic tendency to establish orientation whenever full or partial orientation is lacking or is impaired by a change in stimulation. In other words, the cue value of a stimulus representation in its context is determined through meaning actions. If the initial meaning action fails, orienting responses are elicited to furnish material for further meaning action. The gradually evolving product of meaning action is orientation. As often reiterated, the attainment of orientation is an indispensable antecedent to action other than orienting responses. Since orientation consists of a network of meanings we suggest calling it *cognitive orientation* (CO).

It is intuitively plausible to assume that there exist many levels and types of cognitive orientation, differing in complexity and degree of consciousness. The CO sufficient for eliciting a defensive conditioned response would probably not suffice for steering an act of molar behavior. Further, a CO may be highly elaborate or not; it may be differentially veridical, rational, and realistic; it may be presently formed or almost fully retrieved from memory; it may be more or less conscious; it may be related directly or indirectly to action or not evoke any present behavior at all; its establishment may reduce fear, anxiety, and tension or be completely independent of the immediate requirements of a present situation. But in any of its manifestations CO is an expression of the basic tendency toward orientation.

At this point, it may be appropriate to recall the three basic hypotheses of our theory, mentioned in Chapter 1. They may serve as a summary for the theoretical assumptions presented in this chapter and as a bridge to the central theme of our empirical studies, which is molar behavior and its relations to cognitive orientation. The first hypothesis is that human beings and perhaps also higher animals have a basic tendency to establish, preserve, reestablish, and develop cognitive orientation. We may add that the tendency is primarily innate but may be modified within limits through learning. The second hypothesis is that behavior above the level of spinal reflexes is steered or directed by cognitive orientation and/or by the tendency to establish cognitive orientation. The third and final hypothesis is that detailed information about a specific cognitive orientation is a sufficient basis for predicting the form and direction of ensuing behavior, provided that one knows the actual stimuli in the situation and the forms of behavior available to the individual as abilities and/or tendencies. To this we may add as a corollary that experimentally induced changes in cognitive orientation are expected to produce predicted change(s) in behavior, that is, in its form and direction.

It is hoped that the present chapter has contributed to rendering these hypotheses plausible. Insofar as an assumption about basic tendencies is concerned, it may be accepted at least temporarily if it is shown to be plausible and to lead to better interpretations of known phenomena than other competing assumptions. This is not the case with regard to the second and third hypotheses. Although equally basic, they highlight that type of relation which requires empirical demonstrations before the hypotheses can be accepted even temporarily, or at least not rejected. Later chapters will present many studies prompted by the second and third hypotheses with regard to the molar level of behavior.

Cognitive Orientation on the Molar Level: The Elements

ELICITATION OF MOLAR BEHAVIOR

Whenever we try to distinguish different levels of behavior we have to resign ourselves to highly blurred boundaries. It may be that segmental reflexes, such as the flexion and extension reflexes, can be considered even today as a relatively neat and well-distinguished class of behaviors in spite of increasing evidence that functional and structural systems beyond a specific segment of the spinal cord are involved in their elicitation. But the behaviors above this relatively low level are much more difficult to order and locate. The orienting, defensive, adaptive, and conditioned responses discussed in Chapter 3 are not only very complex behaviors that involve high neuronal centers; they also differ from each other in so many respects that it is doubtful whether they all belong to the same class or represent the same behavioral level. If we sometimes call them reflexes it is not because the label is in any way justified but simply because this term is still used. Indeed, while these behaviors have very little in common with the classical reflex arc, they can hardly be distinguished from what is commonly called molar behavior.

Interestingly, it is precisely the orienting reflex that exemplifies the difficulty of characterizing the differences between the molar and submolar levels. As long as we focus globally on dominant components of orienting such as GSR, decreased heart rate, vasoconstriction and dilation, EEG changes, and the like, they may seem to belong to the same behavioral level. But the motor components of orienting blur the picture considerably. Turning the head in the direction of the stimulus may still pass for reflex behavior, but turning the whole body or even moving toward the stimulus source may frequently resemble molar behavior rather than a reflex. The same goes for more or less elaborate forms of exploratory behavior, notwithstanding the fact that often we can hardly draw the demarcation line between the orienting response and exploratory behavior.

Indeed, none of the common criteria, such as temporal duration, complexity, voluntary control, awareness, and so on, is sufficiently clear and valid to make possible a distinction between molar and submolar behaviors along the whole range of this continuum. Nevertheless, the distinction corresponds to the pervasive assumption that some behaviors are more elaborate than others. This assumption reflects the principle of economy. Applied to behavior it implies that an organism will try first the less elaborate behavior, and will resort to the more elaborate forms only if the simpler ones have failed or are blocked in some sense. Accordingly, the extremes of the behavioral continuum are outlined with sufficient clarity to urge us to accept the distinction between the molar and submolar levels in our attempt to characterize major differences as well as sequential interrelations between them.

One frequently mentioned example of the interrelations between submolar and molar behaviors is the transition from the orienting response to the more elaborate forms of exploratory behavior—those which involve locomotor exploration, investigatory manipulations of objects, and the like. It is safe to conclude on the basis of available evidence (Berlyne, 1960) that exploration proper sets in when the orienting responses, that is, the mere sharpening of sensory organs and simple motor actions, fail to furnish the information necessary for establishing initial meaning, that is, the minimal meaning required for eliciting an unconditioned or conditioned response. In a certain sense exploration may be viewed as an extension in depth and comprehensiveness of the second stage of orienting (Chapter 3).

A similar situation may arise in the case of defensive or adaptive responses. For example, a hot object brought near to the hand elicits a thermoregulatory reflex of vasodilation in the head and hand, accompanied perhaps by a slight reflexive withdrawal of the hand. Yet if the feedback shows that this action was not sufficiently effective in coping with the stimulus of heat, we may resort to more comprehensive actions, such as making a bigger move away from the source of heat, shielding our hand, or engaging in another more or less predictable molar behavior. Transition to the molar level is thus contingent upon failure to cope regardless of the cause of this failure.

Obviously, before molar behavior is mobilized the not-fully-adequate response may be repeated, even more than once. This may reflect an assumption on the part of the organism that the same response will prove adequate in an additional attempt, either because of summated effect or because the repeated elicitation will not be disrupted by some factor that has impeded former elicitations. Again, it is possible that before molar behavior is elicited other responses are elicited on the same behavioral level as the response that proved inadequate, for example, in accordance with the principle of the habit family hierarchy. The outcomes of these new or repeated responses, like those of the original response, are again subjected to meaning action in order to establish their initial meaning so as to determine whether they have been adequate to cope with the situation. At this point it should be mentioned that the criteria for determining the adequacy (or inadequacy) of coping form a part of the meaning of the response. For example, the meaning of a defensive response is avoidance. Checking the success of coping consists in matching the meaning of the result of the response or of the postactional situation against the coping criteria implied in the meaning of the response, for example, the criteria for avoidance. If the testing produces a match, the cycle of action may be regarded as completed. Otherwise transition to the molar level is most likely.

There are, however, stimuli that seem to evoke highly complex forms of molar behavior straightaway, without passing through the initial stage of an unconditioned or conditioned response. Tinbergen (1951) and Thorpe (1956) report that in certain animal species the male starts to attack if another male with particular colors enters its territory. By using dummies, Tinbergen was able to show that a specific shade of a particular color suffices to elicit the sequence of action called instinctive behavior. It is still largely controversial to what extent this whole behavioral sequence is innate or acquired and which of its aspects are innate or acquired. Again, there are no observations that convincingly suggest the existence of innate full-fledged behavioral sequences on the human level. However it may be, there is no doubt that everyday life is full of complex reactions and sequences of behavior elicited directly by some input. Indeed, the greater part of human actions are of this kind. Responding to a question, stopping the car at the signal of a red traffic light, noting down an idea before it is forgotten, perceptual scanning of a situation— these are just a few examples, more or less characteristic.

We thus have three conditions under which transition to molar behavior is most likely:

1. when in spite of improved perception produced by the orienting response, no further information about the stimulus object and the stimulus situation is forthcoming, whereas the already received and processed information is insufficient for establishing the initial meaning necessary to identify the stimulus and subsequently to inhibit the orienting response and release an unconditioned or conditioned response;

2. when the initial meaning necessary for identification of the stimulus has been established and some innate or learned adaptive or defensive response has been triggered off, but feedback information reveals that the response was insufficient to cope with the stimulus and has not led to an adequate mastery of the situation;

3. when the established initial meaning contains the requirement for molar action, that is, the stimulus is interpreted as a signal for a complex behavioral sequence.

These three conditions outline the border region between the submolar and molar levels. Each condition describes in fact a certain sequence. It is to be noted that meaning action is the basic process in all the sequences cited. No control mechanism or decision process beyond meaning action is necessary on the submolar level. All the actions or responses discussed, including the orienting response, are elicited directly by the meaning values established with regard to the input. If we imagine the input as a ball, then it is its meaning that directly determines into which of the "holes" on the board it will fall, that is, to which response it will give rise—unconditioned, conditioned, orienting, molar, or none.

MEANING GENERATION

Our discussion of conditions that mark the transition to the molar level may have created the erroneous impression that the molar level is separated from other levels. As we have mentioned, it is only a region in a continuum. The demand for molar behavior neither inhibits suddenly the processes previously active nor occasions the onset of entirely new processes in an all-or-nothing manner. It merely marks the progressive emergence of more complex forms of behavior. The gradual emergence of these behaviors is mediated by the continuation of meaning action in a more expanded, elaborated, and complex form. In the course of this process, more meaning values are produced, more meaning dimensions are used, and more complex relations are formed among the meaning values themselves and between the meaning values and the referent(s). In this manner the denocepts, which are the meaning values characteristic of meaning action, are replaced by concepts. The product is *comprehensive meaning*. In order to distinguish this process from the relatively simple meaning action, we suggest calling it *meaning generation*.

The characterization of meaning generation may best be understood by comparing it with meaning action, whose expansion and elaboration it represents.

First, we shall compare the two processes from the viewpoint of eliciting conditions. Whereas meaning action is initiated by the representation of incoming stimuli, meaning generation is initiated either by the initial meaning established through meaning action or by both the stimulus representation and previously established meaning values. The latter is the case when no initial meaning could be established at all, or not to the degree and extent sufficient for eliciting some defensive or adaptive response. Under these circumstances the combination of the meaning values attained through meaning action generally yields such an ambiguous profile, full of gaps and uncertainty nodes, that the representation of the original stimulus, insofar as it still exists or can be reconstructed or reestablished, must be resorted to.

Incidentally, the latter remarks reveal that we do not accept the habit, so common recently, of identifying representation as such with cognition. As already mentioned, RNA structures may represent genetic information, but it would be misleading to designate them as cognition. Again, a certain exteroceptive or interoceptive input may be cortically represented by a changed brain-wave pattern without eliciting processes that resemble in any way the subject matter of cognitive psychology. At the risk of redundancy, we must emphasize that cognition starts with meaning action and that its basic static unit is the meaning value, the denocept.

Second, from the viewpoint of function, the task of meaning action is to establish those meaning values which by virtue of their signal or cue function may trigger adequate defensive or adaptive responses, or, alternately, orienting responses. Thus the role of meaning action could not be regarded as providing for a full-fledged identification of the input. Nonetheless, the combination of the meaning values yielded by meaning action makes possible some kind of identification of input. It is, however, a highly restricted or general identification, because it is established merely for the purposes of immediate reaction. As a rule, initial meaning does not include anything that might correspond to a "conception" of the input but only the bare minimum of meaning values with signal value. At its poorest, initial meaning consists only of one meaning value, as in the case of the male stickleback, who in the breeding season attacks within his territory anything with a red patch, the patch sufficing to identify an adult male stickleback with the nuptial markings of an intensely red throat and belly (Tinbergen, 1951). At its best, however, initial meaning includes a few meaning values that may mediate identification in a pars-pro-toto manner. In contrast, the task of meaning generation is to establish comprehensive meaning, which not only provides for identification of the input on a much broader basis but also includes the personal relevance of the stimulus situation for the individual. By virtue of its orientative contents (see "The Orientativeness of Beliefs," this chapter) this comprehensive meaning predisposes the individual toward a certain course of molar action. Thus, comprehensive meaning is anchored in action, unfolds for the sake of action, and directs action to no lesser degree than initial meaning. But while the orientative impact of initial meaning is much more immediate and direct, the orientative impact of comprehensive meaning is the product of more meaning values, interrelated through more complex relations, and subjected to further cognitive elaborations (to be described later). Hence the bond of comprehensive meaning to action is less direct and immediate, more complex and equivocal. However, it is evident that molar no less than submolar behavior is directed and shaped by meaning from its origins to its completion, marked by evaluation of its outcomes. Even exploratory behavior is not elicited automatically whenever repeated meaning actions following several evocations of orienting responses have failed to establish an adequate and sufficient initial meaning. As in the case of other forms of molar behavior, its elicitation depends on the products of meaning generation and certain elaborations of these products (to be discussed in Chapter 5).

Third, from the viewpoint of processes, meaning action may be described as scanning stored schemata, reconstructing these schemata into meaning values, and matching these reconstructed models against the stimulus representation. This set of processes, designed to establish initial meaning, is enacted at least partly in parallel. Meaning generation, too, is anchored in this triad of scanning-reconstructing-matching processes, but each process in the triad is more elaborate than in the case of meaning action. Within the framework of meaning generation more meaning dimensions are used as questions, general hypotheses, or restricted expectations that guide the scanning process. Moreover, the scanning procedures themselves may be more complex. If we assume that there exist search strategies different in complexity and refinement, then meaning action is restricted to the use of the simplest, fastest, and most superficial strategy, whereas meaning generation also utilizes the more elaborate, intensive, and sophisticated ones—for example, those for which Sarbin, Taft, and Bailey (1960) suggest the terms scrutinizing, probing, and soliciting. Similarly, in meaning action reconstructing is manifested mainly in *combining* the retrieved elements into some kind of model; in meaning generation it is manifested also in *generating* the elements to be combined in the model. As a consequence of the relative complexity of scanning and reconstructing, the product of meaning generation and the matching procedure to which it is subjected with regard to the input representation are also far more elaborate. For example, as compared to initial meaning, comprehensive meaning consists of many more meaning values representing many more meaning dimensions. In fact, potentially any of the 21 meaning dimensions may be used. The relations between the meaning values themselves are rendered more complex, for instance, by bonding two meaning values, each reflecting a different meaning dimension, by means of a relation reflecting a third meaning dimension different from those reflected by the bonded meaning values. Also, the complexity of the relations increases in view of the fact that any two meaning values may be related in terms of more than one relation, and may be embedded within the context of several units of interrelated meaning values. This would exemplify enhanced use of the principle of successive contextual embedding characteristic of meaning (Chapter 2). Further, the relations between meaning values and the referent are also richer in the case of comprehensive meaning. Whereas initial meaning makes use primarily of the attributive and comparative relations and perhaps minimally also of the exemplifying-illustrative relation between meaning values and referent, comprehensive meaning also uses to no small extent the metaphoric-symbolic relation. This implies that comprehensive meaning also includes elements of personal-subjective symbolic meanings and not only components of interpersonally shared lexical meaning. Inclusion of personal symbolic components introduces into comprehensive meaning the complex interactions characteristic of this mode of meaning. In sum, both meaning action and meaning generation are sets of processes for the elaboration of meaning. Yet since meaning generation uses more widely and extensively the available possibilities for the elaboration of meaning, the product of meaning generation is richer in contents, more complex and differentiated in structure, as well as stronger and more general in impact than the product of meaning action.

Fourth, from the viewpoint of major directing factors, it should be stressed that the only focal object of meaning action is the exteroceptive and/or proprioceptive input. Meaning action is designed merely to furnish material for answering the question "What is it?" insofar as it refers to the input. The relation between the resulting answer or absence of answer, on the one hand, and the ensuing response, on the other hand, is regulated either by innate factors or by prior learning. In any case, the meaning values established through meaning action suffice either to elicit innate or conditioned responses or to bring about transfer to higher levels of elaboration. Whatever the result, there is clearly no need for assuming a "What-to-do?" question in addition to the basic "What-is-it?" question. In contrast, meaning generation is assumed to establish the comprehensive meaning of the input. This also includes

the personal relevance of the input. Hence, meaning generation is regulated by two focal questions: "What does it mean?" and "What does it
mean to me and for me?" Whereas the first question is an elaborate
form of the central question "What is it?" that guides meaning action,
the second question is new and specific to meaning generation. It raises
the issue of personal relevance, but only insofar as action is concerned.
For the sake of clarifying this question it seems advisable to present it
also in some rephrased forms, such as, "Does it affect me at all?", "In
what way does it affect me?", "Am I concerned in any way?", "Should I
be concerned?" ,"Am I involved personally?", "Should I be involved?",
"Is any action required on my part?", "Am I to act or not?" Foreshad-
owing concepts and processes explained and discussed later, we venture
to introduce yet another more technical rephrasing of the same question: "In which sense(s) does it or may it affect (or concern) my goals,
my norms, my beliefs about myself, and my beliefs about the environment or any of its aspects?" Evidently, the formulation "What does it
mean to me or for me?" is merely a label summarizing these different
variants of the question.

It should, however, be emphasized that in reality the two questions
assumed to guide meaning generation are mostly inextricably intermingled with each other, and an act of abstraction is necessary to conceive
of their distinctness. They have been presented as two separate questions
in order to highlight the different processes that may result from each of
these aspects of meaning generation.

Fifth, from the viewpoint of conditions specifying termination of the
process, meaning action and meaning generation again differ markedly.
Meaning action either terminates when meaning values are established
that trigger innate or conditioned responses, or it develops gradually into
meaning generation owing to the occurrence of signals for molar action,
as outlined above. The conditions under which meaning generation terminates are far less clearly delineated. All too often the meaning values
established in the course of meaning generation do not pertain directly
to the referent, that is, the input itself, but to aspects of its meaning
established in previous stages of meaning processing. Thus, they are
meaning values of meaning values. This is obviously the case with regard
to those aspects of comprehensive meaning that relate to the personal
relevance of the input. In principle, meaning generation could go on for
a very long time. Moreover, even in the next stage of cognitive elaboration, conditions may arise that necessitate repeated meaning generation
in order to produce missing information. Thus, in a certain sense, meaning generation overlaps with the next stage, or at least is kept smoldering
in anticipation of further possible utilization. Hence the difficulty of

specifying precisely when meaning generation stops. In practice, how-ever, meaning generation subsides and is replaced by other forms of cog-nitive activity when sufficient information has accumulated to make pos-sible an answer to the question "What does it mean to me and for me?" insofar as action is concerned. If the answer specifies "action is required," the next stage of cognitive elaboration is initiated by the new question "What am I to do?" If, however, the answer is "no action required," meaning generation does not necessarily stop. It may con-tinue for a while in order to attain adequate coding for the purpose of memory storage or simply for the sake of curiosity or maintaining cogni-tive activity. Yet it usually terminates because new inputs may dominate the scene of cognitive processing.

Sixth, meaning action and meaning generation differ in the units that form their material and their product. The units of initial meaning are simple meaning values or labels, or both. In view of their primarily de-notative function and close relation to percepts, we suggested (Chapter 3) the term denocepts for the combination of these units of meaning action. In contrast, the units of meaning generation are intimately linked to concepts. Sometimes they are outright concepts, at other times they designate groupings akin to concepts or equivalent to them. The products of meaning generation are combinations of concepts. We sug-gest the term *beliefs* for these units of meaning generation (see "Beliefs," this chapter).

It should be stressed that belief is a basic unit of cognitive contents only on the level of those processes which are involved in the elicitation and steering of molar behavior. On the submolar level this role is ful-filled by denocepts. As far as the regulation of action is concerned, this implies that denocepts, which result from meaning action, may elicit meaning generation and form one of its objects, but they do not deter-mine the direction of molar behavior. A behavioral sequence starting with a reflexive retraction of the hand from a pain-evoking source of heat stimuli may well continue on the molar level by approaching that very source of heat. But even when the ensuing molar action takes the same direction as a preceding but unsuccessful conditioned response, the denocepts that have elicited this conditioned response would be an un-reliable predictor of the form and direction characteristic of the molar behavior. The emergence of molar behavior must indeed be traced back to meaning action and to the denocepts that interpret the representation of the input, but the initial meaning of the input is evidently only one of the many determinants of molar behavior.

Of course, just as meaning generation can be viewed as an enlarged and more elaborate version of meaning action, beliefs could be seen as a more complex form of denocepts, or alternately, denocepts could be regarded as the rudimentary or incipient form of beliefs. Yet such an attempt at a merging of terms would neither promote greater clarity nor contribute to the understanding of the determinants of molar behavior. For—as gestalt psychologists have shown almost half a century ago—the properties of a combination of elements cannot be deduced from, nor determined through, the summation of the properties of the constituent elements and their various interrelations. Just as comprehensive meaning is not simply more of initial meaning but rather a different kind of meaning, beliefs are not merely more varied or more complexly interrelated denocepts but a new unit of cognitive contents that may make use of elements also applied in denocepts or represented by them.

Having followed closely the list of six characteristics differentiating meaning action and meaning generation, the reader may perhaps wonder why we have not named the products of meaning action and meaning generation denotative meaning and connotative meaning, respectively. Indeed, in an earlier version of our model we did adopt these terms (Kreitler & Kreitler, 1972a). We were, however, forced to abandon this practice in view of the amazing diversity of definitions that weighs down upon these terms. Perusal of the different definitions cited by Cohen and Nagel (1934), Frankena (1958), or Martin (1964) should easily convince the skeptic that the best one can do is to avoid such overworked terms, which necessarily retain overtones of other definitions even when a new or existing definition is clearly stated in some text. Figure 4.1 summarizes the major processes involved directly and indirectly in meaning generation.

BELIEFS

We define belief as at least two meaning values related explicitly or implicitly by means of a third meaning value. This definition emphasizes the nature of the elements of belief and of the relation between the elements. Identifying the elements of belief as meaning values differentiates our concept of belief from other apparently similar cognitive units like attitude, "module" (Sarbin, Taft & Bailey, 1960), "schema" (Stotland & Cannon, 1972), chunk (Tulving, 1962; Wood, 1972), cognition (Insko & Schopler, 1967), or "belief" as defined by Ackoff and Emery (1972), Fishbein (1967a), and others. For example, attitude is often regarded as comprising one (Asch, 1952; DeFleur & Westie, 1958; Fishbein, 1961; McGuire, 1960; Rosenberg, 1956; Sherif, Sherif & Nebergall, 1965; Triandis, 1964a) or more (Rokeach, 1968, chap. 5; Rosenberg & Hovland, 1960, p. 3) of three types of components—the affective, the

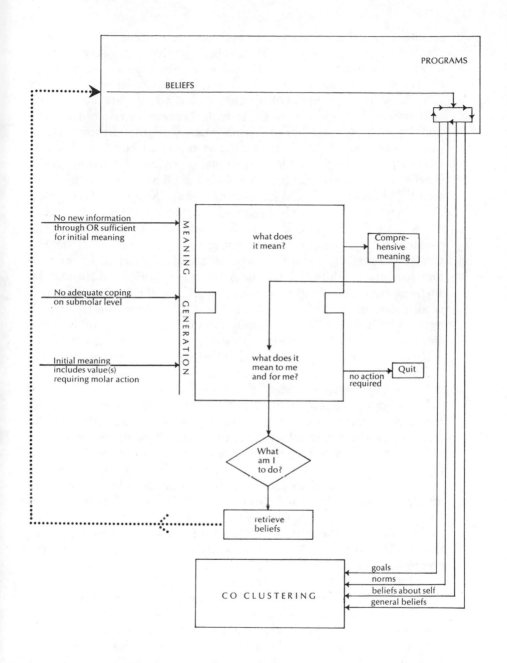

FIGURE 4.1 Meaning generation and evocation of the four CO components. The dotted lines represent connections with memory.

cognitive, and the behavioral. Indeed, our term "belief" may include affective evaluations insofar as these reflect positive or negative relations between the meaning value "I" and some other person, object, etc. referred to in a meaning value. Moreover, belief may accommodate not only the cognitive component of attitudes but also the actional component insofar as it refers to verbal statements about behavior. Yet these would reflect certain types of beliefs rather than the elements out of which beliefs are built. Defining the elements of belief as meaning values seems to us preferable to the usual procedure of referring to the elements as concepts (Colby, 1968; Colby & Gilbert, 1964), objects or events (Mandler, 1967), arguments or nouns (Kintsch, 1972), predicates (Suppes, 1957), words (Stone et al., 1966), attribute lists (Abelson & Carroll, 1965), or classes, all of which limit unnecessarily the potential range of beliefs without solving the major problem of the elements' meaning. It is also preferable to the alternatives of referring to the elements as "things" (Abelson & Rosenberg, 1958), which may be anything from everything to nothing, or defining the elements in terms of all the actual or potential information tied to them directly or indirectly (Quillian, 1967). In contrast, viewing the elements of belief as meaning values makes possible identifying the elements with sufficient specificity in terms of a well-founded, empirically tested, and relatively comprehensive set of meaning dimensions, without placing on them any restrictions of reference, existence, abstractness, etc.

Similarly our suggestion to view the relation itself between the elements of a belief as a meaning value helps to avoid the pitfalls of the prevalent procedures, which concentrate on specifying the relation either in a formal manner or through examples. Whereas the former approach is promoted mainly by linguists and logicians, the latter is preferred by psychologists. It is obvious that describing a relation as an "association" or "dissociation" (Abelson & Rosenberg, 1958), or as "similarity" and "proximity" (Collins & Quillian, 1972a, 1972b), is too formal to do justice to the meaning of the relation, while lists of relations (Rokeach & Rothman, 1965; Weick, 1968) are necessarily restricted and, being unsupported by any underlying principle of some generality or validity, degenerate into a series of instances that cannot be applied to any wider context or system beyond themselves. In contrast, viewing this relation between meaning values as a meaning value enables an integration of all relations mentioned by others within a unitary framework. It is clear that no restriction is to be imposed on the mode of the relation or its form of expression. Accordingly we suggest that a relation may assume any of the following possible modes: the attributive, the comparative, the exemplifying-illustrative, or the metaphoric-symbolic (Chapter 2).

Further, regardless of its mode, the relation may be expressed in any form—linguistic, mathematical, perceptual, or imaginal. If expressed verbally, the relation is either reflected syntactically (e.g., "He lives") or stated explicitly by a meaning value whose function it is to relate the other meaning values (e.g., "The book *belongs* to Nancy"). Since in an image a relation may be manifested through location and spatial proximity or distance, our definition of belief emphasizes that a relation may be expressed not only explicitly but also implicitly.

However, the relation binding the meaning values together is not merely another element of a belief. It is through the relation that the meaning of a belief is different from the meaning(s) of each of the constituent elements singly or even from the sum of their meanings. This fact is a major justification for viewing the belief as a unit, different from other lower-level and higher-level units.

We will now list seven major properties of beliefs, which underlie the important role played by beliefs in the processes involved in directing behavior.

First, a belief is a cognitive unit and not a behavior or a predisposition to behavior. This is another of the major features distinguishing the concepts of belief and attitude. In contrast to attitude, which is often regarded as a predisposition to action (Allport, 1954; Fishbein, 1967b; Rokeach, 1968, chap. 5) and sometimes as referring to actual emotions, perceptions, or behaviors, belief remains always sharply distinct from the behavioral output. Unlike attitude (Campbell, 1950; Cook & Selltiz, 1964) it cannot even be inferred from any behavioral act other than verbal or nonverbal communication of the belief. Similarly, an important reason that precludes identifying belief with a proposition in the logical sense is that a proposition depends on the possibility of assigning to the statement a truth value, which is often equivalent to the operational implications of the proposition. Nonetheless, belief has behavioral implications, which are reflected in what we call its orientative aspect ("The Orientativeness of Beliefs," this chapter). Since the orientative value of a belief may change indefinitely in different contexts it makes no sense to us to identify belief with its behavioral implications or, for that matter, with its truth-functional value.

Second, there are no restrictions on the object, source, foundation, or informational support of the meaning values that comprise a belief, nor on the contents, source, rationality, consistency, commonness, salience, foundation, or veridicality of the belief itself. In other words, all these qualities seem to us immaterial to the characterization of belief as a unit. In this respect as well beliefs differ from most other similar cognitive units. For example, whereas the object of attitude is mostly assumed to be some class of stimuli represented through an object or some abstraction endowed with a minimal degree of constancy, the object of beliefs may be any aspect of the external or internal environment regardless of its constancy or endurance. Similarly, qualities of attitudes like centrality or salience (Rokeach, 1968, chap. 1; Zajonc, 1960) seem to us inconsequential since they are apt to change with the behavioral context. In other words, any belief may become prominent in a situation that sets a priority on the meaning of the specific belief.

Major among the qualities we would like to discount in this context is the veridicality or interpersonally gauged validity of a belief. A belief of any degree of veridicality, that is, a veridical as well as a mistaken belief, may play a role in directing behavior. Even the orientative aspect of a belief is independent of its truth or falsity.

Third, beliefs may be conscious, not conscious but accessible to consciousness, or entirely subconscious. This implies that an individual need not be aware of a belief or of its implications for the belief to be a functionally active unit. Indeed, it is plausible that all too often we ignore, if not our beliefs, at least most of their implications. Here again belief differs from attitude and other cognitive units.

Fourth, many different media can be used for expressing beliefs. Consequently, no special connection should be assumed between beliefs and language (Armstrong, 1968) or between beliefs and sentences in general or even a particular syntactic form of a sentence. Not only are there subverbal beliefs in the prelinguistic stage (Natsoulas, 1970), but even human adults have many beliefs that are wholly or partly averbal or subverbal. Yet we assume that in principle any belief can be expressed verbally in the form of a sentence. Nonetheless, the precise linguistic form through which a belief is expressed seems to us irrelevant. For example, the forms "His mother loves him," "He is loved by his mother," "His mother's love for him," etc., are all equivalent from our point of view.

Fifth, beliefs are not necessarily permanent or even enduring units. In this too beliefs differ from attitudes and other cognitive units, which are commonly endowed with at least some degree of endurance (Fishbein, 1967b; Sarbin et al., 1960; Scheibe, 1970). Some beliefs are retrieved from memory or stored in memory for later use. These are permanent to some extent. Others may reflect an enduring core of meaning but be transient in form, that is, they may be expressed in a certain context in a particular linguistic or other mode that is later discarded or forgotten. Beliefs may also be produced on the spur of the moment simply to serve some specific purpose. Such beliefs, which are the products of instantaneous generation, may be of varying endurance.

Sixth, a belief is a unit of indeterminate size that may be contracted or extended to a certain degree in accordance with the requirements of a situation and of an individual. In this respect a belief resembles such cognitive units as "chunks" in learning (e.g., Bower, 1972; Kintsch, 1970; Wood, 1972), sentence in linguistics, and proposition in logic (Suppes, 1957), but differs from other units, mainly attitudes. The extensions occur in the form of elaborations appended to a certain nucleus that functions as the core of the belief. These elaborations often assume the role of specifications imposed on the more general meaning of the nucleus (Chapter 13). For example, the nuclear unit may be "Belief is a cognitive unit," whereas potential appendable specifications could be "of indeterminate size," "with an important function for molar behavior," "consisting of concepts," "accepted by some investigators," etc. The number of these appended elaborations is potentially infinite but is practically limited through the requirements of the context.

Seventh, as a unit of meaning each belief is embedded in networks of beliefs and other units on the same level as beliefs, as well as on other higher and lower levels of comprehensiveness. In this respect belief resembles all other major types of cognitive units, although the nature and extent of the auxiliary networks differ. Contextual embeddedness not only implies relations with the preceding and succeeding beliefs that form a kind of immediate environment for the focal belief; it also includes relations with beliefs that may not actually occur in a particular situation but are closely allied to the focal belief. For example, there may be beliefs that support the focal belief; exemplify it, for instance by personal memories (Kreitler & Kreitler, 1968a); are derived from it, perhaps by a method similar to "evaluative assertion analysis" (Osgood, Saporta, & Nunnally, 1956); or form presuppositions necessary for its understanding (Lakoff, 1971; McCawley, 1968; Schmidt, 1973, chap. 5). Frequently beliefs are embedded in a hierarchy as, for instance, a hierarchy ordered in accordance with preference, generality, credibility, or utility with regard to a particular purpose, and so on. Finally, each belief is also embedded in more comprehensive structures. These include, for example, constellations of beliefs centered on some criterial referent as the "belief system" discussed by Abelson (1959), the group of attitudes described by Kerlinger (1967), or the "semantic field" as conceived in linguistics (Öhman, 1953; Trier, 1931). A similar group of beliefs, which we call *belief cluster*, is of importance in our context. We define it as a constellation of beliefs focused on a certain theme, which is represented by means of at least one specific meaning value shared by all the beliefs included in the belief cluster. On a higher level, the grouping of beliefs may become more inclusive and take the form of a doctrine, ideology, or faith (Cooper & McGaugh, 1966), or even of the totality of all the individual's knowledge (Colby, 1968; Kintsch, 1972). We do not share the common assumption (Abelson et al., 1968; Newcomb, 1959; Osgood & Tannenbaum, 1955; Rokeach, 1968) that more inclusive groupings of beliefs are necessarily subject to the striving for consonance and balance.

The wider and narrower contexts in which a belief is embedded constitute a kind of tacit knowledge (Polanyi, 1966) that turns each belief into the vertex of a pyramid, a point beyond which increasingly large domains of knowledge unfold the closer we approach it. This implies that each belief is a sample from a much larger constellation of beliefs on various levels. Practically it means not only that the strength or utility of a belief for the individual as well as for a researcher depend on this submerged population of beliefs but also that certain margins of error are allowed the researcher in sampling beliefs from the invisible, actual, and potential ocean of beliefs.

THE FOUR COMPONENTS
OF COGNITIVE ORIENTATION

As the product of meaning generation, beliefs relate to the different aspects of the input and thus are of paramount importance for answering the question "What does it mean?" that underlies the formation of comprehensive meaning. Comprehensive meaning in turn contributes to the evocation and generation of further beliefs designed to answer the question "What does this input mean to me and for me?" More often than not it is not asked explicitly but remains implicit. If the answer to this question, based on the elicited beliefs, indicates the necessity of any action, then the next stage of the process consists in producing additional beliefs and reorganizing those formerly produced beliefs that are particularly suited to answering the crucial question "What am I to do?" (see Figure 4.1). Beliefs point to an answer or answers to this question owing to their orientative aspect. It is important to emphasize that all beliefs, even the most neutral ones, contain potential cues for orientation. Under some circumstances these cues remain subdued or implicit, under other circumstances they become more salient, and they are most prominent in those beliefs that relate directly to the question "What am I to do?" Again, the term "question," as used here and in other places, should not be understood as indicating an internal dialogue. We use this term as a descriptive label for an assumed cognitive process considered from the viewpoint of its immediate results.

By recognizing the orientative aspect of beliefs (to be discussed in greater detail in "The Orientativeness of Beliefs," later in this chapter) we could hypothesize that beliefs predispose the individual to make a particular behavioral choice out of the available behavioral alternatives.

This hypothesis implies the more specific hypotheses—underlying the experiments described in Part II—that beliefs are crucial for the prediction of molar behavior, and that substituting for some beliefs other beliefs with different meanings and hence with different orientative impacts would result in a predictable change of molar behavior.

It goes without saying that these hypotheses are derived from the more general assumption, basic to our theory, that cognitive orientation —its content and processes—directs behavior. The assumption of a close relationship between cognitive orientation and beliefs requires explanation and specification. It is also likely to raise the seemingly well-substantiated objection: Why postulate that beliefs may be used as a major factor for behavior prediction while the findings of so many experimental studies repeatedly show either no correlation or a very low correlation between beliefs and behavior? In fact, most of these studies have been conducted in order to investigate the relation between attitudes and behavior. Nonetheless, since attitudes may be considered as operationally equivalent to beliefs, the demonstrated absence of relation between attitudes and behavior (e.g., Wicker, 1969) makes any assumption of such a relation utterly unrealistic, even though it is frequently presented (e.g., Cohen, 1964, pp. 137–138).

The objection could be countered simply by pointing to our own research findings, discussed in Part II of this book. However, to our mind this would be too behavioristic a way of arguing and moreover would constitute only half an answer, leaving open the question of why we succeeded where so many others failed. Our explanation for the very intriguing lack of correlation between attitudes and behavior is threefold.

First, many, if not all, of the researchers investigating the impact of attitudes upon behavior accepted the attitudinal beliefs expressed by their subjects at face value. That is, they took it for granted that the attitude stated by the subject had the same meaning for the subject that it had for the investigator. This, however, is an unfounded and frequently very misleading assumption. For example, if a subject states his belief that no human being should be discriminated against it could well be that for him the meaning of the term "discriminate" does not include anything relating to social intercourse. Or, even worse, for a subject inflicted by nazism the term "human" may not include certain races or minority groups. In other words, when looking for a correlation between beliefs and behavior the experimenter should determine—as a precondition—which meaning the belief has for the subject and whether this meaning is related to the meaning the subject has about the behavior expected to be correlated with the belief.

Second, in simply expecting a correlation between beliefs and behavior without controlling what lies in between, investigators have ignored the already impressive bulk of data and theories in regard to intention, decision making, availability of plans for performance and their adaptation to the particular behavioral situation, not to speak of conflicts on different levels. Stated crudely, an architect's belief that a building should be well designed does not warrant the expectation that he will actually take the necessary trouble to design well.

Third, most of the studies dealing with attitudes and behavior are based on the attempt to correlate behavior with only one or two types of belief (Chapter 12). However, outside the domain of psychological research psychologists and laymen alike are well aware of the fact that a person who fully agrees with the statement "Decent people do not steal" may still hold the conviction that he himself is in this respect not entirely decent, or alternatively that given his own decency, the statement should not be binding if it proves to be at odds with one's most important goals. In everyday life many people, when considering the probable behavior of a friend or a neighbor, intuitively take more than one type of belief into account and sometimes even consider the interactions of beliefs. In failing to exploit and systematize this intuitive knowledge psychologists have a poor chance of proving a significant relation between beliefs and behavior.

It goes without saying that we tried to avoid these three mistakes by paying great attention to the meaning of beliefs (Chapters 2, 7–11), by analyzing theoretically and controlling experimentally the stage most relevant for behavior evocation (Chapters 5–6, 7–11), and by developing a broader and more systematic approach to beliefs than has hitherto been adopted in this domain of research. In the present context we will explore only the last of these points.

Our awareness that more than one type of belief may be necessary for predicting molar behavior was first aroused while we were analyzing empirical data collected for a study of the schizophrenic belief matrix and its relation to prominent schizophrenic symptoms (H. & S. Kreitler, 1965; see also Chapter 10). We observed that whereas beliefs belonging to a specific homogeneous type are either not at all or very slightly correlated with behavior, beliefs belonging to a variety of types and themes show a high and meaningful correlation with the behavior in question. Those belief clusters that yielded high correlations with behavior consisted not only of beliefs of the normative type or about the behavior of other people but also beliefs about personal aspirations, convictions of the subject with regard to his own abilities and shortcomings, as well as statements that can best be characterized as expressions of general knowledge. Moreover, the analysis of those clusters containing contradictory beliefs revealed clear indications of belief interaction. Of course, our understanding of these findings was still too shallow and general for immediate application to our study of the schizophrenic belief matrix. It sufficed, however, to initiate and spur our attempt to categorize beliefs.

This attempt was aided by relevant hypotheses and observations of other workers in this field. Some psychologists (e.g., Ajzen & Fishbein, 1969; Campbell, 1963; Dillehay, Bruvold, & Siegel, 1969; Fishbein, 1967a; Schwartz, 1970; Wicker, 1969) presented hypotheses and studies purporting to explain the observed inconsistency between attitudinal beliefs and actual behavior. Most specify hitherto neglected belief types and suggest their consideration in predicting behavior. For example, Fishbein (1967a) proposes adding personal and social normative beliefs, each weighted by the individual's motivation to comply with the norm; Insko and Schopler (1967) argue for also considering beliefs about the future consequences of behavior; Warner and DeFleur (1969) proved the role of beliefs about the community to which the subject belongs; Berkowitz (1972, pp. 83–84) demonstrated the importance of beliefs about one's own previous behavior, whereas Schwartz (1970) showed the function of beliefs about personal responsibility for one's own actions and their consequences for the welfare of others. These suggestions are encouraging for the endeavor to specify basic belief types that may be relevant for the prediction of behavior. Yet they are disjointed and unsystematized to a degree that renders them of little use theoretically or experimentally. Similarly, categorizations of beliefs such as those offered by Fishbein (1967b), Lazarus (1966) and others (Rokeach, 1968; Scheibe, 1970) are too closely bound in a post hoc manner to specific types of data, and lack a convincing theoretical background. Moreover, they do not seem to have been applied in studies in a manner that provided proof of their theoretical or practical utility.

Somewhat more systematic and theoretically better-founded suggestions have come from investigators in fields allied to psychology. For instance, Parson, Shils, and Olds (1951, pp. 162–164) classify cultural elements into cognitive (factual), affective (desired), and evaluative (normative, desirable); Kluckhohn (1951) differentiates values (desirable), goals (desired), and existential (factual) propositions; whereas Ackoff and Emery (1972) distinguish between beliefs about the environment, course of action, response capabilities, etc. (factual) and beliefs in intentions and utilities (the desired). These classifications are based on generalized classes of cognitive content. As already indicated by the words in parentheses, these generalized cognitive contents can be identified as statements or beliefs expressing something desired, something desirable, and something factual, although these terms are not used by the authors mentioned. The terms suggested by us were, however, stimulated to a certain degree by the conception of relations underlying logically defined modal operators along the lines indicated, for example, by Hintikka (1969). Thus, beliefs expressing the desirable may be regarded as reflecting necessity ("It is necessary that . . . ," "It ought to be the case that . . ."); beliefs expressing the factual may be regarded as reflecting actuality and possibility ("It is the case . . . ," "It is possible that . . ."); whereas beliefs expressing the desired may be regarded as reflecting an operator such as, "I wish it to be the case that . . .".

Guided by our analysis of these ideas and explorations of preliminary data provided by interviewing various pretest subjects, we conjectured the types of beliefs most necessary for reaching a decision with regard to behavior: beliefs reflecting the personally desired state of affairs, beliefs reflecting what is generally considered desirable, beliefs reflecting relevant factual information, and beliefs reflecting information pertaining to one's own personality, that is, abilities, habits, inclinations, and the like. In utilizing this scheme of beliefs to order our belief collection we found that it constitutes a satisfactory characterization of those beliefs most frequently mentioned by our subjects as relevant for behavioral decisions.

Considered from a more formal point of view, the four belief types appear to belong to two distinct groups: beliefs a person has with regard to his internal world, with regard to his "I," and beliefs a person has with regard to the external world, with regard to everything that is "not I." Thus there emerge two kinds of classificatory criteria that underlie our belief types: one reflects whether a belief refers to the I or to the non-I; the other reflects whether a belief expresses the desired, the desirable, or the factual. All the possible combinations of categories specified by the two classificatory criteria yield six belief types. However, since beliefs about other people's desires and norms have the same psychological and epistemological status as beliefs about other human actions, physical events, and social laws, with which they were highly ($r=.80$–$.85$) correlated in pretest studies, and since beliefs about the personally desirable are in fact general norms endorsed by the self with regard to oneself, we decided in favor of a fourfold categorization of beliefs. The resulting four belief types fulfill in our theory the role of the four CO components.

The four belief types are:

1. *Beliefs about self* (BS). Formally the belief consists of the meaning value "I" as subject, linked to one or more meaning values by means of a meaning value that reflects a factual relation (is so, is not so). Beliefs of this type express information about oneself or any aspect of the self

—one's habits, actions, abilities, feelings, sensations, etc. (e.g., "I never lie").

2. *General beliefs* (GB). Formally the belief consists of a non-I meaning value serving as subject, linked to one or more meaning values by means of a meaning value that reflects a factual relation. Beliefs of this type express information about people, objects, events, situations, or any aggregate or aspect of these, in the present, past, or future (e.g., "People lie a lot"; "Lying is not punished").

3. *Beliefs about norms and rules* (N). Formally the belief consists of a non-I meaning value serving as subject, linked to one or more meaning values by means of a meaning value that reflects a normative relation (should, ought not). Beliefs of this type express norms, rules, and standards of an ethical or nonethical nature, applied to people, behavior, objects, situations, events, etc., or any aggregate or aspect of these (e.g., "People should not lie"; "Life should not be based on lies").

4. *Beliefs about goals* (Go). Formally the belief consists of the meaning value "I" as subject, linked to one or more meaning values by means of a meaning value that reflects a desired relation (wanted, rejected). Beliefs of this type express future actions, behavior, objects, situations, etc., or any aggregate or aspect of these desired or aspired to by the self (e.g., "I want to lie with fewer guilt feelings").

The evidence in support of this fourfold classification of beliefs derives from the empirical studies described in Part II. Here we will only summarize the main findings. The most important finding is that beliefs of the four types make possible predictions of actual behaviors as diverse as achievement behavior, behavior following success and failure, coming late, reactions to pain, curiosity, etc. (see in particular Chapters 7, 8, and 10). The studies show specifically that consideration of each of the four types of beliefs and not merely of their sum total is necessary for predicting behavior. This suggests that each belief type contributes uniquely to predicting behavior. The studies do not and cannot show that there are no other belief types of relevance. This, however, is a purely empirical question; if it is shown that the four belief types do not suffice for predicting a certain class of behavior or even any one single behavior, then an attempt should be made to define further types or to split up one or more of our four types into their component parts—e.g., general beliefs could be split into beliefs about other persons and beliefs about nonperson aspects of the environment.

The second finding of importance is that the differentiation of the four belief types exists already in children (Chapter 8; Kreitler & Kreitler, 1967a; Kreitler, Kreitler, & Zigler, 1974). This again strengthens the status of the four belief types as authentic factors in cognitive contents.

The third type of empirical support for our fourfold classification is of a different order. It consists in showing that the four belief types are probably more than an intervening variable. Already in earlier studies we found that when subjects—adults or children—were asked open-ended general questions, they often referred in their answers to beliefs of more than one of the four types, provided that the questions related to behavior or its motives (H. & S. Kreitler, 1965; Kreitler & Kreitler, 1967a). In a more recent study (Chapter 11, Study II), however, we found that when subjects are asked to select from long lists of beliefs those beliefs which could underlie or lead to a decision to act in a particular way, they check beliefs of all four CO components and even do so to an equal degree.

The fourth point focuses on the comprehensiveness of our fourfold classification. As will be shown in Chapter 12, the four belief types suffice for classifying all items of many attitude scales in the most varied domains. The same is true with regard to personality inventories. In fact, our classification includes practically all content types of beliefs suggested by other investigators (e.g., Fishbein, 1967b; Lazarus, 1966; Rokeach, 1968). The comprehensiveness and adequacy of the classification for different kinds of cognitive material support our claim that the four belief types reflect four essential facets or levels of reality, distinguishable with regard to any object, such as a work of art (Kreitler & Kreitler, 1972c, chap. 15), no less than with regard to personality.

Finally, in order to avoid misunderstanding, two points should be emphasized. The first is that beliefs of the four types are closely interrelated. This point would be too obvious to deserve mention were it not for our emphasis on the relative independence of each type as a separate cognitive component. Belief types interact not only in directing behavior (Chapter 5) but also in providing rationales for beliefs (e.g., "I want to be rich because money buys things": goals–general beliefs) and in giving rise to further beliefs. For example, Bem (1972) showed that general beliefs may be the source of beliefs about self with respect to emotions. Similarly, we demonstrated (Kreitler & Kreitler, 1967b) that the readiness to act for the attainment of general ideals (beliefs about self) depends on availability of beliefs about ways for attaining these ideals (general beliefs).

The second point of clarification is designed to forestall the erroneous identification of the four CO components with apparently similar psychological concepts. Thus, beliefs about norms are not identical with conscience, first because norms need not have a moral content, and second because, in addition to ethically oriented norms, conscience includes means for internal control, such as feelings of guilt and shame

(Sears, Maccoby, & Lewin, 1957, pp. 376–393). Similarly, beliefs about goals should not be identified with the ideal self. The ideal self refers exclusively to personal goals and consists operationally in positively evaluated traits. Beliefs about goals, on the other hand, are not limited to traits but also designate situations, events, objects, etc. Nor do they refer exclusively to the self, although the person desires or rejects them (e.g., "I do not want people to become apathetic and withdrawn"). Likewise, the class of beliefs about self is not identical with self-concept as it is often defined. For example, it differs from Allport's (1961) concept of self, which exercises such functions as self-extension and rational coping, from Freud's (1927) concept of the ego as the agent of compromise between different demands, and from Sullivan's (1947) self-dynamism, which is in charge of monitoring anxiety-free behavior. But it has a lot in common with the various conceptions of the self as a configuration of perceptions and hypotheses about oneself (Epstein, 1973; Rogers, 1959, p. 200; Snygg & Combs, 1949).

THE ORIENTATIVENESS OF BELIEFS

Beliefs direct behavior. But experimental findings, theoretical considerations, and the dictates of plausibility clearly suggest that beliefs have no direct impact upon behavior. Instead, we assume some intermediate indispensable stages between the evocation of beliefs and the resulting behavioral acts (Chapters 5 and 6). The major stages include CO clustering, formation of a behavioral intent, and programming, which transforms the intent into a precise plan of performance. In CO clustering, the first of these stages, the directionality of the presently active beliefs becomes operative and enables interactions between the beliefs so that they may be integrated into a CO cluster. The various processes that constitute clustering are anchored in the orientative property of beliefs. Indeed, orientativeness is the one basic concept that is absolutely necessary for postulating the impact of beliefs upon behavior.

Such an impact is openly declared or covertly assumed not only in cognitive theories but even in essentially noncognitive or anticognitive frameworks. Although it may seem incongruent to many, Skinner—in some prominent passages notably ignored by behaviorists and cognitivists alike—assigns to subaudible self-mands and self-tacts the capacity to control and direct ensuing motor behavior by increasing its probability. The examples he cites reveal these self-mands and self-tacts to be equivalent to if not fully identical with what we call beliefs. Thus, according to Skinner, expressions of "ought" and "should'" describe contingencies of reinforcement. "When, then, a man tells himself *I ought to say* 'No,' he is asserting that 'No' would have certain reinforcing consequences . . . and may increase its [the reinforcing contingency's] effect on the speaker" (Skinner, 1957, pp. 443–444). Similarly, "the hunter who can tell himself *stand still* is probably at an advantage in controlling himself in the field" (ibid., p. 440). In contrast, the self-mands do not necessarily reflect formerly reinforced actions, but may derive from other thought elements. Accordingly, their reinforcement may not be an expected action and its outcome, but consists in what they are and do to the individual, e.g., "as the artist paints what reinforces him visually" or "the writer composes verbal stimuli which arouse (in himself and, incidentally, in others) emotional or other kinds of responses, or serve as prompts or probes to permit him to behave verbally" (ibid., p. 439).

Similarly, Freud, although diametrically opposed to what Skinner represents, implicitly assumes and practically exploits the presumed impact of beliefs on behavior. This he does regardless of whether he finds in the course of therapy that the beliefs reflect reality or a defense-like rationalization or projection. This same assumption, that a belief predisposes towards a certain course of action, underlies his definition of thinking as a trial action in fantasy designed to test the best opportunities for drive reduction. Notably, the better part of psychoanalytical treatment consists in changing the patient's belief matrix by making its subconscious parts conscious and subjecting them to rational reevaluation.

Of course, the agreement between Skinner and Freud in this matter should not be overrated. Skinner would still claim that the important changes in overt and covert behavior are brought about by operant conditioning or, in the case of covert thinking activities, by automatic self-administered reinforcement. Psychoanalysis, in its turn, sticks to the hypothesis that regardless of therapeutic intervention, changes in behavior or in the belief matrix are due to shifts in cathexis or substitution of defenses. Common to both theories is the lack of any indication about the manner in which the impact of cognitive contents on behavior takes place. How is this impact exerted? Which property of cognitive contents or of behavior makes this impact possible?

The concept that best reflects the directive power of beliefs is orientativeness. Orientativeness is an aspect of the contents of any belief. Thus, it is a cognitive property of beliefs. Functionally it may be defined as the potential power of specific meaning values of a belief to direct a cognitive process in a specific direction. Orientativeness salient in one situation may be irrelevant in another and is liable to be replaced by a different orientativeness. Any single meaning value may in principle have some orientativeness in some situation under certain circumstances. Orientativeness is thus a potential quality that becomes emergent in a particular context through interaction with other beliefs and under the pressure of the overall required directiveness.

Theoretically, one may conceive of orientativeness from different viewpoints, such as moral, aesthetic, interpersonal, and so on. The orientativeness on which we focus is behavioral. It is a purely action-oriented concept. In order to stress this point as well as to emphasize the cognitive nature of orientativeness, we have coined the term *cognitive orientativeness*. As distinct from general orientativeness, cognitive orientativeness designates a more limited set of concepts specifically bound to our theory. It may be defined as the potential power of the meaning values of beliefs, functioning singly or in interaction, to promote the formation of a specific behavioral intent and thus to predispose the individual toward a certain overt molar behavior. The major product of cognitive orientativeness is a cluster of beliefs—the cognitive orientation (CO) cluster. It includes beliefs of the four types, which have been evoked in response to the question "What am I to do?" and the comprehensive meaning, and which in turn mostly give rise to a behavioral intent. Thus, the cognitive orientation cluster predisposes the individual toward a specific behavior by virtue of the cognitive orientativeness inherent in the meaning values of the beliefs and their interactions.

The concept of cognitive orientativeness rests upon the assumption that every single belief of the four types described earlier has at least one behavioral facet. In other words, at least one of its meaning values refers to some action or behavior. The meaning dimensions most likely to reflect or to prompt reference to an action are "action(s) and potentialities for action" (dimension 4, Chapter 2), "function, purpose, or role" (dimension 3, Chapter 2), and "consequences and results" (dimension 7, Chapter 2). However, in principle, reference to action may occur in conjunction with any of the other meaning dimensions as well.

Cognitive orientativeness seems self-evident in the case of simple goal beliefs. Many of these beliefs include a meaning value that refers directly to some well-defined action. "I want to drink a glass of Scotch" and "I want to go home" are trivial examples of this. Other goal beliefs contain a less direct reference to action. This is true of goal beliefs that refer to desired or rejected events or situations, such as "I want to be near my family" or "I would like to be admired." In order to uncover the behavioral facet of such beliefs it is often necessary to explore the meaning values of the beliefs, particularly along the dimensions just mentioned, which are most likely to reflect references to actions. Such an exploration might reveal, for example, that the meaning of "I want to be near my family" includes meaning values like "I take only those jobs which do not involve traveling," or "Being near my family frees me from the necessity to do my own cooking," or "Being near my family means that I go with them to the synagogue every Saturday morning." Such beliefs resemble, in a certain sense, general goal beliefs, which do not refer to any single well-defined behavior. Common examples are "I want to be happy" or "I want to be successful." Closer analysis reveals, however, that the meaning of such beliefs includes many meaning values that refer to behaviors involved in the attainment of the goal as antecedents, consequents, accompaniments, or in any other way. To quote an example from a study reported in Chapter 11: for one subject the meaning of the goal "I want to be happy" was "I want to get up in the morning, kiss my wife and children, then go to work, come back late, and fall asleep while watching our prime minister on TV," while another subject said "I want to get up in the morning, but I do not want to go to work, or to smile at anybody, or to answer the phone, or watch TV, or write letters, or put my money in the bank."

These examples show that sometimes a goal belief may refer to more than one behavior. In such cases, subjects usually find it natural to comply with a request to order the cited behaviors in some hierarchy from the viewpoint of instrumentality (i.e., relatedness to the label goal) or substitutability.

The same procedure is necessary for spotting the cognitive orientativeness of norms, beliefs about self, and general beliefs. In this respect norms highly resemble goals. Many simple norms are very similar to simple active goal beliefs, since their meaning values often refer directly to actions that should be performed or should be avoided. Many other norms do not refer to any specific action but elicit meaning values of a rather wide range of behaviors. For instance, the norm "Honest people do not steal" points to diverse acts, some of which fall only marginally into the group of stealing proper. Obviously, some norms do not directly suggest any behaviors at all. "Love your fellow man as yourself" is a famous or notorious example. In such cases the cognitive orientativeness resides in the meaning values of the comprehensive meaning of the norm. When more than one action is elicited, they may be ranged in hierarchies reflecting degrees of importance or necessity in regard to the focal norm, degrees of prohibition, or permission, and so on.

The cognitive orientativeness of beliefs about self and general beliefs is rarely manifested directly in the meaning values that comprise the belief. Moreover, not infrequently even meaning values of the belief's comprehensive meaning do not suggest any behavior. Only through juxtaposition with other beliefs may the cognitive orientativeness of such a belief become manifest. For example, a general belief like "Tomorrow the sun will rise at 5 o'clock and 52 minutes" may seem devoid of cognitive orientativeness unless considered in conjunction with a goal belief like "I want to see the sunrise," or a norm belief like "People should get up before sunrise" or a belief about self like "I enjoy returning home from a night party after sunrise."

All beliefs evoked in order to answer the question "What am I to do?" in a specific context may contribute to the formation of the cognitive orientation cluster. This contribution depends upon the cognitive orientativeness of the beliefs. Thus, every belief is a potential contributor to the cognitive orientation cluster. As we have seen, its actual contribution is determined by its context, that is, indirectly by the meaning of the input and directly by the beliefs evoked concomitantly in answering the question "What am I to do?" This is true regardless of whether the cognitive orientativeness of the belief is reflected directly in its meaning values or indirectly in other elicited meaning values expressing the meaning of that belief. Thus, cognitive orientativeness is a specific aspect of the meaning of a belief.

MECHANISMS OF BELIEF EVOCATION

In describing crucial processes of input elaboration we characterized meaning action as a cognitive attempt to answer the implicit question "What is it?" and meaning generation as the cognitive attempt to furnish answers to the questions "What does it mean?" and "What does it mean to me and for me?" If the answer to the latter question indicates the need for action, a process reflecting the question "What am I to do?" initiates the evocation of beliefs of the four types that constitute the material for CO clustering (see Figure 4.1). The processes that could be conceived as different kinds of clustering strategies will be described in the next chapter. Here we will discuss the basic mechanisms that, if used alternately or concomitantly, bring about belief evocation.

Proper understanding of the mechanisms mediating belief evocation requires consideration of a basic quality manifested by every belief: its capacity to activate other beliefs by functioning as a cue. This cue function can be fulfilled, on the one hand, because of the indeterminate size of every belief, a kind of openness that allows for complementation of the basic unit by other beliefs and even seems to incite such a complementation in a manner similar to the "gestalt pressure" of incomplete gestalts. Thus every belief appears as an active extensible core, a nucleus open to amendments by further meanings. On the other hand, every belief is embedded in several more or less permanent belief structures and groupings. If a belief is activated, the activation seems to spread along the embedding beliefs, setting them, so to speak, into a state of increased readiness. When our subjects were instructed to name a belief and then to tell us what it reminded them of, they tended to recall beliefs related to the focal belief and to one another as members of a belief hierarchy or of an otherwise organized belief cluster. More often than not they recalled beliefs that lent support to the focal belief. For example, the norm "You should not steal" seems to be strengthened by the norm "Theft should be severely punished." Likewise it would be weakened by the norm "One should not be too meticulous in regard to laws." Frequently, hierarchies are not only indicated by content but also by the sequence of beliefs, proceeding mostly from the highest member downward.

Keeping in mind the indeterminate size and the embeddedness of beliefs, the mechanisms that bring about belief evocation appear merely as technical derivatives of the cue function of beliefs.

The three mechanisms are:

1. *Selective activation by similarity.* From the viewpoint of meaning innumerable similarities exist among beliefs. Two beliefs may be similar to each other because they share a greater or lesser number of identical meaning values; because their overall meanings manifest the same meaning dimension(s); or because their overall meanings manifest different meaning dimensions that are related to each other as, for example, in the case of the dimensions "antecedents and causes" and "consequences and results," and so on. Had mere similarity sufficed for activation, every focal belief would have evoked most if not all stored beliefs. Our own observations as well as the observations of others in the field make it likely that the activation by similarities is selective. For instance, in semantic conditioning adult subjects react to similarity in meaning but ignore similarity in sound (Luria & Vinogradova, 1959). However, within a selected area similarity-mediated belief evocation is very frequent (Abelson & Carroll, 1965). The greater the number of shared meaning values the higher the chance of belief retrieval (Colby, 1968). Belief evocation due to similarity in meaning is accorded tacit recognition or implicit status in such diverse models of search and retrieval as those suggested by Collins and Quillian (1972a, 1972b), Kintsch (1970), Rumelhart, Lindsay, and Norman (1972), Shiffrin (1970), and others. Of course, the details of the retrieval or evocation process vary from model to model. Before unequivocal information is available, one may assume that the focal belief and the posed problem or task form a set of memory addresses, elicit a search set, constitute a plan for memory scanning, initiate a multipath search in terms of Quillian's intersection technique, and so on, until the adequate beliefs are retrieved.

Of special interest to us is the case in which comprehensive meaning constitutes the focal beliefs that are subjected to the question "What am I to do?" We assume that under these circumstances the activation is restricted to similarity in orientativeness. This means that only those beliefs of the four types are evoked that point positively or negatively in the same behavioral direction. In other words, the question "What am I to do?" functions as a kind of determining tendency that evokes beliefs with similar orientative aspects. Whether one of the already existing retrieval models could account for this process or whether it is necessary to develop other models will be decided by future research.

2. *Inferential generation.* In contrast to belief recall with little or no reconstruction (Tulving, 1972), some beliefs are partly or completely generated, mostly by inference, from the focal belief. For instance, the focal beliefs "People should not harm one another" and "Stealing may harm another person" may—by substituting "stealing" for "harm"—give rise to the new norm belief "People should not steal from one another." Some instances of inference are restricted to beliefs of only one of the four belief types; others take place across belief types. For example, Kukla (1970) and Weiner and Kukla (1970) observed inferences within one and the same belief component. They showed that if an individual believes that he has succeeded in a task (belief about self) he infers from this the further belief that he has expended a lot of effort on it (belief about self), while if he believes a task is difficult and unusual (general belief) he tends to interpret success in it as indicative of ability (general belief). Inference of goal beliefs from general beliefs was demonstrated by studies carried out in the framework of social learning theory. It was found that preferential choice of a goal, that is, the decision to strive for this goal (goal belief), depends on the expectancy of occurrence of a particular reinforcement (general belief) (Dunlap, 1953; Hunt, 1955) and on the generally assumed delay in its delivery (general belief) (Mischel & Staub, 1965). Belief inference without a generative aspect forms the implicit core of the James-Lange theory of emotions and the more explicitly stated thesis of Bem's attribution theory (i.e., "I am crying therefore I believe that I am sad"). Formal logic makes heavy use of more or less generative belief inference and it is the means of reasoning most prominently exemplified by Descartes' "Cogito ergo sum."

3. *Hierarchical substitution.* People form many more or less permanent belief hierarchies, some consciously represented, others preconscious or subconscious. Besides the well-known hierarchies of beliefs in accordance with preference, importance, relevance, probability of occurrence and so on, there are the less frequently mentioned but no less important hierarchies of instrumentality, especially in regard to many goals (e.g., "For attaining Goal A I have first to attain Goal B," or, "I

want to attain Goal C so that it may help me to attain Goal D" and so on), the early-established hierarchy of graded prohibition in regard to beliefs about norms, and many more. Hierarchies serve not only orientation but constitute a ready pool for belief substitution. Dozens of psychological studies demonstrate that assumed or experienced inability to attain a particular goal evokes the goal belief that proves to be the next highest in a hierarchy of goal preference. Sometimes it is not the goal highest or next highest in the hierarchy that is evoked but another goal lower in the hierarchy that seems to the subject to stand better chances of being attained or seems to enable concomitantly the attainment of an additional goal (Kreitler & Kreitler, unpublished). Such an outcome is due to the impact of two interacting hierarchies—one reflecting preferences for goals and the other the subjective probability of attaining one or even more than one goal at a time. Yet the goal eventually evoked is the hierarchically highest of those goals that satisfy the criteria of both hierarchies. Of course, even the lowest goal belief in a preference hierarchy has a chance of being evoked and serving as a substitute for a higher goal since, according to Rotter (1972), there exists a minimal goal level that marks "the lowest goal in a continuum of potential reinforcements . . . which will be perceived by the person as satisfactory to him" (ibid., p. 36). Transient goal hierarchies of value in a certain situation are involved in the evocation of multiple goal beliefs (Crandall, Good, & Crandall, 1963) and in substituting one goal belief for another. It goes without saying that belief substitution can also be initiated by meaning relatedness of beliefs, by inference, and by the different kinds of nonhierarchial embeddedness of beliefs. However, our studies of goal and norm preferences of normals and schizophrenics (Kreitler & Kreitler, unpublished) shows that hierarchically guided substitution is the most common process of belief substitution.

Since the comprehensive meaning of an input as well as the answer to the question "What does it mean to me and for me?" constitute a set of explicitly and implicitly represented beliefs, the belief evocation elicited by the question "What am I to do?" is mediated by the cue function of beliefs and its three underlying mechanisms. Belief evocation accompanies clustering continuously. It may dwindle in the advanced stages of clustering but stops only when clustering itself is completed. The manner in which activation and evocation of beliefs with common orientative aspects is amended by generative inference and hierarchical substitution for bringing about an operational CO cluster will be explored in the next chapter.

CO Clustering
and CO Clusters

FORMATION OF CO CLUSTERS

While meaning generation and belief evocation furnish the cognitive material for elicitation of molar behavior it is the CO cluster which gives rise to a behavioral intent that eventually may be turned into actual behavior by adoption and performance of a behavioral program. The CO cluster determines the direction of molar behavior. Therefore it is a key concept in our theory, deserving special attention, in particular since it constitutes the basis for behavioral predictions and behavior change.

The CO cluster is a product of clustering among beliefs of the four types that form the four CO components. As indicated in Chapter 4, the selective evocation of relevant beliefs is monitored by the comprehensive meaning of the input and the question "What am I to do?" Our observations lead us to assume that belief evocation usually occurs in one of four sequences. The most frequent sequence is characterized by the evocation of one or more goal beliefs at the very beginning of the process. Comprehensive meaning leads first of all to eliciting goal beliefs, which in turn, by virtue of their specific meaning, bring about the evocation of beliefs of the other three types. Indeed, this is the most trivial and most usual sequence to be expected. For, let us say, in the absence of a goal belief like "I want to kiss this girl," there is little sense in evoking the belief about self "I am too shy to approach her" or the general belief "She looks like the type of girl likely to reject me." In a sequence of this type, the goal belief forms the core of the CO cluster. All other evoked beliefs are related to it in one way or another.

A different, less frequent situation arises when a belief about a norm, or a belief about self, or a general belief serves as core for the CO cluster. This means that the sequence starts with the elicitation of a belief of one of these three types, whereas all the other beliefs, evoked later, are related to it. Yet if the CO cluster is to lead to an action, it must also include goal beliefs. In a CO cluster of this kind the goal belief is subservient to a belief of another type. For example, if the CO cluster is focused on a norm, the goal belief would be "I want to behave so as to uphold this norm," whereas if the CO cluster is focused on a belief about self the goal belief might be "I want to behave so that this belief about myself is confirmed (or supported, or made manifest, or weakened, etc.)."

A third possibility arises when the whole CO cluster relates directly to the comprehensive meaning of the input. The evoked beliefs of each CO component, elicited in any order whatsoever, relate to a clearly set course of action delineated by the comprehensive meaning, which thus remains in a sense the focal determinant of the clustering. This often seems to be the case in experimental situations when the input itself, for instance a light, signals to the subject that he has to perform a certain action, such as press a red button. The situation may be similar whenever an individual pledges himself to follow signaled instructions or orders. However, the cases in which these pledged instructions are not fulfilled, for instance, immoral orders given by a hypnotizer or in a military setting, indicate that concomitantly a CO cluster is also produced and hence may nullify the pledge.

A fourth possibility also needs to be considered. It arises when the meaning of the input and the question "What am I to do?" do not lead directly or indirectly, through one of the other beliefs, to the evocation of a goal belief. We assume that in such a case the CO cluster would not give rise to a behavioral intent. As a matter of fact, it might be more apt to describe the situation in other terms. In the course of our studies we got the impression that a CO cluster that appeared to be devoid of a goal belief upon closer examination often turned out to be a CO cluster with a goal belief like "I do not want to become involved," "I do not want to do anything now," etc. In any case, no behavioral intent was formed. However, this rule may not hold for memorization. The absence of the explicit goal to remember the input does not necessarily exclude its memory registration. Rather, we assume the existence of a general intent—based on a general CO—to register in memory relevant information, and an attached mechanism for scanning external and internal situations for items relevant enough to be stored in memory. This mechanism is probably set in operation whenever there arises a cue denoting information of relevance or particular importance, the completion of any stage in a preparatory or behavioral sequence, and so on. Thus, the absence of the explicit goal to remember need not prevent remembering the input. The same is true for active forgetting of certain types of material.

Common to all four possibilities described is the assumption that goal beliefs are indispensable for action. This assumption has important connotations and implications. On the metatheoretical level, it reflects the tenet, basic to the systems approach, that living organisms are purposeful, goal-directed systems (Ashby, 1956; Bertalanffy, 1952; Sommerhoff, 1969). Obviously an enormous difference exists between the purposefulness of unicellular organisms and the goal-directedness of human beings. There is nonetheless little doubt that the high-level organization of cognitive contents and behavior patterns required for goal-directed human action reflects essentially the same underlying biological principle as the initial gropings of purposefulness and directive correlation (Sommerhoff, 1969) on the lowest levels of living matter.

The assumption that goal beliefs are indispensable for action is of central importance within the framework of the cognitive orientation theory. It turns goal beliefs into the backbone of the clustering process. Thus, it makes possible the emergence of the behavioral intent as the best possible answer under the given circumstances to the question "What am I to do?"

With goal beliefs forming the backbone of the process, in what does clustering consist? How does it take place? Our hypothesis is that the major element in this process is the interaction of meaning values of different beliefs, unfolding in the form of successive contextual embedding. Let us first illustrate this interaction by a simplified example. For instance, I may notice a nicely pointed pencil on the desk of an absent colleague. The question "What am I to do?" elicits directly the goal belief "I want to take this pencil and keep it." Further related beliefs are retrieved or constructed. These may include the general belief "Taking something without its owner's permission is a kind of stealing unfit for honest persons," the norm "One should not steal," and the belief about self "I am an honest, law-abiding person." Two of these beliefs, the general belief and the belief about the norm, relate to a wide variety of actions. The belief about self does not refer in its surface meaning to any specific action. In contrast, the meaning values of the goal belief designate a highly specific course of action. Checking the goal belief "I want to take this pencil and keep it" against the behavior defined as stealing in the cited general belief readily reveals that the action denoted by the goal belief falls into the range of application of "stealing." Thus, the meaning value "stealing" may replace, or at least accompany, the meaning value "take" in the goal belief. In a complementary sense, the matching also occasions the focusing of the meaning value "stealing" in the general belief on the more specific meaning value of taking the pencil mentioned in the goal belief. Similarly, matching the goal belief against the norm shows that the action denoted by the goal is to be included among those actions prohibited by the norm. Or, in more operational terms, plotting all major classes of stealing prohibited by the stated norm would reveal that the action suggested in the goal belief is included under one of these headings. Hence, the actual behavioral meaning of the norm is reduced to the meaning value that corresponds to the most prominent actional meaning value of the goal belief and of the general belief. In the case of the belief about self, the process of matching can be applied only after elaborating the meaning values of "honest" and "law-abiding" in terms of meaning dimensions likely to include actional components. Such an elaboration will reveal a series, indeed a hierarchy, of acts that an honest and law-abiding person rarely, if ever, commits. When we check the major action denoted by the goal belief against this series or hierarchy of listed acts, we are again likely to hit the meaning value "stealing." Thus also the meaning of the belief about self is reduced to the major meaning value of the goal belief.

In more general terms, we assume that the interaction among beliefs consists in matching meaning values of the different beliefs one against the other. Multiple acts of matching may take place, some serially, others in a parallel manner. The meaning values that serve as focus for the matchings are those highest in the hierarchy of actions designated by the goal belief. If only one well-defined action is denoted by the meaning value of the goal belief, this meaning value will serve as a focus for the matchings. If there are more than one, they are tested sequentially. The focal behavior may be stated positively or negatively (see forms of relation between meaning values and referent in "Value-Referent Relations and the Modes of Meaning," Chapter 2). The matchings between meaning values are direct when both meaning values contain identical referents, as in the following pair of beliefs: "*Hatred* is abominable" and "I want to abolish all *hatred*." When, however, the referents differ, preparatory processes have to occur before the matching proper can take place. These preparatory processes consist of meaning elaboration of the meaning values, both those in the goal belief and those in the other types of belief. The meaning elaboration makes possible substitution of meaning values. Obvious examples of substitution include instantiation (e.g., "stealing" is a form of "causing harm" to another person), or replacing one meaning value with another that constitutes a superordinate concept or system (e.g., using the word "crime" instead of "theft." The first example represents substitution in terms of the meaning dimension "range of inclusion" (dimension 2, Chapter 2), whereas the second illustrates the use of the meaning dimension "contextual allocation" (dimension 1, Chapter 2). Substitution may occur in terms of any of the meaning dimensions, so that a referent may be replaced by its presumed cause (dimension 6), or consequence (dimension 7), or an act it does (dimension 4), or any of its parts (dimension 9), and so on. If we take into account the possibility that in the course of substitution the forms and types of relations between the meaning values and the referent (Chapter 2) may also be changed, from, say, assertive to negative, or from attributive to metaphoric-symbolic, it is evident that substitution affords ample ground for the operation of repression and other defense mechanisms.

Probably the substitutions with regard to the two meaning values involved go on independently, each item—new or old—being constantly checked against all those evoked in the framework of the other meaning values until a meaning value common to the two paths, so to speak, is located. It is this common meaning value that makes possible the matching between the two beliefs involved.

Obviously, the same process of interaction takes place with regard to all the evoked beliefs of the four CO components. The interactions may occur in a parallel manner. As we have seen, the interaction involves repeated acts of matching of meaning values. The matching may be aided through substitution of meaning values, replacement of forms and types of relations between meaning values and the referent, and auxiliary judgments about existing or acceptable degrees of congruity or consonance of the involved meaning values. In this manner, the interaction of beliefs brings about a reduction in the meanings of the beliefs to those meaning values that match each other best. In terms of set theory, if we consider the sphere of meanings anchored on each belief as a set, the matching may be viewed as producing an intersection of all the relevant meaning values of the various sets. In this context, the matching is defined in terms of and with regard to the focal meaning value of the goal belief denoting a specific action. It is this focal meaning value that guides the whole set of matchings. Accordingly, the effectiveness of a CO cluster is not due to the combined cognitive orientativeness of the meaning values in the beliefs it includes. Rather, it reflects the cognitive orientativeness of the *common meaning values* of the various beliefs with regard to a specific action. The CO cluster is in some sense a colligation of these common meaning values, since it brings them together in juxtaposition in one structural framework without, however, impairing their distinctness.

As already indicated, the interaction among beliefs consists mainly of recurrent acts of matching, direct or indirect. These repeated matchings make possible a successive contextual embedding of the focal meaning value of the goal belief denoting a behavior. Thus, each completed act of matching leads to viewing the behavior denoted by the goal belief from the viewpoint(s) suggested by the other meaning values singly or in the form of beliefs. These meaning values or beliefs form momentary contexts for the focal behavior. The successive embedding of the focal behavior in these shifting contexts brings about a gradual clarification of its meaning and an increasingly sharp delineation of its behavioral directionality. It is clear that the emergence of a well-defined behavioral directionality depends upon the collocation of the beliefs in pairs, in triads, in clusters, or in chains and is subserved by such processes as deduction, implication, assimilation, and fusion.

In the course of clustering, tentative solutions may emerge in the form of prefinal CO clusters. Their emergence is a manifestation of a gestalt-like pressure for closure. These tentative CO clusters are checked for congruence in orientativeness between the colligated meaning values. If, by some predetermined criterion, the degree of congruence is found to be too low, the tentative CO cluster is immediately disjoined. This serves as a cue for continuing the process of clustering until another tentative CO cluster is formed. The process continues either until the degree of congruence of the colligated meaning values is high enough to make possible the emergence of a definite course of behavior from the CO cluster, or until it becomes evident that the sufficient and necessary degree of congruence cannot be attained or that the search for it would be too long and too strenuous to be possible and justifiable.

However, the congruence of the meaning values of the beliefs in the prefinal CO cluster may be too low to enable the emergence of a behavioral intent. This is by no means always the case. Sometimes no behavioral intent can be formed, most notably when there is a stalemate between beliefs supporting the behavior connoted by the goal belief and those opposing it, or when there are more opposing than supporting beliefs. However, many of these stalemate situations are only transient, owing to the possibilities inherent in the belief hierarchies. When a stalemate occurs, one or more of the colliding beliefs can be replaced by other beliefs from the same respective hierarchies. In the case of our previous example, the highly restrictive norm "One should not steal" could, for instance, be replaced by the more lenient norm "One should not take valuable property without the owner's permission." This norm would probably prove to be more manageable than the former, especially when it is accompanied by the common general belief that a pencil is not to be regarded as valuable property. Another possibility would be to change the original goal belief "I want to take this pencil and keep it," substituting for it a similar goal belief, say, "I want to take this pencil and return it later" or "I want to take this pencil now and ask for permission later when the owner returns." These goal beliefs are indeed lower in the preference hierarchy, but stand better chances of being supported by norms, beliefs about self, and general beliefs. It may be assumed that the goal belief of a cluster is changed only after attempts to change beliefs of the other types have not sufficed to increase the congruence within the prefinal CO cluster to the point at which a behavioral intent can be crystallized.

The range of these replacements of beliefs is potentially very wide. The object of substitution may be a single belief or even a cluster of beliefs within which the "disturbing" belief is embedded. Moreover, the impact of such replacements may be crucial. Since many of the hierarchies within each of the four belief types are structured in terms of general meaning criteria that are almost formal in nature, such as degree of preference, prohibition, importance, probability, and so on, the hierarchies may contain highly different and even contradictory beliefs in close formal proximity. Thus, substitution of beliefs may in principle change a prefinal CO cluster in a drastic manner. For instance, in an achievement task situation it may happen that the dominant goal belief "I want to be the best" is only slightly higher in the preference hierarchy than the goal belief "I want to avoid effort." Substituting one goal belief for the other may make a lot of a difference. Indeed, in order to play an active role in clustering, a belief must also prove to be relevant or must resonate to the appropriate cues. But even if we take into account the possibility that beliefs near to each other in the belief hierarchies may not all be relevant for a particular behavioral situation, there usually remain enough beliefs adequate for substitution to make possible the resolution of most clustering stalemates.

However, the main factor determining whether a belief will be replaced by another is not its meaning collision with beliefs of another type, but rather the extent of support it enjoys from beliefs of the same CO component. Thus, a goal belief colliding with one or more beliefs of the other CO components may still not be replaced if it is supported by similar goals or by goals whose attainment may be facilitated through it.

Hence, even after some substituting and reshuffling, the final CO cluster may still contain some colliding beliefs, sometimes more, sometimes less. This implies that the congruence of the beliefs included in the CO cluster need not be perfect for a behavioral intent to emerge. In other words, congruence in orientativeness is not the single and ultimate criterion whose fulfillment serves as a cue for forming a behavioral intent.

Two other criteria are the degree of preference for the particular goal belief and the number of different goals that may be satisfied by a specific behavior under the given circumstances. Clearly a certain degree of congruence of the clustered beliefs is indispensable for the formation of a behavioral intent; otherwise the intent would not have sufficient support. However, beyond this minimal level of congruence the other criteria may be used. For example, if the prefinal CO cluster is anchored on one or even two highly preferred goals, a lower degree of intercluster congruence may be taken as sufficient for intent formation. Under such circumstances additional beliefs may be evoked to support the course of action implied in the highly preferred goal beliefs or at least its choice in these conditions. Individual differences in tolerance of incongruities within the CO cluster may also play a role. Some people may be ready to settle for lower degrees of intracluster congruence than others beyond the minimal degree indispensable for intent formation.

If CO clusters may contain colliding beliefs, what happens to the beliefs that do not support the action reflected in the resulting behavioral intent? Similar questions arise with regard to meaning values of beliefs in the cluster that do not match one another. What, then, is the fate of nonmatching meaning values and beliefs? It is plausible to assume that they are subjected to the set of rules subserving "selecting out" in psychological functioning (Abramovici, 1972). These rules include processes such as suppression (Cohen, 1960), denial, differentiation (Abelson, 1959), discounting (Shepard, 1964), ignoring, and overlooking (Brown, 1953; Pollack, 1962; Sarbin, 1942). The result, however, is not necessarily repression or forgetting. Other possibilities should also be considered. For example, the discounted meaning values or beliefs may merely be pushed into the background and put into a state of suspension, ready for use at any instant in the course of subsequent clustering. An analogous situation is evident in the phenomenon of fusion and rivalry, when different information is fed to the two eyes or two ears (Woodworth & Schlosberg, 1954, pp. 397–402).

Sometimes—and this is of great importance—it may happen that repeated attempts at forming prefinal CO clusters do not lead to the emergence of a CO cluster with minimal congruence of its beliefs. Or, the secondary criteria relating to highly preferred goal beliefs or multiple goal beliefs may not be prominent enough, in either absolute or relative terms, to compensate for a sufficient but nonetheless precariously low degree of congruence. Under such circumstances a deadlock arises. The situation is labeled as stalemate either after a certain predetermined amount of time has been spent attempting to create a viable CO cluster or after a certain set of processes has been applied for this purpose without success. The first condition corresponds to what Simon (1967) called "impatience," the second, to what he called "discouragement." Both reflect common criteria for the completion of actions or loops of processes. Yet even a total stalemate does not exclude intent formation and eventual action. The tentative CO cluster may be split into two CO clusters. The likelihood of such a development is indicated by similar developments in other domains. For instance, experimental studies of judgment and evaluation of stimuli suggest that a polarization and eventual splitting are likely to occur when the stimuli differ in more than one dimension (Shepard, 1964), when the distance between the stimuli is relatively large (Sherif & Hovland, 1961), and when the initial beliefs reflect rather extreme positions (Eiser & Stroebe, 1972, chaps. 6–7). In any case, two separate CO clusters can be formed. And if they are formed they will give rise to two behavioral intents, thus creating one of the typical conflict situations envisaged in our model.

In describing the possibility of resolving stalemates by replacing beliefs with other beliefs in the same hierarchy, we mentioned the assumption that the resistance of a belief to substitution depends on the degree to which other beliefs of the same CO component support it. This assumption is based on a modified version of the well-known strength hypothesis frequently used in models of memory retrieval. According to this hypothesis the strength of a belief is determined by the number of other beliefs in the same CO component that support it, subtracting from it, or disregarding, the number of beliefs that contradict it or collide with it. If the contradicting beliefs are subtracted they get a negative value, whereas if they are disregarded they get the value of zero. When only two behavioral alternatives are considered, the number of contradicting beliefs need not be subtracted but may simply be ignored. Although this assumption about the strength of a belief was vindicated in our experiments dealing with predicting behavior (Chapters 7, 8, 10, and 11), we have to mention two reservations. First, there seems to be an upper limit for gain in strength through belief summation within any of the four CO components. Analysis of our data suggests that adding further supporting beliefs beyond a certain limit either does not change the extent of support for the particular belief or yields only progressively diminishing increases in strength until a plateau is reached. The curve leading to this plateau is very steep. The same may be true regardless of whether the relevant unit within the CO component is taken to be a specific belief or a cluster of beliefs. However, we are not yet able to estimate the optimal number of effective beliefs within any of the components. Nor do we know whether this presumed limit, or, possibly, range, changes across CO components, behavioral situations, and individuals. Our second reservation, grounded much more firmly in empirical findings, concerns the differential weight of beliefs from the four CO components. Our studies show that the relative order of dominance of the four CO components changes from one behavioral situation to another (Chapter 13). Yet so far neither the regularity of the changes nor their causes are clear.

Both of these reservations are tentative, pending further research. Neither was taken into account in our predictive studies to date. The method we used was much simpler than warranted or required by the theoretical analysis of the clustering process, as described above. The method, which is fully described in Chapters 7 and 8, is based on an additive model that has been used successfully in many fields in psychology, for instance, impression formation (Anderson & Fishbein, 1965; Tversky & Krantz, 1969), clinical evaluation (Tversky, 1967), discrimination learning (Eninger, 1952), and conditioned behavior (Miller, 1939; Schoeffler, 1954). In spite of its relative crudeness, the method yielded clearcut findings that lent support to our basic assumption, which is that beliefs of the four CO components, when combined in a manner preserving their distinctions, are highly reliable predictors of behavioral intent, and—if behavioral programs are kept constant—also of actual molar behavior. Developments at present are designed to refine the method so that it will reflect more closely the theoretical assumptions underlying the clustering process and thus lead via new findings to further theoretical progress.

It seems advisable now to sum up the major conclusions set forth in this section. We assume that the CO cluster consists of beliefs elicited by the question "What am I to do?", and that the CO cluster constitutes an answer to this question by figuring a behavioral intent. The beliefs are either evoked directly, in response to the input meaning (the comprehensive meaning), or indirectly, by being related to another belief, generally a goal belief. Goal beliefs are often the first to be elicited. Each belief of the four CO components is strengthened or weakened by related beliefs of the same CO component, which are set in a state of readiness when the actually elicited belief is evoked. The clustering of beliefs of the four CO components is facilitated by meaning interaction between them. The interaction proceeds in terms of matching the meaning values one against the other, wherein one of the major meaning values of the goal belief with actional connotations serves as focus for the process. The matching may take place directly, or—in the case that divergences between meaning values are too large—through the intermediation of substitution. Substitution enables the replacement of one or more meaning values in the dominant belief or even the whole belief by other meaning values or beliefs that are sufficiently similar in meaning or adjacent in the hierarchies. Of course, substitution depends on the availability of suitable meaning values or beliefs. Repeated acts of matching bring about a reduction in the meanings of the beliefs to those meaning values which match each other and, mainly, the action-oriented meaning value of the focal goal belief. The process of clustering itself consists in this gradual narrowing down of the range of action-oriented meaning values common to the beliefs and an increasing specification of the behavioral directionality implied by the goal belief. It proceeds through successive contextual embeddings of the goal belief or its major action-oriented meaning value and the formation of one or more tentative prefinal CO clusters. These prefinal CO clusters reflect, from the viewpoint of content, the gradual transformation of the goal belief into a behavioral intent, and, from a formal viewpoint, a gestalt pressure for closure.

The process of CO cluster formation terminates under any one of the following conditions:

1. The degree of congruence of meaning values within the tentative CO cluster is sufficiently high to make possible the emergence of a behavioral intent. This implies that the support for the goal belief is stronger than the opposition to it. Yet the satisfactory degree of congruence may not be judged in absolute terms. Beyond a minimal required congruence a lower level may be judged as sufficient if the goal belief is particularly high in preference or the CO cluster supports satisfaction of multiple goals.

2. The degree of congruence of meaning values within the tentative CO cluster is judged by all standards to be too low to make possible the emergence of a behavioral intent. This implies that the goal belief is overwhelmingly opposed by the other beliefs, and that no substitute goal could be established. The opposition may stem mainly from beliefs of one CO component or reflect lack of support from beliefs of all three CO components. The termination of clustering occurs after a certain predetermined amount of time has been spent and a certain set of processes has been applied in clustering with no success.

3. The degree of congruence of meaning values within the tentative CO cluster is too low to make possible the emergence of a behavioral intent. But since equally strong support is given to two competing goals, the tentative CO cluster is split and two behavioral intents are formed.

4. Scanning and rescanning reveal that the evoked or readily evocable beliefs do not contain any goal. Hence, the rudimentary beginnings of the clustering process that may have been set in motion are immediately stopped.

(Figure 5.1 summarizes the major processes involved in CO clustering and formation of the behavioral intent.)

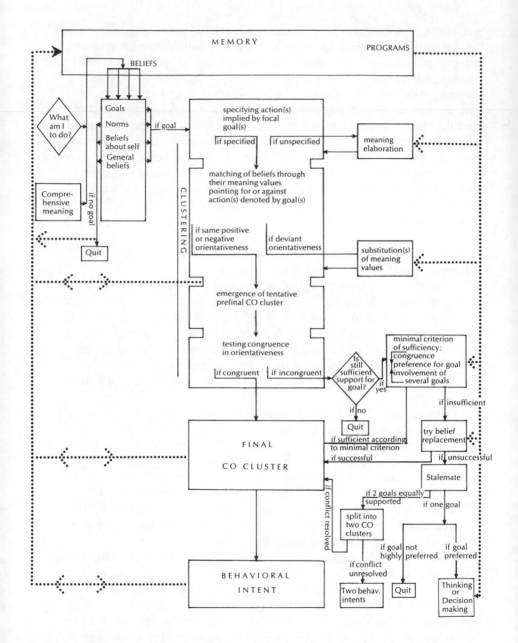

FIGURE 5.1 Major processes involved in CO clustering and formation of the be-havioral intent. The constellation schematized in this figure relates to CO clustering initiated directly by a goal belief. The dotted lines represent connections with memory.

RETRIEVAL AND ADJUSTMENT OF CO CLUSTERS

The summary of the clustering process we have just set forth implies two major properties of CO clusters. CO clusters are aconscious and, strictly speaking, unique. These properties are important for understanding how CO clusters operate.

First, let us take up the issue of consciousness. It has often been re-iterated that a CO cluster is a structure composed of beliefs in multiple interrelations. Since interrelations among cognitive units, structural qualities, and the effects of interactions are difficult to verbalize, the CO cluster eludes direct observation and possibly even awareness. Also, it is of such short duration that the individual can hardly be expected to attend to it and to communicate it. Hence, the CO cluster is neither conscious nor amenable to being made fully conscious. Nevertheless, the intent supported by the CO cluster may be consciously manifested, for instance, in the form of a belief about self, say, "I shall do x now." Moreover, a CO cluster is neither retrievable by the individual nor reconstructable post hoc, that is, in the stage of adjusting or performing behavioral programs or after completion of the action. Indeed, a person may sometimes recall or reproduce after an action several "beliefs" that may or may not have been involved in the CO cluster; but these beliefs do not constitute a CO cluster, nor do they provide clues to its nature and structure. Since the CO cluster is not retrievable, it is clear that motivation, or at least the directive aspect of motivation as manifested in the CO cluster, is not conscious. Yet this does not necessarily make it subconscious in the strictly Freudian sense. Rather, it is essentially aconscious. The closest experimental approximation to the CO cluster so far is some kind of combination of matching beliefs of the four CO components.

The second major property of CO clusters is their uniqueness. Uniqueness implies that for any specific behavioral intent, or for that matter, any specific behavior, a particular CO cluster is formed. This assumption is a necessary implication of our basic hypothesis that human behavior above the level of spinal reflexes is steered by cognitive orientation. Since behaviors are specific, being always adapted to particular situations, which never recur twice in exactly the same form, the directing CO clusters must also reflect these situational changes. Wherein resides the uniqueness of a CO cluster? It seems to depend on the meaning values of each belief, on the collocated beliefs, and on their interrelations. Since the CO cluster is a product of interactions among beliefs, the addition of even a single belief to a preexisting set of beliefs may change the resulting CO cluster. Further, which meaning value of a belief will emerge, be emphasized, or be dropped—that is, which aspect of the meaning of a belief will be allowed to manifest its cognitive orientativeness—depends to no small extent on the other beliefs against which the belief is matched.

The theoretical importance of the property of uniqueness becomes evident when one considers the possible physiological correlates of clustering, for example in terms of the model of brain activity described by Pribram (1971). On the basis of rich material, Pribram (chap. 1) distinguishes between two types of neuroelectric activity: nerve impulse unit discharges and graded slow potential changes. Only nerve impulses are propagated, and only they can bring about a synchronization of the activity of a large number of units. In contrast, the graded slow potentials increase and decrease locally in the brain tissue and are highly sensitive to local influences, both neuronal and chemical. In more general terms, the slow potentials reflect the state of the system, by defining its microstructure, whereas the impulses are the operators regulating its organized action. Applying this to cognitive activity, it is only too tempting to view the slow potentials as the substratum of the constantly ongoing cognitive activity of coding and recoding, and to regard coordinated nerve impulses as the correlate of clustering. At this point it is important to mention two major opposing views concerning neuronal activity. One view maintains that the integration of units necessary for behavior is accomplished mainly through permanent—inborn or learned—associative links between neurons. The other view holds that permanent links cannot account for the major part of the neuronal interactions indispensable for the organization of behavior. The uniqueness of each CO cluster is in line with the second view. It may, therefore, be most stimulating to note that the three main arguments raised by Lashley (1960) in favor of the second view apply to CO clusters no less than to neuronal activity. We shall mention them here since modern research has lent them full support (Pribram, 1971). The three arguments are: (1) equivalence in receptor function, which implies that "the absolute properties of the stimulus are relatively unimportant for behavior and that reactions are determined by ratios of excitation which are equally effective when applied to any group of receptor cells within the system" (Lashley, 1960, pp. 238–239); (2) spontaneous reorganization in motor functions, which consists in preserving the essential motor patterns when some dysfunction of the habitually used muscles necessitates the use of other muscles; and (3) survival of behavior after destruction of any part of a brain system whose total destruction abolishes the behavior. This implies substitutability among parts of the functional systems involved in organizing the behavior.

Now, we would like to suggest first that, with regard to CO clusters, there is within certain limits equivalence in input function. Virtually the same CO cluster, sometimes differing in only one of its meaning values, may be formed or evoked in response to widely different inputs. This may be expected when the different inputs share at least a number of basic meaning values that render them similar in a most characteristic and essential way. This similarity underlies what we call *orientational equivalence* and makes possible the successful use of the same CO cluster for predicting apparently different behaviors. For example, CO clusters of curiosity proved to be effective also in predicting certain behaviors manifested in a setting of probability learning (Chapter 8). Second, the pattern of interactions among beliefs which characterizes a CO cluster and is responsible for generating a specific behavioral intent is not dependent exclusively upon a particular set of beliefs. Indeed, this is an absolutely necessary assumption if we are to account for the evident fact that many different individuals, who must be in possession of widely different beliefs, often form functionally similar behavioral intents, say, "I will try to achieve a high grade" or "I will try to invite this girl to my home tonight." Third, there exists a certain substitutability among parts of the system, that is, among beliefs within hierarchies and belief clusters and perhaps even among the clusters themselves. We have often referred to the substitutability of beliefs when describing clustering in general and resolution of stalemates in particular.

The uniqueness of CO clusters is thus a property well coordinated with the flexibility and autonomy of cognitive functioning in general. On the other hand, however, assuming the uniqueness of CO clusters involves us in certain difficulties. If each CO cluster is unique, then no transfer of CO clusters from one behavioral situation to another should be possible. Yet in our studies we found that the same CO cluster could be used for predicting successfully more than a dozen different curiosity behaviors, and, on top of this, a few additional behaviors related to curiosity that were manifested in the context of probability learning (Chapter 8). Similarly, a CO cluster relating to achievement proved adequate for predicting a whole series of different achievement-related behaviors (Chapters 7, 8, and 11). These findings show that there must be some possibility of using previous CO clusters fully or partially in new behavioral situations. This conclusion is also supported by the observation that people form behavioral intents with tremendous speed, particularly when faced with a familiar situation and when the elicited behavior turns out to be an often reiterated behavior.

If people make use of former CO clusters, how can each CO cluster still be unique? The resolution of this apparent paradox is obvious. Most beliefs have a wide spectrum of applicability, that is, they are less specific than the situation to which they apply and the intent which they produce. The norm "You shall not steal" relates to taking without authorization pencils, pocketbooks, cars, and all other things which are not your legal property. Hence virtually the same CO cluster may promote or prevent varied acts of stealing, the sole difference between the CO clusters being a single meaning value, mostly in the goal belief, which may change in accordance with the specificity of the input, e.g., "I want to take this pencil," "I want to take this pocketbook," and so on. In some cases a change crucial for the ensuing behavioral intent may not even show up in the CO cluster itself since it involves merely one of the background beliefs. A CO cluster orienting against any act of violence may still allow for forming the intent to spank a child if one of the beliefs in the hierarchy of general beliefs states that spanking a child is a beneficial educational means.

All in all, CO clusters are more general than the ensuing behavioral intents, just as intents are more general than the adopted behavioral programs, which in turn are more general than the ensuing behaviors. Hence, in the strictest sense of the word, that is, if we take into account all the meaning values, all the beliefs of supporting hierarchies, and all belief interactions, CO clusters are unique. Viewed with less rigor, virtually the same CO cluster may be evoked in somehow different situations and, provided that behavioral programs are kept constant, may make possible predicting more than one behavioral act.

The problem of retrieving stored CO clusters versus forming new and unique CO clusters may best be grasped in the form of a continuum. One pole of the continuum marks situations in which the clustering process is applied from scratch and in a full-fledged manner, faithful in all details to the model described above. The product of this clustering would be an absolutely unique, new, and original CO cluster. This might occur in situations with which the individual is not at all familiar. Such situations rarely, if ever, occur in the life of a normal adult. The opposite pole of the continuum marks those situations in which no clustering at all should take place. Such situations allow for the application of retrieved CO clusters, without any adjustments to the present cue constellations. Of course, both poles of the continuum represent ideal but unrealistic situations. The possibility of forming an original CO cluster different in all details—contents and structure—from other CO clusters formed previously by the same individual is no more likely than the possibility of retrieving from storage a CO cluster that fits in all details the demands of a present situation. The recurrence of behavioral situations and the relative constancy of many personality tendencies are a sufficient guarantee for the realistic assumption that most situations lie between the two poles. Theoretically this means that we may most often expect adaptations, that is, slight modifications and variations of the basic clustering model described earlier. This implies in practice that a great many situations recur with sufficient similarity to warrant the formation of the same or similar CO clusters. Therefore, it is justified to assume that individuals learn to store recurring CO clusters for retrieval in case of need. That which is stored is probably a kind of generalized schema that upon retrieval is to be filled with details—specific beliefs and interactions among them. The retrieval of the schema, however, may help to shorten the clustering process. The schema may be highly abstract, similar perhaps to the stored structure of a general sentence type, or it may be more concrete, rather like the outline of a specific image. In other cases, partial CO clusters or rules for the reconstruction of various parts of the CO cluster may be stored.

The preceding paragraph is not intended to express the opinion that most people attain an adequate balance between exploiting stored CO clusters and forming new CO clusters. The impressive number of stereotypes in social relations and science seems to testify rather to the overwhelming impact of retrieved CO clusters. Nonetheless, even a stored CO cluster that has been subjected to frequent retrievals and used recurrently with success contains some features due to new clustering. If, for instance, a person in the streets of Tel Aviv, London, or New York is asked about the time or about the location of a certain square, he either answers the question or indicates that he does not know, all this in a manner so prompt and spontaneous that it seems to him practically automatic. He has probably responded in this way hundreds of times and may not be aware that once, a long time ago, a CO cluster had to be formed for eliciting the intent to answer this kind of question. However, if any one of the beliefs colligated in the CO cluster is invalidated through situational conditions, his intent as well as his ensuing behavior change immediately. For instance, if the individual happens to entertain concomitantly the dominant goal to reach a certain place as quickly as possible, he may neither stop nor answer. Again, if the question were asked in an obviously rude manner, thus invalidating the norm of mutual politeness, or if the day before the person acquired the general belief that pickpockets use such questions in order to stop potential victims in the street, he might behave in a very different fashion. Behavioral changes of this type may derive either from the formation of a new CO cluster or from the adjustment of a retrieved CO cluster to the peculiarities of the given situation as mirrored in the generated comprehensive meaning. But what is the difference between adjusting a retrieved CO cluster and forming a new CO cluster? For the time being, we will speak of CO cluster adjustment if the retrieved CO cluster may be rendered fit to meet the situational requirements by replacing one or more of its beliefs with other beliefs from the hierarchies supporting this cluster. If, however, beliefs from outside these hierarchies have to be introduced in order to do justice to the peculiarities of a situation, we will speak of forming a new CO cluster. The new CO cluster may of course include one or more beliefs from the retrieved but discarded CO cluster.

INCOMPLETE CO CLUSTERS

Up to now our description of clustering has been paradigmatic. Therefore we have not yet mentioned the more exceptional or deviant courses or products of clustering. For example, hitherto we have dealt only with CO clusters that consist of beliefs of the four CO components. This rule, however, has exceptions (see Figure 5.1). Some of them are even rather regular. Take, for example, the case of window shopping. While scanning the displays, the glance of a window shopper may be attracted by the slender form of a jar. This may elicit in him a belief cluster consisting of the general belief "Many people place such objects in an empty corner of their living room," the norm belief "One should keep up with fashion," the belief about self "I used to buy such objects," and the further general belief "In the living room there is at present no empty corner." The cluster lacks a goal belief. This person evidently neither wants to change the furniture in his living room nor to possess the jar. In fact, he is window shopping without wanting to buy anything. But while looking at the jar or at some other items, he may have introduced into the elicited but incomplete clusters imagined goals or conditional goals, like "In case I would like to buy something. . . ." Such conditional goals could bring about a tentative closure of the incomplete cluster into a tentative or conditional CO cluster. Thus, our window shopper may even form the behavioral intent to buy that folding table in the corner in case he ever wishes to do some camping. Or he may only store the conditional CO cluster pending substitution of a real goal for the imagined goal.

Often it is a norm that initiates the storage of an incomplete cluster. A person may see a book that deals with a subject unknown to him. This may be reflected in the general belief "The book is about x" and the belief about self "I know nothing about x." Both beliefs would be replaced by beliefs pertaining to another percept, were it not for the elicitation of a norm, say, "Educated people should know about x," followed by the belief about self "I am an educated person." But he does not want to study this subject now, nor does he want even to commit himself for the future by deciding to study it at a later point in time. Still, the incomplete cluster may be stored, producing a vague set for future formation of a behavioral intent. Incidentally, we venture to sug gest that the storage of recurrent incomplete clusters of a certain type may produce a generalized set for intent formations of a particular kind, for example, for studying certain themes, helping people of a specific type, and so on. Such generalized sets may resemble Rotter's concept of generalized expectancies, major among which are internal versus external control of reinforcement and interpersonal trust (Rotter, Chance, & Phares, 1972).

We have mentioned the case of a CO cluster rendered incomplete by the absence of an adequate goal. Sometimes, however, a cluster may be incomplete if there are no relevant general beliefs or beliefs about self, or at least not in sufficient number to support the formation of a behavioral intent. For example, a person may be confronted with the necessity to decide whether he will join a certain club, work in a certain place, or collaborate with certain people on a given project. Although this individual may have goal beliefs and norms that support joining a club, starting to work, or collaborating on the project, he may be unable to form a complete CO cluster. The reason is that he does not have enough general beliefs about the particular club, place of work, or the people with whom he would have to collaborate on the project. Or again, he might not be able to evoke or generate enough beliefs about self regarding his relevant probable reactions to the club, the place of work, or the collaborators on the project. In such a case, an incomplete cluster may be formed and even perhaps a tentative behavioral intent outlined, pending the acquisition or generation of the necessary beliefs. Probably the number of general beliefs and/or beliefs about self a person requires before being able to complete a CO cluster is subject to individual differences, and reflects perhaps the overall weight characteristic of beliefs of that CO component in determining or predicting that person's behavior. It is possible that many people have a ready program for acquiring the missing beliefs necessary for closure of the belief cluster. If this is so, then the definitive formation of the major behavioral intent may be viewed as dependent on the results attained through a secondary intent implemented through a prefabricated program.

Less frequent, though similar, is the case of the cluster rendered incomplete through the absence of relevant norm beliefs. Norm beliefs are usually of such a general nature that they may apply to a variety of situations. Therefore, normless clusters are relatively rare. One type of situation in which such clusters may occur deserves consideration; it arises when a person has to act under conditions unfamiliar to him, perhaps in a foreign country or with people he does not know well. Under these circumstances the difficulty is due to the fact that the comprehensive meaning of the situation as well as the question "What am I to do?" include too many cues for norm beliefs. Some of the cues may even give rise to conflicting norms. At the same time, the other elicited beliefs do not contain sufficiently strong cues for delimiting the range of applicable norms. Under these circumstances, the final closure of the incomplete cluster has to be delayed until elaboration of the input's meaning or further beliefs make possible inserting the proper norm or norms.

We have discussed incomplete clusters of three types: clusters without goals, clusters without general beliefs or beliefs about self, and normless clusters. All these clusters are rendered incomplete by the absence of beliefs from one or more of the four CO components. They occur frequently in daily life and are perhaps the rule in states of reduced consciousness caused by hypnosis, drunkenness, pentothal, and other types of drug intoxication. Incomplete clusters are probably also a common manifestation of impaired clustering in cases of organic brain pathology, for example, in patients with the frontal lobe syndrome suffering from perseveration and the inability to accommodate their goal in a situation with rules established for the task (B. Milner, 1964), or in patients with limbic lesions suffering from disabilities of short-term memory (P. M. Milner, 1970, pp. 444ff.).

But the most remarkable and important incomplete clusters are of a different kind. Although they may consist of beliefs of all four CO components, the clusters are not sufficiently organized or supported to make possible the formation of a proper behavioral intent. Sometimes no clear-cut behavioral intent can be crystallized, sometimes the tentatively formed cluster supports the formation of more than one behavioral intent—each subserving the same goal. Hence, the cluster is incomplete in the sense that it is too weak and unstructured. The weakness may result from the absence of enough supporting beliefs, from a relatively great number of ambiguous beliefs, or from a diversity of beliefs pointing simultaneously in different directions. This state of affairs may be reflected in beliefs about self such as "I do not understand this situation," or "I do not know what to decide." Sometimes, however, there is just a feeling of uneasiness or no subjective response at all. However it may be, under such circumstances the automatic clustering is replaced by other forms of cognitive activity: thinking, in the sense of problem elaboration and problem solving, or decision making, or both. For reasons that will become clearer at a later stage, we suggest regarding thinking and decision making as two different types of cognitive activity and as distinguishable from conflict resolution. Essentially, thinking is a more basic, pervasive, and wide-ranging activity, including many subroutines, strategies, and specific abilities that enable binding, transforming, differentiating, coding, recoding, etc. of cognitive elements. Decision making is a more specific cognitive activity, employed in situations of choice. It consists in considering and comparing certain given alternatives with regard to respective utilities, risk, probabilities, and preferences. Decision making is thus affected by thinking and may often be interrupted by it. In case thinking or decision making is postponed, an incomplete CO cluster is likely to result.

In view of what has beeen said about storage and retrieval of clusters, we assume that also this type of incomplete cluster, which indicates the need for thinking or decision making, may be stored. When stored, such clusters are probably accompanied by their attached meaning patterns. Thus, if at any time later the same or a similar meaning pattern results from some act of meaning generation, this incomplete cluster may be retrieved and contribute to answering the question "What am I to do?" There are, however, other types of incomplete clusters stored with the indication that decision making is necessary. For example, there may be an incomplete cluster that includes at the very least one of the permanent goals of the individual—for example, to preserve one's life—and the general belief "decision making is necessary in this case." Such clusters perhaps result from the binding of comprehensive meaning to one of the permanent goals that has previously led to the elicitation of decision making.

It should, however, be noted that thinking and decision making are not restricted to the stage of clustering. They are often elicited in situations of conflict and represent one possible mode of conflict resolution. For example, thinking and decision making may be elicited when two or more equally supported intents have been formed, or when there arises the need to choose one out of several available behavioral programs for implementing an intent. The latter represent the majority of experimental situations designed to study problem solving or decision making. A behavioral intent is declared or assumed by the experimenter, whereas the subject is required to find a solution to the presented problem, to select a program or course of action, and so on (see Chapter 6).

Finally, there is another remarkable type of incomplete clusters, whose incompleteness resides in the tentative character of the formed intent. These are the CO clusters that seem to steer the course of daydreams. Daydreams are behavioral sequences enacted fully or partially in fantasy, often accompanied by emotional responses of differential intensity. As such, they are to be distinguished from the fleeting or fragmentary imagery that occurs in presleep stages, or that is used in tasks of learning, recall, perception, or problem solving (McKellar, 1972; Paivio, 1972). The stimuli or situations most likely to elicit daydreaming include delay in or impossibility of satisfying a drive in reality (Freud, 1911), interruption of performance of some task or plan, and perceived necessity to implement some behavioral intent under novel or threatening conditions (Singer, 1970). The circumstances that support recourse to daydreaming are often characterized by low or medium levels of arousal, ongoing work on some task that does not demand full attention, and a dull or threatening external situation (Singer, 1970). Examination of findings and theories about daydreaming supports the assumption that most of the goal beliefs that dominate CO clusters formed in daydreaming are highly similar, if not actually identical, to the goals of everyday life. Indeed, sometimes they appear in a more radical, daring, and extravagant form than in "normal" CO clusters, but they hardly differ from the latter in their essential contents, as attested to by the recurrence of such basic daydreaming themes as sex, heroism, achievement, love, success, and aggression. Also, most if not all of the norm beliefs are brought over into daydreams from real-life situations. What are changed in CO clusters of daydreams are general beliefs and beliefs about self. The manner in which these types of beliefs are changed becomes clearer in view of the two patterns of daydreaming identified by Singer and Antrobus (1972). One type of daydreamer is an emotionally unstable person, intolerant and distractible, who tends to daydream about sexual, hostile, and fearful themes. The other type is the "happy daydreamer," who is a creative person, thoughtful and curious about people, and who tends to use daydreaming as an ideational activity and as a means of exploring the future.

It seems to us plausible to assume that the first type, who seeks satisfaction through daydreams, tends to change mainly beliefs about self. Further, he changes them in a direction that enhances his presumed abilities or qualities in dealing with real-life situations, which are reflected in relatively authentic general beliefs. Since the changes in beliefs about self—and sometimes, if necessary, even in a few general beliefs—support wish fulfillment, the formed intents are often emotionally more satisfying than those formed in everyday life. In contrast, the "happy daydreamer" probably seldom changes beliefs about self but concentrates mainly on changing general beliefs. Since his major concern is experimenting with reality, understanding reality, and inventing reality rather than obtaining direct personal satisfaction, it is only logical to expect that he will transfer into the CO clusters directing his daydreaming many of his usual beliefs about self, but will insert into each such

CO cluster one or more different sets of general beliefs. Indeed, sometimes he may have to change beliefs about self, for example, when as a child he plays the role of some animal, or when as an adult engaged in creative thinking he plays the role of a straying electron. Yet even in such cases the changes in beliefs about self are introduced mainly for the sake of exploring and understanding reality. Of course, most daydreamers belong to both types, striving at the same time or on different occasions for satisfaction as well as for exploration.

In any case, changes in beliefs about self and general beliefs endow daydreaming with its as-if character, or, as Sarbin (1972) noted, with its suppositional and hypothetical nature. Changes in beliefs of these two CO components also highlight the affinity between daydreaming, roleplaying games in childhood, imitation, and creative thinking. In the absence of relevant research, it is premature to conjecture whether the beliefs brought over from reality into the daydream (i.e., the combination of goal and norm beliefs plus either general beliefs or beliefs about self) form a kind of incomplete cluster that is completed imaginatively for the sake of the daydream, or whether the whole cluster formation is actually carried out for the sake of the daydream. Possibly both cases exist. For the moment, however, it is more important to note that CO clusters which guide the course of daydreams may also be stored. This is attested to by the recurrence of the same or similar daydreams over extended periods of time, sometimes years (Singer, 1966). These stored CO clusters may form a set that may become active in an appropriate situation or may even affect activities destined to create such a situation.

It goes without saying that CO clusters containing unrealistic beliefs may lead to unrealistic or even pathological modes of behavior. More will be said about this in Chapter 10 when we discuss psychopathology. At present it should suffice to point out that if meaning generation is not itself deviant, it may function as a safeguard against attempts to implement in reality the behavioral intent resulting from the not fully realistic CO cluster in daydreams. Yet, under the somewhat relaxed reality rules of the daydream situation, a bond may be established between a pattern of meaning and an unrealistic CO cluster. This bond would then be stored together with the cluster. If at any point later in time this pattern of meaning reappears, the retrieved CO cluster may not be carefully checked belief for belief. Thus if for some reason, say, frustration, the individual tends to adopt the resulting behavioral intent, he may accept it as such without too much probing. Hence, the behavioral intent may lead to deviant behavior. Moreover, the set produced by stored CO clusters of daydreams may generate a striving for situations that make possible the application of these clusters. Under these circumstances, the incomplete or as-if CO cluster may be made to play the role of the complete CO cluster. The actions it produces may sometimes lead to great achievements, at other times to pathological behavior. Whichever turn development may take depends in small part on reality, in great part on the nature, constitution, and structure of the CO cluster. Figure 5.2 summarizes the preceding discussion of incomplete CO clusters.

CO CLUSTERS IN CHILDREN

As mentioned, children of preschool age have well-distinguished beliefs of the four CO components in many domains (Kreitler & Kreitler, 1967a; Kreitler, Kreitler, & Zigler, 1974). On the other hand, it is plausible to assume that children have difficulties in combining different beliefs and particularly in weighing and comparing several beliefs one against the other. Hence, the ability of children to form a CO cluster in the full sense of the word cannot be taken for granted. This ability has to be gradually acquired and developed.

Following Piaget, the difficulty children have in combining different beliefs derives from the limited character of the schemas and operations in the sensorimotor period (0–2 years) and in the stage of preoperational representations (2–7 years). In Piagetian terms, the full-fledged model of clustering we have described presupposes at the very least the ability to form cognitive structures corresponding to "groups." This is evident when one considers that "group" is defined as a specified set of elements (i.e., beliefs) and a specified operation (e.g., clustering) performed on these elements, satisfying the following conditions: composition, associativity, identity, and reversibility (i.e., inversion). "Groups" in the full sense of the term do not appear before the stage of operational thinking, which starts at approximately 11 years of age. CO clusters, however, occur much earlier. Hence, we would have to conclude that children form CO clusters on the basis of cognitive processes more primitive than abstract groups. Major among these are groupings based upon addition or multiplication of classes and relations (Piaget, 1949), and perhaps "subjective" groups (Piaget & Inhelder, 1956).

A different approach to the problem besetting the development of CO clusters may be based on Luria's (1959, 1961) observations and hypotheses. Starting from the assumption that behavior is first under the control of physical stimuli and is gradually subjected to the control of verbal stimuli, Luria traces the development of the regulative function of speech. The major axes of this development are the progression from external to internal verbal control and the shift from control of behavior

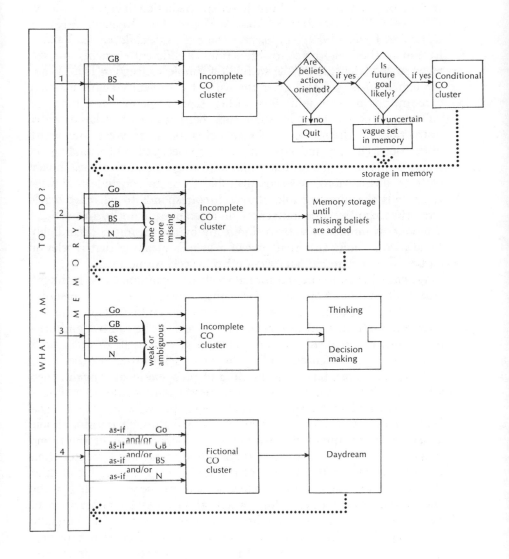

FIGURE 5.2 Formation of three types of incomplete CO clusters. The dotted lines represent connections with memory. (Go = goals; GB = general beliefs; BS = beliefs about self; N = norms.)

through the physical properties of speech to control through the semantic content of the utterance. Indeed, many observations testify that the control of overt behavior through verbal mediation increases with age (Horowitz, 1936; Kendler, Kendler, & Wells, 1960; Kuenne, 1946). In particular, Luria (1959) emphasizes the difficulty children (2–3 years) have in synthesizing the control functions of different elements in a sentence so that they are unable to fulfill a simple instruction like "When the light flashes, you will press the ball"; the difficulty children experience in obeying an inhibitory rather than a permissive order; the difficulty children have in subjecting behavior to a delayed verbal instruction by themselves or in changing behavior when the verbal instructions change; and especially the gap between understanding the semantic meaning of a sentence and following its directive role. In view of these observations, it seems plausible to us to conclude that what Luria calls the directive role of speech corresponds to what we would term the cognitive orientativeness of utterances, namely, the actional components implied directly or indirectly by the meaning. Accordingly, Luria's work shows that that part of a belief's meaning that is relevant for behavior is acquired later than other aspects of meaning.

Whereas Piaget focuses on formal facets of cognition, Luria highlights aspects of content. Both lines of evidence converge, however, in similar conclusions. Up to the age of 5 or 6 years the child develops the cognitive orientativeness of utterances and beliefs in the positive and negative forms. He gradually becomes able to give himself an order or to perform an action corresponding to some self-instruction, belief, or "intent." However, following the rules of preoperational thought, these self-instructions or quasi-intents usually reflect some single belief or cluster of beliefs of one single CO component, probably most often goal beliefs, rather than a system of beliefs formed through transformations and interactions among beliefs. The major impediments to the formation of CO clusters at this stage are the child's tendency to center attention on a single striking feature of the situation to the neglect of other features, his preference for concrete aspects to the neglect of the possible and nonimmediate aspects, his concentration on states rather than on transformations, and his inability to attain reversibility in thinking. Thus, the child is likely to act in accordance with beliefs that happen to gain dominance, mostly because the relevant objects or events are concretely present or because of some associative processes. Since the factors likely to affect the dominance of beliefs are fortuitous, the child's behavior lacks consistency and is mostly difficult to predict. The first clustering attempts may already be observed in children 2 to 3 years old who still verbalize their thoughts. These attempts mostly consist in interrelating two, sometimes even three, sequentially occurring "thoughts" or beliefs. For instance, a child may utter the goal belief "I want the ball," then bring up the general belief "The ball is so big," and complete the sequence with a belief about self "I can reach the ball." Yet the single beliefs frequently seem to remain unrelated. This is most evident, for example, in the case of the 4-year-old child who soliloquized, "I want this chocolate; Mama said a good boy should not take chocolate; I am a good boy," and while saying this took the chocolate and ate it.

Both Luria's and Piaget's observations lead to the expectation that at about the age of 6 or 7 years children may already form CO clusters consisting of beliefs of the four CO components. The experimental confirmation of this hypothesis stems from the success in predicting the curiosity behaviors of children 6 to 7 years old (Chapter 8). However, replication of the experiment with children 5 years old showed that the behavior of a certain number of children could not be adequately predicted. Piaget's (1948) observations about the development of moral judgment indicate that the clusters formed by children 6 to 8 years old are still dominated either by a goal belief or by a norm belief, but rarely by a goal belief fitting some norm. Moreover, it is likely that children in the stage of concrete operations still cannot exploit belief hierarchies for the sake of harmonizing contradicting beliefs, determine the identity of differently formulated beliefs, or perform the reversal necessary for exploiting or even for disbanding a tentative CO cluster. Yet in relying increasingly on the cognitive structures called "groupings" and on initial analogues of "groups," they become gradually capable of forming CO clusters by combining various partial clusters into a larger structure. A full-fledged clustering activity requires the ability to form cognitive structures of the type of "groups" and perhaps even of lattices. These abilities are acquired around the age of 10 to 11 years, but continue to develop all through one's lifetime. So do the extent and depth of meaning. This implies that, on the one hand, more and more CO clusters of recurring situations are formed and stored. On the other hand, however, the wider range of perceived meanings results in the continuous formation of new clusters. But it also increases the extent of necessary adaptations within stored CO clusters so as to render them adequate for use in constantly recurring, yet continuously changing situations.

CHAPTER 6

Intent Formation and Output Program

THE BEHAVIORAL INTENT: PROPERTIES

The term "behavioral intent" designates the link between the CO cluster and the behavioral program. It may be recalled that the behavioral intent was defined as the output of the CO cluster. However, the process of clustering alone cannot guarantee the emergence of a behavioral intent. The formation of a behavioral intent depends on several conditions. The major condition is a minimal degree of congruence of the behaviorally orientative meaning values of the beliefs colligated in the CO cluster. The degree of congruence reflects the amount of support for the behavioral tendency that eventually turns into the behavioral intent. The other conditions are the degree of preference for the goal that plays the focal role in the CO cluster, and the number of different goals that could be satisfied or—to borrow Simon's (1956) term—at least be satisficed if the particular behavioral intent were adopted.

If these conditions are met, the automatic clustering process culminates in the crystallization of the behavioral intent and terminates it. In case no goal belief was evoked or none of the evoked goals had sufficient preference or support to pass the critical threshold of congruence, no behavioral intent is formed—so that no action specific to the input can be taken. If, however, two CO clusters were formed, two separate behavioral intents emerge, and a classical conflict situation is established (Chapter 10).

We assume that the transition from the CO cluster to the behavioral intent is a simple one-step process. The behavioral intent represents the specification and elaboration of the behaviorally oriented meaning value of the most supported goal belief on which the cluster is anchored. Thus, before its full-fledged emergence the intent plays the role of a determining tendency, sometimes manifested in one or more prefinal CO clusters that give rise to tentative behavioral intents.

Our concept of behavioral intent is similar to some concepts of intention proposed by other investigators, and very different from others. For the purpose of describing the particular properties of behavioral intent in our context we shall allude to some of these similarities and dissimilarities.

A most important quality of the behavioral intent emerges from its comparison with the concept of intention forming the basis of Ryan's (1970) voluminous compilation of material. Ryan views intention as comparable to a decision, and the process of its formation as analogous to decision making. Although he is very generous in postulating a list of the varied factors involved in establishing intention, he is explicit in emphasizing the particular role of perceived freedom of choice in characterizing intentional behavior. Behavior is intentional only if "there are alternative possibilities perceived by the individual and he makes a conscious choice among these alternatives" (p. 30). A similar view is propounded by Irwin (1971) in his most carefully constructed theory of intentional behavior. He (chaps. 1 & 6) defines an act as intentional if it is one of a pair of alternative acts, and if the expected outcome of the act is preferred while the expected outcome of the alternative—not chosen—act is dispreferred. The conceptions of Ryan and Irwin are akin to the original definition of "commitment" or "decision" in the framework of cognitive dissonance theory. Both Festinger (1964) and Brehm and Cohen (1962) point out that the performance of an act or the feeling of having made up one's mind are an outcome of the activity of "deciding."

To our mind it would be a mistake to equate intent formation with decision making. We regard decision making as a cognitive activity initiated under specific conditions, such as the existence of an incomplete CO cluster with an insufficient number of beliefs for forming a behavioral intent, the existence of two conflicting behavioral intents, or the existence of two or more programs that seem equally well suited for implementing the same behavioral intent but on closer inspection might turn out to differ in personal preference and ultimate utility. Hence, instead of a behavioral program, a program for decision making is adopted. It is this latter situation that is dealt with by most decision-making models. According to a decision-making model developed by Dan Zakay (1976), the chain of events can best be conceptualized as a subroutine within the executive CO model of behavior evocation. The subroutine starts with the decision to decide, then feeds the competing programs together with their common behavioral intent back as input to further meaning generation and CO clustering. Meaning generation clarifies the different aspects of the given alternatives in relation to the behavioral intent. In the course of CO clustering beliefs about the respective utilities and preferential features of the programs are evoked until a behavioral intent to choose one of the alternative programs emerges. Extensive experiments carried out in line with this subroutine model, which of course is more complex than could be indicated here, demonstrated its amazing predictive superiority over the best-known psychological and mathematical models of decision making. Thus, decision making is essentially a reasoning process, primarily conscious, and subject to voluntary manipulations, reversals, and transformations in all its stages. In contrast, CO clustering and intent formation are not guided by any conscious considerations and inferences but occur automatically through interactions among beliefs of the four CO components.

These remarks raise the question of the consciousness of the behavioral intent. Our position is that whereas CO clustering and even the CO cluster are not accessible to full consciousness—though beliefs as such are—the behavioral intent can in principle be conscious. The behavioral intent often assumes the cognitive form of a belief about self, say, "I will make x," "I have decided to go abroad," "I will think this problem over," "I shall kiss her," "I will take this pencil now," "I have made up my mind to buy these shares," and so on. The familiar character of these statements testifies to the fact that behavioral intents are frequent visitors on the conscious screen of cognition. However, this does not mean that all intents are necessarily conscious or should be conscious. For instance, there is enough evidence to support the existence of determining tendencies in thinking, which operate without awareness on the part of the individual (Humphrey, 1963, chap. 3). Ach (1935) even goes so far as to conclude from his studies that the determining tendency appears in consciousness only under special circumstances and as a means of attaining the goal, for example, when there are special difficulties, inhibitions, lack of concentration, or earlier errors in performance. Another case in point is behavior under particular stress or in danger situations. Here, too, a behavioral intent may produce an action so quickly that a person remains completely unaware of the intent. On other occasions we become aware of not having been conscious of an intent only when the intent has in some sense been lost track of. Most people have had the disconcerting experience of entering a room in the office or at home, suddenly stopping at a loss, and asking themselves: "What did I come here for?" This quite frequent experience suggests that an intent may trigger behavior—say, going to some room in order to . . .(?)— without the person's being aware of the intention until something goes wrong.

Finally, there are the notorious unconscious intentions belabored by depth psychology. All we know of such cases testifies to two possibilities, which at this stage are still merely vague hypotheses. One possibility is that under specific conditions two CO clusters and two corresponding intents are formed, one conscious and the other unconscious. The antecedent conditions propitious for this eventuality probably include a sharp conflict between two goals, one of which is highly preferred but strongly rejected by other beliefs, while the other is less preferred but widely supported by other beliefs. It is possible that if under such conditions two intents emerge, the one representing the goal rejected by many other beliefs is automatically made unconscious. The second possibility is that only one CO cluster is formed but its intent is replaced by an apparently different intent due to feedback from a defensive behavioral program, such as sublimation, projection, and so on. Thus only the replaced behavioral intent would remain unconscious whereas the replacing behavioral intent may become conscious. The antecedent condition propitious for this development is the once reached and permanently upheld decision to replace a particular kind of behavioral intents by certain other behavioral intents. Presumably, the process of replacement as well as the permanent decision to perform it remain unconscious because both are a part of the "defense mechanism" program.

In sum, the behavioral intent may be conscious and often is conscious, but it need not be conscious, and many different circumstances promote its remaining outside consciousness. In this respect we accept Lewin's (1951) and Tolman's (1935) suggestion that an intent may operate without full cognitive representation. However, it may be assumed that if an intent is conscious it affects action in a way different from an aconscious or unconscious intent. This assumption is supported, for example, by the mass of studies on the role of awareness in verbal conditioning (Eriksen, 1962; Kanfer, 1968) and in learning (Ryan, 1970, chaps. 6 & 7).

A different aspect of the behavioral intent is highlighted through its comparison with Heider's (1958, chap. 4) concept of intention. Heider assigns to intention an important motivational status in regarding it as one of the two elements of "trying" (the other being "exertion"), which together with "power" constitute the "effective personal force" of action. Hence, he views intention as the major manifestation of personal causality, which lends direction, coordination, persistence, and equifinality to specifically human acts. Although some of the factors Heider mentions as important in shaping intention, e.g., want, ability, and fear of punishment, are similar to beliefs of the various CO components, his concept of intention reflects "volition" to an extent that makes it incompatible with our concept. Of course, this reservation on our part should be amplified by the comment that volition in this case means self-initiation, personal responsibility, control over performance, often awareness, and always a dynamic quality of pushing forward until the goal is attained—all of which are foreign to our concept of the behavioral intent. Although the behavioral intent plays some role in the control of ensuing action, particularly in its regulation and completion as an element in the feedback mechanisms, it is neither a guarantee that an action will follow nor the epitome of motivational directionality.

On the other hand, it is mainly the energetic aspect of motivation that sets our concept of behavioral intent apart from Lewin's concept. Lewin (1935, p. 242ff.) views intention as a quasi-need, that is, as a tension system that drives towards discharge through attainment of goal and causes activities that serve the execution of the purpose. The analogy between intention and the classical homeostatic model of biological drives introduces the spurious equivalence of intention, on the one hand, and force and energy, on the other hand. Cognition processes meanings, not forces. Hence, the behavioral intent is like an arrow pointing in a certain direction; it may have the function of regulating the flow and transformations of energy, but it is neither a force in itself nor does it set up a motive.

Theoretically there is much more affinity between our concept of behavioral intent and the concept of intention as developed by Fishbein (1967a) and by Ajzen and Fishbein (1973), following Dulany (1968). The affinity consists in the determinants of the intent. Fishbein and his associates assume that the two major factors determining behavioral intentions are the attitude toward the act, measured by rating the specific act on a few evaluative semantic differential scales, and normative beliefs, measured by questions about perceived expectations of other people multiplied by degree of motivation to comply with these expectations. When given empirical weights the two factors, combined in a multiple-regression equation, were shown to predict various behavioral intentions ranging from intentions to decide in a specific manner in hypothetical situations of risk (Ajzen & Fishbein, 1972), to choosing particular strategies in Prisoner's Dilemma games (Ajzen & Fishbein, 1970), engaging in eight different behaviors on a Friday night (Ajzen & Fishbein, 1969), and behaving in specific ways with respect to an African Negro person (Carlson, 1968). An examination of the assessment instruments used in predicting intentions in these and similar studies and recent findings about the determinants of the two predictors reveals that these two predictors—attitude toward the act and normative beliefs—include elements from the four CO components, though often in an indirect, garbled manner. The CO component that seems to be least considered in these studies and conceptualizations is beliefs about goals. These goal beliefs may be represented only marginally in the motivation to comply with the norms. Nevertheless, the correlations between the two factors and behavioral intentions are high owing to a particular property characteristic of the experimental situations. Either these situations are hypothetical, which means that the formed CO clusters are incomplete and may include an as-if tentative goal, or the goal is predetermined for the subject by the experimenter, as in the Prisoner's Dilemma games. In both cases subjects vary so little in the relevant goal beliefs that this component is practically constant and may thus even be overlooked for prediction.

These remarks suggest the importance we attribute to goal beliefs in determining the behavioral intent. This assumption is supported both by theoretical considerations and by empirical findings. The description of the process of clustering makes it abundantly clear that the behavioral intent reflects the action-oriented meaning value of the goal that was supported by the greater number of other beliefs in the CO cluster. Yet the intent appears in a somewhat reformulated or elaborated form. If, say, the goal belief is "I want to have this pencil," and its supported action-oriented meaning value is "to take the pencil and return it later," then the intent may get the form "I will take it." A study of the meaning of behavioral intents (Chapter 11, Study III) also showed the intimate relation between goals and behavioral intents. The desired end appears in the meaning of both terms; but while it forms the focus in the meaning of goals, in the meaning of intents it is the ulterior motive for the described actions.

However, the close relation between goal belief and behavioral intent, and particularly between the action-oriented meaning value of the goal belief and the resulting intent, raise the question whether it is at all justified to postulate behavioral intents. The answer is definitely yes. They fulfill different functions in eliciting behavior. The goal belief operates within the CO cluster, often being its most dynamic force or center of gravity, sometimes being neutralized or modified by other beliefs. In contrast, the behavioral intent is the result of clustering and thus reflects only the particularly supported goal or even merely some of its action-oriented meaning values. Even if the goal is highly specific, such as "I want to marry this girl as soon as possible," it does not thereby become identical with an intent before the completion of clustering. Hence, while the function of the goal is centered within the CO cluster, the function of the intent lies outside it. It consists in triggering the phase of programming, either at once or at some later stage. The behavioral intent is the first step toward actual output production, the bridge between input elaboration and output programming. Moreover, experimentally there is a big difference between remembering a goal that has not yet been attained and a behavioral intent that has not yet been performed. The retrieved goal will not produce action before it is checked against other beliefs, which may lead to modifying it or even dropping it. The behavioral intent no longer stands in need of this checking procedure. It may be acted upon without further elaboration.

The problem of the intimate relations between the behavioral intent and actual output may best be elucidated by comparing our conception with other hypotheses that emphasize a similar aspect of intention. First, a behavioral intent, as we conceive it, always refers only to a particular behavior in a specific situation. Hence it does not represent a general behavioral disposition, as does the concept of behavioral intention in the studies of Bogardus (1925) and particularly of Triandis (Triandis, 1964a; Triandis & Triandis, 1965). For instance, the behavioral intention of friendship as defined by Triandis may mean readiness to eat, gossip, or engage in athletics with a certain person, without specifying any particular behavior designed to take place at a specified time and location. Triandis' concept is perhaps more akin to what we have called generalized sets for intent formation (Chapter 5), which result from the storage of multiple tentative intents produced by incomplete clusters.

Indeed, behavioral intents may differ in the degree of their specificity. Both "I will go to Jerusalem" and "I will go to Jerusalem tomorrow" may qualify as behavioral intents. As noted, the degree of specificity of an intent reflects the degree of specificity of the goal belief focal in the CO cluster. Accordingly, a behavioral intent remains specific even if it refers explicitly or implicitly to more than one particular action, that is, to a family of actions viewed as possibly instrumental in attaining a certain goal. Indeed, the latter may be the rule rather than the exception. A study dealing with the meaning of behavioral intents (Chapter 11) showed that most of the subjects referred to some goal and in addition stated several courses of action envisaged as leading to this goal. The commonness with which such series of actions accompany an intent is reflected also in the emphasis placed by Tolman (1926, p. 355) on the multiplicity of expected means-ends relations in any situation, and by Heider (1958) on equifinality in human motivation.

The behavioral intent shares the property of specificity in behavioral direction with two other hypotheses about intention. One was suggested by Atkinson and Birch, the other by Miller, Galanter, and Pribram. Atkinson and Birch (1970) advance the thesis that intention, as a tendency on the level of covert perceptual and imaginal activity, has nothing to do with overt motoric activity, although both may be instigated by the same stimulus. Since the covert activity often begins before the overt activity people tend mistakenly to explain the latter by reference to the former. Obviously we reject this view of pure parallelism which is supported neither by scientific evidence nor by the subjective experience of every human being. In the CO theory the intent is not an analogue of behavior but a preparatory stage for it. Without assigning to intention any causal function, Miller et al. (1960) bind intention to action by defining it as "the uncompleted parts of a Plan, whose execution has already begun" (p. 61). This implies that intention is identical with or depends on the internal representation of a plan in the course of execution, that it reflects the special status of such a plan, and that it may be involved in controlling the execution. We might adopt these implications. But we do not adopt their major assertion that there can be no intention without a plan whose execution has begun. Many well-attested observations invalidate this assertion. Penfield (1938) reports that while exploring the human brain electrically before surgery he occasionally elicited a nonreflex motor response that the patient described as having occurred without any intention on his part, while at other times he elicited what the patient described as a strong intention to make a certain response, which, however, did not occur. This demonstrates that intention and behavior not only are separate but also may have different physiological correlates. Furthermore, we may point to the common phenomenon of storing behavioral intents for performance at some later period, which may even be far removed from the present. At the moment of storage, however, there may not be even the slightest indication of a program for actual behavior. Moreover, the stored intent may never be retrieved, and if it is may not be acted upon. These and similar observations support the conclusion that intention and behavior should be kept theoretically distinct even though in practice they merge into each other along a continuum and often even appear interwoven.

These remarks raise the more fundamental question whether behavioral intent is a prerequisite for every act of behavior. Our answer is definitely no. First, there are all those acts of behavior on the so-called submolar level, which include mainly the unconditioned and conditioned responses, that is, adaptive and defensive reactions, the orienting response, and so on. All these are triggered by processes simpler than meaning generation and clustering of beliefs (Chapter 3). Hence, the behavioral intent is not involved in their evocation. Moreover, there is evidence that when a specific response can be performed either in a conditioned manner or in a manner mediated by an intention, the physical properties of these two responses differ greatly. The conditioned eyeblink, for instance, differs in form and latency from the intentional blink

(Kimble, 1964, pp. 56–58). Further, subjects who respond on the basis of an intention are better able than conditioned subjects to use general class concepts for discrimination between reinforced and nonreinforced stimuli when various discriminating stimuli are available (Grant, 1968).

Second, a dissociation between the behavioral intent and an action may occur in patients with various types of brain pathology. For instance, Luria and Homskaya (1964) demonstrated that patients with tumors in the frontal lobe are often unable to obey experimental instructions calling for certain motor acts though they are perfectly able to repeat the instructions verbally and correctly identify the relevant cues in the situation. The fact that they try to perform motorically in line with the instructions testifies that they probably have the right kind of behavioral intent, too. This hypothesis suggests the possibility that in other cases of incomplete clusters as well there may occur a dissociation between the behavioral intent and a behavioral act.

There is a third type of acts that perhaps are not fully guided by a behavioral intent adequately supported by a CO cluster. These are behaviors triggered by incomplete CO clusters. Of the various types of incomplete CO clusters described in Chapter 5, those most likely to trigger behavior are the incomplete clusters formed by children and those formed under conditions of reduced control, due for instance to alcoholic drunkenness, various drugs, perhaps hypnosis, extreme panic, stress or duress, and so on. The feature common to all these different states and situations is reduced control, which, on the one hand, may prevent the completion of the clustering process and, on the other hand, may prevent the inhibition of various responses set in a state of preparedness for action. Thus tentative behavioral intents, reflecting CO clusters deficient in various respects, may elicit behaviors. It is possible that such behaviors may not always be experienced as ego-syntonic by the individual at the stage of performance or at a later point in time.

We have mentioned three types of behaviors not mediated by a behavioral intent in the full sense assigned to this term in the framework of the CO model. But we should keep in mind that many of the examples routinely brought up in order to demonstrate the independence of behavior from behavioral intent are in no way convincing. Thus it is often mentioned that people who voluntarily seek help to reduce smoking, excessive eating, and the like nevertheless discontinue therapy or do not maintain the newly acquired beneficial habits a sufficiently long time. Dropout and recidivism rates as high as 70 or 80 percent are not unusual (e.g., McFarland, Gimbel, Donald, & Folkenberg, 1964; Silverstone & Solomon, 1965). A similar case in point is the frequent "determination" of criminals, drug addicts, and alcoholics to stop their noxious behaviors. Yet psychologists should not be misled into believing that the road to hell is paved only with good intents. Some "bad" intents may not be completely absent.

It is evident that the behavioral intent declared by people or suggested by their behavior need not be their actual intent. To wit, a drug addict may undergo withdrawal treatment with the behavioral intent to undergo the treatment so as to reduce the necessary drug doses, and an obese patient may start a dietary regime to pacify his conscience or his marital partner but not with the behavioral intent actually to carry through the treatment. How misleading it may be to accept declarations of behavioral intents at face value was demonstrated in our study of modifying smoking behavior (Chapter 9). We found that of the 40 smokers selected from those answering our newspaper advertisement for volunteers for a smoking withdrawal treatment, only 10 percent had a full-fledged behavioral intent to stop smoking and another 20 percent had a similar though weaker behavioral intent. Indeed, no behavioral context is univocal enough in its meaning to make possible a clear-cut inference about the dominant behavioral intents of individuals acting in that context. Clients in psychotherapy should be attributed the behavioral intent to recover no more than school children should automatically be presumed to be primarily intent on learning.

In summary, the behavioral intent is the product of clustering and reflects the CO cluster. It represents the most supported goal belief and points toward a specific behavioral direction. Hence, it forms the first step toward actual output programming. Nonetheless, it is distinct from behavior and is not a sufficient guarantee of the occurrence of behavior. Further, the behavioral intent is often conscious but need not be fully conscious. Again, the behavioral intent is not identical with volition, motivation, behavioral disposition, energy, or force. Finally, following Ryan (1970, p. 20 ff.), we may mention some dimensions of variation of behavioral intents. Thus, behavioral intents may vary in temporal characteristics, that is, in delay of initiation and duration of performance; in degree of specification of means and details of behavior; in complexity, that is, in the number and homogeneity of behavioral units to which it refers; as well as in intensity, importance, and salience.

THE BEHAVIORAL INTENT: FUNCTIONS

The list of properties just cited may help in outlining the major functions assigned to the behavioral intent in the CO model. All the mentioned properties of the behavioral intent indicate its special role with regard to output behavior. To our mind, this role may be made explicit in terms of three related functions: (1) triggering output programming; (2) regulating the course of action; and (3) completing the action.

The function of triggering the programming behavior reveals the special status of the behavioral intent as a crucial link in the action chain connecting input elaboration and output behavior, or, more specifically, as a bridge between clustering and programming. Indeed, it would be just as adequate to define the function of the behavioral intent as stopping the processes of clustering. Yet due to the intimate relation of the behavioral intent to action, we consider the emphasis on the onset of programming to reflect a more integral aspect of the behavioral intent's function. However, initiating the phase of programming does not imply merely being or emitting a signal "operate" to a certain set of processes. We hypothesize that the behavioral intent channels the phase of programming in a specific direction, biasing it, as it were, in line with certain programs. The empirical support for this hypothesis to date is the finding that behavioral programs, mostly merely outline sketches of programs, constitute an integral part of the meaning of statements concerning behavioral intents (Chapter 11, Study III). More concretely, when the behavioral intent is formed the individual does not have to start from scratch exploring the possibilities and alternatives of programs. Rather, the behavioral intent implies particular programs that can merely be unfolded, explicated, and further specified. This problem, however, will be discussed more fully after we have elucidated the concept of programming.

We know much less both theoretically and empirically about the second function of the behavioral intent, which has to do with controlling the course of action. Three types of observations have led us to attribute such a role to the behavioral intent. The first refers to the persistence of ends and the flexibility of means characteristic of human action. If one course of action or one attempt fails, the individual often repeats it or embarks on another course of action designed to attain the same end. Like Heider (1958) we assume that this equifinality reflects an intent. The second observation is that a normal individual immersed in acting is usually aware in some sense of what he is attempting to do or attain (but not necessarily of *what* he is doing), although he may not be able to verbalize his awareness or even pinpoint it precisely. In this context it may be meaningful to cite Ach's (1905, p. 230) finding that his subjects were immediately aware whether some act of behavior they performed conformed to their previous determination or not, regardless of whether the behavior was self-initiated. How important this awareness may be for action is glaringly demonstrated in cases where it is probably absent. It is reported of patients with lesions in the limbic system that they are able to perform each link in a behavioral chain but often remain stuck when required to initiate a new link in the chain (Miller et al., 1960, pp. 203–204). We assume that a smooth self-evident passage from one link to another requires awareness of a behavioral intent in some sense or on some level. Finally, the third observation is that people persist in an action in spite of various distractions and return to it after an interruption. This observation has indeed been differently interpreted by various investigators. According to one major trend of the interpretation the tendency to complete an interrupted action derives from some force or motive or intent outside the action itself (e.g., Lewin, 1935); according to the other major trend, it is due to the internal dynamics of the course of action (e.g., Mandler, 1964; Miller et al., 1960). For reasons that will become clearer later (see "The Nature of Programs," this chapter) we prefer a third interpretation, linked to our concept of "programs." According to this interpretation the tendency of completion derives from the cortical representation of intended action, which makes the performance of this action possible. The behavioral intent initiates the representation and serves as a basic criterion for evaluating feedback information about the progress of action. Thus the behavioral intent provides a general context-like frame of reference for the action or its cortical representation. Hence, the behavioral intent may elicit signals about whether the action is completed or not, and may initiate further or renewed programming whenever necessary in view of information about external or internal situations. On the basis of such information, the behavioral intent could also regulate the flow of energy made available for output behavior, for example, by signalling the possibility of lowering its level when action is proceeding smoothly or the necessity of raising its level when obstacles, difficulties, and obstructions are encountered. However, this latter suggestion is at present purely speculative.

The conception of the behavioral intent as the general frame of reference for guiding the action reveals that the third function we have attributed to the behavioral intent is inseparable from the second function. That is, completing action is an integral aspect of controlling the course of action. The mechanism that makes it possible to ascertain that an action is not yet completed also provides the cues for stopping when the action is completed. The existence of stop mechanisms for biologically regulated behaviors such as eating and drinking has long been uncovered (Milner, 1970). The conception that mechanisms with a similar function for other behaviors would have to be assumed was forwarded by Mandler (1964), Miller et al. (1960), N. E. Miller (1963), and others. Our suggestion is that the behavioral intent plays an essential role in any such mechanism monitoring behaviors not subject to biological regulation. To use a term suggested by Held (1961), the behavioral intent is a kind of comparator that makes possible evaluating feedback in terms of some state-to-be-achieved. It reflects a certain standard against which feedback information about the proceeding action can be checked. However, in the case of the biologically determined mechanisms the criterion is essentially general and not geared to the peculiarities of a specific action. Moreover, it is largely preset and only marginally modifiable by learning and active response to changing environmental conditions. In contrast, the behavioral intent represents a criterion, or rather a set of criteria, specific to a particular action, and reflects the product of clustering rather than of evolutionary biological trends. But in essence, though perhaps not in details, the process of evaluating the results of action in view of the standard is comparable in behaviors monitored "biologically" and "intentionally."

This conception of the behavioral intent suggests that there exist different types of feedback, or more specifically, that there are different types of feedback information and that this information is evaluated on different levels or by different mechanisms. The behavioral intent would be a crucial element on one such level. The idea of multiple feedbacks is not new. Fitts (1965) assumed the existence of different feedback loops necessary for performance, e.g., central control of perceptual mechanisms, proprioceptive stimuli, inter- and intramuscular feedback, and so on. R. B. Miller (1953) distinguished between action feedback, which can be used for controlling a response, and learning feedback, which comes after completion of the response and can only be used for subsequent responses. Adams (1968) suggests a differentiation between classical feedback, as evident in proprioception and response chaining, and closed-loop feedback, which may emit the signal for stopping a response when completed. Of course, he shows that in view of the evidence the impact of learning on the "reference mechanism" is unavoidable. Further, Annett (1969) demonstrates the necessity of distinguishing between intrinsic knowledge of results, which includes the intermuscular feedback loop as well as the feedback to muscular receptors registering forces resisting movement, and extrinsic knowledge of results, which is based on evaluating visible effects of the act, information provided by the experimenter, and so on.

In view of this and other evidence (Walcher & Peters, 1971), it seems warranted to assume a hierarchy of self-regulatory mechanisms, extending from primary biologically conditioned feedback loops to learned systems of regulation that apply to whole sets or sequences of behavior. Our suggestion is that the behavioral intent plays a crucial role on the highest level of evaluating feedback information about the progress and outcomes of action. Borrowing Walcher and Peter's (1971, pp. 8ff., 232ff.) terminology, this level may perhaps be called the level of thoughtful (or intellectually mediated) self-regulation. In line with the empirical evidence cited by Annett (1969) and by Locke, Cartledge, and Koeppel (1968), we identify this comparator function of the behavioral intent as a phenomenon of knowledge of results. It is focused not merely on movements but on "acts," that is, to use Pribram's definition, "the environmental consequences of movement" (Pribram, 1971, p. 301). In view of Locke et al.'s (1968) careful analysis, the impact of the knowledge of results depends on evaluating the results of action in terms of the goal set by the individual with regard to that action. Again, Annett (1969) shows cogently that the major aspect of knowledge of results is informative, and that its impact depends mainly on the nature of the information and what is done with it, that is, to which conclusions it leads and how it is used. Hence the important role it plays in learning, although limited learning may also take place without it, merely on the basis of lower-level feedback loops. Finally, since it was shown (Moray, 1969b, chap. 7) that output behavior depends to a certain degree on attention, we assume that the process that requires attention, at least intermittently, is the evaluation of progress in which the behavioral intent is involved.

To sum up, the behavioral intent appears to be involved in initiating the programming of output behavior, in regulating the course and flow of output behavior, and in eliciting cues for stopping it after completion. All three functions are interrelated and all three depend on the intervention of meaning—though in different senses. As mentioned above, regulating action and eliciting "stop" signals depend on evaluating feedback information in view of the contents of the behavioral intent. Such an evaluation clearly implies comparison of meaning values, those of the current input with those of the temporarily stored behavioral intent. Since identical meaning values are rare, the comparison often necessitates transformations of meaning values. But also initiating programming depends on meaning. This mediating role of meaning will be explained in the next section.

THE NATURE OF PROGRAMS

Even in the case of behaviors that depend on the prior formation of a behavioral intent, a behavioral intent is a necessary but not a sufficient condition for eliciting actual behavior. The intent is an answer to the question "What am I to do?", but it does not delineate all the details of

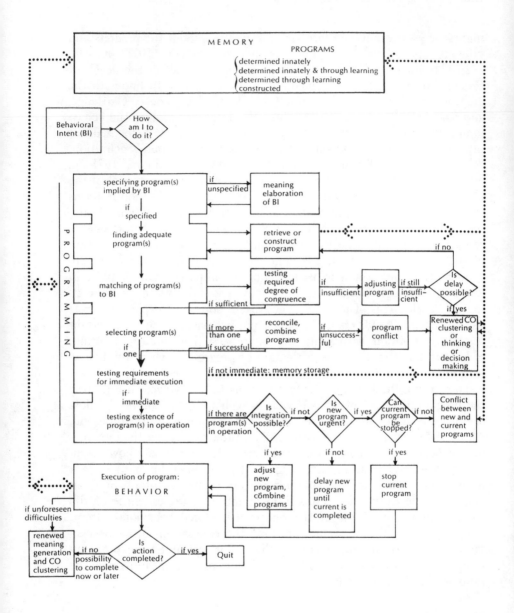

FIGURE 6.1 Major processes involved in programming and the control of output behavior. The dotted lines represent connections with memory.

the exact course of action that must be adopted in practice. In other words, the behavioral intent answers the "what" of behavior but not the details of the "how." The process of programming and the elicitation of output programs fill in the gap between the decision to act for a specific goal and the actual action.

That a certain amount of programming is a necessary prelude to human action was generally assumed long before behaviorism blurred this issue by insisting on a direct connection between stimuli and responses. Considerable empirical evidence has accumulated to support the assumption of programming. First, it was shown that patterns of motor-system firing can occur without triggering overt responses and may be held in readiness for several seconds. This inhibition of response is associated with a sustained negative potential on the cortex surface. The negative shift occurs when a delay in responding is required, disappears when the subject has decided to refrain from responding, and is enhanced when the intended response requires increased effort (Milner, 1970, pp. 97–98). Milner concludes that this phenomenon represents "a mechanism for preventing the response tendency that is active in the brain from reaching the musculature prematurely" (p. 98), that is, before the animal has had time to try out various response possibilities in its mind prior to selecting the most appropriate one. The second observation refers to what Pribram (1970, p. 90) called "intention patterns" and Milner (1971, p. 100) called "thinking about" the next response. Pribram, Spinelli, and Kamback (1967) showed that identifiable waveform patterns may be recorded from the visual cortex of monkeys *prior* to the onset of a response. These patterns are specific to a particular response and occur only after the monkey has learned the correct responses to the presented stimuli. Similarly, Jasper, Ricci, and Doane (1960) found that after aversion conditioning has been established, some of the neurons in the motor cortex fire more rapidly during the application of the conditioned stimulus well in advance of any muscular response. According to Evarts (1966, 1968), this intensified firing occurs also with regard to positively reinforced instrumental responses, and its rate is mostly related to the force to be exerted in action by the muscle associated with the neuron.

These physiological findings indicate that there are probably two types of or stages in programming. One is more general and probably consists in selecting and outlining a specific course of action out of those implied by the behavioral intent, whereas the other is more specific and refers to programming the particular motor steps that constitute the selected action, or at least the very next step to be performed. Taking up this lead we suggest distinguishing between two distinct concepts relevant for the behavioral program: *program scheme* and *operational program*. In order to demonstrate why this distinction is needed and what kind of problem it is designed to solve we have to discuss traditional theories about planning and guidance of output behavior.

THEORIES OF PROGRAMMING
AND GUIDANCE OF ACTION

Resuscitating the concept of programming again raises a problem that had lain dormant during the years of the S-R model domination. Practically the question is simply: What is programmed? What does the organism prepare or activate for the sake of an action? On a more general level the problem is essentially whether a response consists of discrete small units tied to each other so that each link activates the following one, or whether it consists of some structure, one or more rules, a scheme, or some other relatively general organization.

Traditionally, the more cognitive theories have tended to support the second alternative, which is to be expected, both because this alternative assumes that "cognitive" entities or processes such as rules, structures, or expectations underlie behavior and because it is not associationist in nature. There are, however, many additional and more matter-of-fact arguments against the strict S-R model of response. One of the major arguments is that its unit is a response, so that it fails to consider the ubiquitous operation of feedback. Another argument is that the Markov-type chaining that characterizes responses according to the S-R model is too slow and too amenable to error to account for the speed and smoothness of human action. Again, the insistence on specific units as the major elements allows neither for the easy adaptation of particular movements to changing environmental conditions nor for the whole quality of an action, which does not seem to be identical with the sum total of particular movements. Arguments of this kind indicate that the S-R associationist model cannot be the ultimate answer to the problem of action. Nonetheless, these criticisms do not exclude the possibility, perhaps even the necessity, that the S-R model fulfills a certain role within the framework of a more comprehensive theory of action.

Among the nonassociationist anti–S-R conceptions of action the hypothesis of "plans" forwarded by Miller et al. (1960) has assumed a most prominent status. This is due in no small measure to its affinity with computer terms and procedures. According to Miller et al. "a plan is any hierarchical process in the organism that can control the order in which a sequence of operations is to be performed" (p. 16). Every plan is defined as a sequence of Test-Operate-Test-Exit (TOTE) units, but if viewed as a whole, it is itself a TOTE unit frequently containing sub-plans and constituting the subplan of a more encompassing plan. If a "test" indicates "operation," this "operation" takes place, either in the form of direct control of behavior followed by "test," or in the form of delegation to a subplan, which itself consists of the TOTE sequence. The subplans on the lowest level operate only to control behavior, and "exit" from them always implies reentry to a higher level plan.

It has often been noted that Miller et al. failed to clarify the all-important relations between plan and "image," leaving the concept of plan hovering in a theoretical void. Without contesting this very substantial claim, in the present context we have to emphasize another shortcoming of their plan concept, namely, its heavy reliance on principles borrowed from computer simulation. As "a hierarchy of instructions," the plan consists of general instructions gradually branching down to the most specific instructions for the smallest parts in the action sequence, each tiny phase being regulated by the feedback circuit of the TOTE. Such a conception might be appropriate for a computer, which has to perform a limited number of actions, but it will not do for human beings with their enormous versatility and almost unlimited ability to react to unforeseen situations. Even a motor performance as simple as driving a nail into a piece of rough wood is difficult, if not impossible, to perform if guided only by a set of detailed instructions. If the nail hits a knot and hence bends to one side the correcting action depends on a great many factors. The angle of the bend, the size and strength of the nail, the depth into which it has already penetrated, the quality of the wood, the availability of tools, the purpose of the whole action—these are only some of the more important factors that have to be taken into consideration. To translate all these possibilities into exact instructions, even if one has at one's disposal what Miller et al. call plans for adjusting plans, would require a considerable number of precise instructions; yet these would account for only some of the major relatively simple eventualities of driving nails into wood. Since there are probably millions of actions a human being can readily perform, the mere storage of the necessary billions of detailed instructions would create both a space and a retrieval problem. But even if we assume they could all be stored, scanned, and retrieved, they would hardly suffice for guiding a human in the performance of his most trivial activities such as entering a car, lifting a glass, and the like. There are too many small but unforeseeable irregularities to be accounted for by precise instructions and a priori clear criteria guiding the feedback mechanism. Again, not only response units must be assumed to be freely substitutable. Even feedbacks cannot be rigidly planned, for one or another form of feedback is often lacking or difficult to evaluate. Flexibility of plans as postulated by Miller et al. does not solve these problems, for a flexible plan is defined as a plan whose parts can be performed in any order (ibid, p. 67). Hence, even in a flexible plan only the sequence of instructions can be changed, for the sake of ad hoc adjustments, but not the instructions themselves, which control the elementary feedback units.

In sum, the concept of plan leaves us a long way from the solution of the basic problem of action, which Lashley (1951) identified as the puzzle of the serial ordering of movements, and Sherrington (1947) as the singleness and unity of action from one moment to another. Essentially the problem is that whereas we perform movements sequentially, at any moment we seem to have a rather precise representation of what the entire action is and how it is to be achieved. Detailed instructions for action cannot substitute for knowledge about the action without leaving a considerable gap. The conceptual error of Miller et al. was to define plans merely as sequences of instructions, at the same time restricting knowledge under the term "image" only to the choice of the plan.

The concept of schema in its various forms has been the rival of the plan hypothesis from the very beginning. In spite of attempts like those of Lunzer (1968) to reduce the apparent distance between them, the schema conception has been persistently focused on the more general informational aspects that seem to be indispensable for each response. Head (1920), who is credited with establishing the respectability of the schema in modern physiology and psychology, suggested this concept in order to explain how innate and learned action sequences, particularly motor ones, can match the multitude of different constellations encountered in daily life. He defined the schema as a plastic model that serves as a standard for further processes, which, however, change the model itself. For instance, the body image is a schema which is constantly set in such a way as to correspond to the actual posture, and to which both perception and the initiation of movement are automatically referred. Whereas Head made the schema particularly involved in and dependent upon sensory processes, Bartlett (1932) has restored balance by emphasizing the role of the schema in actual response. He conceived of the schema as a flexible frame of reference serving as a guide or model for the present behavior. Schematic behavior occurs at all levels of nervous organization and not merely on the highest. Further, schemas are developed through the organization of previous responses in similar situations. The building-up process is active, however. So too is the reference of incoming information to the schema and the modification of the schema to conform to the specificity of the present situation.

While many of those who used the schema concept have emphasized either its sensory-perceptual aspects (e.g., Stotland & Canon, 1972) or its involvement in the domain of responses (e.g., Allport, 1947), Piaget has tried to accommodate both trends. For Piaget a scheme is "the internal general form of a specific knowing activity . . . the generalizable aspect of coordinating actions that can be applied to analogous situations" (Furth, 1969, p. 264). On the other hand, Piaget reserves the phonetically similar term "schema" for a figurative model, that is, "the symbolic-imaginative support for a knowledge that is directly focused on the figural aspect of an object" (ibid, p. 102). In a valiant attempt to interpret the somewhat different definitions of "scheme" scattered in Piaget's writings, Flavell (1963, pp. 52–55) used phrases such as "a cognitive structure which has reference to a class of similar action sequences," "ensemble of sensorimotor elements mutually dependent or unable to function without each other," "a kind of concept, category, or underlying strategy," or "the motor equivalent of a system of relations and classes." The major underlying idea is that a scheme denotes a cognitive organization of coordinate elements that guides motor behavior and thinking. The guidance is not, however, conceived of as precise instructions but rather as a principle materialized by means of the feedback loop, whose two main stages are accommodation to the changing aspects of a situation and the resulting assimilation into the scheme.

As a matter of fact, any unbiased observer must agree that the various vague formulations of the scheme concept express some essential features of human and animal behavior. These features include flexibility, recurrence of certain patterns but in a dynamically adaptable form, smoothness and rapidity in execution, and independence of the sequence from particular response units. Further, frequent errors of performance in the verbal and motor spheres, such as anticipation errors, "slips" of the tongue or of fingers, inversions in the order of elements, location of the errors (Johnson, 1968; Lashley, 1951), and the like also testify to the presence of features reflecting overall organization and integration in action. This organizational character seems to have all the earmarks of a gestalt, evident not only in the possibility of introducing numerous adaptional modifications in performance without thereby losing the essential identity of the whole, but also in the tendency for closure and the affect attendant upon disruption or interruption of action (Mandler, 1964). It seems not too speculative to assume that these features depend upon or reflect a more or less complex conception, strategy, or system of rules that expresses certain regularities in the relations among events or response units and that implies a kind of understanding of how to act in a certain situation in view of a certain goal by applying specific principles of coordination, seriation, and correspondence of equivalences. This "understanding" is mostly subconscious and rarely, if ever, verbalizable. Its mode of representation is probably sensory, motor, or symbolic in some sense.

It is noteworthy that physiologists have reached a similar conclusion by studying physiological processes underlying movements and action. In view of the evidence (e.g., Taub & Berman, 1968; Weiss, 1952) Milner (1970, p. 92) concludes that "some process of 'mental' organization occurs before the movements of a response begin, and the preparations are by no means confined to the first movement of the contemplated response" but refer to the whole response as well as to its more comprehensive context. This central and essentially cognitive representation guides actual action. Pribram (1971) even goes one step further. He explicitly assumes the dependence of action on some kind of configuration in the motor cortex, a momentary "Image-of-Achievement" that contains all input and outcome information about environmental contingencies (e.g., forces) necessary for the action, and that regulates behavior not by direct control of muscle contractions but by signals to the receptors embedded in the muscles. Pribram takes special pains to emphasize that these "Images" are not patterns of muscle contractions but representations of relevant aspects of the environment (p. 251), "patterns of know-*how*" (p. 250), sensory representations of achievements (p. 301). It may not be superfluous to recall the affinity of these concepts to less modern conceptions about images of consequences (James, 1890) and schemas of order (Lashley, 1951) that shape an action.

However, we do not think that a schema, an image, a representation of order, a "mental" organization, or the like could account for all the essential features of action. There are mainly two reasons for this. Since the schema is a relatively general and abstract structure, whereas action is a highly specific and concrete phenomenon, there is an unfilled gap between the two. Further, since the schema does not include detailed instructions of operation, whereas the muscles require such instructions because they are unable to generate them themselves, there is a need for some intermediate mechanism.

PROGRAM SCHEME AND OPERATIONAL PROGRAM

To our mind, the various considerations and the variegated evidence cited in the previous section indicate the necessity and plausibility of a bileveled or bifaceted conception of programs directing output behavior. One level or facet would refer to an ideationally, verbally, figuratively, or kinaesthetically represented structure, gestalt, schema, image, overall plan, strategy, "competence," or set of rules which reflects some rough blueprint of an action, the major outlines of its sequence until the goal is reached, and the kind of elements indispensable for its execution. Without committing ourselves to any particular form or contents we would assume that this representation has the character of wholeness, is amenable to transformations, and is plastic in the sense of being open to accommodations and assimilations. In contrast, the other level or facet of program would refer to a sequence of detailed instructions to the motor neurons or muscles which sketches each particular step down to the necessary specifications. Hence, we have suggested calling the former aspect of a program the *program scheme* and the latter aspect the *operational program*. Both together constitute what we call *program*.

Existing evidence indicates with sufficient clarity that the two aspects of program differ at least in contents, structure, and development. For example, whereas generalizability and tight organization appear to be the major criteria for evaluating the program scheme, ease of performance and economy in energy expenditure are much more adequate criteria for the operational program. Again, whereas the program scheme could be characterized structurally by function-like rules relating classes, sets (Scandura, 1970), or some other units of representation, the operational program is most probably structured hierarchically.

There are various possible views of the relations between the program scheme and the operational program. Certain studies in the domain of learning (e.g., Grice, 1965; Mandler, 1954, 1962) could be interpreted as indicating the possibility that what we call the program scheme is acquired or constructed at a later stage in the process of learning than the operational program, which it could perhaps even displace. Insofar as this view implies the superiority, autonomy, and indispensability of the program scheme in contrast to the relative inferiority, lack of autonomy, and lesser importance of the operational program, we find that it is too partial and distorting. Another possibility of conceptualizing the relations between the program scheme and the operational program is a hierarchical model similar in some respects to the one suggested by Tinbergen (1950) for instinctive behavior. According to such a model the program scheme would constitute the highest level of integration activated by input, whereas activation of the operational program would depend on the presence of further adequate inputs—mainly external. A model of this type also suggests the possibility that one program scheme may correspond to several related operational programs. Another possibility is based on the views expressed by Milner (1970) and Pribram (1971). Accordingly, activation of the program scheme is a necessary antecedent to eliciting the operational program. The latter, however, constitutes a decoding of the former, a version or translation made to fit the capabilities of muscles. Needless to say, according to both models the program scheme and the operational program are assumed to be mediated by different anatomical structures. Again, the two models assume that the program scheme and the operational program differ in function and structure but that both are indispensable for action.

Another formulation of program scheme and operational program, which is more in line with our views about cognitive processes and which may highlight distinctions and interrelations between these two concepts, may be attained by using the meaning dimensions presented in Chapter 2. Accordingly, the program scheme could be envisaged as consisting of meaning values along one or more of the following meaning dimensions: "action and potentialities for action," "domain of application," "antecedents and causes," "consequences and results," "state and possible changes in it," and "structure." Meaning values along these dimensions provide in some sense answers to such questions as: What can the program be expected to do or accomplish? Which consequences or effects may be expected to result from its operation? With which items (objects, events, etc.) does it interact or which items could be affected by it? Under which conditions is it to be elicited? What is the overall structure or organization of the act? and, Which modifications could be introduced into it? In contrast, the operational program may be conceptualized as consisting of meaning values along one or more of the following meaning dimensions: "manner of occurrence or operation," "what the referent consists of," "range of inclusion," "temporal qualities," and "qualities of location." Meaning values along these dimensions provide in some sense answers to such questions as: What are the various parts or stages of the action? Which specific response units, organs, muscles, and so on are involved in the action? Where are they located? In which temporal order are they activated? and, How precisely is each of them to operate?

Obviously, we do not assume that the meaning values appear in a verbalizable form or that the individual is aware of the involved meaning dimensions. It seems to us, however, that defining the program scheme and the operational program in terms of meaning dimensions reveals in an advantageous manner the similarities, the differences and the possible interaction and interrelations between these two aspects of program.

THE FUNCTIONING OF PROGRAMS

We have discussed in this chapter three concepts basic for understanding performance: the behavioral intent, programming, and programs (see Fig. 6.1). Each of these concepts denotes a specific stage on the way to actual behavior. The first two stages precede performance; the last occurs concomitantly with performance. This description of the sequence implies the widely held view that action is separate from the so-called information processing stages. This view may have been prompted by the externally striking similarity in structure between computers and human beings. Very soon it was given fresh impetus by physiological findings suggesting the division of the cerebrum into two intrinsic sectors (distinct from the extrinsic sector): a frontal one involved mainly in action, and a posterior one involved mainly in perceiving, recognizing, and "making sense of" inputs (Pribram, 1960). Yet the possibility of separation should not make us overlook the need to explain the relation between these parts, which form in fact stages in a unitary sequence. Indeed, we have often stressed the point that the knowledge implied in the CO cluster and the resulting behavioral intent differs from the knowledge implied in the bileveled program. While the behavioral intent reflects mainly the knowledge "what to do," the program reflects mainly the knowledge "how to do it." Nevertheless, the behavioral intent and the program must be intimately related. Otherwise the behavioral intent to drink a cup of coffee would elicit a program adequate to control writing movements. It is to be noted that Miller et al. (1960, p. 18) identify this problem as the central problem of their book, but they have scarcely elaborated on it. Dealing with it, however, is imperative if cognitive processing is ever to be conceptualized as eventuating in behavior. What then is the relation between the behavioral intent and the program?

One possibility would be to explain it in terms of some association or habit formation of the S-R type. We mention this alternative not because it is plausible, but mainly because it is still prominent in psychology. It would lead us to assume that every single behavioral intent has become related to a specific program through contiguity and reinforcement. Since each behavioral intent is unique, the number of behavioral intents is practically unlimited. Nevertheless, individuals mostly seem to be able to locate an appropriate program within a relatively short time. Consequently, barring the possibility of precognition on the part of individuals engaged in acquiring connections between intents and programs, we would have to assume that this problem is handled through generalization. This implies that humans are almost always forced to select a program that fits the behavioral intent only approximately. In other words, we almost never do what we intend to do.

A plausible alternative to this sad conclusion is that we are almost always able to select a program adequate for the behavioral intent, and that this selection is mediated through meaning. This assumption introduces program selection into the domain of cognitive relations, that is, relations which depend upon the elaboration or use of meaning values.

The evidence we have so far in favor of this hypothesis consists in the finding that programs most often constitute an integral part, or at least an implied aspect, of the meaning of statements reflecting behavioral intents (Chapter 11, Study III). For example, if the behavioral intent is "I will go to Jerusalem," the meaning of this statement may be "Tomorrow I will get up early enough to catch the 7 o'clock train to Jerusalem" or "I must phone my friend who travels every day by car to Jerusalem and ask him if I may join him on Wednesday." These examples illustrate some of the major types of meaning values that together reflect the program implied by a behavioral intent. These are meaning values along the meaning dimensions "temporal qualities" (e.g., I will go to Jerusalem tomorrow, on Wednesday, etc.), "manner of occurrence or operation" (e.g., means—I will go to Jerusalem by train, by car, etc.—or major stages of operation—get up early, phone friend, etc.), "location," and "consequences and results." It is noteworthy that the meaning dimension "manner of occurrence or operation" is the prominent one in the meaning constellation of behavioral intents. Indeed, it appears to form the pivot to which the other meaning values of "when," "where," etc. are attached according to need or context. However, theoretically, too, this meaning dimension is precisely fitted to form the bridge from intent to action since by definition it refers to "the stages, processes, acts, instruments, means, organs, etc. involved in the occurrence or operation of the referent, i.e., which make it possible or of which its operation consists" (Chapter 2, p. 26). Implication of the program by the behavioral intent may be viewed as a natural extension of the cognitive orientativeness, that is, actional implications, highlighted in all beliefs involved in providing for an action. As we saw in Chapter 4, in the course of clustering the cognitive orientativeness of beliefs consists in the prominence of meaning values mainly along the following three meaning dimensions: "action and potentialities for action"; "function, purpose, and role"; and "consequences and results." These meaning dimensions seem most likely to provide meaning values relevant for answering the question "What am I to do?" However, after the formation of the behavioral intent that answers this question, there arises a new question: "How am I to do it?" The meaning dimensions most likely to provide meaning values relevant for answering this new question are of course different from those most likely to provide meaning values relevant to the question answered by the behavioral intent. Yet both sets of meaning dimensions emphasize actional aspects.

As noted, the meaning values relevant to the question "How am I to do it?" occur as part of the meaning of the behavioral intent. However, the behavioral intent itself is a product of the clustering of different beliefs forming the CO cluster. Therefore, we assume that also the meaning values of the intent which outline the program reflect meaning values of the beliefs that entered into the clustering process, but that these meaning values are, as mentioned, different from those on which the clustering process focused. Further, we assume that just as the goal beliefs played a central role in the process of clustering that terminated with intent formation, it is the meaning values of the goal beliefs that contribute most to shaping the answer to the question "How am I to do it?" Nonetheless, the meaning values crucial to the question of "How" are, of course, the meaning values of the behavioral intent and not of any specific belief that entered into its making. In fact, when these various meaning values are added to the behavioral intent they constitute an increasing extension and specification of its content. For example, "I will go to Jerusalem" is much less precise and definite than the extended form "I will go to Jerusalem alone, tomorrow morning, by the 7 o'clock train from the new station and will pay for the ticket on the train." The more specifications of this type are added, the more detailed becomes the program of action. As mentioned earlier in this chapter ("The Behavioral Intent: Properties"), behavioral intents vary in specification. Therefore, it may not always be univocally clear where the boundary between behavioral intent and programming should be located. Again, it may be recalled that the behavioral intent itself was also regarded as a specification of the major preceding goal belief(s). Thus, it appears that starting from the initial goal belief, the processes of clustering, intent formation, and programming consist in fact in an increasing specification of the goal belief(s), culminating in the elicitation of the output program. This specification is made possible through a gradual elaboration and interactive matching of the various beliefs' meanings and is prompted by successive contextual embedding in other beliefs and their meanings.

Although behavioral intents are more specific than goals, they still allow for the adoption of slightly differing behavioral programs. Just as goal beliefs usually contain several actional meaning values, only one of which is transformed into the behavioral intent, so the behavioral intent mostly includes several meaning values along the pivotal meaning dimension "manner of occurrence or operation" and other meaning dimensions crucial for the question of "How." Even in the case of a very specific behavioral intent, like "drinking this cup of coffee placed before me on the table," there are almost always many possible ways of performance. One may lift the cup with the right or with the left hand, one may hold the handle, encircle the cup, or place it between three fingers behind and one in front, one may lift the saucer below the cup or bend a little forward, and so on. How then is a program selected when several are possible? And how is the relevant program elicited?

As long as current experiments do not suggest different hypotheses, we assume that the selection and/or elicitation of an output program occurs through matching the various meaning values of the behavioral intent against the meaning values of the programs, that is, the program scheme and/or the operational program. As noted in Chapter 3, matching is the simplest cognitive activity, so simple that it mostly occurs automatically according to predetermined strategies of operation. Moreover, the matching activity is further facilitated by the fact that all the relevant meaning dimensions of the behavioral intent—"manner of occurrence or operation," "temporal and locational qualities," as well as "consequences and results"—are also the meaning dimensions most likely to characterize the program. Owing to this matching process the program eventually adopted is that which shows in terms of meaning values the best fit to the behavioral program. A minimal degree of indispensable congruence is probably required. The closer the fit between the program and the behavioral intent the less necessary it is to subject the program to adjustments or accommodations such as combinations of programs, fragmentation of programs, omission of one or more components, changing the sequence of units, and so on. If none of the available programs passes the previously acquired criteria of a minimal but still acceptable fit it is possible that the input situation, viewed in the light of the behavioral intent and the available programs, is reexamined by way of further meaning generation and CO clustering. It may be recalled that the meaning of the input situation is not necessarily a part of the meaning of the behavioral intent. Hence, its reexamination may provide cues, that is, meaning values, matching those of one of the programs, and thus tilt the balance in favor of one program.

However, some of the difficulties that may arise in selecting programs cannot be resolved through the processes just mentioned. For example, two or more equally adequate but completely different programs could be elicited. This type of conflict—the "program conflict"—differs from the conflict between two behavioral intents discussed earlier. Its resolution may come about either through the retrieval and application of any one of the available programs for coping with such conflict situations or through further meaning elaboration and even additional CO clustering. As noted earlier ("The Behavioral Intent: Properties"), it seems that the greater part of decision-making theory and models is devoted to describing and devising strategies for the resolution of program conflicts.

Another complex situation may arise if no congruence can be attained between the meaning values of the behavioral intent, and sometimes of the input situation as well, and those of the scanned programs. Practically this means that the available programs are not adequate in view of the intent and the input situation, or that no programs at all are available for implementing that specific behavioral intent. Again, in these and similar cases further meaning elaboration and CO clustering may often be necessary. It is not infrequent in such situations that there arises the behavioral intent to think the problem over, to plan an adequate course of action, to analyze the available programs more carefully, and so on. A behavioral intent of this type implies a delay in performance and replacement of an activity designed to implement the original behavioral intent by an activity that is distinct from CO clustering. Figure 6.1 summarizes the major processes involved in programming.

The programs elicited for the purpose of implementing a behavioral intent may differ in several aspects. Those which seem to us most relevant in this context are content area, type of program, and characteristics of the program and program users.

The content area of a program is simply a designation of the kind of expected output behavior. Many research findings suggest that programs in each behavioral domain are specific to that domain and differ from those possible and dominant in another domain. For example, programs adequate for problem solving (Newell & Simon, 1972) may have very little in common with learning programs (Gagné, 1970) or general coding programs like those subsumed under the unfortunate labels of cognitive style or cognitive control (Gardner, Holzman, Klein, Linton, & Spence, 1959).

In addition to content area, programs also differ in type. By type we mean differences between programs in terms of the manner in which they were acquired and in overall structure. Following some suggestions by Miller et al. (1960) and others, we assume four major types of programs:

1. Innately determined programs consisting of one or more schemes and/or operations. Such programs underlie reflex behavior, tropisms, and conditioned responses of the classical type. Hence, their domain of application mostly lies below the level of molar behavior, but sometimes they may guide partial aspects of behavior on the molar level as well. Although neither the units themselves nor their sequence may be changed, the execution of such programs allows for small adjustments to the peculiarities of the given situation.

2. Programs including both innate and acquired schemes and/or operations. Such programs underlie most of instinctive behavior as described by Lorenz (1969), Tinbergen (1951), and other ethologists. It appears that the first stages of instinctive behavior, the "appetitive" ones, show the earmarks of individual learning, whereas the later more stereotyped stages are guided by characteristically innate programs. However, the role of learning and inheritance in instinct is still controversial (Burg-

hardt, 1973). Also, defense mechanisms, as described by psychoanalysts, seem to contain inherited elements, perhaps merely at the level of
the program scheme. Obviously the sequence and even the constituent
elements of defense mechanisms are far less fixed than those of instinctive behavior. Recently it has been claimed that linguistic behavior also
shows the traces of innate programs (McNeill, 1970). If that is so, then
their role is comparatively very small.

3. Learned programs. This type includes the majority of programs
used by human beings in their daily behavior. The learning may be
formal, informal, based on modeling, incidental, and so on. Accordingly, such programs may be more culturally determined or reflect personal experience and idiosyncracies. Examples include anything from
logical rules of thinking and problem-solving strategies to social habits
and behaviors such as rigidity, introversion, impulsiveness, avoiding eye
contact or touching people while talking to them, and so on. Programs
of this type are in principle highly flexible and adaptable, though in any
specific case the degree of their flexibility may depend on factors like
habit strength, functional fixedness, and the like.

4. Constructed programs, which may be viewed as a subtype of
learned programs. Programs are constructed when no adequate program
is available for the implementation of a specific previously formed
behavioral intent. Sometimes programs are constructed when a situation
and the formed behavioral intent are imagined, as in the course of daydreaming. Miller et al. (1960) assume that new programs are formed by
using programs specifically designed for program construction. Yet in
order to escape from the regressus ad infinitum implied in this assumption, they suggest that humans are told how to construct programs, and
that this instruction probably constitutes the most important part of
formal education. Nevertheless, this hypothesis does not explain how
society ever attained programs for program construction. Further, it even
implies that a child would not be able to form a new program if not
told specifically how to go about this task. Yet every parent casually
observing his 2- to 3-year-old child has plenty of opportunity to overhear
verbalizations of new action sequences programmed to greater or lesser
detail, which the child may or may not eventually perform.

Using Piagetian concepts, we assume that program construction does
not necessarily stop when the formal aspects of an action, that is, its
sequence and coordination, are internalized and abstracted. Rather, it
will eventually include the principle of sequence construction, which is
made possible by the increasing understanding of reversibility. Indeed,
the main function of reversibility appears to be precisely to make possible the construction of programs. Hence, by reviewing what he has

done, the child acquires programs for programming long before he is told how to program. Moreover, there is no reason to assume that children or adults can construct further programs only by exploiting learned or acquired programs for programming. On the contrary, we assume that the best part of thinking consists in ad hoc programming or in constructing new ad hoc programs for programming with or without exploiting previously acquired programs for this purpose. This conclusion becomes all the more plausible if one considers that cognitive activity goes on all the time and that it consists largely in elaborating meanings in various senses. Since programs may be viewed as constellations of meaning values along specific meaning dimensions ("The Nature of Programs," above), the constructing of programs could be conceived of as an integral part of the constantly ongoing flow of cognitive activity. However it may be, constructing a program mostly requires better understanding of principles of coordination and structure than does learning a program. It is, therefore, plausible to expect that constructed programs are generally more flexible than programs of the other three types. This seems to be the case even in regard to constructed programs that have been stored in memory before being retrieved for the purpose of performance.

These last remarks bring us to the third significant aspect in which programs may differ—characteristics of programs and of program users. Flexibility is naturally only one of the properties of programs; many others have been cited. Miller et al. (1960) mention such properties as complexity, openness, systematization, efficiency, fixedness, comprehension or span, etc. Klinger (1971, p. 171) emphasizes in addition the following two variables: "the width of motor variation in the population from which a particular schematic component must recruit one instance" and "the degree to which the use of feedback is integrated into the behavioral flow." There is no reason other than utility to limit the number of possible dimensions along which programs may vary. Yet, in view of the large number of such dimensions, it seems to us more profitable to anchor the variation in individual differences. This means that instead of attempting to classify programs we should perhaps try to characterize also the users of programs. Studying the cross-situational constancy of tendencies such as using or constructing flexible versus inflexible programs, or one-track versus multiple-alternative programs, may contribute toward uncovering those dimensions of variation in programs most relevant for understanding, predicting, and manipulating behavior.

Selecting a program and programming do not in any way imply that the program has to be carried out immediately. More often than not programming takes place while the organism is still busy with the performance of some other ongoing programs. This is so not only because the organism is never quiescent, but also because CO clustering and intent formation are presumably much faster processes than the execution and feedback control of output. Moreover, programs are sometimes constructed not for immediate use but for performance at some other more or less precisely determined future situation or occasion. When that time arrives, the organism is probably doing something or other. Since the organism is so constructed that mostly no more than one program can be executed at any one time (Shallice, 1972), it must be assumed that the individual is often faced with the problem of choosing between or reconciling intended programs and those in the process of being executed.

In principle, there are three possible types of solution in such a situation. The first is delaying the performance of the new program until the completion of the current program or activity. The second possibility is to interrupt the program in the course of performance for the sake of a new program. The third possibility consists in some form of integration between programs, for example, changing somewhat the two programs so that they may be coordinated into a single stream of action, combining them by selecting at least some subprograms that may be identical for both, and so on. Studies devoted to this problem show, for example, that stopping one activity for the sake of another depends on personality tendencies such as the achievement motive and fear of failure, on the goals being satisfied by each of the activities, and on situational characteristics like the relative difficulties of the tasks (Feather, 1961). Atkinson and Birch (1970) regard an activity in progress as reflecting the relatively strongest action tendency out of those aroused at any given time. Thus, a change in activity occurs when another action tendency gains dominance. The strength of any action tendency reflects the strength of the instigating and inhibiting forces of the stimulus situation for that activity, and the functional or consummatory significance of the intended behavior.

These examples demonstrate that the problem of reconciling or choosing between the intended and current programs is a basic problem of action. This conclusion, as well as the cited findings, suggest that the fate of a new program with respect to a current program is an integral part of the behavioral intent or the program itself, or both. In other words, whether to interrupt an ongoing program in favor of a new one, whether to wait until the current program is completed, whether to check specific characteristics of the current program before interrupting it, etc.—all these are only partly and indirectly determined by the meaning of the input situation. Their major and direct determinants are the behavioral intent and possibly also particular features of the new program. Following Simon's (1967) suggestion, we find it plausible to assume that certain activities have a peremptory character about them, an urgency that reflects basic biological or other existential emergencies. Yet, in contrast to Simon, we do not think it necessary to introduce a special "interrupt system" for coping theoretically and practically with such eventualities. Essentially, we agree with Atkinson and Birch (1970), who would regard such emergencies as instances of the consummatory value of an activity, which strengthen the tendency to perform that activity. Accordingly, we assume that the behavioral intent, and sometimes also the particular program selected and prepared for its implementation, contain enough cues urging the immediate execution of specific programs regardless of which program happens to be performed.

Nonetheless, conflicts may arise. For example, it may prove to be very difficult to interrupt an ongoing program because it is highly organized, the interruption occurs in an inopportune stage of performance, and so on (Mandler, 1964). At other times, the intended program and the performed program are both endowed with urgency. Such unforeseen circumstances may generate a conflict, which differs from the two other types of conflict mentioned earlier—the conflict between two or more behavioral intents and the conflict between two or more programs for implementing the same behavioral intent. Essentially it is an approach-approach conflict and revolves on technicalities of the "How" of performance. Yet, as in the case of the two other types of conflict, we assume that the resolution may require renewed CO clustering unless programs are available for coping with this problem situation. Observations of animal behavior (Burghardt, 1973) suggest, however, that many of the predetermined programs for dealing with conflicts, such as displacement activities or redirected behavior, may not be specific to one type of conflict alone. The same could be true of acquired programs to cope with the problem on the human level.

For the actual execution of a program, regardless of its content area, we do not assume any special mechanism or system. Since programs consist of sequences of program schemes and operational programs, not only are they basic for thinking or cognitive regulation but they also guide and control actual motor performance directly, if so required by the program. Therefore, a start signal should suffice to set the program in motion, and thus produce what is regarded in the CO model as output, that is, execution of an action or a behavioral sequence. As we have seen, control of performance during execution is taken care of by a successive set of feedbacks on various levels. The major levels are probably

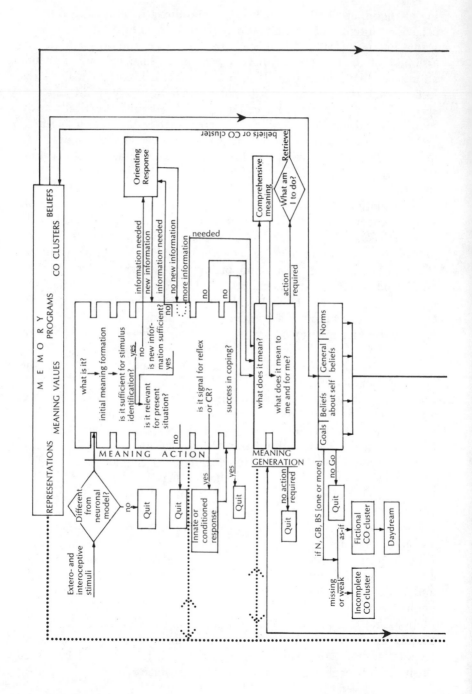

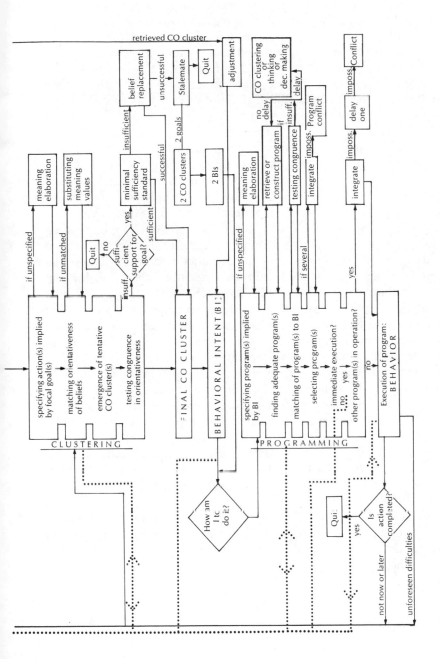

FIGURE 6.2 Overview of the main processes postulated by the CO theory.

the level of the effectors involved in execution per se, the level of the operational program, the level of the program scheme, and the level of the behavioral intent, which provides a kind of context for evaluating the progress made in the action and determining whether it may be viewed as completed. Yet we should not overlook the possibility that unforeseen difficulties may arise that cannot be coped with through these feedback mechanisms. These circumstances define, in fact, a new situation, which requires renewed meaning generation and CO clustering (see Figure 6.1).

These latter remarks imply a principle that is basic to the whole process of behavior generation and execution. In outlining the cognitive elaboration of inputs down—or up—to the production of the behavioral output, we proceeded step by step, mentioning only occasionally the need to resort to prior stages of feedback circles. However, this procedure may give rise to a misleading conception of the CO model unless the following principle is kept in mind. Whenever in clustering, intent formation, programming, or program execution a difficulty arises that cannot be coped with by the mechanisms described above, or, for that matter, by mechanisms that could be viewed as thinking or decision making, the resulting situation constitutes a new input in the sense that it is referred to further meaning generation. Such situations arise not only in view of unforeseen external circumstances but also in the case of inputs from the internal or surrounding environments that interfere with ongoing activities owing to their biological, emotional, or other physio-psycho-social significance. For the sake of model construction, it is opportune to visualize and describe the model in sequential linear terms. In reality, however, we should not expect a simple linearity between input and output, but rather a development that often follows the spiral path of progress and regress along complex feedback loops. Indeed, even the final stage of behavior completion is not simply output. It is also input in multiple senses, for each completed act of behavior may contribute to enriching the elements of the meaning system, the processes of clustering, and the mechanisms of programming, as well as to elaborating programs and perfecting feedback control. Thus, the CO model generates itself through the generation of the behavior whose production it helps to explain, to predict, and to manipulate (see Figure 6.2).

PART TWO

The Experiments

Predicting Everyday Behavior

COMMON BACKGROUND CHARACTERISTICS

Underlying the six independent studies we present here is a common general hypothesis: information about a specific cognitive orientation makes possible predicting the direction of ensuing behavior, provided that the stimuli and forms of behavior available in the situation are known. This hypothesis is in turn derived from our basic hypothesis that cognitive orientation fulfills a directive role with regard to behavior. Accordingly, the goal common to all six studies is to demonstrate that the four CO components predict behavior.

While other studies (notably those reported in Chapters 8 and 10) also deal with predicting behavior, the particular characteristic of the experiments described here is that the behavior predicted is common, ordinary behavior, that is, frequent and familiar. It ranges from acting in an achievement-oriented manner to being late and giving up smoking. In every case the predicted behavior is actually enacted, not merely reported by others from hearsay, or by the subjects through self-observation. We emphasize this point since in certain domains of psychology, especially attitude research and personality study, the term "behavior" more often denotes pencil-and-paper performance than the actual behavior the verbal description is supposed to represent.

Common to all six studies reported in this chapter, as well as to the behavior prediction studies reported later, is the method we used to assess the subject's cognitive orientation. Its two major aspects are construction of cognitive orientation questionnaires and assignment of cognitive orientation (CO) scores to the individuals.

In constructing a cognitive orientation questionnaire we followed a procedure consisting of several steps. First we identified the relevant aspects of the situation and the behavior to be studied that should be represented in the questionnaire. This was done by using the procedure developed for determining meaning (Kreitler & Kreitler, 1968; see also Chapter 2) because relevant aspects of a situation or a behavior are essentially aspects of meaning. Insofar as data collection is concerned, this procedure consists in asking individuals to communicate the meaning of a certain referent to a hypothetical partner in as comprehensive and clear a manner as possible, using any verbal or nonverbal means of expression. In some studies (e.g., in the study on postsuccess and postfailure performance) this procedure was applied after the experimental situation and tasks were demonstrated to the subjects. In other studies (e.g., on achievement behavior and on being late), the subjects were requested to communicate the meaning of the behavior stated in verbal terms, i.e., "achievement," "being late," or "coming on time." The stimuli that served as "referents" always referred to the various behavioral alternatives in the situation. These alternatives were known from the design of the experimental situation. Sometimes pretest subjects were interviewed in order to define these alternatives in a more definite and comprehensive manner.

For exploratory purposes, the general question about the meaning of the situation and behavior(s) was sometimes supplemented by more specific questions, like, "What would you like to know about (the referent)?" "What would you ask a friend about (the referent)?" "If you had to decide about (the referent) which aspects would you consider?" "Which of the following presented aspects do you consider as most important for the characterization of (the referent)?" These specific questions did not yield results deviating from those obtained by means of the more general and basic question. In any case, the responses of the subjects were subjected to a content analysis that revealed the frequency with which various concepts recurred in these communications of meaning. Concepts mentioned by at least 50% of the subjects were selected for the questionnaire. In most studies (e.g., achievement, accuracy, postsuccess and postfailure performance, curiosity—Chapter 8) we used in this first pretest stage 25 to 35 subjects drawn from the same population from which the later samples were drawn. Sometimes, however, we used only 5 to 10 selected subjects in the role of a purposive sample (e.g., cessation of smoking, being late, reactions to pain).

The second step in constructing the questionnaire consisted in formulating the beliefs to be included in it. This was done by making use of several meaning dimensions shown (Kreitler & Kreitler, 1977) to be most relevant for behavior: function, antecedents and causes, consequents and results, manner of occurrence or operation, action and potentialities for action, domain of application, feelings and emotions, judgments, opinions and values. Thus, for each belief we used one or more of the concepts (that is, meaning values) found to be relevant in the first stage, joined to each other or to the referent, or both, in terms of one of these meaning dimensions. For example, if the referent is "achievement," and "ability" is a recurring meaning value, a belief using the meaning dimension "antecedents or causes" would be "Achievement depends mainly on ability"; a belief using the meaning dimension "consequences and results" would be "Achievement promotes the development of abilities." We thus constructed several beliefs focused on the major meaning values determined in the pretests of the first stage, a procedure that ensured an adequate and proper sampling of beliefs. The criteria we used in selecting beliefs for the questionnaire were mainly clarity, plausibility, and the orientative value of a belief with regard to any of the relevant behavioral alternatives.

We then reformulated the selected beliefs in terms of the four CO components: beliefs about norms (N), beliefs about goals (Go), beliefs about self (BS), and general beliefs (GB) (see Chapter 4). Formally, the differences among the four CO components consist in the nature of the meaning value that serves as a subject and the meaning value that serves to interrelate the other two meaning values. For example, in a belief about norms the subject is not the self and the interrelation is of the "ought" or "should" type; in a belief about self the self is the meaning value that serves as subject and the interrelation is declarative or assertive, reflecting some presumed or denied fact. Thus, a norm belief like "People should make efforts in order to succeed in life" was also reformulated as a belief about goals ("I want to make efforts in order to succeed in life"), as a belief about self ("I usually make efforts in order to succeed in life"), and as a general belief ("People make efforts in order to succeed in life"). Positive ("People should make efforts . . .") and negative ("People should not make efforts . . .") forms of the beliefs were counterbalanced. An effort was made to formulate the same contents in terms of all four CO components, although the wording sometimes differed.

The beliefs of each CO component were grouped into a separate part of the questionnaire. Thus, the questionnaire consisted of four parts, each of which had different instructions to the subjects. The instructions preceding beliefs about norms emphasized that the statements following reflected rules about how people should or should not behave and not about how they actually behave. The subject was requested to respond only in terms of the norm character of the statements. Similarly, the instructions preceding goal beliefs emphasized that the statements represented wishes and goals and that the subject was to express only his acceptance or rejection of these goals. The instructions preceding beliefs about self emphasized that the statements were supposed to apply to the subject and requested a response reflecting only the subject's opinion of how true these statements were, how well they actually described him or her. The instructions preceding general beliefs emphasized the factual character of the statements and requested a response reflecting only the subject's opinion of how true the statements actually were.

The four parts of the questionnaire were presented together in random sequence. An exception was made only in the study on curiosity (Chapter 8), in which questions of the four types were grouped together and focused on core themes, such as learning a new game or asking questions of adults.

The form in which the subject was requested to respond varied from study to study. For example, in the studies on achievement, accuracy, and postsuccess and postfailure performance the subject was asked, in the parts referring to norms and beliefs about self, to select a certain number of statements out of each group of statements presented. The groups included an equal number of statements supporting each of two behavioral alternatives. In the general beliefs part he had to select the "more correct" statement in each pair of statements, whereas in the goals part he was requested to respond to each statement by checking the appropriate location on a scale defined by the two poles "applies to me very much" and "does not apply to me at all." The variation in tasks was designed to insure the subject's continued attention and interest. In the study on being late, the subject was instructed, in the parts on norms, general beliefs, and beliefs about self, to check his or her response in terms of one of the following possibilities: agree completely, agree, disagree, disagree completely. In the goals part the response alternatives were: very true about me, true about me, untrue about me, very untrue about me. Here the difference in response modes was dictated more by the contents of the beliefs in the four parts.

The constructed questionnaire was presented to three or four judges, who were asked independently to rate each belief in terms of its clarity and assumed orientative function. Beliefs that were rated as low in these respects as well as beliefs that received inconsistent ratings by the judges were deleted.

The third and final state of constructing the questionnaire consisted in administering it to a sample of 30 to 50 subjects. The questionnaire always included the four parts, presented in random order. These pretest results were used for purposes of item analysis and checking the reliability of each of the four parts of the questionnaire separately. Reliability was mostly of the split-half type. In the studies on quitting smoking and curiosity data on test-retest reliability were also available. Beliefs low in discriminability or reliability were deleted. Thus, the number of statements in the four parts of the questionnaire was not equal. Yet, an attempt was made to keep the number of questions within a range of approximate similarity.

Also common to the various studies predicting behavior is the procedure for assigning cognitive orientation scores to the subjects. First we counted the number of responses the subject gave supporting each behavioral alternative in each of the four parts of the questionnaire. Where only two behavioral alternatives were represented, each subject was assigned four separate scores, reflecting his responses in the four parts of the questionnaire. Otherwise, more scores per each part were necessary (e.g., study of defense mechanisms, Chapter 10). In order to combine the four scores, the median (or the mean, in cases of more homogeneous distributions) of the distribution of scores in each part of the questionnaire was computed. This enabled the conversion of each individual score to a binary scale: if the score lay above the median in the respective distribution, it was assigned a value of 1; if below, it was assigned a value of 0. The four binary scores were added, resulting in a unitary score that ranged from a maximum of 4 to a minimum of 0. The unitary score we call the CO score. Theoretically we view CO scores as reflecting the underlying CO clusters. The CO score enabled us to classify the subjects into groups and compare their actual behavior(s) with each other and with that implied by the cognitive orientation each group held.

The major statistical comparison was always based on the paradigm of analysis of variance. We opted for this procedure, as against a multiple correlation taking the four CO components as predictors, because the distributions of the four CO components were not always appropriate for this kind of analysis.

STUDY 1
CO and Achievement Behavior

PURPOSE AND HYPOTHESES

The major purpose of the study was to test the predictive power of CO clusters in the domain of achievement behaviors. Achievement

The authors wish to express their gratitude to Dr. Z. Kasif, the principal, and to the staff of his school for their help and kindness, which enabled the collection of the data; to Mrs. Miriam Nehari, Mrs. Avivya Raz, and Mr. Amos Spektor for their help in collecting and analyzing the data; to Miss Henrietta Gallagher and Mr. Richard Harrison of the Educational Testing Service, Princeton, N.J., for their assistance in analyzing the data; and to Dr. N. Frederiksen and Dr. M. Lewis of the Educational Testing Service for their helpful suggestions.

behaviors are commonly viewed as determined by motivational but not purely cognitive factors, which are assessed by the measures of n Ach reflecting the achievement motive (Atkinson, 1958; McClelland et al., 1953, chap. 2) and the Test Anxiety Questionnaire (TAQ) reflecting fear of failure (Atkinson & Litwin, 1960; Mandler & Sarason, 1952). Thus a secondary purpose of the study was to compare the predictive power of the four CO components with that of the measures n Ach and the TAQ in respect to achievement behaviors and to examine the interrelations between these two sets of measures.

Accordingly, the major hypothesis of the study was that the combination of beliefs of all four types in the form of CO scores would be related positively to the quantity and quality of performance in tasks designed to assess achievement behavior under neutral, postfailure, and postsuccess conditions.

The second hypothesis was that CO scores would be related more highly to, and to a wider range of, achievement behaviors than the traditional measures of n Ach and TAQ. The rationale for this expectation was our assumption, also underlying the first hypothesis, that achievement behaviors are determined mainly by cognitive factors and thus should be predictable by CO scores reflecting the CO clusters concerning achievement. Since CO scores are purer measures of the relevant cognitive factors than n Ach and TAQ, they should prove to be better predictors.

The third hypothesis was that the measures of n Ach and TAQ would be related, at least partially, to the measures of the four CO components. The rationale for this hypothesis was our assumption that n Ach and TAQ reflect in part cognitive contents, although in a more restricted, implicit, and unsystematic manner than the four CO components. This assumption was based on analyzing the measures themselves as well as the many references to them that highlight their affinity to cognitive factors. Thus, according to McClelland et al. (1953, chap. 4), n Ach is designed to assess the individual's concern for success in competition with standards of excellence, i.e., it reflects norms and values (Rosen, 1956), as well as information that enables evaluation of people and situations (general beliefs?). According to Atkinson (1957) the achievement motive denotes the disposition to strive for the satisfaction expected to ensue from accomplishment; whereby "expectancy" reflects information about the self in the past and about the present situation (i.e., beliefs about self and general beliefs). Similarly, insofar as the TAQ is conceived as a measure of the tendency to avoid failure (Atkinson & Litwin, 1960) or "to do well" (Mandler, 1966), it reflects learned judgments and cognitive expectations and thus assumes reference to norms and general information; yet insofar as it is regarded as a self-report measure of anxiety in achievement situations (I. G. Sarason, 1960), or of defensiveness with regard to anxiety (S. B. Sarason, 1966), or as a correlate of self-imposed achievement demands (Argyle & Robinson, 1962), it may be assumed to include elements of beliefs about self. These examples strongly suggest that the n Ach and TAQ tap cognitive elements to some extent. However, contradictory results of former attempts to investigate relations between n Ach and verbal measures of self-report or attitudes (negative results, e.g., Atkinson & Litwin, 1960; Holmes & Tyler, 1968; positive results, e.g., Mehrabian, 1968; Sherwood, 1966), as well as the diversity of opinions about the processes tapped by n Ach and TAQ, preclude the statement of a hypothesis about precise interrelations between these two variables and the CO components.

METHOD

Subjects. The subjects were 50 high school students, 26 boys and 24 girls, 15–16 years old, chosen randomly from the population of second-year students in high schools in Tel Aviv, Israel.

Procedure and Materials. Each subject was seen by an experimenter for two individual sessions, each of about an hour's duration, separated by an interval of 3–10 days. In one session he was administered three performance tasks, in the other the CO questionnaire of achievement. The order of the sessions was randomized, so that about half the subjects answered the questionnaire in the first session, and about half in the second session. The n Ach and TAQ measures were administered at about the same time in a separate group session under neutral classroom conditions.

The performance tasks were administered under three experimental conditions, previously shown to affect the relation of n Ach and TAQ to performance (e.g., Feather, 1966; McClelland et al., 1953): the first task was administered under neutral conditions, the second under postsuccess conditions, and the third under postfailure conditions. The instructions for all three tasks were equally achievement-oriented, in line with findings that show the relation of n Ach and TAQ to performance to be highest when performance is assessed under achievement-aroused conditions (Heckhausen, 1967; Klinger, 1966). All three tasks, commonly used in achievement studies, were routine tasks, requiring well-trained abilities, that would enable the manifestation of individual differences in effort and achievement striving rather than in training or speed of learning. All the arithmetic tasks were simple enough to exclude contamination of the results by individual or sex differences in mathematical ability and knowledge. The first task, which was called by the fictional name

"Test of Combinatorial Thinking," was Düker's (1949) two-step arith-metic task. After explanation of the task the subject was told: "You are requested to work with precision, avoiding mistakes, and as quickly as possible. Please proceed according to the given order of exercises. When you finish one sheet, please take another one from the pile. I shall tell you when to begin and when to stop." The duration of the task was 15 minutes.

The second task was a set of subtraction exercises, each of which con-sisted of two 10-digit rows. The subject was instructed to calculate the results as quickly and as correctly as possible. After the first 8 minutes, the experimenter gave the impression of checking the subject's results against his own set of results and norms and remarked: "Now, this is extraordinary! You have done remarkably well. But go on, go on quickly, I don't want to delay you." After this remark, the subject went on work-ing for another 8 minutes. It is only the data of this second set of 8 min-utes, following the induction of "success," that form the data of the second performance task in this study.

The third task was a set of addition exercises, each of which consisted of three 6-digit rows. The subject was instructed to calculate the results as quickly and as correctly as possible. After the first 8 minutes, the experimenter gave the impression of checking the subject's results against his own set of results and norms and remarked: "Well, you have not done too well. But go on, go on quickly, I don't want to disturb you." After this remark, the subject went on working for another 8 min-utes. As in the former task, it is only the data of this second set of 8 minutes, following the induction of "failure," that form the data of the third performance task in this study.

The performance variables based on these three tasks were: (a) the number of exercises solved by the subject in each task; (b) the number of exercises solved correctly by the subject in each task; (c) an index representing variables a and b, constructed so that each exercise solved correctly got a 2-point weight and each exercise solved incorrectly got a 1-point weight.

Although these three variables are positively intercorrelated within and across tasks or conditions (mean of within-task correlation being .90-.92), the correlations across tasks reveal independent variation high enough to warrant a separate treatment (the correlation between the variables of tasks one and two is .62; one and three, .45; two and three, .63). Variable a is the most stable across tasks (mean $r = .70$); variable c, the least stable (mean $r = .40$); and variable b, intermediate (mean $r = .59$).

The questionnaire of cognitive orientation of achievement was constructed in line with the procedure described in "Common Background Characteristics" (*ibid.*). The norms (N) part consisted of 16 statements presented in two groups of 8 statements, 4 reflecting achievement-oriented norms, and 4 antiachievement-oriented norms. The subject was shown the statements of each group together, each statement typed on a separate card, and was requested to choose out of each group the 4 statements that reflected his opinion. Each achievement-oriented norm scored as 1 point, so that the maximum proachievement score was 8 points. The general beliefs (GB) part consisted of 15 pairs of statements in a questionnaire form, 1 achievement-orienting and 1 antiachievement-orienting. The subject was to select 1 statement in each pair. The maximum proachievement score was 15 points. The beliefs about self (BS) part consisted of one group of 6 statements and another of 8 statements, half of the statements in each group being achievement-orienting and half antiachievement-orienting. The subject was requested to check 3 statements in the first group and 4 in the second group, the maximum proachievement score being 7 points. The goals (Go) part included 12 statements, 6 proachievement and 6 antiachievement. The subject was requested to express his degree of acceptance of each statement by placing a check sign on a scale defined by the poles "applies to me very much" and "does not apply to me at all." The scoring was dichotomous and represented the number of endorsed proachievement goals minus the number of endorsed antiachievement goals. Scores ranged from a maximum of 6 to a minimum of −6.

Some examples of beliefs included in the questionnaires are: "Whatever a person does he should do as well as he can, regardless of whether he likes it or not" (N); "Effort and striving help to develop the special abilities and potentialities of a person" (GB); "I tend to demand more from myself than others expect from me" (BS); "I would like to lead a life whose essence is effort, striving, and achievement" (Go).

Split-half reliability coefficients are .82 for the N part, .81 for the GB part, .77 for the BS part, and .71 for the Go part. The average interitem correlation ranged from .22 to .60 for the four parts. The average correlation between individual items and the total score of the respective questionnaire part ranged from .45 to .59 for the different parts, with a minimum of .29 for any item. Table 13.5 reports the correlations among the four components as well as the CO score. The medians of the distributions used in constructing CO scores were 6.5 in the N part, 9.5 in the GB part, 4.6 in the BS part, and 1.8 in the Go part.

The French Test of Insight was used as a measure of *n* Ach since it

was shown to be related to behavior in more cases than the TAT measure (Klinger, 1966, p. 297). Scoring was done in accordance with the
standard procedure applied in regard to the TAT measure (Kreitler,
Nehari, & Kreitler, 1971). The TAQ was used as a measure of fear of
failure.

RESULTS AND CONCLUSIONS

All the data were analyzed together since preliminary checks showed
no significant differences between boys and girls or between subjects
who answered the CO questionnaire before the performance tasks and
those who answered it after.

Table 7.1 shows that the three groups of subjects formed on the basis
of CO scores differ in their mean performance as measured by the index
variable in the expected direction under all three experimental conditions. That is, the higher the CO score of the subjects, the higher the
level of their performance. Under postsuccess conditions, the three
groups differ also in their mean performance as measured by the variables of number of items solved and number of items solved correctly.
Under neutral and postfailure conditions the differences among the
three groups in these two variables are significant only beyond the .10
level. But even when the overall differences only exceed the .10 level, the
differences between the extreme groups, i.e., CO scores 4 versus 1 and 0,
are significant beyond the .05 level. Moreover, in all cases without exception the differences in performance are in the expected direction so that
rank correlations between CO scores and means of performance are
equal to 1 across all measures and experimental conditions.

In view of the demonstrated differences between males and females in
achievement motivation (Alper, 1974; Heckhausen, 1967), the data were
also analyzed in terms of a 2×3 factorial design, wherein the first
factor represented the two sexes and the second factor, three levels of
CO scores. In all cases, the effects of the sex factor and of the interaction were nonsignificant, whereas the effect of the CO factor was of the
same order of significance as that reported in Table 7.1.

The data were also subjected to three types of control analysis
designed to examine the role of the four CO components in the demonstrated relation of CO scores to performance level. The first control
analysis was devoted to checking whether all four CO components were
indeed necessary for predicting performance. It consisted in comparing
performance levels of groups formed on the basis of less than the four
CO components. This analysis involved four comparisons between
groups formed on the basis of median splits in each of the four CO

TABLE 7.1

Achievement Performance on Tasks under Three Experimental Conditions, by Subjects Classified According to CO Scores

CO SCORES	n	NO. OF ITEMS SOLVED		NO. OF ITEMS SOLVED CORRECTLY		INDEX OF ITEMS SOLVED & SOLVED CORRECTLY	
		$\overline{X}$	SD	$\overline{X}$	SD	$\overline{X}$	SD
		1. Neutral Task					
a. 4	3	77.00	7.87	56.67	10.49	133.66	27.58
b. 3 & 2	24	57.83	18.40	45.00	19.47	102.83	37.08
c. 1 & 0	23	55.47	15.67	42.04	16.19	95.78	30.46
Significance of differences		$F = 2.02, p < .10$ $t_{a,b} = 1.72*$ $t_{a,c} = 2.25*$		$F = .88, p < .10$ $t_{a,c} = 1.46, p < .10$		$F = 10.85***$ $t_{a,b} = 1.34, p < .10$ $t_{a,c} = 1.97*$	
		2. Postsuccess Task					
a. 4	3	25.33	2.51	21.00	2.16	46.33	3.05
b. 3 & 2	23	18.69	4.46	13.89	4.83	32.84	8.77
c. 1 & 0	23	16.80	5.13	12.89	4.43	29.69	9.08
Significance of differences		$F = 4.53*$ $t_{a,b} = 2.49**$ $t_{a,c} = 2.80**$ $t_{b,c} = 1.33, p < .10$		$F = 4.00*$ $t_{a,b} = 2.42*$ $t_{a,c} = 3.01**$		$F = 4.91*$ $t_{a,b} = 2.60**$ $t_{a,c} = 3.10**$	
		3. Postfailure Task					
a. 4	3	23.83	2.46	17.83	1.31	41.66	4.04
b. 3 & 2	24	16.47	5.28	11.25	4.26	27.72	9.12
c. 1 & 0	23	16.08	6.26	11.27	5.49	27.45	10.95
Significance of differences		$F = 2.51, p < .10$ $t_{a,b} = 2.35*$ $t_{a,c} = 2.09*$		$F = 2.51, p. < .10$ $t_{a,b} = 2.57**$ $t_{a,c} = 1.98*$		$F = 3.01*$ $t_{a,b} = 2.58**$ $t_{a,c} = 2.19*$	

ᵃ The reported significance levels of t-values are one-tailed.
* $p < .05$.
** $p < .01$.
*** $p < .001$.

components separately, six comparisons among groups formed on the basis of the CO components taken two at a time, and four comparisons among groups formed on the basis of the CO components taken three at a time. These comparisons were done across the three experimental situations. Table 7.2 exemplifies the analyses for two criteria of perform-

TABLE 7.2
Comparisons of Performance under Neutral Conditions
(Number of Items and Index) of Subjects Classified
According to All Possible Combinations of CO Components

CO COMPONENTS		POSITION OF CO COMPONENTS RELATIVE TO MEDIAN									SIGNIFICANCE OF DIFFERENCES
		Above	Below	2 Above	2 Below	1 Above, 1 Below	3 Above	2 Above, 2 Below	1 Above, 2 Below	3 Below	
N											
Number:	n	23	27								
	$\overline{X}$	62.43	54.03								$t = 1.64$
	SD	18.14	17.21								
Index:	$\overline{X}$	109.21	94.81								$t = 1.47$
	SD	11.32	10.01								
GB											
Number:	n	20	30								
	$\overline{X}$	54.65	60.06								$t = -1.06$
	SD	17.45	17.07								
Index:	$\overline{X}$	96.10	105.00								$t = -.88$
	SD	31.21	35.83								
BS											
Number:	n	23	27								
	$\overline{X}$	58.26	57.59								$t = .13$
	SD	16.69	18.00								
Index:	$\overline{X}$	101.91	101.03								$t = .08$
	SD	33.73	34.87								
Go											
Number:	n	20	30								
	$\overline{X}$	58.60	57.43								$t = .22$
	SD	18.61	16.55								
Index:	$\overline{X}$	104.20	99.60								$t = .45$
	SD	35.69	33.27								

					F
N, GB					
Number:	n	9	16	25	
	$\bar{X}$	63.55	58.62	55.40	$F = .72$
	SD	13.15	16.20	18.93	
Index:	$\bar{X}$	110.55	102.06	99.60	$F = 4.90^*$
	SD	24.70	31.32	37.12	
N, BS					
Number:	n	13	17	20	
	$\bar{X}$	62.23	54.58	57.89	$F = .69$
	SD	17.44	19.22	15.38	
Index:	$\bar{X}$	108.15	95.41	102.20	$F = .53$
	SD	37.51	35.65	29.89	
N, Go					
Number:	n	12	19	19	
	$\bar{X}$	64.33	55.73	55.86	$F = 1.06$
	SD	16.53	16.88	17.21	
Index:	$\bar{X}$	112.75	96.26	99.46	$F = .87$
	SD	34.07	32.35	34.51	
GB, BS					
Number:	n	11	18	21	
	$\bar{X}$	58.81	61.61	53.50	$F = 1.67$
	SD	16.33	16.89	17.54	
Index:	$\bar{X}$	101.18	106.61	95.73	$F = 1.74$
	SD	29.44	34.79	35.87	
GB, Go					
Number:	n	8	18	24	
	$\bar{X}$	57.12	60.38	56.28	$F = .28$
	SD	21.58	17.56	15.40	
Index:	$\bar{X}$	101.25	104.22	99.40	$F = .25$
	SD	37.74	36.91	30.87	
BS, Go					
Number:	n	11	18	21	
	$\bar{X}$	61.09	58.61	55.62	$F = .07$
	SD	17.22	16.95	17.64	
Index:	$\bar{X}$	106.27	100.72	99.51	$F = .80$
	SD	34.71	33.86	34.36	

TABLE 7.2 (cont'd.)

CO COMPONENTS		POSITION OF CO COMPONENTS RELATIVE TO MEDIAN									SIGNIFICANCE OF DIFFERENCES
		Above	Below	2 Above	2 Below	1 Above, 1 Below	3 Above	2 Above, 2 Below	1 Above, 2 Below	3 Below	
N, GB, BS											
Number:	n						5	17	16	12	
	$\bar{X}$						69.00	56.41	55.12	59.08	$F = .85$
	SD						11.54	16.31	18.63	17.40	
Index:	$\bar{X}$						115.80	101.17	96.50	102.41	$F = .38$
	SD						25.77	34.99	34.46	33.63	
GB, BS, Go											
Number:	n						5	13	20	12	
	$\bar{X}$						67.20	51.84	56.60	60.83	$F = 1.48$
	SD						18.68	11.43	19.44	16.50	
Index:	$\bar{X}$						117.60	92.46	102.80	102.08	$F = 2.08$
	SD						32.83	26.64	38.26	35.14	
N, GB, Go											
Number:	n						5	13	21	11	
	$\bar{X}$						66.40	57.53	54.85	60.27	$F = .65$
	SD						14.37	19.93	15.52	17.34	
Index:	$\bar{X}$						117.60	99.69	98.28	102.18	$F = .42$
	SD						23.75	41.85	32.22	18.39	
N, BS, Go											
Number:	n						7	15	15	14	
	$\bar{X}$						63.71	61.00	49.73	56.28	$F = 1.73$
	SD						15.84	18.72	18.04	19.25	
Index:	$\bar{X}$						108.71	109.66	91.13	96.85	$F = 1.28$
	SD						34.53	38.43	26.88	36.38	

ance in the case of the task administered under neutral conditions. Out of the 126 comparisons, the only comparisons that yielded significant results were the combination of N and GB with respect to the index variable under neutral conditions (see Table 7.2: $F = 4.90$, $df = 1, 46$, $p < .05$), and the combination N, GB, and Go with respect to the number of items solved under postfailure conditions ($F = 4.12$, $df = 2$, 46, $p < .05$). These significant findings, which constitute 1.56% of the total number of comparisons, can be safely interpreted as due to chance.

The second control analysis was designed to examine whether the predictive utility of CO scores is due to the fact that they are based on a quadripartition of the beliefs or merely to the fact that they reflect a large number of beliefs. The analysis consisted in comparing the performance levels of groups formed on the basis of a median split in the sum of all beliefs pooled together, regardless of the distinctions among the four CO components (median = 21.5). None of these comparisons yielded significant results (the t statistic ranged from .08 to 1.73).

The third control analysis consisted in classifying the beliefs *randomly* into four groups, so that a fictional score, analogous formally to the CO score, could be assigned to each subject, and comparing the performance levels of subjects who differed in these fictional scores. This analysis was performed in order to control for the possibility that any quadripartition and not just the theoretically defined four CO components would yield significant differences. However, none of the nine comparisons resulted in significant differences (the F ratios for $df = 1, 46$ ranged from .25 to 2.38).

In sum, the findings support the first hypothesis, first, by demonstrating an overall positive relation between CO scores and the performance variables, particularly the index, across the three tasks and experimental conditions; and, second, by showing that all four CO components are crucial for the demonstrated relation. Table 13.11 shows that N and BS are the variables with the relatively greatest weight in the relation across all tasks.

Table 7.3 shows that the variables n Ach and TAQ are related to performance only in the postsuccess task, the interaction Sex $\times$ TAQ being, moreover, in a direction counter to that expected. Considering the fact that also in other domains related to achievement n Ach and TAQ did not predict as well as CO scores (with regard to grade point average see note, p. 215, and with regard to commitments to action see note, p. 336) it may be concluded that at least in samples like the one used in this study (i.e., adolescents of both sexes), the predictive power of CO scores is greater than that of n Ach and TAQ (Kreitler, Nehari, & Kreitler, 1971). These findings fully confirm the second hypothesis.

Testing the third hypothesis consisted in analyzing the correlations between the two sets of predictors. The analysis revealed that n Ach is related positively to GB ($r = .28$, $p = .05$), while the TAQ is related positively to BS ($r = .33$, $p < .05$). It is interesting to note that these findings correspond to the external forms of the two measures. The n Ach measure is based on statements the subject makes about others, and the

TABLE 7.3
Analysis of Variance of Performance on Three Tasks
under Three Experimental Conditions by Subjects
Classified as High or Low in n Ach and TAQ

SOURCE	df	NUMBER SOLVED MS	F	NUMBER RIGHT MS	F	INDEX MS	F
		1. Neutral Task					
Sex (S)	1	484.31	1.54	130.86	<1	1118.68	<1
n Ach (N)	1	255.69	<1	168.83	<1	8.98	<1
TAQ (T)	1	.20	<1	56.39	<1	49.82	<1
S × N	1	538.20	1.72	1048.18	3.01[1]	3088.56	2.59
S × T	1	425.02	1.36	1298.29	3.72[1]	3208.98	2.69[1]
N × T	1	348.67	1.11	.95	<1	386.06	<1
S × N × T	1	333.11	1.06	447.26	1.28	1552.36	1.30
Error	38	313.43		348.64		1193.40	
		2. Postsuccess Task					
Sex (S)	1	.20	<1	15.73	<1	39.93	<1
n Ach (N)	1	3.15	<1	.10	<1	11.75	<1
TAQ (T)	1	3.98	<1	4.88	<1	4.83	<1
S × N	1	130.98	5.01*	21.69	<1	197.53	2.12
S × T	1	134.13	5.13*	217.04	8.01**	580.56	6.24*
N × T	1	.11	<1	.67	<1	2.23	<1
S × N × T	1	18.79	<1	48.20	1.78	84.47	<1
Error	37	26.15		27.08		93.04	
		3. Postfailure Task					
Sex (S)	1	29.92	<1	4.33	<1	57.03	<1
n Ach (N)	1	74.06	1.87	59.46	2.16	266.24	2.26
TAQ (T)	1	1.34	<1	1.02	<1	4.70	<1
S × N	1	14.66	<1	7.69	<1	1.11	<1
S × T	1	52.86	1.34	46.52	1.69	198.57	1.68
N × T	1	2.14	<1	21.54	<1	37.27	<1
S × N × T	1	1.26	<1	1.26	<1	.00	<1
Error	38	39.54		27.48		117.85	

[1] $p < .10$. * $p < .05$. ** $p < .01$.

TAQ measure is based on self-report statements. The occurrence of the two correlations provides some support for the third hypothesis. The low incidence of elements from other CO components in the n Ach and TAQ measures is surprising, but it might explain why together they predict behaviors better than each separately but not as well as CO scores, at least in samples of adolescent boys and girls.

STUDY II
Accuracy

PURPOSE AND HYPOTHESES

The purpose of the study was to test the predictive power of CO clusters with regard to accuracy. We chose accuracy not only because of the ubiquity of its manifestations but also because, being a habit, it seemed to us to reflect a general program of behavior rather than a motivational tendency or a specific form of behavior. Hence, the importance of demonstrating its correlation with CO scores. An allied though secondary purpose was to examine whether accuracy is independent of achievement and, if so, to demonstrate that prediction of behavior requires specificity of the beliefs included in the four CO components.

Accordingly, the major hypothesis of the study was that pertinent CO scores would be related positively to accuracy in behavior manifested in diverse tasks.

METHOD

Subjects. The subjects were 50 high school students, 25 boys and 25 girls, chosen randomly from the population of first- and second-year students in high schools in the suburbs of Tel Aviv.

Procedure and Materials. Each subject was seen by an experimenter for two individual sessions, separated by an interval of 5–8 days. In one session he or she was administered five performance tasks, and in the other he or she was asked to answer questionnaires: the CO questionnaire of accuracy, the CO questionnaire of achievement, and two other sham questionnaires about preferences in sports and in movies. The order of the sessions was randomized so that half of the subjects answered the questionnaires in the first session, and half in the second.

The five performance tasks were all routine tasks requiring well-trained abilities and apt to become boring after a short time. They were chosen in order to enable the manifestation of individual differences in the general program of accuracy, if there exists one, rather than general or temporary motivations and interests.

The tasks were varied in order to make possible the study of accuracy in different domains. The instructions to all five tasks emphasized the need to work as accurately as possible, avoiding all mistakes.

The five tasks, administered in random order to each subject, were:

1. Computing pairs of simple additions and subtractions (Düker, 1949), which required writing the sum of the two results if the first was larger than the second and their difference if the first was smaller than the second. The results never exceeded the limit of 10. Duration—20 minutes.

2. Underlining in pages with rows of numbers every cipher 3 that was either preceded by the ciphers 5 or 8 or followed by 6 or 8. Duration—8 minutes.

3. Copying Latin-type letters combined into nonsense words. (It is to be remembered that the subjects do not use Latin letters in their native language.) Duration—10 minutes.

4. Computing results of subtraction exercises, each of which consisted of two 10-digit rows. Duration—8 minutes.

5. Computing results of addition exercises, each of which consisted of six three-digit rows. Duration—8 minutes.

The variable defined on the basis of the raw data was the proportion of correct items out of the total number of items done by the subject in a particular task. Thus, the speed of performance was neutralized. Since the correlations between these accuracy variables across the five tasks were very high (mean of the 10 correlations = .94), the five variables were averaged into one variable, which was interpreted as an index of a generalized accuracy program.

The CO questionnaire of accuracy, constructed in line with the procedure described above ("Common Background Characteristics"), included four beliefs in the N part, of which the subject was to select two; two pairs of beliefs in the GB part, of which the subject was to select one from each pair; four beliefs in the BS part, of which the subject was to select two; and two beliefs in the Go part, with regard to each of which the subject had to check his degree of acceptance on a continuous scale reduced in scoring to a dichotomy. Examples of beliefs in the questionnaire are: "In most domains the main thing is correct and precise performance even if the quantity is thereby reduced" (GB), "I would like to be able to function without being concerned about how clean and precise my work is" (Go). The average interitem correlation ranged from .25 to .60 within each questionnaire part. The correlation between the individual items and the total score in the corresponding part of the questionnaire always exceeded the .05 level of significance.

Table 13.5 reports the correlations among the four components and the CO scores. The medians of the distributions used in constructing CO scores were 2.8 for N, 2.4 for GB, .80 for BS, and 1.5 for Go.

The CO questionnaire of achievement administered to the subjects was described above, in Study I.

RESULTS AND CONCLUSIONS

Table 7.4 shows that the relation between CO scores of accuracy and the index variable of accuracy in performance is positive and in the expected direction, that is, the higher the CO score, the higher the degree of accuracy evidenced in behavior. This finding fully supports the hypothesis of the study. Furthermore, no differences were found between subjects who answered the CO questionnaire before the behavioral tasks and those who did so afterwards.

In addition Table 7.4 shows that the variable of accuracy in performance is not at all related to CO scores of achievement. This finding demonstrates the independence of accuracy from achievement as defined by our CO questionnaire. It may be remembered that in Study I as well the CO scores of achievement were not as strongly related to the number of items solved correctly—presumably a variable with an affinity to accuracy—as to the index variable reflecting both quantity and quality of performance. It seems warranted to conclude that when the quantitative aspect of performance is largely partialed out, as in the case of the variable of accuracy, the CO of achievement does not play any appreciable role in directing this behavior. Thus, the study demonstrates that behavior is predicted best by beliefs that are specifically relevant for the particular behavior, even if their number is as excessively small as two beliefs per component.

TABLE 7.4
The Relation of Accuracy in Performance (Index Reflecting Accuracy in Five Tasks) to CO Scores of Accuracy and to CO Scores of Achievement

CO Score of Accuracy	n	$\overline{X}$	SD	F	CO Score of Achievement	n	$\overline{X}$	SD	F
4	7	.82	.07		4 & 3	13	.78	.24	
3	16	.78	.07		2	14	.79	.69	
2	21	.75	.09		1	13	.79	.24	
1	6	.73	.09		0	10	.73	.28	
				3.19*					.00

* $p < .05$.

Control analyses showed that the accuracy index was related neither to the overall sum of beliefs orienting toward accuracy of all four components nor to any combination of CO components based on less than the four components. Table 13.11 shows that none of the components singly correlated significantly with accuracy.

STUDY III
Behavioral Reactions to Success and Failure

PURPOSE AND HYPOTHESES

The major purpose of the study was to examine the relation of the four CO components to behavior following success and failure. This attempt was spurred by two considerations. The first was the observation that individual variation in responses to success and failure is so great that it often casts doubt on the common generalization of increase in performance following success and decrease following failure. The second consideration was that cognitive elements figured as the common denominator in many of the attempts to account for postsuccess and postfailure behavior (e.g., Feather, 1966; Weiner et al., 1971). Yet these attempts were highly restricted in scope and timid in formulating the explicit role of cognition.

A secondary purpose of the study was to examine the relations between postsuccess and postfailure behaviors as well as between the CO scores for these behaviors. Analysis of research findings in this domain (e.g., Atkinson, 1964; Birney et al., 1969; Weiner, 1972) has led us to assume that behaviors in these two situations are independent of each other. This assumption has implications with regard to predicting behavior after success and after failure (see our first two hypotheses) as well as with regard to the specificity of the relations between the relevant CO scores and behaviors after success and failure (see our third hypothesis).

The first of the three hypotheses was that CO scores for postsuccess behavior would be related positively to changes in performance after success. More specifically, it was expected that subjects with high CO scores for postsuccess behavior, reflecting orientation toward expending more effort after success, would raise their level of performance after success, whereas those with low CO scores for postsuccess behavior, reflecting lack of interest in success, would lower their perfomance after success, or maintain it at the same level as prior to success. The second hypothesis was that CO scores for postfailure behavior would be related positively to changes in performance after failure. That is, subjects with high CO scores for postfailure behavior, reflecting orientation toward expending more effort after failure, were expected to raise or at least maintain their level of performance after failure, whereas those with low CO scores for postfailure behavior, reflecting discouragement and loss of motivation after failure, were expected to lower their performance after failure. The third hypothesis was that the changes in level of performance after success would be unrelated to the changes in level of performance after failure, that the CO for postsuccess behavior would be unrelated to the CO for postfailure behavior, that the CO for postsuccess behavior would *not* be related to changes in performance after failure, and that the CO for postfailure behavior would *not* be related to changes in performance after success.

METHOD

Subjects. The subjects were 50 randomly chosen high school students from Tel Aviv, Israel, 25 boys and 25 girls, ranging in age from 16 to 18 years.

Procedure and Materials. Each subject was seen by an experimenter for two individual sessions, separated by an interval of 6–13 days. In one session the subject was administered the performance tasks and in the other CO questionnaires for postsuccess and postfailure behavior. The order of the sessions was randomized, so that about half of the subjects completed the questionnaires in the first session, and the other half answered them in the second session.

In the performance session the subject was first administered three routine copying tasks, each of 5 minutes' duration, which were irrelevant to the present study. The performance tasks pertaining to the present study were administered immediately afterwards with no intervening break. The two tasks were of the type requiring well-trained abilities, so as to enable the manifestation of individual differences in CO rather than in training or speed of learning. The task designed to assess the effect of failure on performance level consisted of a series of addition exercises, each with three 6-digit rows. The subject was instructed to calculate the given exercises as quickly and as correctly as possible. After the first 8 minutes, the experimenter gave the impression of checking the subject's results against a set of norms, and remarked: "Well, you have not done too well. The norms for your age group are higher. But go on, go on quickly, I don't want to disturb you." After these remarks, the subject continued working on the remaining exercises for another 8 minutes. The task used to assess the effects of success on the level of performance consisted of a series of subtraction exercises, each with two 10-digit rows. The subject was instructed to calculate the given exercises as quickly and as correctly as possible. After the first 8 minutes the experimenter gave the impression of checking the subject's results against a set of norms and remarked: "Now, this is extraordinary! You have done remarkably well. But go on, go on quickly, I don't want to delay you." After these remarks, the subject continued working on the remaining exercises for another 8 minutes. The order of presenting the two tasks was randomized.

The measures provided by these tasks are:

1. The change in performance after failure measured by the difference in scores between the second 8-minute unit and the first 8-minute unit, as reflected in the total number of solved exercises, in the number of exercises solved correctly, and in an index constructed so that each exercise solved correctly got a 2-point weight, and each exercise solved incorrectly got a 1-point weight.

2. The change in performance after success measured by the difference in scores between the second 8-minute unit and the first 8-minute unit, as reflected in the total number of solved exercises, in the number of exercises solved correctly, and in an index constructed so that each exercise solved correctly got a 2-point weight, and each exercise solved incorrectly got a 1-point weight.

Two different cognitive orientation questionnaires were used: one was designed to enable assessment of beliefs orienting toward postsuccess behaviors, and the other, those orienting toward postfailure behaviors. Accordingly, each subject got two separate CO scores: one for postsuccess and one for postfailure behavior.

The two different questionnaires were constructed in line with the procedure described in "Common Background Characteristics" at the beginning of this chapter. The four parts of each questionnaire consisted of groups of statements, i.e., two, four, or six, half of which reflected beliefs orienting toward greater effort and half of which reflected beliefs orienting toward lesser effort after success or failure. In the N, GB, and BS parts the subject's task was to select a specified number of statements, e.g., one out of two, that reflected his opinion. In the Go part he was requested to check his degree of acceptance of each goal statement, and this was later converted into a dichotomous score, representing the number of "positive" goals minus the number of "negative" goals endorsed by the subject. The maximum scores in the postsuccess questionnaire were 5, 7, 8, and 6, in the postfailure questionnaire, 8, 12, 6, and 8, for the N, GB, BS, and Go parts, respectively. The following are examples of statements used in the questionnaires: "If I go on doing too long something in which I have previously succeeded, I usually have problems and eventually fail" (BS, postsuccess); "Difficulties and failures are a good basis for learning in life" (GB, postfailure). The split-half reliability coefficients ranged from .72 to .85 and from .74 to .89 for the four parts of the postsuccess and postfailure questionnaires respectively. The range of the test-retest reliability coefficients over an interval of three weeks was .70 to .91 and .78 to .85 for the four parts of the postsuccess and postfailure questionnaires respectively. The average interitem correlation ranged from .28 to .59 for both questionnaires. The range of correlations between items and total score of the respective part of the questionnaire was .25 to .60. Table 13.5 presents the intercorrelations between the different parts of each questionnaire as well as the respective CO scores.

RESULTS AND CONCLUSIONS

Table 7.5 indicates that since the performance levels in the two tasks do not differ in the first 8-minute unit, the tasks may be viewed as essentially comparable. On the other hand, the existence of differences in the expected direction, that is, increase in group performance after success and decrease after failure, in the second 8-minute unit demonstrates the effectiveness of the administered treatments.

The findings relevant to the first and second hypotheses are summarized in Tables 7.6 and 7.7. Table 7.6 shows that CO scores for postsuccess behavior are related in the expected direction to changes in performance after success as reflected in the index variable (first hypothesis) and that CO scores for postfailure behavior are related in the expected direction to changes in performance after failure as reflected in the index variable (second hypothesis). Table 7.7 shows that the

TABLE 7.5
Level of Performance before and after Success
and before and after Failure

TASK	PERFORMANCE BEFORE AND AFTER SUCCESS		PERFORMANCE BEFORE AND AFTER FAILURE		
	$\bar{X}$	SD	$\bar{X}$	SD	t^a
Part 1					
No. of solved items	17.06	5.44	17.95	5.66	1.51
No. of correct items	12.10	5.24	12.39	5.29	.37
Index	29.16	9.80	30.34	10.18	1.01
Part 2					
No. of solved items	18.09	5.07	16.74	5.80	2.53*
No. of correct items	13.86	4.90	11.66	5.02	2.94**
Index	31.95	9.48	28.40	10.15	3.00**

[a] The t values reflect the differences between the correlated means.
* $p < .02$, two-tailed.
** $p < .01$, two-tailed.

TABLE 7.6

Relation of CO Scores to Changes in Performance
after Success and after Failure

CO SCORES		CHANGE IN NO. OF SOLVED ITEMS		CHANGE IN NO. OF CORRECT ITEMS		CHANGE IN INDEX OF NO. OF SOLVED AND CORRECT ITEMS	
	n	$\overline{X}$	SD	$\overline{X}$	SD	$\overline{X}$	SD
Postsuccess							
a. 4 and 3	8	2.00	2.15	6.31	3.64	8.31	5.09
b. 2	14	1.50	2.15	1.46	5.46	2.96	6.20
c. 1 and 0	27	.50	2.52	.98	3.49	1.48	5.45
Significance of differences		$F = 1.62$ $t_{a,c} = 1.73^1$		$F = 2.74^1$ $t_{a,c} = 5.33^{**}$ $t_{a,b} = 4.85^{**}$		$F = 3.62^*$ $t_{a,c} = 3.28^{**}$ $t_{a,b} = 2.18^*$	
Postfailure							
a. 4 and 3	19	−1.08	1.88	.24	4.58	− .84	3.50
b. 2 and 1	18	− .33	2.09	− .65	2.43	− .98	4.10
c. 0	13	−2.62	3.85	−2.26	2.65	−4.88	6.10
Significance of differences		$F = 2.99^1$ $t_{b,c} = 1.96^1$		$F = 2.37^1$ $t_{a,c} = 1.95^1$ $t_{b,c} = 1.73^1$		$F = 3.62^*$ $t_{a,c} = 3.06^{**}$ $t_{b,c} = 2.00^1$	

Note. Data are available for 49 subjects only. One subject had to stop in the middle of the experiment for health reasons.
$^1 p < .10.$ $^* p < .05.$ $^{**} p < .01.$

differences between the CO groups remain significant even after a statistical adjustment has been made through covariance analysis for the possible effects of the pretreatment level of performance. In the case of the other two subcriteria of performance, the changes are all in the expected direction, and when examined for pairs of groups are also often highly significant, as in the case of the number of correct items after success. But since not all pairs of groups differ significantly, in three of the four cases the overall F coefficient reaches only the .10 level of significance. Since analyses performed with regard to the third hypothesis (see next paragraph) show the index criterion to be sufficiently sensitive to the treatments of success and failure, the findings provide full support for the two hypotheses concerning the relation between CO scores and changes in performance following success and failure. It may be noted that in Study I as well, it was the index variable that showed the closest relation to CO scores of achievement.

An analysis of the findings separately for those subjects who answered the CO questionnaires before the behavioral tasks and those who did so

TABLE 7.7
Analyses of Variance and Covariance
for Changes in Postsuccess and Postfailure Index Measures

TASK	SOURCE OF VARIATION	ANALYSIS OF VARIANCE			ANALYSIS OF COVARIANCE		
		df	MS	F	df	MS	F
Postsuccess	Treatments (CO)	2	111.25	3.62*	2	90.89	3.43*
	Error	46	30.74		45	26.53	
Postfailure	Treatments (CO)	2	79.86	3.62*	2	93.96	3.25*
	Error	47	22.06		46	28.91	

* $p < .05$.

afterwards showed no differences between these two groups in CO scores, behavioral change scores, and the relation between the two.

Two types of analysis were performed in order to check whether all four CO components are necessary for predicting behavior. The first analysis consisted in comparing changes in performance according to the index of groups formed on the basis of all possible combinations of less than the four CO components taken one at a time, two at a time, and three at a time. Out of the 56 comparisons, that is, 14 for postsuccess performance changes and 14 for postfailure performance changes, only one yielded a significant finding, which can be attributed to chance (the variable GB for postsuccess performance change, $t = 1.88$, $p < .05$, one-tailed, in the expected direction). The other type of analysis consisted in comparing changes in performance levels, according to the index, of groups formed on the basis of a median split in the sum of all responses to beliefs pooled together, regardless of the distinctions among the four CO components. None of these four comparisons yielded significant results. This indicates that the predictive utility of CO scores is due to the fact that they represent four distinct CO components and not merely a large number of beliefs.

The findings in regard to the third hypothesis refer to three aspects. The first aspect concerns correlations between changes in performance after success and after failure. The correlations are: for total number of solved items .32 ($p < .05$), for number of items solved correctly $-.02$ (nonsignificant), and for the index .20 (nonsignificant). These findings show that apart from the 10% of shared variance in the variable of total number of solved items, the changes in postsuccess and postfailure performance reflect factors specific to these two situations and not general factors, such as the tendency to increase or decrease performance after an interval, or achievement motivation, and so on. Incidentally, these findings also show that the total number of solved items is a relatively less appropriate variable for checking the first two hypotheses than are the index and the number of items solved correctly. This conclusion strengthens the findings concerning the first two hypotheses. The second aspect of the findings relevant to the third hypothesis concerns correlations between the CO scores for postsuccess and postfailure behavior and their components. The correlation between the two CO scores was nonsignificant ($r = -.04$). Moreover, none of the correlations between the respective four CO components of the two CO questionnaires was significant. Finally, the third relevant aspect of the findings concerns the use of CO scores for postsuccess behavior for predicting changes in performance after failure, and the use of CO scores for postfailure behavior for predicting changes in performance after success. In contrast to our expectation, the CO score for postsuccess behavior was found to be related to performance changes after failure according to the index (for CO scores 4 & 3, 2, 1 & 0: $\bar{X} = 1.56$, $SD = 3.27$; $\bar{X} = -.43$, $SD = 5.11$; $\bar{X} = -3.27$, $SD = 4.40$, respectively; $F = 4.48$, $df = 2/47$, $p<.05$). This finding, which partly disconfirms our third hypothesis, indicates that similar changes in performance after failure could derive from two different CO clusters. The level of performance may rise after failure either because the subject sees an incentive in success and tries to turn the failure into success (high CO for postsuccess behavior) or because the subject regards failure as a signal for trying harder so as to avoid failure. Similarly, the level of performance may decrease after failure either because the subject does not see success as an incentive and hence is not interested in attaining it (low CO for postsuccess behavior) or because the subject is not challenged by failure but is rather discouraged by it (low CO for postfailure behavior).* Since the CO for postsuccess behavior and the CO for postfailure behavior are uncorrelated, it is in principle possible to determine the motives for changes in performance on the level of individual subjects. It may be hypothesized that subjects who increase performance after "failure" in order to attain success would also increase their performance after "success," while those who increase performance after "failure" in order to avoid failure would not necessarily increase their performance after "success." Similarly, subjects who decrease per-

---

* The expectation that under certain circumstances subjects high in CO for postsuccess behavior and low in CO for postfailure behavior may behave similarly to subjects low in CO for postsuccess behavior and high in CO for postfailure behavior is borne out by the findings concerning commitments to risky alternatives (see Chapter 11, Study IV).

formance after "failure" because they are discouraged by failure might still increase their performance after "success."

At least two of the outlined patterns have already been identified in research. For example, Weiner (1969) reports that subjects high in fear of failure, as determined by a combined score of low *n* Ach and high TAQ, perform worst following failure and perform best following success. These would seem to be subjects with a low CO score for postfailure behavior and a higher score on the CO for postsuccess behavior. In contrast, subjects high in "fear of failure," according to Birney et al.'s (1969) measure of Hostile Press, are interested mainly in avoiding failure but not in success per se; that is, they choose to avoid achievement situations, but when forced into an achievement situation with clearly defined standards of failure and success, they try to avoid failure by the only device possible under such circumstances—working harder and succeeding (Birney et al., 1969, chap. 4). These subjects would probably have a high CO score for postfailure behavior and a low CO score for post-success behavior.

STUDY IV
CO and the Prediction of Being Late or Coming on Time

PURPOSE AND HYPOTHESES

This study focused on the prediction of being late or coming on time. Whereas Studies I, II, and III dealt with behaviors elicited under laboratory conditions, it was the major purpose of this study to examine the adequacy of CO scores in predicting behaviors observed in real-life situations over long periods of time.

A secondary purpose of the study was to examine the possibility of improving the predictive power of CO scores by adding to the usual set of CO scores reflecting support for a certain behavior a complementary set of CO scores reflecting the subject's opposition to the alternative behavior possible under the given circumstances. More concretely, a person who has a CO score predisposing coming on time does not necessarily have a CO score that sets him against being late. Borrowing the terminology used by Sherif and Sherif (1967) without the theoretical underpinning and implications, we may suggest that there could be a difference between the latitudes of noncommitment and rejection.

Accordingly, our first hypothesis was that CO scores dealing primarily

This study was carried out by Mr. David Azikri and Mr. Nehemya Geva under the supervision of Shulamith Kreitler, at the Department of Psychology, Tel Aviv University, in 1971–72.

with coming on time would predict the behaviors of coming on time or being late. More specifically, the expectation was that subjects with high CO scores for coming on time would come on time more often than subjects with low CO scores for coming on time. Our second hypothesis was that CO scores dealing primarily with opposition to being late would predict the behaviors of coming on time or being late. More specifically, the expectation was that subjects with high CO scores reflecting opposition to being late would come on time more often than subjects with low CO scores reflecting opposition to being late. Our third hypothesis was that a combination of the two sets of CO scores—those reflecting support for the studied behavior (coming on time) and those reflecting opposition to the alternative behavior available in the situation (being late)—would be more highly related to behavior than either of the constituent CO scores separately.

METHOD

Subjects. The subjects were 70 randomly chosen boys and girls ranging in age from 16 to 18 years, who were high school students from eight different classrooms in Israel.

Procedure and Materials. The CO questionnaires for coming on time and being late were administered to the subjects in group sessions under normal classroom conditions. The questionnaires were constructed in line with the procedure described in "Common Background Characteristics." Each part of the questionnaire included in random order items of the two kinds of COs: those referring to coming on time (i.e., in favor of coming on time) and those referring to being late (i.e., opposed to being late). The mode of response in all four parts of the CO questionnaire was in terms of a 4-point Likert scale. Thus, in the N and GB parts the scale points were "agree completely," "agree," "reject," and "reject completely," while in the BS and Go part the scale points were "very true of me," "true of me," "untrue of me," "very untrue of me." There were 47 statements in the N part, 55 in the GB part, 45 in the BS part, and 41 in the Go part.

The following are some examples of statements included in the questionnaire: "It is desirable to liberate oneself from dependence on the watch" (N), "Some students come late to school in order to draw attention to themselves" (GB), "When on my way to a meeting, I sometimes ignore acquaintances I see on the street in order not to be late" (BS), "I want to be always on time so as to give other people the feeling that I respect them" (Go).

Three kinds of CO scores were computed on the basis of the subject's responses: CO scores in favor of coming on time, CO scores opposed to being late, and CO scores based on a combination of these two CO scores.

The minimum correlation between any item and the total score on the corresponding part of the questionnaire was .28. Table 13.5 presents the intercorrelations among the different parts of the questionnaire, as well as between them and the corresponding CO scores, for the three types of CO scores.

The dependent variable was the total number of times the student was late to school in the 3 months preceding administration of the CO questionnaires. This number was extracted from the regular school files. The recordings were absolutely reliable and were made by people— teachers and secretaries separately—who could not know anything of the study when they made the recordings.

RESULTS AND CONCLUSIONS

In presenting the results we shall deal first with the interrelations between the two kinds of CO scores in order to establish to what extent they are actually different.

Table 7.8 shows that three components of the CO in favor of coming on time and of the CO opposed to being late are interrelated significantly, the exception being the component of general beliefs. Thus, the mean intercorrelation between the components of the two COs is .35, whereas it is .80 and .84 between the components of the combined CO (CO_3) and the CO in favor of coming on time (CO_1) and the CO opposed to being late (CO_2), respectively. Thus it appears that the two COs are interrelated but are neither identical nor mirror images of each other.

TABLE 7.8
Intercorrelations of Components in Three Sets of CO Scores:
In Favor of Coming on Time (CO_1), Opposed to Being Late (CO_2),
and Combined CO (CO_3)

CO Scores	N & N	GB & GB	BS & BS	Go & Go	CO & CO[a]
CO_1 and CO_2	.43**	.02	.61**	.30*	.36**
CO_1 and CO_3	.82**	.73**	.92**	.64**	.58**
CO_2 and CO_3	.80**	.68**	.87**	.92**	.59**

[a] These intercorrelations refer to CO scores with the range 0–4. The restricted range might have a dampening effect. The corresponding values for the variables that reflect the sum of beliefs endorsed in all four components in the appropriate direction are .53, .86, and .87.

* $p < .05$.
** $p < .01$.

This conclusion is also supported by the results of a normalized vari-max factor analysis (Table 7.9). If we consider only saturations of at least .55, analysis of the findings presented in Table 7.9 shows that the two COs are loaded on different factors. While the components of CO_1 are loaded on Factor I (i.e., GB and BS) and on Factor III (i.e., N and Go), the components of CO_2 are all loaded on Factor II. Thus, the two COs emerge as different to a certain extent. This difference indicates that having a high score on the CO in favor of coming on time does not automatically imply that the individual also has a high score on the CO opposed to being late. Indeed, 74% of those who had a high CO score in favor of being on time (CO 2 and higher) also had a high CO score opposed to being late, but also 39% of those who had a low CO score in favor of coming on time had a high CO score opposed to being late. In sum, it appears plausible to conclude that CO_1 and CO_2 partly sample the same themes but in reverse, which accounts for their interrelation, and partly sample different aspects of meaning of the studied behavior.

Table 7.10 presents the major findings of this study. It shows that all three hypotheses were fully confirmed. There is a relation between the

TABLE 7.9
Factor Analysis of Components of Three Sets of CO Scores:
In Favor of Coming on Time (CO_1), Opposed to Being Late (CO_2),
and Combined CO (CO_3)

VARIABLES	SATURATION OF VARIABLES ON:		
	Factor I	*Factor II*	*Factor III*
N_1	.36	.14	*.74*
N_2	−.04	*.68*	*.60*
N_3	.21	.42	*.80*
GB_1	*.81*	.08	.14
GB_2	.06	*.85*	.06
GB_3	*.64*	*.63*	.06
BS_1	*.80*	.20	.33
BS_2	.54	*.56*	.20
BS_3	*.76*	.40	.30
Go_1	.47	−.13	*.68*
Go_2	.27	*.66*	.42
Go_3	.41	.47	*.61*
CO_1	*.84*	.12	.52
CO_2	.30	*.87*	.36
CO_3	*.64*	*.58*	.49

Note. All saturations above .55 are italicized and underscored for the sake of emphasis.

TABLE 7.10
Relation of Three Sets of CO Scores
to the Behavior of Being Late

CO Scores	n	$\overline{X}$	SD	Significance of Differences
In favor of being on time				
a. 4	13	1.85	1.57	$F = 2.75^*$
b. 2 & 3	32	3.19	3.16	$t_{a,b} = 2.13^*$
c. 0 & 1	25	4.24	3.36	$t_{a,c} = 2.99^{**}$
Opposed to being late				
a. 3 & 4	27	2.56	2.50	$F = 5.37^{**}$
b. 2	18	2.33	2.06	$t_{a,c} = 2.81^{**}$
c. 0 & 1	25	4.84	3.67	$t_{b,c} = 2.59^*$
Combined				
a. 6, 7, & 8	21	2.42	2.40	$F = 6.76^{**}$
b. 3, 4, & 5	29	2.58	2.21	$t_{a,c} = 2.82^*$
c. 0, 1, & 2	20	5.34	3.90	$t_{b,c} = 2.71^*$

$^* p < .05.$
$^{**} p < .01.$

CO in favor of coming on time and the number of times the individual was late to school (first hypothesis), between the CO opposed to being late and the number of times the individual was late to school (second hypothesis), and between a combined CO and the number of times the individual was late to school (third hypothesis).

Moreover, as expected, the relation between behavior and the combined CO appears stronger than the relation in the case of either CO_1 or CO_2 separately. This finding lends further support to the conclusion stated above concerning the interrelation of the two COs. Since the two COs are only partly reverse images of each other, their combination is a better predictor of behavior than either CO alone. The practical implication seems to be that increased precision in predicting behavior may be attained by considering also the behavior or behaviors alternative to the one specifically studied. This may be done either by setting up separate complementary sets of CO scores relating to the alternative behaviors, or—what seems to us more advisable—by increasing in the CO score itself the range of sampled meaning aspects of the studied behavior. The latter would allow for including in the CO score not only rejection of the alternatives but possibly also other aspects that might strengthen the predictive power of the CO score.

STUDY V
CO and Pain Tolerance

PURPOSE AND HYPOTHESES

The major purpose of the study was to examine the predictive power of CO scores with regard to the tolerance of pain. Pain tolerance has been of particular interest to us because of the nature of the phenomenon of pain and the variety of theories developed to account for differential pain tolerance. Pain is a most elusive phenomenon, lying at the borders of the domains of sensations, emotions, and drives. The extent of its manifestations is matched by the variety of definitions offered for its characterization (Buytendijk, 1961; Sternbach, 1968). The same is true of pain tolerance with the reservation that it is defined sufficiently well to justify its treatment as a behavioral variable.

In the course of the last 15 years enough data have been amassed to indicate not only that pain tolerance varies from individual to individual and in the same person on different occasions, but also that it is affected by a great number of factors. Major among these are motivational instructions (Barber, 1965; Gelfand, 1967), direction of attention (Blitz & Dinnerstein, 1971), availability of information concerning future pain (Jones, Bentler, & Petry, 1966), cognitive dissonance with regard to the pain (Zimbardo, Cohen, Weisenberg, Dworkin, & Firestone, 1969), attribution of the pain to certain causal agents (Nisbett & Schachter, 1966), cognitive style of augmenting versus reducing (Petrie, 1967), and culturally determined values and attitudes (Sternbach & Tursky, 1965; Zborowski, 1969). Cognitive contents appear to be the element common to these and many other factors found to increase or decrease the level of pain tolerance. Consequently, it seemed reasonable to expect that if CO scores predicted pain tolerance, CO theory might prove an adequate framework for integrating the findings about the various factors affecting pain tolerance.

Thus, the hypothesis of the study was that CO scores would be related to pain tolerance. Since it was shown (Bandler, Mandaros, & Bem, 1971; Blitz & Dinnerstein, 1968; Gelfand, 1964; Nisbett & Schach-

This study was carried out with Mrs. Talma Lobel. Parts of it were presented by Mrs. Lobel as a Master's thesis in partial fulfillment of the requirements of an M.A. degree at the Department of Psychology, Tel Aviv University, 1974. Special thanks are due to Mr. Jaakov Rinetzky for constructing the instrument for administering electric shocks.

ter, 1966; Wolff, Krasnegor, & Farr, 1965) that various experimental manipulations affect pain tolerance differently from the way they affect the sensitivity threshold, the pain threshold, and pain evaluation, we concluded that pain tolerance differed from these latter variables. Hence, our hypothesis refers specifically and exclusively to pain tolerance, and implies that CO scores are not related to the sensitivity threshold, the pain threshold, and the evaluation of pain.

Finally, it should be mentioned that this study formed the first stage of an experiment whose second stage was devoted to experimental manipulations of the threshold of pain tolerance guided by processes of the CO theory (see Chapter 9, Study II). Hence the importance of first proving that CO scores are related to pain tolerance.

METHOD

Subjects. The subjects were 112 students, 56 males and 56 females, from the departments of psychology and social sciences at Tel Aviv University. The subjects ranged in age from 18 to 27 years. They volunteered for this study in partial fulfillment of their duties during the first two years of study.

Procedure and Materials. Each subject participated in two sessions. One was a group session in which the CO questionnaire of pain tolerance was administered to the subjects. The other was an individual session devoted first to the measurement of the various thresholds and pain evaluation, and later to experimental manipulations (to be described in their proper context in Chapter 9, Study II). The time interval between the two sessions was 4–6 weeks.

In the experimental session the subject was invited to enter the experimental room, where the experimenter showed him or her the instrument for administering electric shocks. This instrument, which was built at the Psychology Laboratory Workshop at Tel Aviv University, resembled in its main features the Shocker No. 5226 manufactured by the LaFayette Company. It consisted of two parts: one part transmitted the electric current and included a direction switch and a dial, invisible to the subject, showing the voltage level of the current being applied; the other part included a small platform with a protruding electrode. By placing a hand on the platform and touching the electrode with the index finger, the subject received an electric shock. There was thus no need, as with the LaFayette shocker, to attach electrodes to the subject's fingers.

The experimenter explained to the subject that the device was designed to deliver weak electric shocks, that it was pretested and found to be absolutely safe, and that consequently there was no reason for fear. Then the procedure for delivery of the shocks was demonstrated. It was explained that starting with subthreshold intensity a series of shocks progressively stronger in intensity would be administered. The subject was requested to report (1) when he or she first felt anything (sensitivity threshold), (2) when the shock first became painful, even if only minimally so (pain threshold), and (3) when the shock was too painful to endure and he or she did not want to receive it any more (tolerance threshold). The subject was told that the shocks would be terminated immediately when he or she said "stop," thus indicating the third phase. The subject was requested to leave his or her hand on the platform at all times, without budging. After answering the various clarification questions posed by the subject, the experimenter wiped the subject's hand with alcohol, presumably for purposes of cleanliness, and asked him or her to place a hand on the small platform of the shocker so that the experiment might begin.

The series of shocks was started with zero μA. The intensity of each administered shock was $5\mu A$ higher than that of the previous one. The shocks were administered only in ascending order; thus the first shock was of zero intensity, the second was $5\mu A$, the third, $10\mu A$, and so on. Each shock was of 2 seconds' duration. The interval between shocks was also 2 seconds.

At the end of the series of shocks each subject was asked to indicate on a scale running from zero ("was not painful at all") to 100 ("was extremely painful") the intensity of the experienced pain at the instant of having said "stop" in order to terminate the shocks. The subject's response, in the form of a check mark placed on the scale, was taken as a measure of the evaluation of pain.

All the subjects were right-handed and all received the shocks on their left hands. In order to control for possible differences in behavior of males and females due to the sex of the experimenter, only male experimenters tested male subjects, and female experimenters female subjects.

The questionnaire dealing with pain tolerance was constructed in line with the procedure described in "Common Background Characteristics" at the beginning of this chapter. Each of the four questionnaire parts included 10 questions, half of which were formulated as supporting pain tolerance and half as not supporting pain tolerance. The questions were in the form of statements, and the subject was requested to check one of three available responses: "True," "Not true," and "?"—the latter designed to reflect inability to decide, conflict between the two response modes, or the conviction that various restrictions apply to both of the two other response modes. Here are some examples of statements included in the four questionnaire parts: "A person should welcome the opportunity of coping with difficulties that arise, in order to develop his ability for self-control" (N), "One of the most admirable human qualities is to suffer in silence" (GB), "If something hurts me, I find it very difficult to concentrate on something different from the pain" (BS), "I would not want to decrease my special sensitivity to pain and to my own and others' suffering" (Go).

The interitem correlations ranged from .27 to .71 for the four parts of the questionnaire. The lowest correlation between any item and the total score on the corresponding part of the questionnaire was .28. The split-half reliability coefficients ranged from .78 to .90 for the four parts. Table 13.5 reports the correlations between the four parts of the questionnaire and between them and the computed CO scores.

In order to increase the clarity of the results in the second and main part of the experiment (Chapter 9, Study II), subjects with a CO 2 were not included in the study.

RESULTS AND CONCLUSIONS

Table 7.11 shows that our hypothesis was fully confirmed. CO scores are related in the expected direction to the threshold of pain tolerance, as well as to the related measure that reflects the difference between the

TABLE 7.11
Two-Factor (CO and Sex) Analyses of Variance of Thresholds
of Sensitivity, Pain, and Tolerance, and of Pain Evaluation

Variable	Source of Variation	SS	df	MS	F
Sensitivity	CO (A)	294.00	1	294.00	2.92
threshold	Sex (B)	1001.04	1	1001.04	9.93**
	A × B	308.17	1	308.17	3.06
	Within cell	9275.76	92	100.82	
Pain	CO (A)	35.04	1	35.04	< 1
threshold	Sex (B)	3577.04	1	3577.04	25.39***
	A × B	112.67	1	112.67	< 1
	Within cell	12959.75	92	140.86	
Tolerance	CO (A)	726.00	1	726.00	4.10*
threshold	Sex (B)	4187.04	1	4187.04	23.62***
	A × B	170.67	1	170.67	< 1
	Within cell	16305.25	92	177.23	
Tolerance	CO (A)	416.67	1	416.67	4.70*
threshold	Sex (B)	35.04	1	35.04	< 1
minus pain	A × B	1.04	1	1.04	< 1
threshold	Within cell	8149.75	92	88.58	
Pain	CO (A)	6.51	1	6.51	< 1
evaluation	Sex (B)	1708.59	1	1708.59	3.19
	A × B	.26	1	.26	< 1
	Within cell	49228.12	92	535.09	

* $p < .05$.   ** $p < .01$.   *** $p < .001$.

tolerance threshold and the pain threshold. Table 13.11 suggests that the CO components of BS and GB probably play relatively the greatest role in the demonstrated relation. Equally important are the findings, also predicted by our hypothesis, that CO scores are not related to the threshold of sensitivity, to the pain threshold, or to the evaluation of pain.

Table 7.12 shows that the derived measure of tolerance threshold minus pain threshold is in a certain sense a purer measure than the tolerance threshold itself, since it is correlated only with the tolerance threshold, while the tolerance threshold is correlated with both the sensitivity and pain thresholds. Table 7.12 also demonstrates the remarkable lack of correlation between pain evaluation and any of the thresholds studied in regard to pain.

Finally, it is worth mentioning that males and females differ greatly in the sensitivity, pain, and tolerance thresholds (Table 7.11), females being significantly lower than males on these thresholds (Table 7.13). However, in no case do the effects of CO and of sex interact. Thus, CO scores were equally predictive of the tolerance threshold of males and females, despite a sizable difference between the sexes.

Again, it may be noted that the derived measure of tolerance threshold minus pain threshold is not subject to sex differences, probably because it does not reflect absolute values but relative differences. Yet the absence of sex differences with regard to pain evaluation is probably due

TABLE 7.12

Intercorrelations between Thresholds of Sensitivity, Pain, and Tolerance and of Pain Evaluation

	Sensitivity threshold	Pain threshold	Tolerance threshold	Tolerance threshold minus pain threshold	Pain evaluation
Sensitivity threshold	—	.54*	.46*	−.03	−.08
Pain threshold		—	.79*	−.14	−.14
Tolerance threshold			—	.49*	−.08
Tolerance minus pain threshold				—	.06
Pain evaluation					—

* $p < .01$.

TABLE 7.13
Means of Thresholds of Sensitivity, Pain, and Tolerance
and of Pain Evaluation for Male and Female Subjects,
High and Low in CO Level

VARIABLE	CO HIGH		CO LOW		CO HIGH Male & Female	CO LOW Male & Female	CO HIGH & LOW Male	CO HIGH & LOW Female
	Male	*Female*	*Male*	*Female*	*Female*	*Female*	*Male*	*Female*
Sensitivity threshold	24.17	14.12	17.08	14.21	19.14	15.64	20.62	14.17
Pain threshold	41.50	31.46	42.46	28.08	36.48	35.27	41.98	29.77
Tolerance threshold	56.62	46.08	53.79	37.92	51.35	45.85	55.21	42.00
Tolerance threshold minus pain threshold	15.21	14.21	11.25	9.83	14.71	10.54	13.23	12.02
Pain evaluation	50.00	58.33	50.42	58.96	54.17	54.69	50.21	58.64

to other causes, and again reveals the difference between this variable and the other various measures concerning pain.

STUDY VI
CO and Quitting Smoking Following Behavior Therapy

PURPOSE AND HYPOTHESES

The rationale for including a study about quitting smoking in a chapter dealing with prediction of everyday behaviors is that quitting smoking *is* a common everyday behavior. As we are reminded by Mark Twain's reported remark—"Stopping smoking? It's very easy, I have done it already fifty times"—this repeatable behavior is ubiquitous, even though not easy.

It has often been found that decreases in smoking due to behavior therapy—the most successful of antismoking treatments—are variable, inconsistent, and transitory (e.g., Marston & McFall, 1971). The major

This study was carried out by Mr. Anton Shahar under the supervision of Shulamith and Hans Kreitler. It was presented by Mr. Anton Shahar as a Master's thesis in partial fulfillment of the requirements of an M.A. degree at the Department of Psychology, Tel Aviv University, 1972. Parts of it were presented in a lecture in the Twelfth Israeli Congress of Psychology, Tel Aviv University, Israel, 1972. A more complete version of this study may be found in Kreitler, Shahar & Kreitler (1976).

purpose of our study was to examine the role of the CO for quitting smoking in determining the cessation of smoking after behavioral therapy, and to compare this role with the role of another motivational variable, reflecting more dynamic and habitual aspects of smoking in the form of a typology. Two types of smokers—the positive affect smoker and the negative affect smoker—were defined on the basis of Tomkins' fourfold classification and other empirical findings (Kahaneman, 1970; McKennel, 1970).

The first hypothesis of the study was that CO scores for quitting smoking would be related to the amount of decrease in smoking following behavior therapy. This hypothesis reflected the conviction that merely undertaking therapy does not imply that the client is willing and ready to give up the controversial behavior. CO would be a much more reliable indicator of this readiness and hence a much better predictor of the ensuing change in behavior.

Our second hypothesis was that predominantly positive affect smokers would benefit more from a saturation therapy than from treatment through desensitization, whereas the reverse would be true of the negative affect smoker. The rationale for the hypothesis was that the accumulation of inhibition by means of saturation may bring about a reduction in the pleasure-providing qualities of smoking as such, while the neutralization through desensitization of situations evoking negative affect may be most helpful to the negative affect smoker.

Finally, the third hypothesis was that there would be an interaction between the effects of CO (first hypothesis) and the effects of adapting the behavioral technique to the type of smoker (second hypothesis), so that subjects with high CO scores who get treatment adequate for their type would decrease smoking most, and those with low CO scores who get treatment inadequate for their type would decrease least.

METHOD

Subjects. The subjects were 40 individuals selected from 142 people responding to a newspaper advertisement asking for volunteers for a study of smoking withdrawal. Twenty-two individuals dropped before the selection and 17 after the selection of 57 subjects. The sole criterion for selection was an extreme score on the Motivational Questionnaire (see "Materials" and "Procedure and Measures," below) presented at a preliminary meeting—a score of at least 26 reflecting negative affect or a score of at least 24 reflecting positive affect. Of the subjects 24 were male, 16 were female. The mean age was 37.5 years. They smoked on the average 31.26 cigarettes per day and the mean number of their former attempts to stop smoking was 3.00 (range: 0 to 10+).

Materials. The Motivational Questionnaire designed to enable the classification of subjects into predominantly positive or negative affect smokers included mainly items from McKennel's (1970) questionnaire, supplemented by a few new items directly reflecting Tomkins' assumptions. It consisted of six groups of six statements. The subject was requested to check in each group the three statements that best applied to him and to rate them on applicability. The maximum possible score was 36.

The cognitive orientation questionnaire for quitting smoking was constructed along the lines described in "Common Background Characteristics." It included 12 questions, 3 in each of the four parts. For example: "When a person undertakes a certain task, such as overcoming the urge to smoke, should he persevere in his attempt even if it is difficult?" (N); "Do you think a person can stop smoking completely or that there always remains a certain tendency to resume smoking?" (GB); "Have you succeeded in the past in getting rid of various habits you wanted to overcome?" (BS); and "Could it be claimed that stopping smoking is a real goal for you or just an interesting attempt?" (Go). The scoring was in terms of three categories: an answer reflecting orientation toward quitting smoking (e.g., "When I think of stopping smoking I feel pleasure and freedom") was assigned two points; an answer reflecting anti-quitting orientation (e.g., "Nothing would improve in my life if I stopped smoking"), no points; and an answer reflecting an indeterminate position, one point.

The test-retest reliability for the four parts of the questionnaire over an interval of one month ($n = 30$ smokers) ranged from .88 to .91. The average interitem correlation across the four parts of the questionnaire was .72. Table 13.5 reports the correlations between the four parts of the questionnaire as well as between them and the computed CO scores.

The medians of the distributions of scores, which served as the basis for computing the CO scores, were: 2.05 (N), 1.62 (GB), 2.21 (BS), and 2.00 (Go).

Procedure and Measures. The study was a 2×4 factorial experiment plus a single control group. The first factor reflected two levels of CO scores: high (CO scores 3 and 4) and low (CO scores 0, 1, and 2). The second factor included four levels, each representing a coupling of a certain type of smoker with a certain type of treatment: (1) negative affect smokers who got desensitization treatment ($n = 9$); (2) negative affect smokers who got saturation treatment ($n = 8$); (3) positive affect smokers who got desensitization treatment ($n = 7$); and (4) positive affect smokers who got saturation treatment ($n = 8$). Factors A and B were uncorrelated ($r = .10$, n.s.; $\chi^2 = .008$, $df = 1$, n.s.). In the control group there were eight subjects. The assignment of negative and positive affect smokers to the various treatment groups or the control was done on a completely random basis.

All subjects were invited first to a general screening meeting in which they answered the CO questionnaire, the Motivational Questionnaire, and a questionnaire designed to provide general information about the subjects and their smoking habits. A few days later the selected subjects were invited to a meeting at which instructions were given about keeping a precise record of the number of cigarettes smoked per week. Administration of treatments started at the end of this week, according to the plan described in Table 7.14. The subjects assigned to any of the treatments were divided randomly into groups of four to six individuals, who met together, once a week for an hour, for 5 consecutive weeks. The control subjects met the same number of times in the same setting and played group games ostensibly necessary as a preliminary to their "special treatment." At the end each subject was paid a sum equivalent to eight dollars for performing the follow-ups.

At the end of the treatments all subjects were instructed to record daily for a week successful abstention from smoking, or else the number

TABLE 7.14
Description of Desensitization and Saturation
Procedures Applied for Control of Smoking

Desensitization	*Saturation*
Meeting 1	
1. Instructions and training in relaxation (Paul, 1966).	1. Explanation of therapeutic rationale following Wolpe (1958) and Yates (1958).
2. Explanation of therapeutic rationale (Pyke, Agnew & Kopperud, 1966) and emphasis on self-control.	2. Distribution of favorite cigarettes and matches.
3. Distribution of typed relaxation instructions for training at home (2–3 times daily).	3. Detailed listing of sensations accompanying smoking.
	4. Instructions to light cigarettes and smoke three in a row, a puff every 10 seconds (at signal), leaving the finished cigarettes burning in ashtrays.
	5. After inhaling deeply the smoke-filled air of the room participants are requested to go to another room with clean air, take a breath, and note the difference. Here they spend a 15-minute recess, without smoking.
	6. Return to original room and repetition of steps 2–5.

TABLE 7.14 (cont'd.)

Meeting 2

1. Discussion of relaxation training at home.
2. Collective performance of relaxation.
3. Instructions for further training of relaxation at home.
4. Instructions for preparing detailed lists of smoking-eliciting stimuli.

Steps 2–6 of Meeting 1.

Meeting 3

1. Free discussion, mainly about relaxation.
2. Information about the desensitization procedure.
3. Checking of lists of stimuli.
4. Instructions for further training of relaxation at home.

Steps 2–6 of Meeting 1.

Meeting 4

1. Free discussion.
2. Checking of lists of stimuli.
3. Training in desensitization: while in relaxation, imagining fixedly an eliciting stimulus for 10 seconds, without change in relaxation or evocation of desire to smoke; if latter occurs, reinstating relaxation; training of all eliciting stimuli sequentially until none evokes change in relaxation or desire to smoke.
4. Instructions for desensitization training at home (typed).

Steps 2–6 of Meeting 1.

Meeting 5

1. Free discussion.
2. Training and instructions for desensitization in real-life situations.
3. Determination of date for stopping smoking, if desired.
4. Discussion of means to help the control of smoking—relaxation, removal of cigarettes, and handling a possibly recurrent desire to smoke.
5. Explanation of follow-up procedures.

1. Steps 2–6 of Meeting 1.
2. Determination of date for stopping smoking, if desired.
3. Discussion of means to help the control of smoking—removal of cigarettes and handling a possible recurrent desire to smoke.
4. Explanation of follow-up procedures.

---

of cigarettes smoked. They were instructed to bring in similar records after 1, 2, and 3 months.

There were two sets of dependent measures. One consisted in converting the four posttreatment records into computed percentages of change, the baseline being the global pretreatment estimate by the subject of the average number of cigarettes he smoked daily. The second set consisted in converting the four posttreatment records into computed percentages of change, the baseline being the precise pretreatment recording by the subject of the number of cigarettes smoked each day for a week. In both sets a decrease in smoking was denoted by a plus sign, and an increase by a minus sign.

Although the two pretreatment baselines were correlated ($r = .82$, $p < .01$), the difference between them was significant ($\bar{X}$ "estimated" $=$ 30.45, $\bar{X}$ recorded $= 25.57$, $t = 2.15$, $p < .05$). To our mind the estimate baseline is more reliable, first because it reflects the fairly precise information a person has about the number of cigarettes he smokes every day, information important for him in terms of both cost and supply; and second because this baseline does not suffer from the decrease in smoking attendant upon any procedure of recording the precise number of cigarettes smoked.

RESULTS AND CONCLUSIONS

Table 7.15 shows that the first hypothesis about the relation of CO scores to changes in smoking following behavior therapy was confirmed according to the "estimate" measures upon the end of treatment and in the first two follow-ups, and according to the "recorded" measures upon the end of treatment and in the second follow-up. A comparison of the means of subjects high and low in CO scores (Winer, 1971, p. 449) confirmed these findings and showed in addition a significant effect in the case of the third "estimate"-type follow-up (CO high $X = 49.17$, CO low $X = 24.25$, $t = 2.11$, $p < .05$). In all cases the differences between the means of the high and low scorers in CO are sizable, mostly of the 2:1 order and always in the expected direction.

Table 13.11 suggests that the CO component BS plays the relatively greatest role in the demonstrated relation between CO scores and the behavioral changes.

In contrast, Table 7.15 shows that the second hypothesis was fully disconfirmed according to all eight measures used in the study. A specific comparison of the means of positive affect smokers treated by the two techniques, and of the negative affect smokers treated by the two techniques, also yielded no significant results. Thus, the findings clearly show that as far as decreases in smoking following behavioral therapy are concerned it does not matter whether the client was a positive or a negative affect smoker, or whether he or she was treated by desensitization or saturation. Moreover, the third hypothesis about interactional effects also received no support whatsoever.

TABLE 7.15
Analyses of Variance of the Effects of
CO Scores and of Treatment-Type of Smoker

Source of Variation	df	ESTIMATED SS	MS	F	df	RECORDED SS	MS	F
End of Treatment								
Between cell	8	14067			8	14075		
Control vs. all others	1	322	322	< 1	1	866	866	1.01
A (CO)	1	5951	5951	8.21**	1	4233	4233	4.93*
B (Type and Treatment)	3	7088	2362.67	3.26[1]	3	5591	1863.67	2.17
A × B	3	706	235.33	< 1	3	3385	1128.33	1.31
Within cell	28	20306	725.21		28	24055	859.11	
First Follow-up								
Between cell	8	17011.14			8	12374		
Control vs. all others	1	739.14	739.14	1.17	1	3447	3447	3.91[1]
A (CO)	1	3817.08	3817.08	6.04*	1	2599	2599	2.95[1]
B (Type and Treatment)	3	7130.95	2376.98	3.76[1]	3	4647	1549	1.76
A × B	3	5323.97	1774.66	2.81	3	1681	560.33	< 1
Within cell	28	17681.40	631.48		28	24691	881.82	
Second Follow-up								
Between cell	8	12489			8	13245		
Control vs. all others	1	606	606	1.00	1	5231	5231	7.89**
A (CO)	1	4867	4867	8.04*	1	3099	3099	4.67*
B (Type and Treatment)	3	5349	1916.33	3.17[1]	3	3769	1256.33	1.89
A × B	3	1267	422.33	< 1	3	1146	382	< 1
Within cell	28	16944	605.14		28	18572	663.29	
Third Follow-up								
Between cell	8	14205			8	17758		
Control vs. all others	1	2605	2605	2.43	1	4875	4875	4.50*
A (CO)	1	2880	2880	2.69	1	1566	1566	1.45
B (Type and Treatment)	3	7369	2456.33	2.29	3	4824	1607.67	1.48
A × B	3	1351	450.33	< 1	3	6493	2164.33	2.00
Within cell	28	29992	1071.14		28	30341	1083.61	

[1] $p < .10$.　　* $p < .05$.　　** $p < .01$.

Finally, a word about the control group is in order. As Table 7.15 shows, in many cases the differences between the decreases in smoking in this group and the experimental groups were not significant. Nevertheless, as Table 7.16 shows, the differences in quantity, regularity, and even direction of change are remarkable. The nonsignificance of many comparisons is due partly to the experimental design, which collapses all the intergroup differences into one coefficient, and partly to the immense variability in the control group, which may reflect in no small part the reactions of the control subjects to the frustrating situation of volunteering for therapy without getting it.

GENERAL CONCLUSIONS

As we have seen, all six studies described in this chapter show that CO scores are related to actual behavior. The significance of this finding is enhanced through its regularity and constancy across the studies. Though the six studies differ in many respects, these differences do not seem to affect the basic relation between CO scores and behavior. Thus, CO scores predict behavior regardless of whether the behavior occurs in a natural setting or under laboratory conditions, whether it is a short-term or long-term behavior, whether it is elicted in an experimental

TABLE 7.16
Percentages of Change in Smoking
in Experimental and Control Groups

PERIOD	% BASED ON ESTIMATE		% BASED ON RECORDED NO.	
	$\overline{X}$	SD	$\overline{X}$	SD
End of Treatment				
Experimental	36.97%	33.72%	25.94%	36.18%
Control	19.31	26.68	−2.50	30.15
First follow-up				
Experimental	33.88	34.10	21.28	35.74
Control	−7.88	44.91	−30.69	38.96
Second Follow-up				
Experimental	35.03	33.06	25.16	33.57
Control	1.13	53.85	−20.63	54.33
Third follow-up				
Experimental	33.59	33.72	23.03	34.22
Control	5.38	39.72	−17.44	36.21

Note: A minus sign indicates increase in smoking. No sign indicates decrease.

subject or takes place on the basis of voluntary exposure to certain stimuli, whether it involves pleasantness or unpleasantness, emotional overtones or none, and so on. Moreover, the relation between CO scores and behavior is also unaffected by such features of the CO questionnaire as its length, or the response mode required of the subject. All these and probably many other aspects may be freely varied provided that three features are preserved: the sampling of the beliefs should reflect major meaning aspects of the studied behavior and/or behavioral situation, the beliefs included in the questionnaire should be of the four basic types (N, GB, BS, and Go), and the final overall CO measure should reflect the independent standing of these four CO components.

Of course, viewed strictly the six studies are merely correlational studies, which implies that they do not point unequivocally to the direction of the causal chain involved in the relation of CO and behavior. Nevertheless, we claim that the studies lend substantial support to the basic theoretical tenet that cognitive orientation plays a role in guiding behavior. It should be noted that the relation between CO scores and behavior was not affected by whether the CO questionnaire was administered before the behavior took place or after it. This invalidates the argument that subjects adjusted their behavior to the CO scores. Moreover, the method of computing CO scores made it difficult if not impossible for subjects to adjust their behavior to such scores. Last but not least, precautions were taken to hide from the subjects the possible relation between the two aspects of each study—the CO questionnaire and behavior. The precautions included administration of the questionnaires and the behavioral tasks in two separate sessions that were often organized differently—for example, one might be an individual session and the other a group session; one might take place in a special laboratory room and the other in the regular classroom or a big hall; sometimes different experimenters were used in the two sessions; sometimes additional experimental tasks unrelated to the focal tasks were administered in the same session (e.g., Study III). Yet, over and beyond these procedural considerations further arguments buttress our claim that the findings of the six studies support the basic tenet of the cognitive orientation theory about the role of cognitive contents in guiding behavior. First, it should be noted that the studies and their design were made possible by the theory of cognitive orientation, and second, that the findings, as well as the three above-mentioned features on which the findings seem to depend, not only derive directly from the cognitive orientation theory but were clearly predicted on the basis of the theory.

Two points concerning the findings seem to us most important. One is the breadth of behavior types shown to be related to CO scores. Chapters 8 and 10 include further examples of behaviors predicted in this manner. This very breadth appears to lend validity to the underlying theoretical principle. The second point concerns the specificity of the relation between CO scores and behavior, which consists in the correspondence of the particular contents and the orientational direction of the beliefs in the CO questionnaire and the particular predicted aspects of the studied behavior. Specificity in this sense reflects the uniqueness of meaning characteristic of every act of behavior. Thus, there is no reason to expect CO scores of pain tolerance to be related to the pain threshold simply because pain is involved in both pain tolerance and pain threshold. However, specificity does not exclude generality. On the contrary, within the bandwidth of the particular meaning(s) involved, there should be no limit on the range of behaviors predictable by the same CO scores other than the relevance and relative prominence of the meaning aspects reflected in the particular CO scores (see Chapter 5). Clear demonstrations of this conclusion are provided by the broad spectrum of behaviors predicted by the CO scores of achievement (this chapter, Study I; Chapter 8, Study I; Chapter 11, Study IV), by the CO scores for postsuccess behavior and the CO scores for postfailure behavior (this chapter, Study III; Chapter 8, Study I; Chapter 11, Study IV), and by the CO scores of curiosity (Chapter 8, Studies III and IV).

Experiments in Learning and School Behavior

THEMES AND METHODOLOGY OF THE STUDIES

The four studies presented in this chapter deal with the relation of CO scores to various aspects of studying and school behavior. The first two studies focus on predicting behaviors related to school grades: grade point average, and the compatibility between IQ and grades, that is, high achievement and so-called underachievement at school. The last two studies focus on predicting curiosity in children and its direct and indirect manifestations in behavioral tasks and in a probability learning setup. Neither curiosity nor grades may be identified with learning or studying as such, but learning and studying ultimately depend on curiosity as one of their main motives, and are reflected in some form in grades, as one of their major manifestations within the framework of formal education. From a certain viewpoint the relations of curiosity and of grades to studying may seem antithetical, curiosity representing an intrinsic motive and grades an extrinsic one. But this viewpoint is too limited to do justice to the complexity of motivation. If we view the CO cluster as a major motivational nexus in which the various orientational directionalities of beliefs are integrated, then the distinction between internal and external sources of motivation is reduced to the distinction between beliefs differing in their subjects, objects, or, perhaps, sources. Since in the CO cluster all beliefs interact intimately, this distinction is mostly superfluous, sometimes misleading, and at best of minor importance. Our major purpose in the four studies was to demonstrate that grades and curiosity behaviors alike are predictable from CO scores.

The four studies have essentially the same design. The major set of variables whose intercorrelations are studied always includes CO scores on the one hand and one or more behavioral variables on the other. The studies also make use of the same methods of constructing the CO questionnaires that make possible the assignment of CO scores to subjects. The four studies share with the studies reported in Chapter 7 the main characteristics of design and procedure of constructing CO question- naires. Therefore we will not describe the latter procedures again but rely instead on the detailed description in "Common Background Char- acteristics," Chapter 7.

STUDY I
CO and Grade Point Average

PURPOSE AND HYPOTHESES

It is commonly recognized that grade point average (GPA) cannot be viewed as a simple and direct reflection of learning. Nor can it be inter- preted as a direct reflection of any other single variable. A major prob- lem associated with GPA is that it represents the product of many fac- tors. The correlation between GPA and IQ being approximately $r =$ .50, it is usually estimated that about 75% of its variance is determined by motivational factors. Nevertheless, as Weiner (1971, p. 222) notes, "a definitive study demonstrating a motivation-GPA relationship does not exist." The most salient candidate for assuming the motivational load in this case is the need for achievement. However, whereas in some studies a relation—at best modest—between grades and n Ach was found (e.g., Atkinson & Litwin, 1960; McClelland et al., 1953, pp. 237, 240; Robinson, 1964; Rosen, 1956; Shaw, 1961; Weiss, Wertheimer, & Groesbeck, 1959), in others no relation was found (e.g., Bendig, 1958; Caron, 1963; Cole, Jacobs, Zubok, Fagot, & Hunter, 1962; Mitchell, 1961), or the relation was not quite interpretable (McKeachie, 1961). No clearer conclusions can be stated about the relation of GPA to success-oriented achievement motivation (Heckhausen, 1963) and anx- iety level (Atkinson & Litwin, 1960; Spielberger & Katzenmeyer, 1959).

The purpose of the present study was to contribute toward clarifica- tion of the determinants of GPA by focusing on CO clusters likely to predict GPA. We were particularly interested in GPA because it is a product of various behaviors extending over a relatively long period of time, approximately 10 months. This fact also provided us with a clue to the probable major CO determinants relevant for GPA. When we focus on the structure of schools and on the different student behaviors that are eventually reflected somehow in GPA, it appears that one salient characteristic of these behaviors is that they are responses to a continu- ous sequence of forthcoming successes and failures. More specifically, getting higher grades seems to depend greatly on the ability to make continuous efforts after having earned a high grade, that is, after success, no less than after having earned a low grade, that is, after failure. Hence, we thought it probable that CO scores for postsuccess and for postfailure performance (Chapter 7, Study III) would be most relevant for predicting students' GPAs. In contrast, the CO of achievement (see Chapter 7, Study I), which focuses on the readiness to make an effort and take pains in order to realize a certain standard in performance, seemed to us of relatively less weight in determining GPA. What counts in behavior at school is the manner in which the student reacts to the various rewards and setbacks that confront him. Thus, the CO of achievement is relevant to GPA only insofar as it deals with making an effort. Consequently, it may be expected to be related to GPA only marginally at best.

Accordingly, our first hypothesis was that CO scores for postsuccess behavior and for postfailure behavior would be jointly related to GPA in the following manner: subjects high in both the CO scores for postsuccess and for postfailure behaviors would have higher grades than subjects low in these two CO scores, whereas subjects high in one of these CO scores and low in the other would have a GPA between the GPAs of the other two groups. Our second hypothesis was that the CO of achievement would be related to GPA only marginally, if at all.

METHOD

Subjects. The subjects were 50 high school students 16–18 years old, selected randomly from three schools in Israel. The group included 27 boys and 23 girls. (The subjects were the same as those in Chapter 11, Study III.)

Procedure and Materials. The CO questionnaires of achievement (Chapter 7, Study I) and for postsuccess and postfailure behavior (Chapter 7, Study III) were administered to the subjects together with other questionnaires in a group session in their classroom. Grade point average was calculated on the basis of the final grades received by the subjects in the academic year preceding the date of the study in the six major humanistic subjects (Bible, literature, composition, Hebrew, English, and French or Arabic languages) and in the four major science subjects (algebra, geometry, physics, and chemistry).

RESULTS AND CONCLUSIONS

Table 8.1 demonstrates that the COs for postsuccess and postfailure behavior are jointly related to GPA in the predicted manner. The subjects high in both CO scores have a higher GPA than those low in both CO scores, the other subjects occupying an intermediate position. Thus, the findings fully support the first hypothesis.

TABLE 8.1

CO Scores for Postsuccess and Postfailure Behavior
and Grade Point Average (GPA)

Group	CO for Postsuccess[a]	CO for Postfailure[a]	n	X̄	SD	X̄	SD
A	High	High	11	7.55	.61		
B	Low	High	17	6.79	.99 ⎫	6.72	.87
C	High	Low	12	6.71	.77 ⎬		
D	Low	Low	9	6.33	.51 ⎭		

Note. For groups A, B + C, D: $F = 5.83$, $df = 2/46$ ($p < .01$).
[a] Subjects were classified as "high" when they received CO scores 4, 3, or 2, and as "low" when they received CO scores 1 or 0.

The described prediction is noteworthy in that it involves two separate and independent CO scores. Also in another study, involving commitments to action (Chapter 11, Study IV), the prediction of the dependent variables was based on the joint use of these two CO scores for postsuccess and for postfailure behaviors. However, the form of interaction between the two CO scores differed in the two cases. In predicting GPA it was found that subjects with the highest grades were high in both COs, whereas subjects with intermediate grades were high in one CO and low in the other. In predicting commitments to action, on the other hand, it was found that subjects who chose the most difficult tasks were high in one of the CO scores and low in the other, whereas subjects who chose tasks of medium difficulty were high in both COs. A conclusion implying an orientative equivalence, for example, between the choice of difficult tasks and intermediate-level grades, or between the choice of less difficult tasks and high grades, lies near at hand. Be that as it may, the findings suggest that one and the same CO or complex of CO clusters may be involved in the determination or prediction of different behaviors. An even more important implication is that different behaviors may be determined not only by different COs but even by similar COs in different combinations.

Concerning our second hypothesis, Table 8.2 shows that the CO scores of achievement were not related to GPA in both sexes. Yet they were related in boys to the mean grade in natural sciences (but not in humanistic subjects), and in girls to the mean grade in humanistic subjects (but not in natural sciences). The absence of a relation to the overall GPA in the whole sample and the conditional and modest nature of the positive relation in the case of boys and girls fully support our second hypothesis about the minor role played by the CO of

TABLE 8.2
Relation of Mean Grades in Natural Sciences, in Humanities,
and Overall GPA to CO Scores of Achievement

GRADES	CO SCORES 4 & 3			CO SCORES 2, 1, & 0			
	n	$\bar{X}$	SD	n	$\bar{X}$	SD	t
Natural sciences							
Male	6	7.32	.92	20	6.67	1.20	1.81*
Female	6	6.78	.90	17	6.69	1.10	< 1
Humanities							
Male	6	6.53	.75	20	6.50	.73	< 1
Female	6	7.55	.73	17	6.89	.70	1.89*
GPA							
Male	6	6.90	.86	20	6.68	.81	< 1
Female	6	7.28	.86	17	6.82	.79	1.15

Note. The scale of grades runs from 0 through 4 (= fail) to 10 (= excellent).
* $p < .05$, one-tailed.

achievement in determining GPA. The moderate degree of the relation is particularly striking when compared to the strong relation of the
CO of achievement to behaviors in the various performance tasks
(Chapter 7, Study III). However, it seems to us important to emphasize
the wide predictive range of the CO of achievement even with regard to
long-range behaviors that are only marginally dependent on it.*

STUDY II
CO and High Achievement or Underachievement in School

PURPOSE AND HYPOTHESES

The major purpose of the study was to identify the CO determinants
of underachievement and to explore the possibility of using CO scores

---

* The availability of n Ach and TAQ scores for these subjects made possible a
three-factor ($2 \times 2 \times 2$) analysis of variance (sex $\times$ n Ach $\times$ TAQ) of grade
point average. There were no significant main effects. The significant results included only a sex $\times$ TAQ interaction ($F = 3.94$, $p < .05$) and a sex $\times$ TAQ $\times$
n Ach interaction ($F = 9.16$, $p < .01$), indicating that girls high in TAQ and
n Ach had higher grades than girls low in these two measures. The findings are
difficult to interpret.

This study was carried out by Mrs. Miriam Nehari under the supervision of
Shulamith Kreitler and Hans Kreitler. It was presented as a Master's thesis by Mrs.
Miriam Nehari in partial fulfillment of the requirements of an M.A. degree at the
Department of Psychology, Tel Aviv University, 1970. Thanks are due to Mrs. Ora

for predicting high achievement and underachievement in school. Attempts to study the personality features and background characteristics of underachievers have mostly led to contradictory results. For exam-ample, while some studies indicated a positive relation between n achievement and underachievement (e.g., Burgess, 1956; Gebhardt & Hoyt, 1958), others found no relation between them (e.g., Bending, 1957; Uhlinger & Stephens, 1960). Again, some (Frenkel, 1960; Shaw, 1962) claim that the underachiever is most actively involved in social interactions, whereas others (Appelbaum, 1964; Gowan, 1955) deplore his social apathy and passivity. Contradictory findings of this type suggest that the roots of the phenomenon are to be sought at a more fundamental level than that of direct or indirect behavioral manifestations.

In our attempt to identify the CO determinants of underachievement, we were guided by the emphasis many researchers placed on the causal role played in underachievement by parents and siblings, by peers and friends, and by the child's attitudes towards school and studying. Indeed, the importance of these three themes in a student's life is evident not only from research findings but also from the viewpoint of any major psychological theory of behavior. The often described role of the overly concerned or apathetic parent, the impact of peers hostile to learning, and the effect of alienation between teacher and student are only some of the more glaring instances that may serve to illustrate the presumed power of these factors in shaping behavior. Accordingly, we included in our CO cluster beliefs representing the three mentioned themes in a sufficient number and adequate representation of the four CO components so as to make possible the assignment of three partial CO scores, one for each of these themes. Our intention was to explore the possible role of these partial CO scores in underachievement. The overall CO score assigned to each subject reflected all the beliefs of the three mentioned themes together.

Consistency among the four CO components in high achievers and underachievers was another theme for our exploration. It could be reasoned that underachievers share with high achievers the general norms of our culture, which are on the whole achievement-oriented, but that their goals and beliefs about self are not as congruent with these norms as are perhaps those of high achievers. Thus, inconsistencies among the four CO components should be greater in underachievers than in high

Margalit and Dr. Avner Ziv, directors of Psychological Service Centers in Tel Aviv, who have so kindly cooperated by making the collection of data possible. Parts of the study were presented in a lecture in the framework of a symposium on "Cognitive Orientation and Behavior" in the Tenth Israeli Congress of Psychology, Bar Ilan University, Israel, 1971.

achievers. But, it could also be argued that since underachievers are often confronted by teachers and parents with the problems of their underachievement, they may thus be forced to deal with the relevant beliefs and resolve some of the more blatant contradictions, which high achievers are never spurred to do. Thus, there should be fewer inconsistencies among the four CO components in underachievers than in high achievers. As there is no empirical basis for choosing between these alternatives, the question had to be left open for exploration.

Accordingly, this study had one major hypothesis and two open-ended questions. The hypothesis was that CO scores would predict whether a subject was a high achiever or an underachiever. High achievement and underachievement were defined in terms of the relation between actual grades and the grades expected in view of the subject's intelligence (see "Subjects"). As in our former studies (Chapter 7), it was assumed that the CO scores are based on beliefs relevant to the predicted behavioral variable of high achievement or underachievement. The first exploratory question concerned the relation of partial CO scores referring to parents and siblings, peers and friends, and school and studies to the phenomena of high achievement and underachievement. The second exploratory question concerned the degree of congruence between the four CO components in high achievers and underachievers.

METHOD

Subjects. The subjects were 92 seventh-grade children, 60 boys and 32 girls, who belonged to two groups: high achievers ($n = 46$, 26 boys and 20 girls), and underachievers ($n = 46$, 34 boys and 12 girls). The seventh-grade age group was chosen as the lowest age group that might justifiably include girls, because girls tend to manifest underachievement only after the sixth grade (Shaw & McOwen, 1960). In order to control for the possible effects of socioeconomic level, ethnic and family background, and level of intelligence, these factors were kept within constant limits. All the selected subjects were from the same socioeconomic class, namely, middle and higher-middle class following the criteria of father's occupation (Lisak, 1967) and number of rooms in apartment relative to size of family; they were all of intact families (i.e., both parents alive and unseparated), and of European or American origin; and their level of intelligence was not below the average (i.e., not less than the 30th percentile).

The subjects were selected from an initial population of over 600 seventh-grade pupils in the metropolitan area of Tel Aviv. A preliminary selection of pupils according to the above-stated criteria of socioeconomic class, family background, ethnic group, and intelligence level reduced the population to 411 pupils (234 boys and 177 girls) of 15 classes in eight different schools, with a mean intelligence score of 46.5 ($SD = 7.71$) as measured by the standard scholastic aptitude test administered to all students, and a mean GPA of 7.24 ($SD = 1.10$) as measured on a scale running from 0 through 4 ($=$ fail) to 10 ($=$ excellent). One class whose GPA distribution deviated markedly from the rest was left out. High achievement and underachievement were defined, following Thorndike (1963), in terms of the gap between actual GPA and the GPA expected on the basis of the regression equation reflecting the relation between intelligence and GPA ($n = 407; r = .57, p < .01$; regression coefficients $a = 3.42, b = .08$). The criterion for high achievement or underachievement was a gap of at least 1.1 SD between actual and expected GPA in the upward or downward direction, respectively. Table 8.3 shows that the gap is significantly wider in underachievers than in high achievers. This is to be expected, first because the actual scale of grades runs from 4 to 10 or even to 9, teachers usually being reluctant to use the grade 10 ($=$ excellent), and second because the GPA in the whole sample was 7.01 (which corresponds with the instructions of the Israeli Ministry of Education).

One hundred twenty individuals were found to meet the described criterion. Of these, 28 dropped out of the sample, or could not participate in the study, or were considered unfit for various reasons. This

TABLE 8.3
Characteristics of High Achievers and Underachievers

Variable	High Achievers	Underachievers	Significance of Differences
GPA			
$\overline{X}$	8.31	5.72	$t = 20.00**$
SD	.49	.71	
Intelligence			
$\overline{X}$	44.35	46.50	$t = 1.45$
SD	6.15	7.79	
Gap between actual and expected GPA			
$\overline{X}$	1.24	1.52	$t = 3.60*$
SD	2.23	4.68	
Socioeconomic level			
Lower middle	14	15	
Middle	23	19	$x^2 = 2.18$
Higher middle	9	12	

* $p < .01$.   ** $p < .001$.

brought the number of actual subjects down to 92. Table 8.3 presents the major relevant characteristics of the two groups of subjects.

Procedure and Materials. The subjects were invited individually to participate in the study. They were tested in groups of ten, each group including randomly invited high achievers and underachievers from different classes and schools. Each group met with an experimenter after school on the precincts of the Psychological Service Centers in the neighborhood of the schools. The subjects were told that they had been selected randomly to participate in a mass study of seventh-graders.

In the course of the session the subjects were administered the CO questionnaire of high achievement and underachievement. Each subject worked separately. The atmosphere was highly liberal and the subjects were encouraged to ask the experimenter about whatever was unclear to them. There was no time limit in answering the questionnaire.

Two experimenters participated in the study. The assignment of experimenters to groups of subjects was random. The experimenters were unaware of the purpose of the study and of the subjects' achievement level.

Intelligence scores and GPAs were taken out of the students' files at schools or at the Psychological Service Centers.

The design of the study consisted in comparing the CO scores of high achievers and underachievers. We chose high achievers rather than regular students, whose GPA corresponds to the GPA expected on the basis of their intelligence, in order to produce optimal conditions for studying the CO characteristics of underachievers.

The CO questionnaire of high achievement and underachievement was constructed in line with the procedure described in "Common Background Characteristics," Chapter 7. The N part consisted of 24 pairs of statements, and the subject's task was to check in each case one of the stated alternatives. The GB part consisted of 28 statements, and the subject's task was to check whether each was "true" or "not true." The BS part included 27 triads of statements, and the subject's task was to check in each case one of the stated alternatives. The Go part included 26 triads of statements, and the subject's task was to check in each case one of the stated alternatives. The scoring of responses was done in accordance with a predetermined system of weights: a response that reflected orientation toward high achievement got a higher weight than a response reflecting orientation toward underachievement. Thus, if there were two response alternatives the former got a weight of 2 and the latter a weight of 1. If there were three response alternatives, the weights ranged from 3 to 1, with 2 assigned to the neutral response.

Each of the four parts of the questionnaire included statements relevant to the three themes of parents and siblings, friends and peers, studying and school. Statements about parents and siblings referred, for example, to parents' interest in the child's studies, their expectations for the child, and whether the child's attainments were compared with those of siblings. Statements about peers and friends referred, for example, to the child's view of his or her popularity, satisfaction with his or her social standing, and the attitudes of his or her friends toward studying. Statements about studying and the school referred, for example, to the child's studying habits, interest in knowledge in general, relations to the teacher, the teacher's fairness, and so on.

Examples of beliefs included in the questionnaires follow: "If a child does not answer a question correctly in class, the other kids sometimes laugh at him" (GB); "A child should always (should not) tell his parents what happens at school and with his friends so that they can participate fully in his life" (N).

Test-retest reliability coefficients over an interval of 2 weeks were .55 for the N part, .38 for the GB part, .72 for the BS part, .70 for the Go part, and .73 for the sum of responses across the four CO components. All coefficients were significant beyond the .01 level. The average split-half reliability coefficient for the four parts of the questionnaire was .53 ($p < .01$). Discriminability of the items was guaranteed by weeding out questions that yielded too skewed a distribution of responses (i.e., less than 10% of the subjects checked one of the response alternatives) and by checking the content of the selected alternative against the total score on the relevant part of the questionnaire (i.e., a question was dropped if there was no correspondence in more than 30% of the subjects). Table 13.5 reports the correlations between the four CO components and between them and the CO scores.

On the basis of his responses, each subject received three partial CO scores—one dealing with parents and siblings, another dealing with school and studying, and a third dealing with peers and friends—and a total CO score reflecting responses to the three themes taken together.

The means of responses in the four CO components that served as the basis for assigning CO scores were: 11.16 (GB), 13.35 (BS), 12.11 (Go), and 10.05 (N) for the parents and siblings theme; 9.96 (GB), 14.74 (BS), 14.16 (Go), and 10.09 (N) for the school and studies theme; 10.38 (GB), 16.49 (BS), 14.40 (Go), and 11.18 (N) for the peers and friends theme; and 31.50 (GB), 44.58 (BS), 40.67 (Go), and 31.33 (N) for the total of all responses.

RESULTS AND CONCLUSIONS

The data fully support our major hypothesis. Table 8.4 shows that the total CO score discriminated significantly between the high achievers and the underachievers. There were almost 2.5 times more high achievers than underachievers with high CO scores and 3 times more under-achievers than high achievers with low CO scores. These findings are valid with regard to males and females equally. No differences were found between the sexes in the distribution of responses to the CO questionnaire or to any of its four parts in the sample as a whole or in the separate groups of high achievers and underachievers separately.

Table 8.4 also affords an answer to our questions about the role of the three partial CO clusters in determining high achievement and under-achievement. It shows that the CO clusters concerning parents and sib-lings and school and studies both discriminate about equally and highly significantly between high achievers and underachievers, whereas the partial CO cluster relating to peers and friends does not discriminate between the groups at all.

As may be expected, the partial CO score concerning peers and friends is not correlated with the CO scores concerning parents ($r = .03$, n.s.) and studies ($r = .19$, n.s.), whereas the latter two CO scores are correlated ($r = .29$, $p < .01$). The fact that the correlation between the partial CO scores concerning parents and studies is so moderate shows

TABLE 8.4
Relations of Partial and Total CO Scores
to High Achievement and Underachievement at School

CO Scores	High Achievers	Underachievers	χ^2
Partial CO cluster: parents			
2.5–4	23	6	
1.5–2	16	19	17.22*
0–1	7	21	
Partial CO cluster: school and studies			
2.5–4	27	11	
1.5–2	16	18	16.66*
0–1	3	17	
Partial CO cluster: peers and friends			
2.5–4	13	15	
1.5–2	23	19	.70
0–1	10	12	
CO total			
2.5–4	26	11	
1.5–2	15	20	11.80*
0–1	5	15	

* $p < .01$.

that these CO scores reflect largely nonoverlapping themes and thus are both necessary for predicting high achievement and underachievement at school. It is obvious that a total CO score based only on the relevant themes of parents and studies would prove to be even more highly discriminating between the groups than a CO score reflecting responses to all three themes (Table 8.4).

Our second question referred to the congruence between the four CO components in the two groups of subjects. Table 8.5 shows that there is no difference in the mean degree of congruence between the CO components in high achievers and underachievers. Moreover, in both groups the congruence is low.

TABLE 8.5
Intercorrelations of the Four CO Components
in High Achievers and Underachievers

| CO COMPONENTS | INTERCORRELATIONS IN: | |
	High Achievers	*Underachievers*
General beliefs and beliefs about self	.18	.13
General beliefs and goals	.23	.13
Beliefs about self and goals	−.05	.21
Norms and goals	.08	.28
Norms and general beliefs	−.05	−.05
Norms and beliefs about self	.05	.30*
Mean of intercorrelations[a]	.07	.17

[a] Z of difference between mean intercorrelations $= .49$, nonsignificant.
* $p < .05$.

STUDY III
CO and Curiosity

PURPOSE AND HYPOTHESES

A major purpose of this study was to clarify the role of the CO cluster in determining the level and form of the behavioral manifestations of curiosity. Another purpose was to examine the suitability of the CO cluster for predicting a broad range of different behaviors, all manifesting the same behavioral trait or motive—in the present case curiosity. A third purpose was to examine the predictive power of CO scores with regard to children, that is, subjects whose awareness and self-control are not as highly developed as they are in most adolescents and adults.

This study was published (Kreitler, Kreitler, & Zigler, 1974) and will therefore be summarized here only briefly.

Accordingly, the hypothesis of the study was that CO scores reflecting beliefs relevant for curiosity would be related in children to the level of curiosity manifested in a broad range of different behaviors reflecting curiosity.

METHOD

Subjects. The subjects were 84 first-graders, 42 boys and 42 girls in the age range 6.66–8.41 years ($\overline{X} = 7.15$ years, $SD = .53$) from two communities in New Jersey, one static and conservative, the other mobile and developing. Of the children, 75 were white and 9 were black; 33 belonged to the low social class and 37 to the middle and high social class (concerning the rest no data were available).

Procedure. In two sessions about a week apart, all children were administered five behavioral tasks in random order (Table 8.6). The tasks yielded 19 variables commonly viewed as reflecting different aspects of curiosity: 18 of these are described briefly in Table 8.6 (nos. 1–18); and the remaining variable was dichotomous, referring to the child's choice of playing with familiar or new toys. There was in addition a further variable (Table 8.6, no. 19), reflecting the teacher's averaged ratings of the child's interest and curiosity.

A factor analysis (Kreitler, Zigler, & Kreitler, 1975) showed that most of the variables were loaded on five factors identified as manipulatory curiosity, perceptual curiosity, conceptual curiosity, curiosity about the complex, and adjustive reactive curiosity (Table 8.6).

Sixty-four of the children, randomly selected, were also administered the CO questionnaire of curiosity in a separate session. About half got the questionnaire before the behavioral tasks and about half afterwards. The interval between these sessions was about 2 weeks. The 20 children who did not take the questionnaire served as a control group for assessing the possible effects of answering the questionnaire.

The questionnaire, constructed in line with the procedure described in "Common Background Characteristics," Chapter 7, included 73 questions (N, GB, BS = 18 questions each, Go = 19 questions) distributed unequally around 10 core themes related to curiosity. Internal consistency ranged from .81 to .90, and split-half reliability coefficients ranged from .79 to .93 for the four parts. Test-retest reliability over a 2-week period was .91. Table 13.5 presents the intercorrelations between the four CO components as well as between them and CO scores.

RESULTS AND CONCLUSIONS

A primary analysis of the data showed that there were no significant differences on any of the curiosity variables between children who answered the questionnaire and those who did not, between children

TABLE 8.6
Means and *SD*s of Responses along Curiosity Variables
in Groups Defined by Cognitive Orientation (CO) Scores

CURIOSITY TASKS AND VARIABLES[a]	FACTOR LOAD- INGS[b]	CO 4		CO 3 & 2		CO 1 & 0		F
		$\bar{X}$	SD	$\bar{X}$	SD	$\bar{X}$	SD	
Observation of simple and complex stimuli								
1. Simple stimuli— observation time	II	24.71	4.97	31.83	11.81	28.11	9.84	2.40[1]
2. Complex stimuli— observation time	II, IV	24.65	14.97	29.66	16.08	21.64	14.45	2.62[1]
3. Mean time difference between complex and simple stimuli	IV	−.06	5.80	−2.17	5.80	−6.46	5.91	21.73***
4. Switching glance— total no.	II, IV	27.49	9.33	23.59	5.95	23.56	3.89	6.57**
5. No. of pairs whose complex stimulus was viewed longer	IV	4.35	1.32	3.87	1.87	4.04	1.80	< 1
Preference for simple or complex stimuli								
6. No. of complex stimuli preferred	IV	2.70	1.21	1.65	.93	2.00	.84	4.82*
7. Switching pref- erence—total no.	II, V	3.32	1.06	3.83	1.98	3.19	1.69	< 1
Preference for the unknown								
8. Choosing the unknown—total no.	V	6.11	2.25	5.94	1.37	4.74	1.29	3.29*
9. Switching choice— total no.	—	3.53	3.15	3.61	2.23	4.04	2.70	< 1
Meaning								
10. No. of meaning values	III	5.30	2.23	5.12	1.41	4.82	2.04	< 1

who got the questionnaire before the behavioral tasks or afterwards, between white and black children, or between children of the two social classes. Boys and girls were found to differ on variables 11, 13, 15, and 16, and on the choice of new versus familiar toys.

Accordingly, the relation of CO scores to curiosity variables was examined both through a one-way analysis of variance with CO scores as the single factor underlying a tripartite grouping (Table 8.6) and through a

TABLE 8.6 (cont'd.)

CURIOSITY TASKS AND VARIABLES[a]	FACTOR LOAD-INGS[b]	CO 4 X	SD	CO 3 & 2 X̄	SD	CO 1 & 0 X	SD	F
11. No. of meaning dimensions	III	11.11	3.65	13.06	4.88	13.07	5.16	1.17
Object manipulations								
12. Time interval of choice	I, III	3.26	6.72	3.28	3.77	4.07	6.44	< 1
13. No. of inspecting manipulations	I	5.11	3.45	2.28	2.63	2.30	1.56	8.18**
14. No. of customary use manipulations	III, V	3.58	2.09	3.50	2.23	3.04	1.91	< 1
15. No. of exploratory manipulations	I	13.63	1.38	12.33	2.59	9.93	3.02	12.88**
16. Total no. of manipulations	I	22.79	9.25	16.94	8.33	16.52	6.91	3.85*
17. Total time of manipulations	I	417.80	125.20	368.90	193.40	383.31	151.20	< 1
18. Weighted index of questions	III	4.26	4.34	3.48	4.68	2.94	2.44	< 1
Teacher's rating								
19. Teacher's rating of curiosity	V	2.22	.85	2.39	.78	1.68	.75	4.05*
Manipulatory curiosity (Factor scores of Factor I)	I	.52	1.11	−.19	.95	−.18	.85	3.57*

[a] In variables 1–5 the number of subjects in the three groups is 19, 15, and 24 respectively. Thus $df = 55/2$. In all other variables (6–19) the number of subjects is 19, 13, and 27 respectively, and $df = 61/2$.
[b] Only factor loadings exceeding .25 are mentioned. Factor I represents manipulatory curiosity; II, perceptual curiosity; III, conceptual curiosity; IV, curiosity about the complex; V, adjustive-reactive curiosity.
[1] $p < .10$.   * $p < .05$.   ** $p < .01$.   *** $p < .001$.

three-way analysis of variance ($3 \times 2 \times 2$) considering CO scores, sex, and social class (Table 8.7). Table 8.6 shows that groups formed on the basis of CO scores differed significantly and as expected in 10 of the 19 variables. Moreover, in four additional variables (nos. 10, 19, 14, and 18) the direction of interrelation corresponded to expectation.

Table 8.7 presents the findings of the three-way analysis of variance, which deviate from the findings of the simpler analysis. It shows that

TABLE 8.7
Three-Factor Analyses of Variance (3 × 2 × 2)
of Responses along Three Curiosity Variables

Variable	Source of Variation	df	MS	F
12. Time interval of choice	CO Score (CO 4, CO 3 & 2 vs. CO 1 & 0(A)	2	63.59	2.63[1]
	Sex (B)	1	13.16	< 1
	Social Class (low vs. middle) (C)	1	74.26	3.07[1]
	A × B	2	28.19	1.16
	A × C	2	150.96	6.23**
	B × C	1	17.88	< 1
	A × B × C	2	18.46	< 1
	Error	33	24.22	
18. Weighted index of questions	A	2	6.41	< 1
	B	1	11.47	< 1
	C	1	21.27	1.09
	A × B	2	21.83	1.11
	A × C	2	66.67	3.41*
	B × C	1	16.74	< 1
	A × B × C	2	27.89	1.42
	Error	33	19.57	
10. Number of meaning values	A	2	24.41	< 1
	B	1	4.01	< 1
	C	1	12.76	< 1
	A × B	2	81.61	2.59[1]
	A × C	2	4.28	< 1
	B × C	1	6.15	< 1
	A × B × C	2	.94	< 1
	Error	33	31.46	

[1] $p < .10.$ * $p < .05.$ ** $p < .01.$

the expected relation between CO scores and behavior is evident in three more variables in an interactive form: in the case of the time interval of choice (no. 12) it is more pronounced in lower-class than in middle-class children; in the case of number of questions ask (no. 18) it is more pronounced in middle-class children than in lower-class children; and in the case of number of meaning values it is more pronounced in girls than in boys.

Tables 8.8 and 8.9 show that CO scores were also related to the choice of new or familiar toys. A chi-square analysis of interactions between CO and the factors of sex and social class (Castellan, 1965) showed that the relation between CO and choice of toys was not affected by sex but was significant only in lower-class children.

In sum, the CO scores of curiosity were related to 14 of the original 20 measures of this study. It is noteworthy that in spite of the high intercorrelations between the four CO components in this study (see Table 13.5), a simpler measure of beliefs that reflected merely the overall sum of all procuriosity beliefs in the four CO components taken together was related only to four of the curiosity measures (nos. 6, 8, 13, and 16 in Table 8.6, on the .05 level). This finding again supports the greater utility of CO scores over other measures that do not take full account of the separate CO components.

In order to appreciate fully the predictive power of the CO scores of curiosity it is important to emphasize that the CO scores were related to eight of the 10 variables with .50–.99 communalities, to four of the seven variables with .10–.50 communalities, and to one of the two variables with communalities lower than .10 (for communalities see Kreitler, Zigler, & Kreitler, 1975). Thus, four of the unpredicted variables had low communalities. And in general, the more characteristic of curiosity a variable is, the higher the chances that it is predicted by the CO scores of curiosity. In other words, the CO scores of curiosity are related as expected to behavioral measures that primarily manifest curiosity.

TABLE 8.8
Frequency of Choosing New and Familiar Objects in Groups Defined by Cognitive Orientation (CO) Scores

CHOICES OF OBJECTS	CO SCORES		
	4 & 3	2 & 1	0
New	23	6	8
Familiar	8	10	9

$\chi^2 = 7.39, df = 2, p < .05.$

TABLE 8.9
Chi-square Analysis of Choosing New and Familiar Objects Partitioned along CO and Social Class

Source	df	χ^2
Within low class	2	11.171**
Within middle and high class	2	.450
Low × high class	1	.348
Total	5	11.969*

* $p < .05.$ ** $p < .01.$

The particular power and versatility of the CO scores of curiosity are evident not merely in the high percentage of curiosity measures that they predicted but also in the broad range of curiosity factors spanned by the predicted measures (four of the five loaded on factor I, three of the four loaded on factor II, three of the five loaded on factor III, four of the five loaded on factor IV, and two of the four loaded on factor V). Thus, the CO scores of curiosity seem to reflect tendencies so basic to curiosity that they predict a wide range of curiosity manifestations that are in part even unrelated to one another.

The study serves to show, first, the breadth of the predictive range of CO scores, and second, the full effectiveness of CO scores on the level of first-grade children.

STUDY IV
CO of Curiosity and Probability Learning

PURPOSE AND HYPOTHESES

The major purpose of the study was to clarify the role of the CO cluster of curiosity in determining the occurrence and intensity of certain behaviors common in the setting of probability learning. Probability learning situations are characterized by the availability of several alternatives of response, only one of which is reinforced randomly at a certain predetermined ratio. Our expectation that curiosity might provide a clue to understanding some behaviors in probability learning was based not merely on the general assumption that an ambiguous and intriguing situation may evoke curiosity in children but also on more specific findings showing that conditions favoring curiosity also favor alternation in responses in contrast to maximization (i.e., concentration on the payoff response) in probability learning—for example, parents who avoid punishment (Maw & Maw, 1965; Gruen & Zigler, 1968), decrease in the value of available reinforcement (Zimbardo & Montgomery, 1957; Brackbill, Kappy, & Starr, 1962), or high aspiration level (Maw & Maw, 1965; Gruen & Zigler, 1968).

This study was carried out with Professor Edward Zigler of Yale University. Thanks are due to Mr. B. Bernstein, principal of the school at Deans, N.J., and to Mr. Robert T. Gavin, Director of Special Services at Dayton School, N.J., for their kind help; to Mr. Charles Armitage for his helpful cooperation; and to the Department of Psychology, Princeton University, and the Research Division of the Educational Testing Service, Princeton, N.J., for making available to us their mobile lab setups. A more complete presentation of the study is available (Kreitler, Kreitler, & Zigler, 1975).

In this study we focused on three behaviors: maximizing, which consists in pressing the payoff knob consistently, regardless of whether reinforcement is continuously forthcoming or not; exploring, which consists in examining the situation and testing hypotheses about reinforcement patterns in an attempt to identify the problem and solve it; and minimizing, which consists in pressing consistently a nonreinforced knob even if reinforcement is never forthcoming. We assumed that exploring reflected a relatively high level of curiosity, whereas maximizing and minimizing reflected low levels of curiosity. We viewed exploring in this context as akin to curiosity because the processes of hypothesis testing and alternating responses characteristic of exploring are major manifestations of curiosity. We interpreted maximizing as reflecting a low level of curiosity not only because in probability learning it cannot occur together with alternation (Gruen & Zigler, 1968), but also because the conditions enhancing it (Estes, 1964) show that maximizing occurs when the subject assumes there is no problem to solve or that the goal is simply to hoard as many rewards as possible. We concluded that minimizing was inimical to curiosity since it consists in turning one's back both on reinforcement and on the intriguing or problematic aspects of the situation.

Accordingly, we hypothesized that CO scores of curiosity would be (1) correlated negatively with the measure reflecting maximizing; (2) correlated negatively with the measure reflecting minimizing; and (3) correlated positively with the measures reflecting exploring.

METHOD

Subjects. The subjects were 64 first graders, 32 boys and 32 girls (mean age = 7.10 years) from two different schools in the United States. Nine were black, the rest were white. Their mean intelligence level on the Otis IQ Test was 5.85 (*SD* = .85) and their mean score on the Metropolitan Achievement Test was 19.36 (*SD* = 1.85). Twenty-five belonged to middle and high social classes, and 26 to the low social class (about the rest no information was available).

Procedure and Variables. Each subject was invited to two individual sessions, 3 to 4 weeks apart. In one session the subject was administered the CO questionnaire of curiosity (see Study III above) and in the other the probability learning task. The order of the sessions and the assignment of one out of six experimenters to each session was random. The testing was done in a mobile lab on the school grounds.

The probability learning task made use of the standard apparatus, which consists of a vertical panel with three identical knobs for pressing, a light signal to denote the beginning of a trial, and a small container for holding the released marbles (Stevenson & Zigler, 1958). After proper demonstration, the subject was given 100 trials of pressing the knobs. For each subject only one randomly determined knob was reinforced, and this in only 66% of the trials following a random schedule. After the task the child was asked whether she or he liked the game, what she or he thought while pressing the knobs, how she or he knew which knob to press, and whether she or he had any questions.

The three behaviors were defined mainly in terms of the subject's response sequences, in line with the more recent emphasis on trial-to-trial changes in responses (Goulet & Goodwin, 1970), and not in terms of summative measures of response frequencies, which are uninformative concerning information-processing strategies. The three-step run was used as a basic unit in view of findings that first graders are capable of taking account of response sequences that long (Wier, 1964). Thus, maximizing was measured by the frequency of three-step sequences of pressing the reinforced knob. This measure ranges from a minimum of 0 to a maximum of 98 for 100 trials and is uncorrelated with the total number of times the reinforced knob was pressed ($r = .00$). Minimizing was measured by the frequency of three-step sequences of pressing a nonreinforced knob. This measure too ranges from 0 to 98. Exploring was measured by the degrees of predictability of three-step, two-step, and one-step sequences as reflected in the third (C_3), second (C_2), and first (C_1) approximations to the Index of Behavioral Stereotypy (Miller & Frick, 1949), respectively. Since exploration in general and hypothesis testing in particular require consideration of one's preceding acts so as to avoid undue repetition, we concluded that the second (C_2) and third (C_3) approximations to the Index of Behavioral Stereotypy, reflecting the degree to which a subject systematically chooses a response different from his last or his two last responses, are indicative of exploring (Miller & Frick, 1949) and not of stereotyped responding (Goodwin, 1969). Accordingly, high exploring should be manifested in relatively high C_2 and C_3 and low C_1 indices, whereas low exploring should be manifested in high C_1 and low C_2 and C_3 indices. Our assumption is borne out by the fact that the indices C_3 and C_2 were found to be correlated positively ($r = .55$, $p < .01$), whereas the indices C_3 and C_1 ($r = -.50$, $p < .01$) and the indices C_2 and C_1 ($r = -.35$, $p < .01$) were found to be correlated negatively. In addition, exploring was also measured by a dichotomous variable that reflected the degree to which the subject looked for a response pattern and/or was engaged in hypothesis testing as determined by three independent judges (100% agreement) on the basis of the subject's verbal responses.

RESULTS AND CONCLUSIONS

The data of the whole sample were analyzed together since preliminary analyses showed no differences on any of the studied variables between the children who received the CO questionnaire of curiosity in the first sesssion and those who received it in the second session, between white and black children, between boys and girls, or between children of the two social classes. Moreover, the studied variables were unrelated to intelligence or academic achievement.

Table 8.10 shows that the higher the curiosity CO scores of the subjects, the lower their level of maximizing. This fully confirms our first hypothesis. In order to characterize more sharply the meaning of this prediction it should be noted that none of the following "traditional" variables was related to CO scores: the total number of "correct" responses, i.e., pressing the payoff knob regardless of reinforcement ($F = .42$, $df = 60/3$, n.s.); the number of "correct" responses on the last block of 20 trials ($F = .20$, $df = 60/3$, n.s.); the amount of progression in "correct" responses from the first 30 trials to the last 30 trials ($F = .45$, $df = 60/3$, n.s.); or the overall rate of change, defined as the maximum number of "correct" responses per 10-trial block divided by the number

TABLE 8.10
Means and SDs of Responses in Groups
Defined by Cognitive Orientation (CO) Scores

VARIABLES[a]	CO 4 ($n = 19$)		CO 3 ($n = 11$)		CO 2 & 1 ($n = 17$)		CO 0 ($n = 17$)		F	DEVIATIONS FROM LINEARITY
	X	SD	X	SD	X	SD	X	SD		
Maximizing	20.63	7.56	30.27	9.84	35.11	10.58	39.58	6.21	3.14*	n.s.
Minimizing	.21	.42	.18	.40	.53	.80	.82	.29	5.76**	n.s.
Index of Behavioral Stereotypy C_1	15.41	12.58	7.19	14.16	9.77	19.16	24.03	19.35	2.86*	$F = 34.05$***
Index of Behavioral Stereotypy C_2	11.45	10.11	15.03	12.09	13.57	10.24	6.08	4.08	4.37**	$F = 36.00$***
Index of Behavioral Stereotypy C_3	10.72	8.52	19.72	9.84	13.86	8.58	8.29	6.06	4.78**	$F = 36.99$***

[a] In CO 3, the difference between C_3 and C_1 is significant at $p < .05$ ($q_r = 4.34$, $CR_{.95} = 3.58$), and between C_2 and C_1 at $p < .10$ ($q_r = 2.71$, $CR_{.95} = 2.95$). In CO 0, the differences between C_3 and C_1 ($q_r = 5.73$, $CR_{.99} = 4.44$) and between C_2 and C_1 ($q_r = 6.53$, $CR_{.99} = 3.89$) are significant at $p < .01$ (Newman-Keuls procedure).
* $p < .05$. ** $p < .01$. *** $p < .001$.

of trials it took the subject to reach this level of "correct" responding ($F = 1.30$, $df = 60/3$,n.s.). These control analyses emphasize that the level of mere "correct" responding, which has usually commanded the interest of researchers, is completely unrelated to the CO of curiosity. In contrast, an overriding interest in reinforcement, reflected in concentrating on the payoff knob without testing any other hypotheses, is related to a low CO score of curiosity, whereas the absence of these features is related to a higher CO score of curiosity.

The findings in Table 8.10 also fully support the second hypothesis. Subjects with high CO scores of curiosity have a low level of minimizing, that is, they perseverate in pressing the nonreinforced knobs, whereas subjects with low scores of curiosity have a high level of minimizing. The minimizers share perseveration with the maximizers. Yet, unlike the maximizers who perseverate on the winning side, they perseverate on the losing side, perhaps because they reject the basic terms of the task or feel too helpless and incompetent to solve the problem. Another possibility is that maximizers and minimizers share basically the same approach but are led to differ in their subsequent behavior through the accident of initially pressing a rewarded or nonrewarded knob.

Concerning the third hypothesis, the findings at first glance seem surprising. As may be recalled, exploring was assumed to be manifested through relatively high second (C_2) and third (C_3) approximations to the Index of Behavioral Stereotypy and a relatively low first approximation (C_1) to the Index. The data show that the expected positive relation between CO scores and the indices C_2 and C_3 and the expected negative relation between CO scores and C_1 seem to hold for all subjects except the CO 4 subgroup. Indeed, findings in this subgroup are the sole factor responsible for the significant deviations from linearity in the case of the three indices of stereotypy. Also, a comparison of the indices in each CO subgroup separately (Table 8.11) shows that the findings conform to expectation in subgroups CO 3, CO 0, and CO 2 & 1, which holds an intermediate position, but not in CO 4, which, contrary to expectation, got a much higher C_1 index and much lower C_2 and C_3 indices than would seem warranted by our assumptions and the behavior of subjects in other subgroups.

What is puzzling about these findings is that they apparently conform to expectation in the case of most subjects but not in the case of precisely those subjects who should have manifested the behaviors in their clearest form. The disturbing character of these findings is greatly reduced if we assume the existence of two modes of exploration: one consists in studying the relation between knobs and reinforcement in a highly systematic and consistent manner, bordering sometimes on perseveration while the other consists in examining the relation in a highly mobile, sometimes inconsistent, and noncontinuous manner, checking several hypotheses and using different patterns in their checking. The two modes are reminiscent of Bruner's (1965) distinction between "extrinsic" and "intrinsic" problem-solving and Achenbach and Zigler's (1968) differentiation between the cue-learning and problem-learning strategies. The first mode would be manifested, as we originally hypothesized, in high C_3 and C_2 indices and a low C_1 index, whereas the second mode would be manifested by lower C_3 and C_2 indices (due to inconsistent exploring) and a higher C_1 index (due to using also one-step sequences in exploring). We assume the first mode to be dominant in subjects with CO 3, and the second to be dominant in subjects with CO 4. This assumption leads to the expectation that subjects with CO 3 would most often use the known patterns of pressing left-middle-right, and right-middle-left, which combine alternation with stereotypy ($\bar{X} =$ 13.42, 17.00, 15.90, 10.53; $SD =$ 10.60, 15.21, 10.51, 9.38, respectively for the four CO subgroups). The trend of findings does conform to expectation and thus lends some support to the view that this kind of alternation is a relatively high-level behavior (Baumeister, 1966) and not

TABLE 8.11
Analyses of Variance on the Three Approximations
to the Index of Behavioral Stereotypy
in Groups Defined by Cognitive Orientation (CO) Scores

CO Score	Source of Variation	SS		df	MS	F
4	Between subjects		2181.71	18		
	Within subjects		4314.86	38		
	Indices	242.50		2	121.25	1.07
	Residual	4072.36		36	113.12	
3	Between subjects		964.18	10		
	Within subjects		4352.33	22		
	Indices	1181.22		2	590.61	3.72*
	Residual	3171.12		20	158.55	
2 & 1	Between subjects		4403.20	16		
	Within subjects		2479.16	34		
	Indices	176.02		2	88.01	1.22
	Residual	2303.14		32	71.97	
0	Between subjects		3449.47	16		
	Within subjects		7360.68	34		
	Indices	3257.12		2	1628.56	12.70***
	Residual	4163.56		32	128.23	

* $p < .05$.   *** $p < .001$.

merely primitive perseveration (Wier, 1964). However, since the two modes of exploring may be equally important and necessary, there is hardly any justification for viewing exploration as inherently contrasting with perseveration.

Owing to the ambiguity in interpreting the C_3 and C_2 indices as manifestations of exploring, the verbal remarks of subjects might be a more reliable and consistent criterion for exploring. Table 8.12 shows that our hypothesis was fully confirmed. Subjects with high CO scores of curiosity were much more often engaged in searching for a pattern or in hypothesis testing than subjects with low CO scores.

In sum, this study demonstrated, first, the utility of using the CO theory for studying learning behaviors and shedding light on unclear issues in this domain, and, second, the utility of CO scores of curiosity in predicting curiosity behaviors in a context far removed from the common settings for studying curiosity.

TABLE 8.12
Preoccupation with Finding a Pattern in Subjects Grouped by Cognitive Orientation (CO) Scores

CO SCORES	PREOCCUPATION	
	Yes	No
4	14	5
3	6	5
2 & 1	7	10
0	4	13

$\chi^2 = 10.22$, $df = 3$, $p < .02$.

GENERAL CONCLUSIONS

The four studies summarized in this chapter demonstrate the predictive power of CO scores with regard to various behaviors related to school, studying, and learning: grades, the disparity between intelligence level and grades in the direction of high achievement and in the direction of underachievement, 14 different types of curiosity behaviors, and various behavioral strategies in the context of probability learning. In this respect, the findings of these studies make it possible to extend further the conclusions stated at the end of Chapter 7. They show how broad the predictive power of CO scores is and how different may be the behaviors related to them.

The findings also shed light on the issue of the generality or specificity of CO scores. In Study I two different sets of CO scores were shown to be necessary for predicting GPA, whereas in Studies III and IV the same set of CO scores was used successfully for predicting 20 different behavioral variables. There is no contradiction between these two facts. Since the relation of CO scores to behavior depends on the relevance or correspondence in meaning of the CO scores to the studied behavior, it is the meaning of the behavior and/or the situation in which it occurs that determine how many different CO scores must be used to predict a given behavior successfully.

On the other hand, one may perhaps speak not of different CO scores but of different subclusters within a particular CO cluster. Is the difference merely superficial? Since subclusters encompassed within a CO cluster do not have to be correlated (Chapter 4), one may well ask when they should be viewed as different subclusters within one overall CO cluster and when they may be viewed as forming separate CO clusters. In the absence of any data to the contrary, it is warranted to assume that if certain subclusters occur sufficiently often together in one or more specific behavioral situations they form a single CO cluster, possibly owing to the fact that they come to share a minimal number of meaning values, though fewer than those shared by the beliefs encompassed within the subclusters. If, however, they occur no more often together than separately, it makes more sense to treat the subclusters as elements in separate CO clusters. For the time being, the problem seems to have more methodological than theoretical implications.

Inducing Behavior Change

PROBLEMS IN CHANGING BEHAVIOR

Having demonstrated that CO clusters enable the prediction of molar behavior (Chapters 7 and 8), we now focus on inducing change of behavior by changing CO clusters. The purpose of this chapter is two-fold. First, we wish to demonstrate that inducing changes in CO clusters actually brings about changes in behavior. This hypothesis, underlying the two studies described in the present chapter, derives directly from our conception about the relation of CO clusters to molar behavior, and thus represents—as may be recalled—a corollary of one of the two major general hypotheses of our theory (Chapter 1). Indeed, the importance of this hypothesis in the framework of our theory can hardly be over-rated. For, if it can be shown that planned changes introduced into CO clusters are followed by expected changes in specific behaviors, the determinative role of CO clusters with regard to molar behavior may be viewed as conclusively proved.

Second, the two studies reported in this chapter explore methods for changing CO components and CO clusters. In this respect this chapter is definitely exploratory. Each study utilizes a different method of change, derived from the two major psychological domains in which change is being practiced: attitude change and psychotherapy. Whereas Study I makes use of discussion, persuasion, and communication of information, Study II relies on role playing as the main tool of change. The method used in Study I has many affinities with traditional methods of attitude change and social influence, which are based on the assumed direct effect of communication (e.g., Cohen, 1964; Hovland, Janis & Kelley, 1953; Sherif & Sherif, 1965) or on its indirect effect, mediated through dissonance reduction (e.g., Rosenberg et al., 1960;

Rokeach, 1973). The analogous psychotherapeutic methods are certain parts of classical psychoanalytic treatment, mainly working through, or particular therapeutic schools, like Frankl's (1973) logotherapy. In contrast, the method of Study II resembles techniques applied in various attitude-change studies (e.g., Elms, 1969), but derives ultimately from Moreno's (1946, 1959) psychodramatic method. Yet its psychotherapeutic analogues are not restricted to psychodrama proper, but also include different variants of the role-playing technique and even fantasy enactment (e.g., Desoille, 1961; Sheehan, 1972).

As emphasized, the two studies reported in this chapter deal with producing actual changes in behavior by changing CO components and clusters. In this respect, the two studies share with many other psychological studies the problems attendant upon producing and evaluating change. The major problems are usually identified as being methodological, for instance, complications involved in repeating after the change manipulation the original or equivalent behavioral measure, or the necessity of controlling for the unknown effect of the premanipulation base level on the amount and direction of ensuing change.

In addition to these relatively traditional problems of change studies, there are problems specific to our domain of interest. First, testing our major hypothesis depends on the possibility of changing experimentally only CO components or CO clusters, or both, without affecting the expected behavior in any other way, indeed without suggesting to the subjects in any form what the expected behavior is. In this respect our studies differ radically from other projects focusing on change, such as those centering on changing achievement behavior (Kolb, 1965; McClelland, 1965; McClelland & Winter, 1969). Since the major aim of these earlier studies was to attain changes in behavior regardless of method, and since their underlying theory supported eclecticism of ways and means, it is only natural that the applied methods were diverse, referring not only to beliefs but also to action strategies, programs, and actual training of habits (see, for example, Alschuler, Tabor, & McIntyre, 1970). Indeed, even psychotherapy proper is not particular about changing any specific factor or inducing change through a particular agent. What restrictions exist within certain schools pertain more to using particular techniques than to barring other techniques that may be—and usually are—used simultaneously. But proving the determinative role of CO with regard to behavior requires focusing on changing only the CO; hence the selection of methods designed to change CO alone becomes a crucial issue. Incidentally, these requirements also entail a major restriction on the technique or techniques that may be used in any one study.

A second and related problem peculiar to this domain consists in our inability, for the time being, to specify the nature and extent of the changes in CO necessary to bring about the expected behavioral changes. Our hypothesis asserts that changes in CO cause changes in behavior. But our present state of ignorance precludes hypothesizing which CO component is changed first, how the change in any one CO component affects other CO components, how changes in CO components proceed after termination of the treatment or manipulation, and how long it takes to change the CO components to any appreciable degree.

A third and final problem, unlike the two just described, is general rather than specific to our domain, and of a psychological rather than methodological nature. It concerns the morality of changing behavior. By morality we are not referring to some metaphysical ethics but to the possible consequences of changing a certain aspect of behavior. The consent of subjects or parents (if subjects are children) to the change process may constitute an adequate response to the legal problem of invasion of privacy, but not to the moral problem. In order to be fully able to decide whether one agrees to a change process, one needs to know all the implications and consequences of changing a certain facet of behavior; yet psychological knowledge is severely limited in this respect. Therefore, in addition to the formal consent of subjects—or their parents—we relied on our own conviction as psychologists that the change, should it occur, would not harm the individuals in any way. Adhering to this conviction has greatly limited the range of behaviors to whose change we could apply ourselves. Furthermore, it sometimes necessitated a departure from common research paradigms, as in Study I, in which we dealt with raising the level of curiosity but not with lowering it.

STUDY I
Changing Curiosity

PURPOSE AND HYPOTHESES

The major purpose of the study was to investigate the relation of experimentally induced changes in CO clusters to resulting changes in behavior. A second purpose was to explore the utility of verbal discussions, persuasion, and communication of information in small groups as a method for inducing changes in CO. A third purpose was to examine

This study was carried out with Mrs. Tirza Boas. It was presented by Mrs. Tirza Boas as a Master's thesis, in partial fulfillment of the requirements of an M.A. degree at the Department of Psychology, Tel Aviv University, 1974.

the dynamics of change over time. Since the changes in CO and in behavior were examined a short time after and again a relatively long time after the experimental treatment, it was possible to explore how the changes on the two levels proceed and possibly interact with the passage of time.

It is evident that the first and the third purposes depend on the second, insofar as changes in CO are assumed to be the necessary and sufficient condition for changes in behavior. Thus, if the method used for inducing changes in CO is inadequate, no resulting behavioral changes can be studied immediately or at any later date. However, studying the adequacy of the method for changing CO is itself dependent on the basic hypothesis that CO can be changed at all.

The fact that the subjects of the study were preschool children imparts special interest to the second purpose. Indeed, attitude-change techniques have been developed only with regard to more adult subjects and have hardly been employed at all with children. Possibly investigators assumed that children are largely inaccessible to verbal persuasion techniques or that they do not have sufficiently stable and well-formed beliefs and attitudes. Neither assumption has been tested. Moreover, regardless of the method applied, there is some question whether children tend to change their beliefs at all under experimental conditions. The problem is far from trivial; if children regard beliefs in an anthropomorphic manner or anchor them in the dictates of some authority figure, they may not feel able or entitled to change beliefs even when convinced of the correctness of other beliefs. In contrast, we assumed that children would change beliefs in response to attitude-change techniques since these rely mainly on persuasion, which is so prominent and ubiquitous in the educational process at all levels. Thus, our attempt to apply attitude-change techniques to children may shed new light on hitherto hardly explored aspects of these techniques as well as on the cognitive life of children.

Curiosity was the domain to which our change efforts were applied. We chose to change the CO and behavior of curiosity mainly because of the beneficial effects shown to accrue from a raised level of curiosity. For example, curiosity is related positively to creativity (Day, 1968; Maw & Maw, 1964; Penney, 1965), to concept formation and adequate understanding of the environment (Minuchin, 1971), to attention to stimuli (Berlyne, 1957, 1958a, b), to motivation for learning (Fowler, 1965; McReynolds, Acker, & Pietila, 1961), to positive changes in IQ over time (Kagan, Sontag, Baker, & Nelson, 1958), to adjustment to the classroom, teacher, or peers (McReynolds et al., 1961), to social competence (Banta, 1970; King, 1969), and so on. Nevertheless, besides some general suggestions (e.g., Bruner, 1966; Day, 1968; Schermann, 1966; Suchman, 1961; Susskind, 1970), no method was devised for raising curiosity in children. Hence the importance of an attempt such as ours to develop a method for changing curiosity in children.

We had two main hypotheses. The first was that there would be changes in CO following the experimental treatment. Since, as mentioned, we dealt only with raising the level of curiosity and not with lowering it, the expected changes in CO were in the direction of higher scores. This hypothesis involves the assumptions that CO is amenable to change, and that persuasion, discussion, and communication of information in small groups are useful for changing beliefs at large and in children specifically. If the hypothesis is disconfirmed, there is of course no way to determine which of these assumptions was wrong. The hypothesis refers in general terms to changes, that is, rises in CO, and not to any specific changes in any one or more CO components, which could not be predicted owing to lack of firm knowledge. We will, however, use the data in order to explore such issues as whether all or only some CO components are affected, whether they are affected equally, whether the extent of change in CO depends on the prior level of CO scores, and how durable the changes in CO are.

The second hypothesis was that changes in CO would lead to expected changes in behavior. More specifically, we expected that those subjects manifesting increases in the CO of curiosity would also have increases in curiosity behaviors relative to their pretreatment stage, as compared to subjects who received the experimental treatment but did not respond by increasing their CO level, and as compared to control subjects who received no experimental treatment. Since experimental subjects with no CO increases might still be affected by the treatment though not in a manner or to a degree that became manifested in their CO, comparisons with this group are not interpretable in a completely unambiguous manner. Thus, the major burden of testing the hypothesis unequivocally and conclusively rests on comparing those subjects in the experimental groups who benefited from the treatment in a manner manifested in CO changes with control subjects who neither underwent experimental treatment nor evidenced any changes in CO. The hypothesis, it should be noted, refers to the effect of changes in CO on behavior in rather general terms. Owing to lack of sufficient knowledge it was not possible to refer in the hypothesis to specific issues such as the nature of the affected behaviors, the extent of the behavioral changes, their durability, and whether they would occur immediately after treatment or at a later date. The data, however, were used to explore these issues.

METHOD

Subjects. The subjects of the study were 59 preschool Israeli children enrolled in the last preschool kindergarten year, which in Israel forms part of the compulsory education system. The children frequented two different kindergartens. The original sample included 63 children, 4 of whom dropped out in the course of the study owing to sickness or refusal to participate. The final sample consisted of 29 boys and 30 girls. The mean age of the children at the beginning of the study was 5.4 years, the age range being 4.10 to 5.11 years. The socioeconomic status of the children's families was middle- or lower-middle class. About half the fathers were workers, mostly professional workers, and the rest were clerks, merchants, or self-employed. They lived in urban quarters characterized by marked social mobility, where the population consisted mainly of essentially lower-class families whose economic level improved sufficiently to afford a move to these relatively better residential surroundings. This socioeconomic background was considered favorable to the goals of the study insofar as the children could be assumed neither to be so positively oriented towards curiosity that no improvement would be possible nor so disadvantaged that no readiness, willingness, or ability to participate in this kind of study could be expected.

Procedure. The study included three stages. In the first stage all subjects were administered the CO questionnaire of curiosity and a series of tasks designed to provide behavioral measures of curiosity (see "Tasks and Variables"). The questionnaire and the various tasks were administered in random order. In the second stage, which took place only a few days after termination of the first stage, the subjects got the experimental treatment designed to raise the level of their procuriosity CO clusters and consequently also of their behavioral curiosity. For this purpose the subjects were divided into three groups on the basis of their responses to the CO questionnaire of curiosity. There were no significant differences in the mean number of procuriosity responses in the three groups. The means were 53.78 ($SD = 24.9$) in one group, 51.18 ($SD = 24.8$) in the second group, and 53.19 ($SD = 23.9$) in the third group. Initially the number of subjects in each group was 21, but because of dropouts it became 19, 19, and 21, respectively. The subjects in the three groups were of the same age, included about the same number of boys and girls, and included about the same number of children from each of the two kindergartens. The three groups were assigned randomly to the roles of experimental or control groups. One of the groups was an experimental group designed to be retested a week after termination of the treatment

TABLE 9.1
An Outline of the Treatment Administered to Experimental Groups 1 and 2

Aims	Auxiliary Materials	Themes of Discussion
	Session 1	
1. Creating a pleasant group atmosphere, allaying possible anxiety, explaining goals, establishing trust in experimenter. 2. Producing awareness of the existence of various modes of exploring and satisfying curiosity.	Small dolls and toy animals that move their limbs in various directions when a certain spot is pressed.	1. Various possible modes of exploring and their advantages and disadvantages. 2. Taking a thing apart—when forbidden and under which conditions permissible and desirable.
	Session 2	
1. Increasing interest in some unknown object. 2. Increasing interest in members of unknown lands and cultures.	A picture book about the life of a black girl in Africa. The book was wrapped in several colored papers and tied with several interesting ties.	1. Finding out about the hidden and not present. 2. Questions about the unknown and not understood as a means for knowing. 3. Learning about people from other countries and about their life and various experiences.
	Session 3	
1. Producing awareness of the adequacy of different modes of exploring for different problems. 2. Clarifying conditions under which it is desirable to ask adults.	A small battery-operated ventilator wrapped in several colored papers and tied with several interesting ties.	1. Finding out about the hidden and unknown. 2. Learning to operate devices. 3. Defining conditions under which child should ask adult. 4. Defining conditions under which adult is capable and willing to answer.

	Session 4		
1. Increasing awareness of the relations between the unknown and the new. 2. Reducing fear of the unknown.	A hidden whistle producing a special sound.	1. Exploring the bizarre. 2. Relations between unfamiliar and novel people, objects, or events. 3. Fear of the unknown and its manifestations. 4. Modes of coping with this fear 5. Defining conditions under which fear is justified and helpful and conditions under which it should be reduced.

	Session 5		
1. Repeating and summarizing themes discussed in sessions 1–4. 2. Clarifying points that remained unclear and strengthening beliefs that remained too weak or unsupported.	All those used in sessions 1–4.	Major themes raised in sessions 1–4.

243

(Experimental 1; $n = 19$), another was an experimental group designed to be retested two months after termination of the treatment (Experimental 2; $n = 19$), and the third served as a control group ($n = 21$). The two experimental groups were treated in an identical manner. For purposes of treatment, each of the three groups was split into two subgroups of 9 to 10 children each. The children assigned to a subgroup belonged to the same kindergarten so that they knew each other. Each subgroup had five experimental treatment sessions, 20–30 minutes long, held on the grounds of the kindergarten. The five sessions took place in the course of two weeks, that is, there were two or three sessions per week.

The experimental treatment consisted in discussing a few themes intimately related to curiosity, as shown by the CO questionnaire of curiosity (see Chapter 8, Study III) and informal conversations with children not included in our sample. The themes centered on the existence of various means of pursuing curiosity and of exploring, the possible problems involved in exploring (e.g., conflict with adults, stumbling against taboos, anxiety, etc.), the beneficial effects of curiosity, and the advantages (or disadvantages) of knowledge. Each session had a central theme (see Table 9.1). A session started with a common summary of the last session, proceeded with a discussion of the central theme, and ended with an outline of the next session's theme. A pleasant atmosphere was maintained throughout the group discussions and liberal use was made of various concrete aids, mainly toys and pictures, to help the children concentrate on the theme being discussed. Special care was taken not to point out behavioral implications or encourage certain behaviors while discouraging others. The experimenter focused on facilitating the participation of the individual children, shaping group discussion, and imparting relevant information whenever necessary. Although the drawing of conclusions was encouraged, no general conclusions or conclusions binding in any sense were reached. Table 9.1 summarizes the major procedural features of the experimental treatment.

The control subgroups met with the experimenter for the same number of sessions as the experimental subgroups. The sessions were of the same duration. However, no themes were discussed or games played that were in any way relevant to curiosity; instead, the experimenter organized various games or told stories that were later discussed by the children. The control subgroups were intended not only to control for the factors of passage of time and group sessions with an unfamiliar experimenter, but also to prevent the teachers in the kindergartens from knowing which children got the procuriosity experimental treatment and which did not.

In the third stage of the study all children were retested on the CO questionnaire of curiosity and the tasks providing behavioral measures of curiosity. As mentioned, Experimental Group 1 and the control group were retested a week after termination of the treatment, while Experimental Group 2 was retested two months after termination of the treatment. The testing in the first and third stages was done by experimenters who did not know the goals of the study and to which groups the children were assigned.

TASKS AND VARIABLES

Two tasks were used to assess the behavioral manifestations of curiosity. The tasks were selected on the basis of previous studies that dealt with identifying the main types of curiosity (Kreitler, Zigler, & Kreitler, 1975) and with predicting these various types of curiosity by means of CO scores of curiosity (Kreitler, Kreitler, & Zigler, 1974; this book, Chapter 8, Study III). The two selected tasks provided measures reflecting three of the curiosity factors: manipulatory curiosity, perceptual curiosity, and curiosity about the complex. There were two reasons for this choice. First, manipulatory and perceptual curiosity were found to be the major, the dominant, and also the best-defined types of curiosity in children. This is not the case with curiosity about the complex, which was included for control purposes, mainly because one measure reflecting it is derived from the same task that provided the measures for perceptual curiosity. Second, the selected tasks were shown to provide measures of curiosity that were predicted significantly on the basis of CO scores. Ease of administration in field conditions outside the laboratory and the possibility of devising parallel sets of measures for repeated administration were additional though secondary factors that influenced the choice of tasks. Hence, some of the tasks were similar but not identical to those used in the studies mentioned above.

The task designed to provide measures of manipulatory curiosity consisted of presenting the child with two toys that lend themselves to many and varied manipulations: a board with a number of moving and removable flaps and bars, and a regular kaleidoscope (in the pretreatment stage); and a concrete truck that could be taken apart or reconstructed, and a kaleidoscope with a turnable headpiece (in the posttreatment stage). The child was invited to play with the toys if he wanted. Maximum duration was 15 minutes. The variables were: (1) total duration of play with the two objects (in seconds); and (2) total number of different manipulations of the two objects, as recorded by an experimenter once every half minute. Variables 1 and 2 reflect manipulatory curiosity.

The task designed to provide measures of perceptual curiosity and curiosity about the complex consisted of presenting the child with 5 pairs of stimuli, drawn in black ink on white cardboard. Each pair included one simple and one complex stimulus, exemplifying 5 complexity dimensions. There were 5 pairs for the pretreatment stage and 5 different pairs for the posttreatment stage. The 10 pairs were selected randomly from the 20 pairs used in Tasks A and B by Kreitler, Zigler, and Kreitler (1975) and were divided randomly into the pretreatment and the posttreatment sets. The experimenter showed the child each pair of stimuli for 1–2 seconds, then turned them upside down and asked the child to turn each picture and observe it as long as he or she wanted. The stimuli pairs were presented in random order. The simple and complex stimuli of each pair were shown randomly on the right and on the left. The variables were: (3) total duration of observing the simple stimuli in the 5 pairs (in seconds); (4) total duration of observing the complex stimuli in the 5 pairs (in seconds); and (5) the difference between the durations of observing complex stimuli and simple stimuli (in seconds). Whereas variable 3 reflects perceptual curiosity, variable 4 is loaded mainly on perceptual curiosity and also, to a small degree, on the factor of curiosity about the complex; variable 5 reflects curiosity about the complex.

The CO questionnaire administered to all children orally was the CO questionnaire of curiosity described in Chapter 8, Study III.

The actual measures used in the study were the difference scores between the post- and pretreatment stages. In order to determine changes in CO, the difference scores along the four CO components were divided by the standard deviation of the differences along the relevant CO component. The four standard scores thus obtained were summed; the summed measure reflected overall changes in CO.

RESULTS AND CONCLUSIONS

Since preliminary checks in the pretreatment stage showed no significant differences in the various measures between children of the three groups, or between the sexes and the kindergartens, the sample was treated as one homogeneous unit.

In order to test the first hypothesis, we first compared the two experimental groups and the control group for changes in the four CO components, singly and together. Table 9.2 shows that only in the case of general beliefs were the changes in one of the experimental groups significantly higher than in the control group. As a second step in testing the first hypothesis, we focused on those subjects who showed rises in CO regardless of how large or small they were. Since in the control group the

TABLE 9.2
Comparisons of the Two Experimental Groups and Control Group
with Respect to Changes (Summed Standard Scores) in CO Components

Variables and Groups	$\overline{X}$	SD	Significance of Differences[a]		
			$q_{r,a-b}$	$q_{r,a-c}$	$q_{r,b-c}$
Beliefs about self					
a. Experimental 1	.25	.68	< 1	2.00	1.36
b. Experimental 2	.16	.63			
c. Control	−.03	.55			
Beliefs about goals					
a. Experimental 1	.28	.93	< 1	1.27	1.00
b. Experimental 2	.22	.85			
c. Control	.00	1.13			
Beliefs about norms					
a. Experimental 1	.06	1.00	< 1	< 1	< 1
b. Experimental 2	.26	1.11			
c. Control	.13	.85			
General beliefs					
a. Experimental 1	.35	1.09	< 1	2.83*	3.11[1]
b. Experimental 2	.41	.85			
c. Control	−.27	.97			
Total					
a. Experimental 1	.94	2.88	< 1	2.22	2.44
b. Experimental 2	1.05	3.25			
c. Control	−.17	2.53			

[a] Testing the significance of differences was done in terms of the q_r statistic following Duncan's (1955) procedure.
[1] $p < .10$, two-tailed.   * $p < .05$, two-tailed.

difference in the summed standard scores of CO changes between subjects with rises in CO ($\overline{X} = 1.47$, $SD = 1.27$) and subjects with no rises, i.e., no changes or decreases ($\overline{X} = −1.66$, $SD = 2.11$) was nonsignificant, the changes in CO that occurred in this group were regarded as random fluctuations and the control group was treated as a homogeneous unit. Table 9.3 shows that in both experimental groups the "risers" (i.e., Experimental 1a and Experimental 2a) differed significantly from the "nonrisers" (i.e., Experimental 1b and Experimental 2b) as well as from the control subjects. In contrast, the "nonrisers" in both experimental groups did not differ significantly from the control subjects in the case of Experimental Group 2 but showed a slight difference from the controls in the case of Experimental Group 1. Comparisons showed that experimental subgroup 1a did not differ significantly in extent of

CO changes from experimental subgroup 2a. It is obvious that also the differences between experimental subgroups 1b and 2b were not significant. These findings imply that in 63.16% of the subjects of Experimental Group 1, and in 52.63% of the subjects of Experimental Group 2, there were appreciable rises in CO, significantly different from the random fluctuations in CO characteristic of the controls. If in addition we consider the fact that in experimental subgroups 1b and 2b as well as in the control group there was a tendency toward decreases in CO, the rises in the experimental subgroups 1a and 2a become all the more significant. The occurrence of essentially the same findings immediately after the experimental treatment and two months later testifies to the durability of the changes in CO. It is noteworthy that in adults as well the applied techniques of discussion, persuasion, and communication of information are far from attaining perfect and dramatic results in all subjects; hence the findings we got seem to us satisfactory, since they show that the method can be used for changing CO in a predictable manner and that it is applicable to children. Thus, the findings lend support to the first hypothesis.

In summary, the findings demonstrate that changes in CO are possible even in children, are variable in extent, subject to individual differ-

TABLE 9.3

Comparisons of Total Change in CO Components (Standard Scores) in the Two Experimental Groups and the Control

Variables and Groups[a]	n	$\overline{X}$	SD	Significance of Differences[b]		
				$q_{r,a-b}$	$q_{r,a-c}$	$q_{r,b-c}$
Total change in CO components (standard scores)						
a. Experimental 1a	12	2.76	1.91	7.17**	4.35**	2.83[1]
b. Experimental 1b	7	−2.04	1.44			
c. Control	21	−.17	2.53			
Total change in CO components (standard score)						
a. Experimental 2a	10	3.46	2.71	7.49**	5.34**	2.15
b. Experimental 2b	9	−1.63	1.57			
c. Control	21	−.17	2.53			

[a] Experimental subgroups "a" included subjects whose CO rose, and experimental subgroups "b" included subjects whose CO did not rise or decreased.

[b] Testing the significance of differences was done in terms of the q_r statistic following Duncan's (1955) procedure.

[1] $p < .10.$ ** $p < .01.$

ences, and sufficiently durable to remain constant after two months. The data were explored further in order to learn more about changes in CO. Accordingly, comparisons of means (Table 9.4) and an analysis of variance (Table 9.5) of the standard scores of subjects with rises in CO show that in both experimental groups the four CO components were affected to an equal degree. Further, comparison of the changes in CO in subjects with high and low initial pretreatment levels of CO scores showed that in the two experimental groups the rises in CO were significantly greater in those subjects with low prior CO scores than in those

TABLE 9.4
Standard Scores of Subjects with Rises in CO Components

Groups	BS	Go	N	GB
Experimental 1a				
$\bar{X}$[a]	.56	.69	.45	1.06
SD	.49	.81	.86	.71
Experimental 2a				
$\bar{X}$[a]	.54	.88	1.10	.94
SD	.52	1.09	.80	.81

[a] None of the differences between the means within each group is significant following the Newman-Keuls procedure.

TABLE 9.5
Analysis of Variance of Standard Scores
of Subjects with Rises in CO Components

SOURCE OF VARIATION	EXPERIMENTAL 1a			EXPERIMENTAL 2a		
	df	MS	F	df	MS	F
Between subjects	11	.89		9	2.04	
Within subjects	36	.51		30	.38	
CO components	3	.84	1.75	3	.66	1.89
Residual	33	.48		27	.35	

with high prior CO scores (Table 9.6). The fact that the difference was not significant in the control group corroborates our earlier conclusion that the changes in the control group were merely random fluctuations.

Practically, the results imply that the rises in CO in experimental subgroups 1a and 2a were sufficiently pronounced to make possible the testing of the second and major hypothesis of the study, which refers to the expected changes in behavior following changes in CO. Obviously, in testing the second hypothesis it is mainly the "risers" in CO who have to be considered relative to the control subjects. Moreover, as men-

TABLE 9.6
Comparisons of Changes in CO Components
in Subjects with High and Low Pretreatment CO Scores

| GROUPS | HIGH PRIOR CO | | | LOW PRIOR CO | | | |
	n	$\overline{X}$	SD	n	$\overline{X}$	SD	t
Experimental 1	12	−.02	2.51	7	2.61	2.70	2.13*
Experimental 2	9	−.55	2.28	10	2.83	3.46	2.49*
Control	11	−.84	2.62	10	.57	1.07	1.58

Note. High CO scores are defined as COs 4, 3, and 2; low CO scores, as COs 1 and 0.
* $p < .05$, two-tailed.

tioned, the subjects of experimental subgroup 1b, who had significantly lower changes in CO than the subjects of experimental subgroup 1a, nevertheless showed sufficient evidence of rises in CO to be slightly distinguishable from the control subjects (Table 9.3). In line with the second hypothesis, these subjects may be expected to evidence behavioral changes corresponding to their CO changes. More specifically, from the viewpoint of changes along the behavioral measures, the subjects of subgroup 1b and perhaps also of 2b will occupy some intermediate position between the experimental "risers" in CO and the control subjects.

In testing the second and major hypothesis we focused on comparisons between those experimental subjects with rises in CO (subgroups 1a and 2a), those experimental subjects with no rises in CO (subgroups 1b and 2b), and the control subjects. The statistical method used in the comparisons was Duncan's procedure for multiple a posteriori comparisons. In spite of the fact that our comparisons were a priori, we selected this a posteriori method, which was strict relative to our design, not only because the comparisons were not independent from each other but also in order to place our major hypothesis under stringent testing conditions. The results, summarized in Table 9.7, show that in the first testing period the experimental subgroup of "risers" in CO (1a) had significantly greater rises than the control group in all the five behavioral measures of curiosity. In the second testing period, the "risers" in CO (2a) had significantly greater rises than the control group in three of the five behavioral measures of curiosity. In the other two measures the differences were only in the expected direction. It should, however, be noted that one of these two measures was the difference between the durations of observing complex and simple stimuli, which reflects curiosity about the complex, a type of curiosity that probably develops in general at a later age than manipulatory and perceptual curiosity.

These results indicate that increases in CO are accompanied by increases in the relevant behavioral measures. This was shown to be true with regard to all behavioral measures in the first testing period, and with regard to most measures even after two months. Indeed, we have no cogent explanation for the nonsignificant finding in the case of two measures in the second testing period. It lies near at hand to suggest that the enormous rates of variance in our measures rendered demonstration of significance particularly difficult. But then these high rates of variance themselves stand in need of explanation. Moreover, they were characteristic of all measures in this study and not only of the two that turned out nonsignificant results in the second testing period. However it may be, the findings lend strong support to the second hypothesis.

Further supportive evidence may be derived from examining the results of the "nonrisers" in the two experimental groups (subgroups 1b and 2b). As predicted, neither the subjects of 1b nor the subjects of 2b differed significantly from the control subjects along any of the five behavioral measures. This finding strengthens our former conclusion regarding the dependence of changes in behavior on changes in CO. Indirectly it also confirms the fact that the experimental treatment focused exclusively on changing CO and not on changing behavior directly. However, as we mentioned, the subjects of 1b and 2b were expected to occupy some sort of an intermediate position, not merely because they were exposed to the experimental treatment but mainly because—at least in regard to subgroup 1b—there was evidence that they had somewhat higher increases in CO than the control subjects (Table 9.3). The intermediate position of these subgroups is evident in the degree of their rises in the behavioral measures of curiosity, which in all cases lies between the extremes of the "risers" in CO and the control subjects. In addition, their intermediate position is indicated by the fact that though their increases in behavior did not differ significantly from those of the control subjects, they differed from the increases of the "risers" in CO in Experimental Group 1 mostly only at the .10 level and did not differ significantly from the increases of the "risers" in CO in Experimental Group 2. In summary, the results concerning the experimental subgroups 1b and 2b suggest that in future studies the second hypothesis can be stated in a quantitative functional form, implying that the extent of changes in CO will determine the extent of changes in the behavioral measures.

Finally, it should be noted that the subjects of experimental subgroup 1a do not differ significantly from the subjects of experimental subgroup 2a in any of the behavioral changes. This finding indicates that the behavioral changes attained through changing CO were durable and constant.

In sum, the results of this study support two major conclusions: CO

TABLE 9.7
Comparisons of Experimental Groups and Control Group
with Respect to Changes in Behavioral Variables

Variables and Groups	$\bar{X}$	SD	Significance of Differences[a]		
			$q_{r,a-b}$	$q_{r,a-c}$	$q_{r,b-c}$
Group 1					
Duration of play					
a. Experimental 1a	278.08	320.15	2.79[1]	4.29**	1.51
b. Experimental 1b	142.71	222.47			
c. Control	69.52	137.84			
Number of manipulations					
a. Experimental 1a	7.83	11.58	2.74[1]	4.71**	1.97
b. Experimental 1b	3.86	6.81			
c. Control	1.00	8.70			
Duration of observation: simple stimuli					
a. Experimental 1a	23.71	26.44	2.08	3.40*	1.32
b. Experimental 1b	2.21	20.18			
c. Control	−11.45	39.50			
Duration of observation: complex stimuli					
a. Experimental 1a	45.54	62.87	2.99*	3.74*	< 1
b. Experimental 1b	.93	29.44			
c. Control	−5.76	47.12			
Difference of observation: complex and simple					
a. Experimental 1a	17.38	23.97	2.76[1]	2.89*	< 1
b. Experimental 1b	−.71	19.98			
c. Control	−1.57	26.13			

can be changed through experimental treatment without undue difficulties, even in children, and experimentally introduced changes in CO bring about expected changes in behavior. Both changes in CO and the corresponding changes in behavior persist at least for two months, which indicates their relative constancy and greatly reinforces our conclusions about the potency of CO changes in bringing about behavioral changes.

TABLE 9.7 (cont'd)

Variables and Groups	X	SD	Significance of Differences[a]		
			$q_{r,a-b}$	$q_{r,a-c}$	$q_{r,b-c}$
Group 2					
Duration of play					
a. Experimental 2a	161.09	310.02	1.41	1.23	< 1
b. Experimental 2b	55.25	137.76			
c. Control	69.52	137.84			
Number of manipulations					
a. Experimental 2a	4.91	9.46	2.19	2.87*	< 1
b. Experimental 2b	1.50	3.97			
c. Control	1.00	8.70			
Duration of observation: simple stimuli					
a. Experimental 2a	34.38	51.09	2.38	4.00**	1.62
b. Experimental 2b	7.14	20.48			
c. Control	−11.45	39.50			
Duration of observation: complex stimuli					
a. Experimental 2a	42.81	61.79	2.15	3.58*	1.43
b. Experimental 2b	13.64	20.45			
c. Control	−5.76	47.12			
Difference of observation: complex and simple					
a. Experimental 2a	8.94	26.13	< 1	1.46	1.12
b. Experimental 2b	6.50	16.69			
c. Control	−1.57	26.13			

[a] Testing the significance of differences was done in terms of the q_r statistic following Duncan's (1955) procedure.
[1] $p < .10$, two-tailed. * $p \leq .05$, two-tailed. ** $p < .01$, two-tailed.

STUDY II
Changing Pain Tolerance

PURPOSE AND HYPOTHESES

The major purpose of the study was to test several hypotheses derived from the CO theory under conditions involving an experimental manipulation of variables. The manipulated variables were beliefs of the four types, the behavioral intent, and the behavioral program. The manipula-

See source note to Chapter 7, Study V.

tion took place by means of induced role playing. The dependent variable was behavioral. It was the threshold of pain tolerance, which was shown to be predictable on the basis of CO scores (Chapter 7, Study V). Thus, all our hypotheses refer specifically to this and related variables and not to other variables in the same domain, such as the sensitivity threshold, the pain threshold, and pain evaluation, that were not related to CO scores.

A secondary purpose of the study was to examine induced role playing as a method for changing factors of major importance for behavior according to the theory of cognitive orientation. The advantages of the method are obvious: it is fast in application, it makes possible a focused and circumscribed change in any of the factors singly or in combination, and it provides far-reaching control over the kind of change induced in the subject. These and other advantages apply, of course, only if the method is of actual operative value, objectively with regard to its effects on the manipulated variables, and subjectively with regard to its psychological effects on the subjects.

The first and main hypothesis was that induced changes in major cognitive factors underlying behavior evocation would result in corresponding changes in behavior, the amount of change being greatest when beliefs of the four CO components are changed, less when the behavioral intent is changed, and least when the program is changed. This order is hypothesized both relatively, when the effects of changes in the three factors are compared, and absolutely, when the experimental subjects and the control subjects are compared. Thus, the effect of changing beliefs is expected to be greatest, the effect of changing the program is expected to be minimal if significant at all, and the effect of changing the behavioral intent is expected to fall between these two extremes. In view of the central role assigned to the four CO components in the CO theory, it is obvious why we hypothesize that changing beliefs would have the strongest effect on behavior, that is, stronger than the effect of changing the behavioral intent without changing its underlying CO cluster, and stronger than the effect of changing the program. This part of the hypothesis not only derives directly from the CO theory but is also supported by many studies that show the dependence of pain tolerance on various cognitive contents, such as causal attributions (Nisbett & Schachter, 1966), information about future pain (Jones, Bentler, & Petry, 1966), cognitive dissonance (Zimbardo et al., 1969), and culturally determined values and attitudes (Zborowski, 1969). Furthermore, since the behavioral program serves mainly to implement the behavioral intent, we expect that changing the behavioral intent would have a greater effect on behavior than changing the behavioral program. The three-stage decreasing order of effectiveness (CO cluster, intent, program) is hypothesized in regard to behavioral changes both in the direction of increased pain tolerance and in the direction of decreased pain tolerance. In addition, it should apply regardless of the sex of the subjects and their CO prior to the experimental manipulations. It is evident that the hypothesized order of effectiveness is in a way counter to common sense since it is based on assigning less effectiveness to a factor the nearer it is to actual behavior. Yet, by the same token, it is a cognitive order par excellence.

The second hypothesis refers to the interaction between the subject's CO prior to the experiment and the direction of the experimental manipulations. The direction of the induced role playing may be in accord with the subject's prior CO score, as when a subject with a high CO for pain tolerance gets instructions supporting increased pain tolerance, or a subject with a low CO gets instructions supporting decreased pain tolerance; or it may run counter to the subject's prior CO score, as when a subject with a high CO gets instructions supporting decreased pain tolerance or vice versa. The second hypothesis was that the effect on pain tolerance of the experimental manipulation would be greater when the manipulations were in accord with the subject's prior CO than when they were counter to it. The rationale for this hypothesis is that if manipulations correspond to the CO level, they strengthen already existing tendencies, whereas if they do not correspond, they are not only unsupported by existing tendencies but may induce in the subject a state of tension or conflict that may further reduce her or his ability to comply with the instructions. Accordingly, a corollary of the second hypothesis was that the assumed conflict of subjects undergoing experimental manipulations counter to their CO would manifest itself in higher ratings of difficulty of the experiment and lower ratings of subjectively felt success in the experiment by these subjects than by subjects who underwent experimental manipulations in accord with their COs.

Finally, we used this experiment to examine the problem of whether responses to CO questionnaires are affected by an immediately preceding behavior relevant to the contents of the CO questionnaire. The problem is important not only because of the light it might throw on the stability and origins of responses to CO questionnaires but also because Bem's (1972) claim about beliefs as the product of behavior would lead us to expect a shift of CO in the direction of the behavior just completed. In contrast, the CO theory, which attributes a primacy to beliefs, would lead us to expect no changes in CO to adapt it to immediately preceding behavior. (Incidentally, this does not refer to the long-term impact of behavior on CO, which is one of the ways output behavior may exert a feedback effect on the formation of future CO clusters.) The fact that the preceding behavior was induced through role playing does not change either the inference from Bem's thesis or the hypothesis deduced from the CO theory, since the particular effectiveness of role playing for changing attitudes has often been demonstrated (Elms, 1969). Thus, the third hypothesis was that CO scores and CO components based on the responses of subjects to a questionnaire administered immediately after termination of the behavioral task would not differ significantly from CO scores and CO components based on the responses of subjects to the same questionnaire administered earlier, before the behavioral task and without any obvious connection to it.

METHOD

Subjects. The subjects were 112 students, 56 males and 56 females, 18 to 27 years old, from the departments of psychology and social sciences at Tel Aviv University. The subjects volunteered for the study in partial fulfillment of their duties during the freshman and sophomore years.

Procedure and Design. All subjects participated in two sessions, 4–6 weeks apart. One session was a group session devoted to the administration of the CO questionnaire of pain tolerance (Chapter 7, Study V). The other session was an individual session consisting of two phases. The first phase, already described (Chapter 7, Study V, "Procedure and Materials"), was devoted to measuring the thresholds of sensitivity, pain, and pain tolerance and getting the subject's pain evaluation. As far as the present study is concerned, the role of this first phase was to provide baseline measures of the relevant dependent variables prior to the manipulations.

There was an interval of 7 minutes between the first and second phases of the experimental session. The second phase was devoted to experimental manipulations designed to check the hypotheses of the present study (concerning the experimental manipulations see also "Role-playing Behavior," below).

The overall structure of the study corresponded to a $3 \times 2 \times 2 \times 2$ factorial design plus a control group. The first factor reflected the type of the experimental manipulation. Its three levels were manipulation of beliefs of the four CO components, manipulation of the behavioral intent, and manipulation of the program. The second factor was the CO of the subject prior to the experimental manipulation. The two levels of this factor were a high CO score (i.e., a CO score of 3 or 4) or a low CO score (i.e., a CO score of 1 or 0). The third factor reflected the direction of the experimental manipulation, which was designed either to raise the threshold of pain tolerance and thus make the subjects tolerant of higher degrees of pain or to lower the threshold of pain tolerance and thus make the subjects tolerant of lower degrees of pain than they were prior to the experimental manipulation. The fourth factor, sex, consisted of males and females, who were found to differ in all three relevant thresholds, females having lower values than males in the thresholds of sensitivity, pain, and pain tolerance (Chapter 7, Study V).

Thus, there were 24 experimental subgroups, with four subjects in each. In addition, there was a control group designed to provide a check on the effects of prior CO and sex in the absence of any experimental manipulations. Thus, it included four males with a high CO, four females with a high CO, four males with a low CO, and four females with a low CO. Prior to beginning the experiment it was determined on a completely random basis which type of manipulation a subject would undergo and in which direction, or whether he or she would be assigned to the control group. The experimenter did not know the subject's CO.

The instructions to the control subjects were: "Now, we will repeat again the same procedure as before [as in the first stage of the experimental session]. I will ask you to put your hand on the instrument [the shock-dispensing device] and will gradually raise the intensity of the electric current from zero on. Your task will be to say 'Now' when you first feel the slightest sensation, to say 'Painful' when you first feel the slightest pain, and to say 'Stop' at the instant you cannot tolerate the pain any more and want it stopped."

The subjects of the groups in which beliefs were manipulated were told that the procedure of the first phase would be repeated but that they were to behave like a person who holds beliefs like those mentioned in a list of beliefs presented to them. The typed list was given to the subject, who was told: "Read attentively the following statements. While you read them try to feel as if *you* are thinking these thoughts, as if they are *your* thoughts and beliefs." After the subject finished reading the list of 11–12 statements, he or she was asked to concentrate on the "thoughts" for approximately 3 minutes, trying to identify with and feel like the person whose thoughts these were. At the end of this period the list of beliefs was taken away, and, as in the control groups, the subject was reminded of the three stages in the procedure referring to the thresholds of sensitivity, pain, and tolerance. The statements in the list included beliefs of the four types, selected from the CO questionnaire of pain tolerance (Chapter 7, Study V) because they had highest discriminability and were evaluated by judges as clear in contents and concise in form. Subjects of the four subgroups designed to undergo a manipulation for the increase of pain tolerance got a list of 12 beliefs supporting high pain tolerance, such as, "A person should learn to suffer relatively slight pain in order to make himself tough and develop his ability to undergo hardships," and "I have never given in because of any difficulty." Subjects of the four subgroups designed to undergo a manipulation for the decrease of pain tolerance got a list of 11 beliefs supporting low pain tolerance, such as, "I would like to learn to accept things as they are without trying to be a hero," and "No reason in the world can justify voluntary exposure to pain."

The subjects of the groups in which the behavioral intent was manipulated were told that the procedure of the first phase would be repeated but that they were to behave like a person who has decided to "tolerate as much pain as possible" (if the manipulation was designed to increase pain tolerance) or "tolerate only a very slight degree of pain" (if the manipulation was designed to decrease pain tolerance). A card with a typed statement of the appropriate behavioral intent was then given to the subject, who was asked to read it, trying "to feel as if *you* decided it, as if this were *your* decision." Then the subject was asked to concentrate on the "decision" for approximately 3 minutes, attempting to identify with it. At the end of this period, the card was withdrawn, and the subject was reminded, as in the control groups, of the three stages of the procedure.

The subjects of the groups in which the behavioral program was manipulated were told that the first phase would be repeated but that they were to behave like a person following a procedure corresponding to the one to be given to them. The typed description was given to the subject, who was asked to read it trying to feel as if this were *his* or *her* procedure. After the reading, the subject was asked to concentrate on the "procedure" for approximately 3 minutes, trying to identify with and feel like the person whose "procedure" it was. At the end of this period the card was taken away and, as in the control groups, the subject was reminded of the three experimental steps. Subjects of the subgroups designed to undergo a manipulation for the increase of pain tolerance got as program a procedure consisting of two steps: first, reclining comfortably in a chair, relaxing, while breathing 20 regular and deep breaths without moving or speaking; and second, imagining that he or she was in a particularly pleasant situation, moving the head slightly as a sign that the mental image was clear, and attempting to maintain the image and keep distant from the experimental situation while getting the electric shocks. The pleasant situation was described by the subject prior to the experiment and its details were repeated in the instructions given by the experimenter. Subjects of the subgroups designed to get a manipulation for the decrease of pain tolerance got as program a procedure consisting of four steps: (1) sitting motionless for a minute concentrating on any slightest bodily sensations of pricking, pain, etc.; (2) repeating to oneself three times regularly and voicelessly: "It will be very painful"; (3) giving the experimenter a sign to start the experiment by moving the head slightly; and (4) repeating to oneself regularly and continuously: "Stop, stop, it is *very* painful." Both "procedures" were pretested for feasibility and efficiency.

The administration of shocks immediately followed the presentation of the instructions. The thresholds of sensitivity, pain, and tolerance were recorded. After the subject asked to stop the shocks (i.e., reached the threshold of pain tolerance), he or she was requested—as in the pre-manipulation phase—to evaluate the intensity of the experienced pain on a scale ranging from 0 ("not at all painful") to 100 ("very painful"). In addition, the subject was asked to evaluate the degree of difficulty and the degree of his or her success in carrying out the instructions of the second phase of the experimental task on two separate scales each ranging from 0 to 100. Finally, before leaving, the subject was requested to answer again the whole of the CO questionnaire of pain tolerance.

In sum, the independent variables of the study were the type of manipulation, the direction of manipulation, prior CO, and sex. The major dependent variables were the difference between the tolerance threshold after and before manipulation in absolute and transformed (i.e., $\Delta x/x$) values, the difference between the tolerance and pain thresholds after manipulation (found in Chapter 7, Study V to be the least contaminated variable), and the evaluation of difficulty and success in performing the task. Other variables were included in the elaboration of data mainly for purposes of comparison.

Role-playing Behavior. Since our experimental manipulation relies heavily on role playing, we consider it necessary to deal at least briefly with doubts raised recently about the adequacy of role playing as a substitute for the "real" behavior of subjects in an experimental situation.

A. G. Miller (1972, p. 626), in reviewing the literature known to him, argued that role playing is a "cognitive construction by the subject of how he might respond were the situation genuine." Similarly, McGuire (1969, p. 52) states that "we feel intuitively that . . . [the] approach of having quasi-subjects tell us how the experiment would probably come out had we done it will prove quite limited." To this Miller (1972, p. 627) adds that "man's actual rather than self-hypothesized behavior is the only ultimate criterion." Miller, however, does not present any empirical evidence demonstrating the inadequacy of role playing as a substitute for experimental behavior. Instead, he tries to support his claim by showing that studies purporting to show the adequacy of role playing (Darroch & Steiner, 1970; Greenberg, 1967; Horowitz & Roths-child, 1970; Willis & Willis, 1970) fail to do so.

However, Miller's argument is theoretically unconvincing and in regard to empirical evidence utterly incomplete. Even the definition of role playing as conceived by Miller and the authors he quotes reveals ignorance of the frequently demonstrated potentialities and applications of role playing. Role playing, as originally introduced by Moreno (1946, 1959) and developed by him and his numerous students, is rarely if ever a verbal report of what the subject would do were he in this or that situation. Mostly it is actually enacted behavior in a situation in which some of the real elements are missing and, hence, have to be imagined, provided that the subject is instructed to enact his or her own role. Which features of the situation are left for construction through imagination depends on the experimental or therapeutic design. For instance, in role playing "conditioned response" the CS may be left to imagination while in role playing "reaction to insulting stimuli" the insulting words may be uttered by the experimenter but the insulting intention has to be imagined by the subject. Conclusions drawn from role-playing behavior about real-life behavior are theoretically as sound and empirically as valid as conclusions drawn from experimental performance in the lab about performance in real life. Reaction times registered in the laboratory do not necessarily hold for performance outside the lab.

From the viewpoint of cognitive orientation both real behavior and psychodramatic behavior are determined by CO clusters and available programs. Hence, the equivalence or difference between real behavior and role-playing behavior depends on the degree of similarity of these elements. This problem is not central for our present study, since, as mentioned, we suggested to our subjects beliefs, behavioral intents, or programs. Thus the role-playing task consisted in imagining that these proposed beliefs or intents or programs were their own for the duration of the experiment.

However, even in those role-playing experiments in which subjects were not presented with a predetermined CO cluster or behavioral intent or program but were merely asked to act as if they were in a certain situation, the recorded behavior of the subjects proved convincingly similar to their behavior as recorded in corresponding life situations. Thus, actual behavior and role-playing enactment were found to correspond with regard to responses to frustration (Borgatta, 1952), social aggressiveness (Rotter & Wickens, 1948), interpersonal competence and autonomy (Stanton, Kurt, & Litwak, 1956), a series of 31 different behaviors including social behaviors, emotional behaviors, behavior in work, behavior with regard to eating, sleeping, etc. (Kreitler & Kreitler, 1968b), and a series of 8 social behaviors such as being active verbally, beginning conversations, etc. (Raz, Kreitler, & Kreitler, 1976). The variety of behaviors and the range of different subjects in these studies greatly reinforce the conclusion that psychodramatic role-playing behavior may faithfully reflect behavior in real-life situations. Moreover, the work of

Moreno and numerous studies by psychodramatists around the world (see the *Journal of Psychodrama* and *Group Psychotherapy*) show that the emotional intensity of psychodramatic role-playing behavior compares well with that observed in everyday life behavior.

Another argument frequently raised against the validity of role-playing behavior is that it reflects attitudes rather than actual behavior (Banuazizi & Movahedi, 1975). If attitude is measured as it usually is (sec Chapter 12), through statements that reflect beliefs of one or two CO components, then role-playing behavior, just as actual behavior, is mostly unrelated to attitudes (Raz, Kreitler, & Kreitler, 1976). Similarly, contrary to the common assumption (Banuazizi & Movahedi, 1975; Bem, 1967) that responses to questions of the type "how would you behave if/when . . ." reflect actual behavior or role-playing behavior, it was shown that role-playing behavior—like actual behavior—is unrelated to such responses (Borgatta, 1952). However, role playing is not a magic wand. Studies and the rich psychodramatic experience show that if role-playing behavior is to reflect reliably behavior in life an adequate technique must be employed. Otherwise the subject may well be induced to play his ideal self, or his conception of what the experimenter might like to observe, and so on.

RESULTS AND CONCLUSIONS

The data of the study were subjected to four-factor analyses of variance complemented by analyses of the differences between the experimental and the control groups (Winer, 1971, pp. 468–473) and comparisons between specific means as dictated by a priori hypotheses (Winer, 1971, p. 384ff.).

Testing the three hypotheses of the study depends on a prior demonstration of the utility of the method used for the experimental manipulations. If the role-playing method was effective then we would expect subjects who got role-playing instructions supporting increase of pain tolerance to tolerate pain more than subjects who got role-playing instructions supporting decrease of pain tolerance. Table 9.8 shows that for all three variables relevant to pain tolerance (see columns 3, 4, and 10) the main effect due to direction of manipulation was significant beyond the .01 level. Further, Table 9.9 shows that the means of pain tolerance in the subgroups that underwent manipulations designed to increase pain tolerance were always higher than the means in the subgroups that underwent manipulations designed to decrease pain tolerance. The interactions between direction of manipulation, type of manipulation, and prior CO level are irrelevant from the viewpoint of the utility of the method and will be dealt with in the appropriate context. It may,

TABLE 9.8
Four-Factor Analyses of Variance of Differences in Thresholds
and of Evaluations Following Experimental Manipulations

SOURCE OF VARIATION	df	DIFFERENCE IN SENSITIVITY THRESHOLD[a]		DIFFERENCE IN PAIN THRESHOLD[a]		DIFFERENCE IN TOLERANCE THRESHOLD[a]		TOLERANCE MINUS PAIN THRESHOLD[b]		DIFFERENCE IN PAIN EVALUATION[a]	
		MS	F	MS	F	MS	F	MS	F	MS	F
Between cell	23										
Control vs. all others	1	.00	<1	201.52	1.55	79.41	<1	3.87	<1	688.10	2.56
Type of manipulation (A)	2	73.70	<1	107.51	<1	116.37	1.39	353.09	4.27*	183.07	<1
CO (B)	1	404.26	3.20	10.67	<1	201.26	2.40	981.76	11.88**	337.50	1.26
Direction of manipulation (C)	1	380.01	3.00	840.17	6.45**	5445.09	64.90**	1007.51	12.19**	10626.04	39.60**
Sex (D)	1	27.09	<1	416.67	3.20	133.01	1.58	173.34	2.10	37.50	<1
A × B	2	3.20	<1	82.88	<1	38.79	<1	15.88	<1	311.72	1.16
A × C	2	.82	<1	37.63	<1	520.87	6.21**	365.01	4.41*	2790.88	10.40**
B × C	1	137.76	1.09	216.00	<1	388.01	4.62*	68.34	<1	651.04	2.43
A × D	1	215.53	1.70	14.26	<1	44.29	<1	258.22	3.12	85.16	<1
B × D	1	1357.51	10.73**	400.17	<1	1.26	<1	201.26	2.43	266.67	<1
C × D	1	184.26	1.46	24.00	<1	364.26	4.34*	98.01	1.19	876.04	3.26
A × B × C	2	188.57	1.49	20.09	<1	50.17	<1	22.72	<1	836.20	3.12
A × B × D	2	140.70	1.11	164.13	1.26	63.29	<1	46.13	<1	62.76	<1
A × C × D	2	126.07	<1	33.22	<1	24.67	<1	2.26	<1	297.13	1.11
B × C × D	1	58.59	<1	4.17	<1	10.01	<1	162.76	1.97	1.04	<1
A × B × C × D	2	326.66	2.58	104.51	1.12	94.29	1.12	.76	<1	583.07	2.19
Within cell	87	126.48		130.15		83.90		82.66		268.32	

SOURCE OF VARIATION	df	DIFFICULTY EVALUATION[b]		SUCCESS EVALUATION[b]		TRANSFORMED DIFFERENCE IN SENSITIVITY THRESHOLD[c]		TRANSFORMED DIFFERENCE IN PAIN THRESHOLD[c]		TRANSFORMED DIFFERENCE IN TOLERANCE THRESHOLD[c]	
		MS	F	MS	F	MS	F	MS	F	MS	F
Between cell	23										
Control vs. all others	1	10529.17	12.42**	12994.08	21.44**	1.84	<1	8.71	1.09	8.31	1.72
Type of manipulation (A)	2	78.38	<1	422.65	<1	4.88	<1	4.91	<1	4.44	<1
CO (B)	1	25.04	<1	2252.34	3.72	15.12	2.01	2.38	<1	25.80	5.36*
Direction of manipulation (C)	1	150.00	<1	219.01	<1	39.07	5.20*	80.24	10.11**	382.52	79.52**
Sex (D)	1	459.37	<1	846.09	1.40	.71	<1	30.27	3.81	5.37	1.12
A×B	2	283.07	<1	1610.15	2.66	.64	<1	2.02	<1	3.69	<1
A×C	2	1969.53	2.32	1204.95	1.99	2.25	<1	2.25	<1	23.38	4.86*
B×C	1	600.00	<1	58.59	<1	15.92	2.12	8.45	1.07	22.69	4.72*
A×D	1	211.72	<1	344.53	<1	13.22	1.76	1.57	<1	2.20	<1
B×D	1	876.04	1.03	283.59	<1	58.37	7.76**	18.68	2.35	.55	<1
C×D	1	104.17	<1	1971.09	3.25	9.75	1.30	.19	<1	12.13	2.52
A×B×C	2	333.59	<1	825.78	1.36	9.67	1.29	1.21	<1	2.61	<1
A×B×D	2	361.20	<1	366.41	<1	20.60	2.74	12.55	1.58	5.90	1.23
A×C×D	2	883.07	<1	1875.78	3.09	3.69	<1	2.99	<1	.39	<1
B×C×D	1	4.16	<1	31.51	<1	4.29	<1	.02	<1	.97	<1
A×B×C×D	2	356.51	<1	176.82	<1	15.60	2.07	11.68	1.47	4.19	<1
Within cell	87	847.63		606.03		7.52		7.94		4.81	

[a] The variable reflects the difference between the measure after and the same measure before the manipulation.

[b] The variable reflects only measures taken after the manipulations.

[c] The variable reflects a transformation $\Delta\chi/\chi$ of the difference between the measure after and the same measure before the manipulation.

* $p < .05$.   ** $p < .01$.

TABLE 9.9

Comparisons Involving the Relations between Direction of Manipulation, Type of Manipulation, and Prior CO

MANIPULATION	DIRECTION OF MANIPULATION		CO (HIGH, LOW) & DIRECTION OF MANIPULATION				CONTROL
	Increase	Decrease	H Increase[a]	L Decrease[b]	H Decrease	L Increase	
Variable: Difference in sensitivity threshold							
Beliefs	2.88	−.75	4.00	3.75*	−5.25	1.75	
Intent	4.13	−.13	4.25	4.50*	−4.75	4.00	
Program	6.06	2.00	2.25	2.62	1.37	9.87	
Total	4.36	.37	3.50	3.62	−2.87	5.21	2.37
	$F = 1.08$	$F = .09$					
Variable: Difference in pain threshold							
Beliefs	1.12	−6.81	1.00	−4.37	−9.25	1.25	
Intent	−.87	−4.50	2.00	−5.50	−3.50	−3.75	
Program	3.50	−2.69	6.25	− .62	−4.75	.75	
Total	1.25	−4.67	3.08	−3.50	−5.83	−.58	2.12
	$F = .27$	$F = 2.52$					
Variable: Difference in tolerance threshold							
Beliefs	10.81	−12.50	11.62	−12.12	−12.88	10.00	
Intent	3.81	−10.87	9.12**	−10.25**	−1.50	−11.25	
Program	3.75	−3.44	8.00**	−2.75	−4.12	−.50	
Total	6.12	−8.94	9.58**	−8.38	−6.17	−.58	1.00
	$F = 7.90**$	$F = 7.67**$					
Variable: Tolerance minus pain threshold							
Beliefs	20.75	14.06	23.50**	9.12	13.50	12.17	
Intent	15.06	11.31	20.75	1.75	5.87	18.00	
Program	12.81	3.81	16.50*	11.25	16.87	9.37	
Total	16.21	9.73	20.25*	7.37	12.08	13.18	12.44
	$F = 10.87**$	$F = 9.26**$					
Variable: Difference in pain evaluation							
Beliefs	17.19	−19.37	23.75	−18.75	−27.50	13.12	
Intent	15.62	−10.62	18.12	−11.25	−2.50	10.62	
Program	−1.87	−2.19	2.50	0.00	−4.37	−6.25	
Total	10.31	−10.73	14.79	−10.00	−11.46	5.83	6.87
	$F = 4.80**$	$F = 4.25*$					

TABLE 9.9 (cont'd)

MANIPULATION	DIRECTION OF MANIPULATION		CO (HIGH, LOW) & DIRECTION OF MANIPULATION				CONTROL
	Increase	*Decrease*	H *Increase*[a]	L *Decrease*[b]	H *Decrease*	L *Increase*	
Variable: Transformed difference in sensitivity threshold							
Beliefs	1.14	−.54	1.63	.41	−1.49	.66	
Intent	1.22	−.24	1.48	.96	−1.45	.96	
Program	1.39	.71	.68	.97	.45	2.10	
Total	1.25	−.02	1.26	.78	−.83	1.24	.98
	$F = 1.36$	$F = .30$					
Variable: Transformed difference in pain threshold							
Beliefs	.67	−1.77	.90	−1.41	−2.14	.44	
Intent	.05	−1.44	.58	−1.77	−.48	−1.11	
Program	.82	−.73	1.42	−.35	−1.11	.22	
Total	.52	−1.31	.97	−1.18	−1.45	.06	.39
	$F = .33$	$F = 1.60$					
Variable: Transformed difference in tolerance threshold							
Beliefs	2.61	−3.04	3.06	−3.18	−2.89	2.15	
Intent	1.29	−2.81	2.84**	−3.07	−2.55	−.27	
Program	1.07	−1.16	2.07**	−.85	.07	−1.47	
Total	1.65	−2.34	2.66**	−2.37	−2.30	.65	.44
	$F = 4.48*$	$F = 8.54**$					

[a] Asterisks in this column mean that the difference between "High, Increase" and "Low, Increase" is significant.
[b] Asterisks in this column mean that the difference between "Low, Decrease" and "High, Decrease" is significant.
* $p < .05$.   ** $p < .01$.

however, be mentioned that role-playing instructions in the "increase" direction had a greater impact on females than males (Table 9.8, column 3). Yet this fact in no way detracts from the utility of the method. In sum, the cited findings clearly demonstrate the effectiveness of the role-playing technique.

The first hypothesis focuses on type of manipulation. The data demonstrate that changing beliefs of the four CO components had a strong effect on behavior, that changing the behavioral intent had a lesser effect, and that changing the program had a mostly nonsignificant effect. Since there is a significant interaction between the type of manipulation and the direction of manipulation (see columns 3, 4, and 10 in Table 9.8), and since the positive and negative effects of the manipulations in the two directions ("increase" and "decrease") tend to cancel each other when combined, the effects of type of manipulation have to be considered separately for the two directions of manipulation. Table 9.9 (i.e., rows 3, 4, and 8) shows that the differences between changed beliefs, changed intent, and changed program are highly significant for all three focal variables, in both directions ("increase" and "decrease"), and the means reflecting the amount of change are always in the hypothesized order of magnitude: the change in pain tolerance was greatest when beliefs were changed, less when the behavioral intent was changed, and least when the behavioral program was changed.

Moreover, overall significant differences of this kind and the hypothesized order of the means occur in the three variables reflecting changes in pain tolerance, and not in the case of changes in the thresholds of sensitivity and pain. However, they do occur with regard to changes in pain evaluation as well. This was not hypothesized, because in the premanipulation stage (Chapter 7, Study V) pain evaluation was found to be related neither to CO scores nor to pain tolerance. Yet, though pain evaluation and pain tolerance remain unrelated for the whole sample also after the manipulations, the moderate premanipulation relation between them in the subgroups with a low CO ($r = .25$, $p < .05$) rises remarkably after the manipulation ($r = .78$, $p < .01$), whereas in the subgroups with a high CO it decreases (before: $r = -.29$, $p < .05$; after: $r = -.11$, n.s.). Moreover, the changes in pain evaluation and in pain tolerance after and before manipulation are also correlated ($r = .52$, $p < .01$). These facts might explain why the first hypothesis was confirmed with regard to pain evaluation as well.

No evaluation of the findings is complete without examining the effectiveness of the three types of manipulations relative to the changes of pain tolerance in the control group. Comparisons between the six experimental subgroups and the control group in terms of our three focal variables (rows 3, 4, and 8 in Table 9.9) show that only the following differences in mean changes are significant: in the variable of difference in tolerance threshold, only the subgroups "beliefs, increase" ($F = 9.18$, $df = 1/87$, $p < .01$), "beliefs, decrease" ($F = 12.61$, $df = 1/87$, $p < .01$), and "intent, decrease" ($F = 9.29$, $df = 1/87$, $p < .01$) differ from the control group; in the variable of tolerance minus pain threshold only the subgroup "beliefs, increase" ($F = 6.68$, $df = 1/87$, $p < .01$) differs from the control; and in the variable of transformed difference in tolerance threshold, "beliefs, increase" ($F = 7.83$, $df = 1/87$, $p < .01$), "beliefs, decrease" ($F = 20.14$, $df = 1/87$, $p < .01$), "intent, decrease" ($F = 17.57$, $df = 1/87$, $p < .01$), and "program, decrease" ($F = 4.26$, $df = 1/87$, $p < .05$) differ from the control group. These findings show that in five out of six cases the subgroups in which beliefs were changed differed from the control group. The changes occurred as often in the direction of "increase" as in the direction of "decrease." In contrast, in only one out of six cases did a subgroup in which the program was changed differ from the control group. The situation with regard to intents is similar: only in two out of six cases did the changes differ from those in the control group.

Notably, the one case in which changing the program had a significant effect and the two cases in which changing the intent had a significant effect involved manipulations designed to decrease pain tolerance. It seems intuitively convincing that it should be easier to lower pain tolerance than to increase it, at least when one does not offer subjects anything more substantial than an intent or a program unsupported by beliefs. The reason for this seems to be the existence of some permanent CO for suffering as little pain as possible.

In sum, changing beliefs is not only a more potent means of causing changes in behavior than changing intents or programs; it is often the only efficient means of doing so. Moreover, the findings also lend support to the validity of the experimental manipulations. Contrary to the possible claim that the manipulations are not independent (since by changing the intent we may have also changed beliefs indirectly, etc.), the findings show that the manipulations were sufficiently independent of one another to demonstrate the clear superiority of changing beliefs over changing intents or programs.

The second hypothesis deals with the interaction between the direction of the manipulation and the subjects' prior CO level. The occurrence of this interaction with regard to the absolute and transformed values of the difference in tolerance threshold (Table 9.8) supports our hypothesis. As a matter of fact, our hypothesis involved a threefold expectation, which may be checked taking into account the type of manipulation as well. The first expectation was that increases in pain tolerance would be higher in the subgroups with a high level of prior CO than in those with a low level of prior CO. Table 9.9 shows that this expectation was confirmed except in the case of beliefs in the variables of absolute and transformed difference in tolerance threshold and in the case of intent in the variable of tolerance minus pain threshold. We venture to suggest that the nonconfirmation of our expectation in those subgroups that underwent belief change testifies to the overpowering impact of changing beliefs, which may be even stronger than the effect of the prior CO level. The second expectation was that decreases in pain tolerance would be greater in subgroups with a low level of prior CO than in those with a high level. This expectation was confirmed only in the case

TABLE 9.10
Mean Evaluations of Difficulty and Success

Manipulation	CO High, Decrease (1)	CO Low, Increase (2)	CO High, Increase (3)	CO Low, Decrease (4)	$\overline{X}$ of (1) & (2)	$\overline{X}$ of (3) & (4)
	Variable: Evaluation of difficulty					
Beliefs	31.87	54.37	35.00	26.87	43.13	30.94
Intent	47.50	33.12	29.37	45.00	40.31	37.19
Program	38.75	41.25	46.25	34.37	40.00	40.31
Total	42.92	39.37	36.87	35.42	41.15	36.15
	Variable: Evaluation of success					
Beliefs	64.37	45.00	47.50	56.87	54.69	52.19
Intent	61.87	46.25	85.00[a]	49.37	54.06*	67.19
Program	62.50	59.37	51.87	58.12	60.94	55.00
Total	62.92	50.21	61.46	54.79	56.56	58.13

[a] This value differs significantly ($p < .10$) from the two values in the same column and from the three corresponding values in the same row.
* $p < .05$.

of the intent in the variable of absolute difference in tolerance threshold. Again, it seems that the impact of the present manipulation is stronger than that of the prior CO. Finally, the third expectation was that subjects undergoing manipulations counter to their prior CO would experience the task as more difficult and their performance as less successful than subjects undergoing manipulations in accord with their COs. The data presented in Table 9.10 do not support this expectation in any way. It is difficult to account for this fact. Since the evaluations of difficulty and success were sensitive only to the gross difference between the experimental groups and the control group (Table 9.8; difficulty was lower and success higher in the control groups), it is possible that these variables were not refined enough to reveal the presence of tension, conflict, or even mere discomfort. In sum, support for the third hypothesis is not convincing. There is indeed evidence for an interaction between the direction of manipulation and prior CO level, but when examined in terms of the subgroups of type of manipulation it appears to be mostly absent when decreases of tolerance are involved and when the manipulated factor is beliefs. These facts as well as the absence of evidence for conflict when the manipulations contrast with the prior CO demonstrate the potency of the method we have used for the experimental manipulations. It seems as if the subject concentrates almost completely on the experimental instructions, immersing himself in the induced role playing to such an extent that even the effects of his own CO tend on occasion to be temporarily suspended. If our conclusion is correct, it should increase confidence in the findings concerning the first and major hypothesis.

The last problem to be raised refers to the third hypothesis, which concerns the effect of an immediately preceding behavior on subjects' responses to the CO questionnaire. As may be remembered, the CO questionnaire was administered in a group session 4–6 weeks before the experimental session, and again immediately upon completion of the behavioral task at the end of the experimental individual session. Comparison of the means in the four CO components and the CO scores before and after the manipulations (Table 9.11) shows that there were absolutely no significant differences in any of the subgroups reflecting type of manipulation, direction of manipulation, CO, or sex, and hence also not in the sample as a whole. As may be expected, the intercorrelations between each of the CO components as well as the CO scores before and after the manipulations are also highly significant (Table 9.12). Moreover, subjecting the differences between the administrations "after"

TABLE 9.11

Means of CO and Its Components before and after Experimental
Manipulations in Subgroups Reflecting Type of Manipulation,
CO, Direction of Manipulation, and Sex

CO	TIME	TYPE OF MANIPULATION			CO		DIRECTION OF MANIPULATION		SEX	
		Beliefs	Intent	Program	High[a]	Low	Increase	Decrease	Male	Female
N	Before	9.75	9.68	9.50	11.48*	7.81	9.67	9.62	9.56	9.73
	After	9.50	9.90	9.84	11.17*	8.33	10.00	9.50	9.87	9.62
GB	Before	11.44	11.53	11.50	13.12*	9.85	11.44	11.54	11.60	11.37
	After	11.06	11.75	11.40	12.71*	10.10	11.35	11.46	11.53	11.23
BS	Before	11.37	13.18	12.41	13.94*	10.71	12.14	12.50	12.83	11.81
	After	11.78	12.72	13.43	14.02*	11.27	12.27	13.02	13.06	12.23
Go	Before	10.53	11.59	11.75	13.17*	9.42	11.68	10.89	11.04	11.54
	After	10.47	11.16	11.62	12.69*	9.48	11.02	11.14	11.33	11.83
CO	Before	2.06	2.09	2.12	3.35*	.83	2.08	2.10	2.12	2.06
	After	1.75	2.12	2.15	2.75*	1.27	1.94	2.08	2.21	1.81

[a] Asterisks in this column denote significant differences between CO high and CO low.
* $p < .01$.

TABLE 9.12
Intercorrelations of CO and CO Components
before and after the Experimental Manipulations

		BEFORE				
		N	GB	BS	Go	CO
AFTER	N	.62*	—	—	—	—
	GB	—	.50*	—	—	—
	BS	—	—	.73*	—	—
	Go	—	—	—	.66*	—
	CO	—	—	—	—	.62*

* $p < .01$.

and "before" in each of the CO components and the CO scores to a four-factor analysis of variance ($3 \times 2 \times 2 \times 2$) in terms of type of manipulation, premanipulation CO level, direction of manipulation, and sex revealed that the differences in the four components could not be attributed to any main effect. The differences in CO scores, while nonsignificant as such, could be attributed to one main effect—not surprisingly, the prior level of CO. Finally, it should also be noted that even the pattern and degree of interrelations among the CO components and between each of them and the appropriate CO scores (Table 13.5) did not change from "before" to "after" the manipulations except in one case (the correlation BS-CO increased from .49 to .60, $z = 2.23, p < .05$). All these facts seem to demonstrate clearly that the experimental manipulations had no effect on responses to the CO questionnaire. Thus, they are in contrast to Bem's thesis but lend full support to the third hypothesis of the present study.

Summing up our findings leads to conclusions in several domains. Concerning the CO theory, the findings lend full support to our theoretical deductions about the crucial role of beliefs of the four types in steering behavior, as contrasted with the lesser role of the behavioral intent and the behavioral program when these are unsupported by an adequate CO. Moreover, our findings show that even if the CO questionnaire is administered immediately after a certain behavior has taken place, subjects do not change their CO to suit the behavior. This indirectly supports our claim that CO directs behavior rather than the other way round, as Bem would have it.

Concerning the method of induced role playing, our findings show that it is both objectively and subjectively a valuable and efficient tool for manipulating basic factors according to the CO theory of behavior and for studying their effects on the behavioral output.

Concerning pain, our findings show that pain tolerance is accessible to control through cognitive means, mainly the four CO components. This conclusion is in accord with the theory of Melzack and Wall (1965) about the role of central processes in pain. Moreover the findings show that manipulation of cognitive factors may affect not only actual pain tolerance but also the very sensation of pain, that is, its experiencing and evaluation. Indeed, pain tolerance and pain evaluation are in general unrelated, but they may become related, for example, in subjects with a low prior level of CO after experimental manipulations of pain tolerance. Our conclusions about the role of cognitive orientation factors with regard to pain tolerance make it possible to integrate varied findings about pain within the framework of one theory. For example, it lies near at hand to interpret the findings of Kanfer and Goldfoot (1966), Gelfand (1964), and Blitz and Dinnerstein (1968) as relating to the relative effectiveness of changing the behavioral intent and behavioral programs, and the findings about interpersonal and intercultural differences in pain tolerance (e.g., Petrie, 1967; Sweeney & Fine, 1965; Zborowski, 1969) as reflecting differences in beliefs of the four CO components with regard to pain tolerance. Concerning the phenomenon of pain as such it was also found contrary to the findings and claims of other investigators (Blitz & Dinnerstein, 1968; Gelfand, 1964; Wolff, Krasnegor, & Farr, 1964) that changing pain tolerance affects the pain threshold, too, but not the sensitivity threshold. Finally, it should be stressed that while females have lower thresholds of sensitivity, pain, and tolerance than males (Chapter 7, Study V), they were affected more than males by the manipulations designed to increase pain tolerance, whereas they reacted like males to the manipulations designed to decrease pain tolerance.

GENERAL CONCLUSIONS

The two studies described in this chapter deal with the problem of inducing changes in behavior by changing CO. The conclusion supported by the findings of both studies is that behaviors change following changes in CO. In Study I the changed behaviors were increased levels of curiosity as manifested in longer playing time with toys, more manipulations performed with each toy, longer durations of viewing simple stimuli, longer durations of viewing complex stimuli, and an increased difference in favor of viewing complex stimuli longer than simple stimuli. Indeed, all the behaviors that were predicted to undergo changes were affected in the expected direction. The same is true of Study II. Here the range of changed behaviors was limited—in line with the design of the experiment—to the threshold of pain tolerance, but it also included in effect pain evaluation. The changes were as expected in the direction of both increased and decreased pain tolerance and pain evaluation.

Our conclusion, that the studies prove that changes in CO bring about changes in behavior, is based mainly on the experimental design and the statistical elaboration. In Study I it was shown that the expected behavioral changes were significantly greater in the experimental subjects than in the untreated control subjects. Furthermore, those experimental subjects who received the treatment but did not evidence manifest changes in CO did not differ significantly in their behavioral changes from the untreated control subjects. In Study II not only were behavioral changes greater in the experimental subjects than in subjects receiving no role-playing instructions, but there were two additional types of control that buttress the causal inferences we are drawing. One consisted in the type of the experimental manipulation, the other in its direction. Thus, it was shown that behavioral changes were greatest following changes in CO components, much less following changes in the behavioral intent, and almost nonexistent following changes in programs —all this precisely in line with the theoretically derived hypotheses. Again, changes in behavior took place in both directions—increase and decrease—in correspondence with the experimental manipulation. In addition, in Study I there was further evidence for the causal link in the demonstration that the assumed changes in CO had actually occurred in subjects with appreciable increases in curiosity behaviors. Thus the two studies provide full support to the major corollary of one of the two general hypotheses of our theory (Chapter 1). The gist of the hypothesis is that knowledge about specific COs enables the prediction of ensuing molar behaviors. Correspondingly, the corollary is that induced changes in COs result in predictable changes in behavior. By supporting this corollary, the two studies provide an important proof for the validity of the CO theory in general and the determinative role played by CO scores with regard to molar behavior in particular. Moreover, since the two studies support the conclusion that CO changes bring about behavioral changes, they also indirectly legitimize a particular reading of the findings reported in Chapters 7 and 8. According to this reading the correlations between CO scores and behaviors are due to the causal relation of the former to the latter.

The major finding of the two studies, that CO changes are followed by behavioral changes, implies the possibility of changing beliefs. To demonstrate this possibility in regard to beliefs relevant for behavior is far from trivial, since in attitude change studies the changes have all too often been restricted to beliefs of relatively little import for the individual. Yet changing beliefs could be important not only for research but also for psychotherapy in the broadest sense of the term. Therefore, it may be useful to mention a few suggestions about conditions that facilitate or inhibit such changes. As the two studies show, subjects with relatively low CO clusters change more beliefs than subjects with relatively high CO clusters. Study II also indicated that certain types of change, viz., increase in the beliefs supporting pain tolerance, may be easier for women than for men. This difference may be due to the initial level or number of such beliefs or to the existence of other beliefs relevant to the issue of pain tolerance. More important indications may be derived from our study about quitting smoking (Chapter 7, Study VI), which did not deal directly with changing CO but rather with predicting which subjects would be behaviorally most affected by exposure to a technique designed to change behavior exclusively. Our success in identifying by means of CO clusters those subjects who changed or did not change behavior clearly suggests the existence of CO clusters orienting the individual toward changing the behavior under study. Two complementary interpretations suggest themselves: there are permanent CO clusters orienting the individual toward change or nonchange in general and/or there are permanent CO clusters orienting the individual toward change or nonchange of particular behaviors or domains in his or her life. Perhaps a general CO cluster of the former type is amplified by means of beliefs referring to the change of specific behaviors whenever such change becomes paramount. However it may be, such issues must be investigated in order to improve the possibilities of identifying subjects amenable to changes in CO and CO clusters amenable to changes.

The two studies also provide suggestive observations about the efficiency of two techniques for inducing changes in CO: the technique of discussion, persuasion, and communicating information in small groups, and role playing in accordance with experimental instructions. The major conclusion supported by the studies is that the two techniques are useful for obtaining the desired type of changes and do not impair the subjects' well-being. In evaluating the success of the method of Study I we have to bear in mind that the method was applied in the form of only five 20-30 minute sessions over 2 weeks; that the subjects were preschoolers; that the verbal comprehension and discussion skills the method requires are not very common at this age, particularly in lower-middle-class children; and that the method is not dramatically successful even with adults. In view of these facts, the attainment of changes in CO significantly different from those in the control group in 63% of the subjects immediately after the treatment and in 53% of the subjects 2 months later seems positive evidence for the method's objective efficiency. However, since the subjects, the domains of research, and the behaviors in the two studies were so different, there is no way to assess the relative efficiency of the two methods.

In any case, neither method for changing CO is perfect. The two methods as used by us so far are not sensitive enough to the particular structure and contents of beliefs to allow us to deal most efficiently with beliefs of the different CO components and to detect fine changes in beliefs. With more sensitive methods we could study the nature of the changes in beliefs of the different CO components, the rate of the changes, their sequence, extent, and interactions between them. Information on such issues would in turn increase the efficiency of the methods applied for changing beliefs, and at the same time enable finer analyses of the relations between changed beliefs and behavioral changes. We would thus be able to answer such questions as: What is the minimal extent of changes in CO necessary for bringing about changes in behavior? Does behavioral change depend on changes of beliefs of specific CO components or not? Must beliefs of all four CO components be changed in order to attain behavioral changes, or does changing beliefs in only some of the components suffice for changing at least certain types of behavior?

Thus, the issue of greater sensitivity in the methods involves not only devising techniques for changing beliefs or belief clusters in a differentiated manner geared to the specific contents and structure of beliefs. It also implies the need for techniques sufficiently sensitive to detect changes in beliefs. The problem is complex, since the changes may first occur on a level different from that of CO components proper. For example, the changes may affect the meaning of the relevant beliefs and thus also their cognitive orientativeness long before the actual phrasing of the beliefs is changed in accord with the transformed meaning; or the changes may affect the interrelations between the relevant beliefs and thus their belongingness to one or another cluster within a CO component, before the belief itself is discarded or otherwise amended. Moreover, sometimes owing to the fact that a particular belief is supported by many other beliefs of the individual himself or beliefs that are shared by other members of his social group or culture, the phrasing of a belief may not undergo change even though its meaning has changed. This possibility is particularly likely since many individuals hold beliefs that are identical or similar in wording but very different in the meanings assigned to them. Truisms are a prime example. Although we still know too little to choose among the possibilities we have suggested—and others not yet formulated—we already know enough to infer that examining the meaning of the beliefs and their meaning values must form integral elements in any method designed to detect and diagnose changes in beliefs.

Abnormal Behavior

MALFUNCTIONING AND SYMPTOMS

Thus far we have presented the CO theory and experiments assuming optimal contents, structure, and functioning of the interacting components. In describing the basic theory we did not discuss the possibility of deviations from the normal course of processes, apart from a passing reference to conflicts; in reporting the experiments individual differences manifested by our subjects were treated as normal variations contributing statistically to the error term. Therefore, before we turn to studies dealing with abnormal behaviors, it is necessary to preface these reports with a short analysis of the possible foci of disturbances and their probable behavioral impacts.

If we view the CO theory as a model of behavior elicitation and guidance we discover two principal sources of pathological output behavior:

1. Pathogenic content or content constellations, e.g., pathogenic meanings, pathogenic beliefs, and pathogenic CO clusters, which were formed by "normal" beliefs but are pathogenic because of their overall meaning and associated pathogenic behavioral programs.

2. Pathogenic functioning, e.g., formation of two CO clusters, two behavioral intents, and/or two behavioral programs; emergence of CO clusters that do not yield any behavioral intents; production of incomplete CO clusters, or of pseudo CO clusters, namely, clusters in which norms fulfill the role of goals, goals the role of norms, etc.; and formation of behavioral intents that do not lead to any behavioral programs.

It is obvious that pathogenic content and pathogenic beliefs are likely to be interrelated. Ambiguous meanings may lead to the formation of incomplete CO clusters. Incompatible beliefs may result in the formation of two CO clusters and two conflicting behavioral intents that in turn may promote the adoption of a pathogenic behavioral program, and so on. Moreover, due to the complexity of neurotic and psychotic symptoms, it is plausible to assume, at least initially as a convenient working hypothesis, that pathogenic content and pathogenic functioning contribute separately, as well as in simultaneous or sequential collaboration, to the formation of the very same symptoms.

Since it is not our intention here to outline a psychopathology based on cognitive orientation (this will be the subject of a forthcoming book), we restrict ourselves to some indications of how cognitive orientation may account for different types of abnormal behavior. In doing so we will focus on the possible psychopathological role of different stages of CO formation and functioning. The reasons for this form of presentation are not only our present interest in demonstrating various aspects of the CO theory, but also two considerations that invalidate the alternative approach of focusing on symptoms or syndromes. First, as noted above, frequently more than one factor contributes to the formation of a particular symptom; second, professional labels like hysteric behavior or schizophrenia designate a great variety of pathological behaviors, which may thus derive from different types of pathogenic content and pathogenic functioning concomitantly or alternately.

The following discussion, then, may be viewed as a series of notes or remarks on the relations between CO theory and psychopathology. Some of these remarks reflect as yet untested hypotheses and deductions from the CO theory, some represent attempts to interpret findings of other investigators in terms of the CO theory, and others are based on our own experiments or on pilot studies and plain observations in the broad domain of abnormal behaviors.

Although there are indications of malfunctioning on the submolar level—e.g., retarded individuals and some schizophrenics evidence protracted orienting responses or even complete failure to inhibit such responses (Luria, 1963; Lynn, 1963; Vinogradova, 1961)—in the present summary only the most likely sources of disturbance on the molar level will be mentioned. So far we have isolated four such sources.

PATHOGENIC MEANING GENERATION

The number of meaning values and dimensions as well as the particular content of meaning values are likely to exert a pathogenic impact. In testing meaning generation, we observed that brain-damaged patients, individuals suffering from schizophrenia simplex, and some chronic catatonics produce extraordinarily few meaning values, most of which are concentrated within the framework of one meaning dimension. Hence, it may be concluded that these patients frequently encounter situations that they misunderstand and are unable to cope with adequately. They constitute the extreme opposite to the overinclusive schizophrenics, for whom, owing to overproduction of meaning values, the meaning of inputs becomes blurred to such an extent that their actions often seem to be unrelated to the stimulus situation. In general, however, schizophrenic patients of the various diagnostic classifications tend to use a more restricted range of meaning dimensions than normals but apply the meaning modes "exemplifying-illustrative" and "metaphoric-symbolic" more often than normals (S. Kreitler, 1965; Wanounou, Kreitler, & Kreitler, 1975).

Pathogenic content of meaning values is most evident in phobic patients who interpret certain exteroceptive inputs as "dangerous" and thus often feel threatened by imminent dangers, whereas their hypochondriac counterparts attach the meaning value "dangerous" unrealistically to a great many interoceptive or proprioceptive inputs, and thus often feel threatened by imminent diseases. The impressive success of behavior therapy in eliminating or at least reducing phobic and, to some extent, also hypochondriac symptoms shows that in these cases an induced change of meaning values may suffice to obtain the desired change of behavior (Valins & Nisbett, 1971). Pathogenic meaning values may also account for some lighter forms of reactive depression and moodiness. This latter point was already demonstrated by the well-known experiments of Schachter and Singer (1962) and others (Valins, 1970).

Frequently, however, the situation is far more complex. It is common knowledge that experimental subjects preoccupied with sex are more likely to interpret neutral inputs in a sexual sense than subjects preoccupied with, say, hunger. Hysterics tend, almost by definition, to oversexualize external and internal inputs to the cognitive system. Yet the hysteric behavior cannot be properly analyzed without considering the CO clusters initiated by these inadequate meaning values and the pathogenic behavioral programs for conflict resolution. The mere fact that a lady attributes to every man on the street sexual intentions toward her does not in itself suffice to make her hasten her steps or avoid walking alone. Particular CO clusters are required to produce the well-known hysteric conflict described by Freud. And even this conflict would not result in overt hysteric behavior without the adoption of a pathogenic behavioral program for the resolution of conflicts of this type. In other words, generation of a pathogenic meaning does not fully determine production of a pathogenic CO cluster nor does a pathogenic CO cluster enforce the adoption of a pathogenic behavioral program for performance.

The production of hallucinations also seems highly complex. Upon first consideration it may appear appropriate to regard hallucinations as resulting from mislabeling an internal stimulus as an external one, probably already on the level of meaning action, which is often regarded as the source of percepts. However, we have reason to believe that the distortion of these products of meaning action derives from previously produced and permanently stored pathogenic CO clusters. This process can be viewed as a kind of model for the genesis of many pathological symptoms. A stored CO cluster, perhaps only slightly pathogenic, interferes with future meaning action or meaning generation, which in turn predispose the production of more pathogenic CO clusters and behaviors, whose feedback again afflicts future meaning production, and so on. We regard this circularity or pathogenic spiral as a basic process of mental disease (H. and S. Kreitler, 1965).

PATHOGENIC CO CLUSTERS

Pathogenic CO clusters are defined as CO clusters that predispose toward pathological behavior. Such CO clusters may obviously result from pathogenic beliefs, that is, beliefs with explicit or implicit pathogenic content. Explicit pathogeneity may become evident in content that clearly deviates from that which is perceived or conceived by the majority of the members in the same sociocultural environment, e.g., "The sun is green," "Some people have the ability to control the minds and bodily functions of others from within," "I am an invisible microorganism," or "Bright colored flowers cause fatal diseases and should therefore be banished." Apart from such obviously pathogenic and unrealistic beliefs there are beliefs whose abnormality is more implicit. Sometimes it resides only in their extreme absoluteness or overgeneralization; at other times it becomes evident only in their implied meaning. Examples of the former type would be such beliefs as "All people should strive to be completely good and pure" or "No human being can ever be trusted." An example of the latter type, derived from our records, is the apparently harmless belief "I am often happy." Its pathogenic nature is revealed only when the meaning of "happy" is known to be "what I feel when I imagine myself thrusting a knife into a human body." Both explicit and implicit pathogenic beliefs may be spotted most frequently in the CO clusters of schizophrenic and manic-depressive patients.

However, deviant beliefs are by no means the only source of pathogenic CO clusters. More often than not pathogenic CO clusters consist of beliefs that, when examined each separately, prove to be rather normal and have no explicit or implicit pathogenic content. There is nothing inherently wrong with, say, the goal "I want to do whatever I do as well as possible," the norm "You should check everything critically, even your own performance" and the general belief "Even reliable people often err." But when these beliefs appear together with the common normal belief about self "I am frequently absent-minded and tend to overlook trivial and small details," they predispose toward obsessive behavior, for instance, returning five times to the entrance door to check and recheck whether it has been locked properly. In other words, the beliefs as such are not pathogenic, but the CO cluster is. Of course, obsessive behavior can also derive from a CO cluster containing one or more clearly pathogenic beliefs, such as "I want to be a hundred percent sure that everything I do is perfect," "I am completely unreliable," "There are always many thieves around my house," and "One should correct a mistake before one finishes committing it."

Psychopathic behavior frequently derives also from CO clusters whose harmful effect results from the juxtaposition of relatively normal beliefs. For instance, when reminded to pay back a debt, the psychopath may produce a CO cluster including such beliefs as "Debts have to be paid," "I want to keep the money for the time being," "There is always time enough to compensate for minor delays," and "Anyway, I am the happy-go-lucky type." Even the CO cluster of the hysteric lady mentioned above, who senses rapists all around the place, may consist of rather normal beliefs like "I am sexually very attractive," "I am often sexually attracted," "I want to stay an honest woman," "One should not have an affair with a stranger," and "Most men dream of raping innocent women."

Our pilot studies indicate, however, that a most important factor predisposing toward neurotic behaviors in general and hysteric behaviors in particular is the formation of two competing CO clusters, one of which is frequently less accessible to awareness than the other. Thus two competing behavioral intents are produced. In conjunction they constitute the classical conflict constellation, which, in turn, may strongly predispose toward the adoption of a pathogenic behavioral program. In the case of hysteric behavior, one CO cluster may consist only of sexually or aggressively toned beliefs while the other CO cluster reflects various moral constraints.

Abnormal behavior, and in particular schizophrenic symptoms, may also derive from faulty CO clusters in which one or two components are overemphasized at the expense of the other CO components, or from pseudo CO clusters, that is, incomplete CO clusters that are often completed by using the same belief for two different CO components. For instance, acting out violently may result from using the goal also as a pseudo norm, while catatonic inaction may result from using a norm as a pseudo goal. Yet in these cases as well the single beliefs seem abnormally extreme and frequently, though not always, based upon faulty meaning generation.

Several different schizophrenic symptoms indicate the probable pathogenic character of the belief hierarchies of schizophrenics. These hierarchies play a prominent role in clustering. In the domain of goals, for example, the second highest belief in a general or specific hierarchy of goal beliefs is often the complementary opposite of the highest goal belief(s) and is mostly equally distorted (see the following section). Thus if for some reason the patient is prevented from behaving in accordance with his predominant CO cluster, the alternative CO cluster may be expected to be no less pathological, and sometimes even more so. In terms of CO clusters the termination of an acute schizophrenic episode would often mean merely that the predominant cluster is relatively normal, while the underlying alternative clusters remain pathogenic. Should performance in accordance with this normal cluster encounter any difficulty, the underlying pathological clusters provide an easily available alternative, and a new episode may begin. Some psychiatrists and clinical psychologists are in the habit of designating this state of affairs as manifesting a "low frustration tolerance," which is often misleading. Usually the schizophrenic patient is admirably persistent in his pathological behavior, notwithstanding the efforts of his environment to discourage or frustrate the behavioral manifestations of his symptoms. Hence, the concept of low frustration tolerance may lead the therapist in the wrong direction, for instance, looking for anxiety or inhibited volition instead of searching for the underlying CO structures.

PATHOGENIC BEHAVIORAL INTENTS

Since the behavioral intent is a direct product of the CO cluster and is fully determined by it, its possible pathogenic nature and effects reflect the pathogeneity of the antecedent CO cluster. As may be recalled, the behavioral intent initiates the behavioral program and is involved in the control and completion of action. It is plausible to assume that there may be disturbances in these three basic functions.

A disturbance in the function of initiation may become manifest in such symptoms as long hesitation periods preceding action, inability to proceed beyond the final stages preparatory to action, and the formation of "delayed" behavioral intents designed for realization at a later, mostly indefinite, time. Operationally these difficulties consist in a weakening of the normally intimate bond between the behavioral intent and the behavioral program, and hence may be reflected in too few meaning values of the meaning dimension "manner of occurrence or operation" in the meaning of the behavioral intent (this chapter, Study III; Chapter 11, Study III). Difficulties in the function of initiation originate in the CO cluster that gives rise to a faulty behavioral intent. For example, a CO cluster predisposing toward indefinite delays in looking for a job may include the following beliefs of the four CO components: "I want to look for a job," "I want to be extremely successful," "A job should be very carefully chosen," "A job should not be changed too often," "I get crazy if I fail," "I can't afford to be unemployed," "There is always an optimal opportunity," and "Haste makes waste."

Disturbances in the function of control may become apparent, for example, in a symptom like the easy distractibility in action often observed in schizophrenics. The distractibility may indicate that, apart from a normal CO cluster from which the action derives, the person also holds a permanent belief such as "Everything I perceive and think is of such great importance that I have to attend to it at once." Another normal-sounding belief that might contribute to the formation of such a symptom is "Only the intellectual conception is important; the rest is merely boring routine."

Again, disturbances in the function of completion may be evident in the difficulty that many neurotic patients experience in completing an action and viewing it as completed without repeatedly attempting to go back to it, or in the difficulty of resuming an action once it is stopped for any reason. The former symptom may derive from a CO cluster including such beliefs as "No act is complete if it is not perfected," "A person should strive for perfection even though he cannot attain it," "I only want to do things I can do well," and "I enjoy work only if I can take my time about it."

The behavioral intent is involved in pathological symptoms also through its prominent role in conflicts. It should be reemphasized that the most common type of conflict is due to the formation of two competing behavioral intents. The CO theory indicates several cores of conflicts. Meaning generation may yield ambiguous or contradictory meaning values that may predispose toward the formation of a conflict on the level of CO clusters. Yet even without these conflict-laden meaning values CO clustering may produce conflicting beliefs that, if not reconciled, may lead to the concomitant emergence of two CO clusters. However, while ambiguous or contradictory meaning values and conflicting beliefs, if they at all enter the scope of awareness, may give rise to what is usually called doubt, the emergence of two concomitant clusters and, in particular, the resulting two behavioral intents always constitute a conflict. This conflict could be called "intentional conflict" and may be further specified as an approach-approach, approach-avoidance, or avoidance-avoidance conflict, in line with the content of the actions implied by the meaning of the relevant behavioral intents.

However, it should be emphasized that not all conflicts are pathogenic and not every pathological behavior pattern derives from conflicts. The pathogeneity of a conflict depends partly on its content but mainly on the character of the behavioral program used for its resolution.

PATHOGENIC BEHAVIORAL PROGRAMS

It is far from trivial to point out that an entirely normal behavioral intent may result in pathological behavior if it is implemented by means of a highly pathogenic behavioral program. Likewise, pathogenic behavioral intents and conflicts may not lead to pathological behavior provided that normal behavioral programs are adopted. Sometimes the pathological behavior of children and even of animals who live in a schizophrenic family setting is at least partly due to imitation and subsequent acquisition of unhealthy behavioral programs. The pathogeneity of a behavioral program consists in its explicit content, that is, the nature of the actions that constitute it, as well as in its intensity. This can be best understood by recalling that defense mechanisms are behavioral programs. The pathogenic character of some of the defenses, say, of regression, resides mainly in the "what" of the programmed action, whereas other defense mechanisms, for instance, repression, denial, and even rationalization, differ from the normal mainly in a quantitative sense. In fact, terms like rationalization, isolation, repression, and so on relate only to what we have called program schemes. They are general and therefore stand in need of an operational program in order to guide actual behavior. Each of these defense schemes is general enough to allow for different operational programs, some still in line with so-called normal behavior, others already considered pathological.

It stands to reason, though not necessarily to psychoanalytic reason, that a behavioral program can be pathogenic without being a defense mechanism (for instance, intolerance of ambiguity; see Kreitler, Maguen, & Kreitler, 1975). Defense mechanisms are behavioral programs for conflict resolution and reduction or avoidance of anxiety. A child may torture an animal because of displaced hatred toward a sibling, because of mere curiosity, or because of pure sadistic impulses that have not yet been curbed by any moral restraints. Considered from the viewpoint of the CO theory the same program of performance may implement behavioral intents deriving from three completely different CO clusters, a fact that should be taken into account if an attempt is made to determine whether the action has to be classified as pathological or not. This brings to mind that adopting identical behavioral programs for different behavioral intents may appear as normal economy, stupid blundering, pathological perseveration, or even fixation, depending upon the underlying CO cluster and the effectiveness of the resulting behavior. Should two equally preferred and promising behavioral programs be available for the same behavioral intent, a conflict situation arises that requires either renewed CO clustering or the adoption of a behavioral program for solving this type of conflict. A rather normal program of this kind—also helpful, incidentally, in cases of intentional conflicts— would be to toss a coin. A pathogenic program would be to forego any action and remain motionless.

Behavioral programs are also involved in another type of conflict, one that arises between a behavioral program in the process of being executed and a behavioral program about to be executed. Such conflicts may be expected not only because every new behavioral act mostly replaces a former act, but because the formation of CO clusters is presumably a much faster process than performance and feedback control of behavioral programs. Usually the problem hardly reaches the stage of real conflict, since there exist two common procedures for dealing with it: (1) delaying the performance of the new program until the present one is completed (Feather, 1960); and (2) interrupting the program in the process of execution for the sake of the new one (Mandler & Watson, 1966; Zeigarnik, 1927). These procedures are applied without any problems being incurred, unless the individual suffers from the above-mentioned difficulties of returning to an interrupted action, completing an action, or resisting distractions in action.

To mention briefly further possible pathogenic effects of behavioral programs: there may be difficulties in adjusting stored behavioral programs to present situations, in devising new behavioral programs if necessary instead of perseverating in the use of stored programs that are inadequate for present situations, in using an adequate variety of programs instead of a few fixated ones, in switching easily from one behavioral program to another, in acting smoothly in accordance with the program without stopping too often to wonder what the next step should be or whether the originally planned next step (or last step) is the right one.

NOTES ABOUT DRIVES AND EMOTIONS

Reading the short summary presented above, the dynamically oriented clinical psychologist or psychiatrist is likely to object by asking: Does the theory ignore pathogenic effects and functions of drives and emotions? To answer this question even briefly requires a short preface about drives and emotions in general as presently viewed within the framework of the CO theory.

As is well known, the central position accorded to drives and emotions in psychology is equalled by the diversity of opinions about their nature. Let us first consider the problem of drives. In the broader domain of motivation there are at least three major approaches to drives. According to one approach drives are conceived mainly as a kind of internal stimulation, peripheral or central (e.g., Dollard & Miller, 1950; Young, 1961); according to the second, as a goal-directed behavior (e.g., Lewin, 1935; McClelland, 1957); and according to the third, as a mode of performance (e.g., Sheffield et al., 1951; Tinbergen, 1951). If drives are viewed as internal stimuli, or as signals of physiological imbalance, then in terms of the CO theory they are a kind of input, which, like the exteroceptive input, has to undergo meaning action and also, if necessary, meaning generation before becoming effective. If, however, the goal-directed aspect of drives is emphasized, then beliefs of the CO component goals are the most appropriate counterpart in the CO theory. Similarly, the conception of drives as innate or acquired performance sequences is reflected in the important function attributed in the CO theory to behavioral programs.

Within the framework of CO theory the conception of drives is based on all three approaches. Drives are defined as physiologically produced and determined tendencies triggered directly by physiological processes and sometimes also indirectly by external signal stimuli. They become manifest in interoceptive stimulation subjected to meaning action and in adult humans also to meaning generation. The interoceptive stimuli relevant for a specific drive are diverse, and in the initial stages many of them may occur together. In the case of some drives the interoceptive stimuli occur cyclically. In infants and perhaps also in animals the meaning action to which the interoceptive stimuli and the external signal stimuli are subjected may affect directly the elicitation of a stored, largely innate behavioral program, sometimes modified to a certain degree by learning, e.g., food-seeking behavior, and so on. In adult humans the elaboration of the interoceptive stimuli and sometimes of the external signal stimuli as well is subjected almost invariably to meaning generation, through which goal beliefs and other beliefs are activated. On this level the clearest representations of the interoceptive and exteroceptive stimuli are goal beliefs (e.g., "I want to eat") or beliefs about self that in this case constitute a kind of mirror-image of the corresponding goal beliefs (e.g., "I am hungry"). These goal beliefs or beliefs about self, or both, strongly predispose toward the adoption of special kinds of behavioral programs, which, though largely learned, often resemble in nuclear form the innate schemes called instincts in animals. Thus, on the human adult level drives could be defined as physiologically produced and determined tendencies cognitively represented in the clearest manner by goal beliefs or their mirror-image, namely, beliefs about self.

The above remarks also apply to so-called secondary or acquired drives. The major differences between them and the primary drives probably resides in the fact that the behavioral programs used to implement the acquired drives are purely learned. However it may be, our suggested conception of drives is based on the crucial function of meaningful elaboration of mostly interoceptive stimuli. In the absence of any such elaboration, we should speak of physiological processes rather than drives.

Needless to say, the extent to which goal beliefs shape ensuing behavior depends on the constellation of their respective CO clusters. Whether the goal belief of a sexually aroused male will or will not guide him to rape the naked woman on a deserted beach is codetermined by his norms concerning rape, his beliefs about his strength, his general beliefs about the gun in her hand, and the like. A drive with pathogenic behavioral implications, for instance the masochistic drives assumed by psychoanalysis, would derive either from an innate tendency (e.g., death drive) coupled with a corresponding goal belief or belief about self, or from a situation in which a goal, say, harming the father, is outweighed by norms and other beliefs and thus has to be replaced by another originally less preferred goal, namely, harming oneself. Should the behavioral implications prove to be somehow satisfactory, the belief cluster may be stored and reactivated later for guidance in similar situations.

Nonetheless, it would be mistaken to assume that goal beliefs or beliefs about self are always or mostly genuine straightforward representations of the relevant drive signals. If the straightforward representation of a wish, say, the goal belief "I want to masturbate," has in the past been outweighed by other beliefs in the evoked CO cluster and therefore replaced by the next meaning-related belief in the goal hierarchy, say, "I want to eat," the present drive signal may be represented at once by what was before merely the substitute goal belief. Under these circumstances the individual will most likely be unaware that he acts in line with a substitute or compromise belief, since awareness is only possible (though not obligatory or always necessary) with regard to beliefs and not with regard to completely unidentified and unlabeled internal signals. Incidentally, as noted earlier (e.g., Chapters 4 and 5), beliefs as such may become conscious, but the CO theory does not assume that their evocation or clustering depends on their being conscious. Mostly beliefs remain in a preconscious state, some or all being available for later recall. More importantly, if the original goal belief led in the first instance to an uncomfortable or frightening conflict, and hence was replaced by a more convenient belief, it is likely not only to remain below the level of awareness (Freud's "preconscious") but actually to be unconscious in a psychoanalytic sense. The individual would then be unable to attain spontaneous awareness of it or would fail to identify it as his own goal belief when confronted with it by his psychotherapist. Again, this type of unconsciousness with regard to beliefs is only possible —or, according to psychoanalysis, likely—owing to prior belief clustering, namely, a conflict situation that led to adoption of the defense mechanism of repression.

As with drives, there exist different approaches to emotions. The major conceptions may be divided roughly into those that grant cognition a major role in the elicitation of emotion (e.g., Arnold, 1960; Köhler, 1929; Lazarus, 1968; Valins, 1970) and those that do not (e.g., Cannon, 1927; Lindsley, 1951). The conception of emotion in the framework of the CO theory belongs essentially to the former class, since it is based on the idea that without elaborations of meaning the input can have no impact.

According to the CO theory, emotions arise as a result of subjecting internal and/or external stimuli to meaning action and sometimes also to meaning generation. The internal stimuli may reflect physiological processes, such as organically induced changes in arousal, in hormonal regulation, and the like. Where only internal input exists one should perhaps speak of "mood," and reserve the term "emotion" for cases in which external input is also involved. Incidentally, it may be noted that changed arousal states may affect the tendency to grasp a stimulus in an emotional sense.

Elaborating the meaning of internal and/or external stimuli predisposes toward the evocation of specific behavioral programs. In infants and animals, and sometimes also in human adults (i.e., perhaps in the case of some fear reactions) the behavioral program may be elicited directly following meaning action. However, in the case of most emotions in adults, meaning generation and not merely meaning action precedes the elicitation of the program. As usual, the meaning generation involves the evocation of various beliefs, but in the case of emotions it does not culminate in the production of a full-fledged CO cluster. The reason for this is the absence of goal beliefs in the primary stage of the process. The beliefs that are elicited include only norms (e.g., "Such behavior on the part of a boss should not be passed over or tolerated"), general beliefs (e.g., "If one disregards the insults of a boss, one may end up being insulted by everyone"), and beliefs about self (e.g., "Such remarks always make me mad"). The resulting incomplete CO cluster may become represented by beliefs about self (e.g., "I am angry"; "It hurts"; "I am joyful"), but it does not lead to the formation of a behavioral intent. Often the incomplete CO cluster is retrieved from memory storage, but it is always complemented by beliefs referring to the present situation.

In the absence of a behavioral intent, no action is elicited. The incomplete CO cluster does, however, predispose to the elicitation of a behavioral program that is autonomic in nature. It involves energetic (arousal), visceral, and postural changes as well as other expressive elements, most of which are innate and only some learned. Being primarily autonomic, such behavioral programs do not require the prior formation of a behavioral intent, as do behavioral programs involving molar acts. The bond between the incomplete CO cluster and the elicited autonomic behavioral program is mostly innate, sometimes learned.

However, the process of emotion formation does not end with this primary stage. It proceeds on the basis of the feedback from the bodily reactions and perhaps also from responses of others to one's own reactions in the primary stage. It is only in this second stage, in elaborating this new internal and external input, that a goal belief may emerge, for example, "I want to take revenge," "I want to remain angry," "I want to destroy," "I want to control my anger and stop being angry." Of course, a goal belief does not always emerge, but if it does the stage is set for the formation of a CO cluster that produces some behavioral intent and thus may lead to a molar act. This act may be called "emotional behavior," but it usually leads the person beyond the experienced and expressed emotion of the primary stage. Needless to say, the goal may affect the autonomic bodily reactions. If, for example, the goal is not to express the emotion publicly, the external manifestations may be suppressed.

The conception of emotions described above leads to several deductions. First, it explains why the emotions of children and animals may seem to be more shallow and of shorter duration than emotions of adults. The reason is that in children and animals probably only the primary stage of emotion occurs, and it is not followed by the second stage, based on the elaboration of the feedback from the first stage. Second, our conception explains why it is difficult to control an emotion in its first stage but possible to do so in the later stage. The reason is that following the primary stage of bodily expression, the emergence of goal beliefs provides a potential means for controlling further behavioral occurrences. Third, our conception explains why there may be no correlation between bodily and self-report measures of emotions, as in veteran parachutists who report little subjective fear despite the presence of marked physiological reactivity (Fenz & Epstein, 1967). The reason for this surprising lack of correlation is that the bodily reactivity is a product of the first stage, whereas the self-report is a product of a behavioral intent formed in the second stage. (A similar finding about pain is reported in Chapter 7, Study V).

What, however, is our explanation of "abnormal" emotions and their pathogenic impact? It seems possible to describe an emotion as pathological or pathogenic if meaning generation or CO clustering are faulty or deviant in some relevant sense. For example, meaning generation may lead to a pathogenic emotion through mislabeling of an input. The mislabeling may consist either in identifying the input deviantly, as when what should be read as sadness is read as anger, or in identifying nonemotional inputs as indicating an emotion and vice versa. Many examples of such faulty meaning generation in regard to emotions were studied in the framework of attribution theory (Valins, 1970; Valins & Nisbett, 1971). Of course, there may be many reasons for mislabeling. For one, our ability to identify our own emotions is poorly developed. Further, mislabeling may occur if some label engenders conflict or evokes other beliefs that are unpleasant to the individual or evaluated by him as undesirable. The original appropriate label may then become unconscious in the sense that it is no longer available for voluntary recall. This conception fully corresponds to Freud's claim that no emotion could be unconscious, and that only its "ideational presentation" could undergo repression (Freud, 1934, pp. 109–111).

Mislabeling as such is not necessarily pathogenic. It may become pathogenic if the inadequate labels are included as beliefs in the CO cluster formed in the second stage. For example, if a person irritated and frustrated by some state of affairs interprets the input as indicating "sorrow" and not "anger," he may in the second stage form a behavioral intent appropriate for "sorrow," such as mourning or self-pity, and thus become even less able than he was originally to cope adequately with the frustrating situation.

However, misidentified inputs are not the only reasons for pathogenic CO clustering in the second stage of the emotional process. Sometimes the labeling of the input in the first stage might be considered adequate, yet the CO cluster is pathogenic since the input is coupled with a pathogenic goal belief (e.g., in the case of sorrow, "I wish that the pain would last"), or with pathogenic general or norm beliefs (e.g., in the case of sorrow, "One should immerse oneself completely in mourning"), or with several normal beliefs that in collocation yield a pathogenic behavioral intent (e.g., the beliefs "I am scared," "I don't want to be scared," "One should not be scared," and "Attacking frees one of fear" may produce the behavioral intent to attack someone when one feels scared). Finally, it should be noted that pathological behavior may ensue when a pathogenic or nonpathogenic behavioral intent is implemented by means of a pathological behavioral program, as when an individual who has been insulted by his or her lover applies the program of abstaining from eating instead of reprimanding the lover or withdrawing from the relation in some form.

ORIENTATIVE BELIEFS OF SCHIZOPHRENICS

Our study of the orientative beliefs of schizophrenics, first published as Part II of a book written in German (H. and S. Kreitler, 1965), was carried out before we embarked upon developing the CO theory and, thus, does not demonstrate the relation between particular CO clusters and particular behaviors. We discuss it in the present context for two reasons. This study formed our first step toward the theory of cognitive orientation since it taught us that it is less productive to treat beliefs as the result of rationalization, sublimation, and so on than to regard them as orientative guides or predispositions to behavior. Second, some of the findings, fragmentary as they may now seem, contain clues for the understanding of schizophrenic behaviors and point toward a new psychotherapeutic technique.

The major purpose of the study was to explore the uncharted domain of the "world view" of schizophrenics, that is, their beliefs about different aspects of life and behavior. The experimental group consisted of 40 hospitalized patients (18 males and 22 females) with a unanimously assigned diagnosis of schizophrenia. Their mean age was 33.13 years ($SD = 9.05$), and the mean duration of their hospitalization was 4.63 ($SD = 4.13$) years. The control group consisted of 40 normal subjects (18 males, 22 females) matched pairwise to the patients in regard to age (mean age = 33.63 years, $SD = 9.08$), ethnic background, socioeconomic level, and years of formal education (for details see H. & S. Kreitler, 1965, pp. 164–167). In order to control for the effects of long-term hospitalization, we posed those questions that were answered differently by schizophrenics than by normals to a group of patients suffering from tuberculosis who had been hospitalized for at least a year before the interview.

The method of inquiry consisted of conducting with the subjects lengthy, individual interviews guided by 40 major questions, including many subquestions, with regard to themes like marriage, profession, family, morality, aggression, sexuality, freedom, work, money, death, and so on (for questionnaire see ibid., pp. 161–163). The answers and statements obtained through this guided interview were classified in accordance with some 100 themes. We considered as characteristic of schizophrenics only answers and statements that were given by at least 80% of the schizophrenic subjects and by no more than 10% of the normal controls and 10% of the tubercular controls. Since the confidence interval on the .05 level is defined by the range 67.75–92.25%, it may be assumed that similar answers would be gotten from at least 67.75% or at the most 92.25% of schizophrenics in other similar potential samples of schizophrenics.

In line with the former criteria, the following beliefs, minimally rephrased in order to reflect the commonest recurrent formulations by schizophrenics, were designated as characteristic of schizophrenics:

1. I want to be the best person in the world. And if this proves impossible, I have to be (or: want to be; or: am) the worst person in the world.

2. Three things are unconditionally bad and forbidden: jealousy, aggression, and sex.

3. Every human being should be absolutely free. (This belief was stated by 100% of the schizophrenic subjects, and by 95% of an additional sample of 80 chronic schizophrenics to whom the relevant question was posed for purposes of rechecking this particular finding).

4. (Through a career) I want to become very famous, be known by everyone and also live a very humble life far from the crowd (or from people, society, etc.).

5. An ideal world could exist, and could be materialized (vivid but different descriptions of this ideal world were given).

6. I do not know what I (or others) could do for creating an ideal world.

7. The human being has a role in life and in the world (specifications of the role differ).

8. (Clear indications are given that death is experienced as a present actuality and as permanently threatening).

At first glance these beliefs appear as rather innocuous, perhaps somewhat bizarre, but certainly not convincingly pathogenic. Yet when regarded as potentially orientative, they prove to predispose those who hold them toward particular kinds of schizophrenic behaviors. Since we have already demonstrated this point in greater detail (H. & S. Kreitler, 1965) and, moreover, intend to furnish further experimental evidence in a forthcoming book, we can restrict the present dicussion to a condensed analysis of two examples.

Whenever human beings start to be emotionally involved they necessarily experience, in the broad sense of these terms, jealousy or aggression or sexual attraction, and sometimes two or even all three together. Therefore a person who believes that each one of these experiences is very bad and should be avoided is strongly predisposed to shy away from intense emotional involvement. It is no wonder that "emotional detachment" is one of the most commonly used phrases for describing schizophrenic behavior. However, when these pathogenic beliefs are clustered together with the conviction that one is already the worst person in the world, and therefore hopelessly free to commit the worst crimes, the scene is set for a strong acting out of jealousy, aggression, and sex.

Again, if a person believes that he should be absolutely and unconditionally free, all the usual social, institutional, and even physical constraints of everyday life will not only cause frequently recurrent frustration but may predispose acts of protest. Other beliefs present in the CO cluster and available programs may determine whether the protest takes the form of hurting oneself, neglecting cleanliness and clothes, distorting common language by inventing neologisms, regressing to infantile logic and childhood habits, or some other of the forms of protest so succinctly described by Binswanger and other sensitive observers of schizophrenic symptomatology.

Also, the orientative content of the other "schizophrenic" beliefs mentioned above pointed toward particular symptoms, thus rendering the observed correlation between beliefs and symptoms more meaningful. However, prior to the CO theory and its supporting experiments we lacked even a provisional conception of the processes responsible for the impact of orientative beliefs upon behavior. In particular, since at that time we had not yet distinguished between different belief types and did not yet know about CO clustering, we could not understand why a particular belief that seemed to orient one subject toward pathological behavior of a certain type was absent in another subject with the same behavioral symptom.

In order to decide whether our findings constituted a promising start or a blind alley, we put our interpretation of these findings to what could be called a psychotherapeutic test. We reasoned that if particular beliefs orient toward a particular behavior, changing these beliefs by psychotherapeutic means should yield an adequate change in behavior. Our methods for obtaining changes in beliefs included individual psychotherapy, group psychotherapy, psychodrama, and a previously devised technique of simultaneously combining all these three methods (Kreitler & Elblinger, 1960). The results were encouraging, in some instances even strikingly impressive. Rechecking our therapeutic work for indications of

292

CHAPTER 10

orientative belief impact we found that the change of one single theme, induced accidentally in the course of one psychodramatic session, produced the immediate breakdown of severe postural catatonic symptoms that had persisted for about 7 years (Kreitler & Bornstein, 1958).

Of course, we knew the methodological limitations of psychotherapeutic research and did not regard psychotherapeutically obtained results as sufficient empirical support for our hypothesis. Yet in retrospect these early findings gain in significance because they are now supported by the results of many well-controlled experiments and are interpretable in terms of the CO theory.

STUDY I
Goal Beliefs of Schizophrenics

PURPOSE AND HYPOTHESES

The purpose of this study was to explore several aspects of the goal beliefs of schizophrenics. Goal beliefs were selected as the theme of the study because of the prominent role they play in CO clustering. In view of the exploratory nature of the study, we included a wide range of aspects. Some were derived directly from the CO theory—mainly the relations between goal beliefs and beliefs about self, norms, and general beliefs, as well as the relation between goal beliefs and conceptions of how to attain the goals. Other aspects, mainly the relations between various rankings of the goals and the dependence between goals, were inspired by the experiments of Dembo (1960) in this domain.

Since so little is known about cognitive contents in mental patients, we replaced specific hypotheses by a series of questions, each relating to one or more of the aspects under study. The questions referred to differences between schizophrenics and normals in (1) the content of basic goals; (2) relations between the rankings of the goals in terms of preference, difficulty of attainment, and sorrow attendant upon nonattainment; (3) the interdependence between goals versus their relative autonomy; (4) confidence in one's ability to attain the goals; (5) support of the goals through beliefs about norms; (6) support of the goals through general beliefs; (7) the existence of present efforts toward attainment of the goals; (8) the readiness to substitute for the stated goals, if unattained, less preferred goals; (9) the role accorded to the mode of attainment of the goals; and (10) the content and structure of the meaning of the goals.

This study was carried out with Miss Rivka Zemet.

METHOD

Subjects. The subjects were 21 schizophrenic patients, of the different diagnostic classifications of schizophrenia, selected randomly from the population of two mental hospitals, and 20 surgical patients, selected randomly from the population of a hospital for patients suffering from various degrees of paralysis or missing limbs following battle injuries or traffic accidents. None of the surgical patients was known to have manifested any psychotic or schizophrenic symptoms. The surgical patients were chosen as control subjects not only because they were normal, at least in the sense of being nonschizophrenic, but also because they were hospitalized for a lengthy period of time as the schizophrenics were. This provided a measure of control over the impact of hospitalization as such on the goal beliefs of the interviewees.

The mean age of the schizophrenics was 27.29 years ($SD = 6.02$) and of the surgical patients, 28.15 years ($SD = 6.75$). The schizophrenic group included 14 males and 7 females, and the surgical patients group included 18 males and 2 females. The range of hospitalization was 5 months to 10 years for the schizophrenics and 2–8 months for the controls. In the schizophrenic group, 2 were married and 19 unmarried; out of the controls 10 were married and 10 unmarried. There were no significant differences between the groups in mean number of years of education (11–12 years), and in the varied sociocultural backgrounds.

PROCEDURE AND MATERIALS

Each subject was interviewed individually, on the grounds of the hospital. The interview was based on a questionnaire that included 13 questions. At first the subject was requested to state three goals if possible, a goal being defined as "something you not only want to happen but also try or could try to attain." Next, the subject was asked to rank these three goals according to his or her preference for them, the difficulty involved in attaining them, and the sorrow attendant upon not attaining them. The relations between any two of these rankings were examined by noting for each subject the number of deviations from perfect correspondence between the two rankings, as computed by subtracting one ranking from the other and disregarding the sign of the result. Thus, the number of deviations is zero when the rankings are identical but it has the maximum value of 4 when the rankings differ as in "1-2-3" and "3-2-1" or "2-1-3" and "3-2-1."

Dependence between the goals was examined by asking the subject whether he or she wanted to attain the two remaining goals if one of the goals could not be attained. Interest in the remaining goals was taken to reflect independence between the goals. When asked with regard to the three goals this question yielded six responses. A response of dependence got zero points, a response clearly reflecting independence got 2 points, and an intermediate response got 1 point.

The other questions, each asked with regard to the three goals separately, referred to how sure the subject felt he or she could attain the goals (responses were given and scored in terms of a 5-point scale); whether he or she thought that all or most people should strive to attain the stated goals (responses reflect norm beliefs); whether he or she thought that all or most people actually strive to attain the stated goal (responses reflect general beliefs); whether the subject thought he or she was doing something at present to attain the goals; whether he or she was ready to be content with other goals if the stated ones cannot be attained; whether he or she was ready to accept immediate attainment of the goals through a fairy; what the meaning of each goal was; and what he or she thought about when thinking about the goals (responses may reflect beliefs about self and daydreams).

After the statement of the goals, all questions were posed in random order. The subject was requested to explain, substantiate, and exemplify his or her responses. In some questions (see Table 10.2) each response was assigned 2 points if it reflected the variable of interest, 1 point if it reflected it unclearly or indecisively, and zero if it did not reflect it at all. The scores for the three goals were always summed so that each subject got one score for each variable. The responses to the question about the contents of one's thoughts about the goal were analyzed in terms of various content categories, of which only three—those deemed of special interest in this context—are mentioned in the relevant summary table (Table 10.3). The responses to the question about the meaning of the goals were analyzed in terms of the meaning dimensions (see Chapter 2 and Chapter 11, Study III). For example, if a subject explained the meaning of the goal "to get healthy" by saying "to exercise as hard as possible until I move my legs and arms from morning till night" the response would be scored in terms of the dimensions "manner of occurrence or operation" (reflected in actions), "actual or potential actions" and "temporal qualities." The response of each subject to each goal mostly referred to more than one meaning dimension. The frequency of the various dimensions in the response patterns of the subjects was tabulated (Table 10.4).

RESULTS AND CONCLUSIONS

A survey of the goals mentioned by our subjects shows that the two groups largely share the same goals (Table 10.1). More normals than schizophrenics referred to "studying," but probably this mainly reflects

TABLE 10.1
Frequencies of Goal Beliefs in Schizophrenics and Normals

Goal Beliefs	% of Schizophrenic Subjects	% of Normal Subjects	Significance of Differences (χ^2)
Health	71.43%	75%	.09
Work and profession	57.14	75	2.41
Studying	14.29	35	8.70**
Family life	80.95	35	18.21***
Economic situation	14.29	10	.76
Happiness	23.81	10	5.65*
Possession of house, car, etc.	19.05	10	2.82
Others[a]	23.81	45	—

[a] Goals classified under this heading were mentioned by only one or two subjects.
* $p < .05$.   ** $p < .01$.   *** $p < .001$.

the fact that most of the normals faced the necessity of changing profession following their injury. More schizophrenics mentioned "family life," probably because most of them were unmarried. The high degree of common goals makes possible meaningful comparisons between the two groups with regard to various aspects of goals.

Table 10.2 shows that in some aspects there are no differences between schizophrenics and normals, in others there tend to be differences, and in still others there are marked and significant differences. Schizophrenics do not differ from normals in the way they relate preference, difficulty, and sorrow at nonattainment of goals, in the essential independence among their goals, and in their moderate tendency to support their goals through norm beliefs. However, schizophrenics tend slightly more than normals to be confident in their ability to attain their goals, and to assume that everyone strives to attain the same goals they do. The major respects in which schizophrenics differ from normals are as follows: fewer schizophrenics than normals claim they do anything at present to attain their goals; and more schizophrenics than normals are ready to substitute other goals for their most preferred ones and to accept immediate miraculous attainment of their goals. This last finding lends special emphasis to the normality of normals. Considering the fact that many of the injured patients had been unable to move their limbs for several months, their rejection of the idea of a fairy even in fantasy is really admirable.

The relative readiness of schizophrenics to replace their goals by others is at first glance striking, since it seems to contradict the schizophrenics' notorious difficulty in renouncing. But in the present context this finding, taken together with the other findings, indicates instead a peculiar aspect of the manner in which the schizophrenic relates to his goals. He seems less bothered than the normal with efforts designed to attain the goals; indeed, he does not even evaluate such efforts as much as the normal. Thus, being uninvolved in actual behaviors designed to

TABLE 10.2
Comparisons of Schizophrenics and Normals
on Various Variables Related to Goals

VARIABLE	SCHIZOPHRENICS		NORMALS		
	$\overline{X}$	SD	$\overline{X}$	SD	t
Relation between rankings of preference and difficulty (no. of deviations)	1.89	1.65	1.40	1.56	.96
Relation between rankings of preference and sorrow if unattained (no. of deviations)	2.53	1.68	2.05	1.63	.87
Relation between rankings of difficulty and sorrow if unattained (no. of deviations)	1.44	1.74	1.55	1.75	.19
Dependence between goals (no. of deviations from dependence)	1.00	1.27	1.50	1.96	.96
Confidence in ability to attain the goals (5-point scale)	9.10	2.42	7.80	2.40	1.71 ($p <.10$)
Support of goals by norm beliefs[a]	3.43	1.71	3.15	1.88	.50
Support of goals by general beliefs	3.57	1.92	2.55	1.56	1.85 ($p < .10$)
Existence of present efforts toward attainment of goals	2.67	1.94	4.15	2.01	2.39*
Readiness to replace goals with less preferred ones	3.52	1.74	2.20	1.94	2.32*
Readiness to accept immediate attainment of goal through a fairy	4.80	1.40	3.00	2.37	2.90**

[a] The variables from here to the bottom of the table were scored by assigning 2, 1, or 0 points for the answers in accordance with the clarity with which they reflected the scored variable. The points for the three goals were summed so that each subject got only one score.
* $p < .05$.   ** $p < .01$.

attain the goals, the schizophrenic may perhaps feel less committed to his goals. Hence, perhaps, his greater readiness to be content with other goals.

The above remarks are greatly reinforced by the findings presented in Tables 10.3 and 10.4. In their daydreams about goals schizophrenics and normals dwell equally on the attainment of the goals. But whereas schizophrenics more than normals tend to think about further consequences of attainment, which often reflect other pleasant actions or states, the normals are concerned more than schizophrenics with the actions leading to attainment of the goals. Precisely the same conclusion is suggested by examining the meaning of the goals (Table 10.4). Here again it is evident that schizophrenics use the dimension "consequences" more often and the dimension "manner of occurrence" much less often than normals. In addition, their meaning communications indicate a tendency to perceive goals less often than normals in terms of actions and correspondingly more often in terms of desired states.

In sum, apart from showing that schizophrenics and normals do not differ in most of the aspects tested, the findings converge in supporting the conclusion that schizophrenics do not regard the mode of attaining a goal as an integral element of the goal to the same degree as normals, and that both in fantasy and in actual behavior they are less concerned about actions designed to further the attainment of their goals.

In order to evaluate adequately the pathogenic significance of these findings it is important to note that mode of attainment is not a promi-

TABLE 10.3
Frequency of Subjects Mentioning Attainment, Consequences or Mode of Attainment when Describing Their Thoughts about Goals

VARIABLE	GOAL 1 Schiz.[a]	Norm.[b]	Sig.	GOAL 2 Schiz.	Norm.	Sig.	GOAL 3 Schiz.	Norm.	Sig.
Description of attainment	7	5	n.s.	7	3	n.s.	10	3	$p = .04$
Consequences of attainment	10	2	$p = .02$	9	2	$p = .03$	9	3	$p = .07$
Mode of attainment	3	13	$p = .01$	2	9	$p = .03$	2	8	$p = .05$

Note. The specific question was: "When you think about (goal ranked by subject as first, second, or third is mentioned), about what do you think?"
[a] "Description" and "consequences" were mentioned in the same response by two subjects in regard to Goal 1, two in regard to Goal 2, and four in regard to Goal 3.
[b] "Description" and "consequences" were mentioned in the same response by one subject in regard to Goal 1 and by one subject in regard to Goal 2; "mode" and "description," by one subject in regard to Goal 2 and one in regard to Goal 3; "description," "mode," and "consequences," by one subject in regard to Goal 1.

TABLE 10.4
Frequencies of Meaning Dimensions in the Meaning of Goals
as Communicated by Normals and Schizophrenics

Meaning Dimensions	Normals[a]	Schizophrenics	Significance of Differences (χ^2)
Action	70%	47.62%	4.26*
State	15	28.56	4.22*
Manner (action)	20	3.14	12.28**
Function	10	3.14	3.58
Antecedents	35	28.56	.65
Location	5	1.57	1.79
Domain of application	5	3.19	.40
Emotion	5	9.52	1.40
Time	5	1.57	1.80
Consequences	20	38.08	5.63*
Range of inclusion	5	9.34	1.31
Beliefs and judgments	10	14.28	.75

Note. The cited percentages of subjects represent means of the percentages in the three goals responded to by each subject. This procedure was adopted in view of nonsignificant differences between responses to the three goals.
[a] The findings for normals do not differ significantly from findings about the meaning of goals obtained in another group of subjects (Chapter 11, Study III, and Table 11.9).
* $p < .05$.   ** $p < .001$.

nent aspect of the meaning of goals in general, that is, in the normal population, nor is it expected to be (Chapter 4; Chapter 11, Study III). Yet the fact that schizophrenics are concerned with this aspect less than the normals in our sample may suggest that the roots of the particular schizophrenic symptom of withdrawal from action may partly lie in the meaning of their goals. If that is so, then the study provides an example of beliefs whose pathogeneity is not apparent from their surface content but becomes evident only through explication of their implied meaning.

STUDY II
Behavioral Intents of Schizophrenics

PURPOSE AND HYPOTHESES

The purpose of the study was to explore the meaning of the behavioral intent of schizophrenic patients and normal controls. Since the behavioral intent is the product of the CO cluster, whatever may be deviant in the CO cluster must be assumed to show up in the behavioral intent. On the basis of this assumption we expected that comparing the meaning of the behavioral intents in the two groups would afford insights into the management of action in schizophrenics. Since generally modes of action figure most prominently in the meaning of the behavioral intent (Chapter 6; Chapter 11, Study III), it seemed only natural to explore the behavioral intent in order to learn more about the tendency of schizophrenics to withdraw from action. As the assumptions underlying this exploration were not definite enough to make possible the formulation of a hypothesis, we restricted ourselves to a general question about the differences in meaning of the behavioral intent in the two groups.

METHOD

Subjects. The normal subjects were 55 individuals (25 males and 30 females) ranging in age from 16 to 46 years, some students in high schools or universities and some clerks or secretaries in various firms. (The same subjects were used in Chapter 11, Study III). They may be considered normal in the sense that they have never been referred for psychotherapeutic help and by their own report have never suffered from any debilitating mental symptoms. The schizophrenic subjects were 25 hospitalized patients, 11 males and 14 females, selected randomly from the schizophrenic population of three mental hospitals. They represented the different diagnostic classifications of schizophrenia. Their mean duration of hospitalization was 1.9 years. In age, educational level, and varied sociocultural background the schizophrenics did not differ significantly from the normal controls.

PROCEDURE AND MATERIALS

The procedure will be described only briefly since it is identical to that described at length in Chapter 11, Study III. The meaning of the behavioral intents was examined in the framework of a study that focused on the meaning of various types of complete and incomplete statements. Altogether there were 14 statements, each presented on a separate card. The two statements that referred to behavioral intents were presented randomly with the others and read: "I intend (to buy a car, to . . .)" and "I made up my mind . . .". The subject was requested to complete the statements as she or he saw fit before proceeding to communicate their meaning. The task of communicating meaning to a hypothetical partner was fully explained and demonstrated to the subject at the beginning of the session. Each subject was interviewed individually by one of five experimenters.

Two independent judges analyzed the responses into meaning values, which were then classified in terms of the meaning dimensions described in Chapter 2. For example, if the meaning communication of the behavioral intent "I intend to study" was "I will get up early and study mathematics before going to work," the response was coded in terms of the meaning dimensions "manner of occurrence or operation" (as manifested in actions), "domain of application," and "temporal qualities."

Interjudge reliability in coding the material was perfect in 98% of the cases.

RESULTS AND CONCLUSIONS

The findings show several major differences between schizophrenics and normals in the meaning of behavioral intents. In communicating the meaning of behavioral intents schizophrenics use less frequently

TABLE 10.5
Frequencies of Meaning Dimensions in the Meaning of
Behavioral Intents in Normals and Schizophrenics

MEANING DIMENSIONS	NORMALS[a]		SCHIZOPHRENICS		SIG. OF DIFF. (χ^2) (BETW. MEAN %[b] IN NORMALS AND SCHIZOPHRENICS)
	Intent 1	Intent 2	Intent 1	Intent 2	
Manner (action)	98.19	100	44	36	25.12***
Function	98.19	90.90	84	88	.40
Antecedents	30.92	50.90	68	60	5.08*
Location	12.73	14.55	—	—	13.64***
Domain of application	1.82	—	—	—	.91
Emotion	10.91	5.45	16	12	1.53
Time	56.37	25.46	12	16	13.20***
Consequences	29.09	1.82	32	36	6.95**
Beliefs and judgments	—	—	12	8	10.00**
Manner (action) and function	87.28	90.90	36	28	26.92***
Manner (action) and time	56.37	25.46	8	12	18.78***
Manner (action) and location	12.73	14.55	—	—	13.64***
Manner (action) and domain of application	1.82	—	—	—	.91
Manner (action) and function and/or time and/or location and/or domain of application	60.01	36.37	8	12	25.07***

[a] The same data are presented in Table 11.9.
[b] The mean percentages represent the average of two behavioral intents in each group.
* $p < .05$.   ** $p < .01$.   *** $p < .001$.

than normals the meaning dimensions "manner of occurrence or operation," "location," and "time," but use more frequently than normals the meaning dimensions "antecedents," "consequences," and "beliefs and judgments," the latter reflecting mainly subjective evaluations of the behavioral intent (Table 10.5). Thus schizophrenics make less use of meaning dimensions that reflect the "what," "when," and "where" of actions. The evident conclusion is that schizophrenics are less concerned than normals with actions designed to promote attainment of their intents. In this sense the findings of the present study fully confirm the findings of Study I (this chapter), which showed that schizophrenics thought less about acts and undertook in reality fewer acts that could lead to the attainment of their goals.

Since the study is merely exploratory, we feel justified at this stage in drawing only the tentative conclusion that schizophrenics may tend to form behavioral intents that are not conducive to action. The pathogeneity of such behavioral intents consists in the element of indefinite delay that is built into their meaning through the absence of a sufficient number of meaning values reflecting action, enabling action, and preparing action. It may be suggested—as a hypothesis in need of testing—that such a pathogenic "delayed" behavioral intent reflects a pathogenic CO cluster, only one of whose possibly pathogenic elements was investigated earlier (this chapter, Study I). Others have to be examined. The pathogenic behavioral intent affects in turn behavior and may underlie the schizophrenic symptom of withdrawal from activity.

STUDY III
Predicting the Use of Defense Mechanisms

PURPOSE AND HYPOTHESES

The purpose of this study was to predict through relevant CO scores the evocation of different defense mechanisms. Predicting from cognitive antecedents which defense mechanisms will be applied is, for a number of reasons, an important and most challenging task. First, if defense mechanisms are conceived as behavioral programs, successfully predicting through CO scores which of these defenses will be used would demonstrate that the choice of a particular behavioral program from among the several available depends upon CO clusters. Second, defense mechanisms have hitherto been widely viewed as processes outside the ken of cognition, probably owing to their function in anxiety

This study has been published (Kreitler & Kreitler, 1969, 1972b) and will therefore be summarized here only briefly.

reduction. Third, the dynamic approaches to personality have failed to explain convincingly why human beings show marked preferences for some defenses over others. The prevalent psychoanalytic explanations are that the choice of defense is determined by the strength of the aroused drive or affect, by the kind of drive aroused, by the nature of the stress situation, by fixations, and by the personality structure and traits of the individual (A. Freud, 1946; Freud, 1933, 1959). Psychoanalysts seem to use these mutually inconsistent and tentative hypotheses indiscriminately. Moreover, though empirical research has lent partial support to some of these hypotheses (e.g., the first hypothesis is supported by Fenz & Epstein, 1962, the fourth by Weinstock, 1967, and the fifth by Byrne, 1964, and Palmer, 1968), it has also supported hypotheses reflecting a contradictory approach, that the choice of defenses is determined by situational features (e.g., Eldow & Kiesler, 1966; Hackett & Weisman, 1964).

The defense mechanisms we studied were rationalization, denial, and projection. They were selected not only because they probably belong to the repertory of every individual but also because they represent defensiveness in the different domains of personal, interpersonal, and general behavior (DeNike & Tiber, 1968).

The specific hypothesis of the study was that a rank ordering of CO clusters assumed to predispose the individual to utilize the three defenses under study would be related to the rank ordering of the behavioral manifestations of these defenses.

METHOD

Subjects. The subjects were 24 (9 male, 15 female) undergraduates at Tel Aviv University, ranging in age from 20 to 27, who volunteered for this study without any reward.

Procedure and Materials. We will limit ourselves to a short description since the full details were published elsewhere (Kreitler & Kreitler, 1969, 1972b). Each subject participated in two experimental sessions. In the first, a group session made to appear unrelated to the second session, the subject was administered the Cognitive Orientation Questionnaire for Defensive Behavior. In the second, which was an individual session 4 to 6 weeks later, the subject was first exposed to a series of incidents designed to evoke anger (i.e., delaying the start of the experiment, requesting the subject to perform an apparently important task of clinically interpreting TAT material in cooperation with a noncooperative accomplice, having the accomplice cut the subject short and present the subject's ideas to the experimenter as if they were his own, failing to attend to what the subject wanted to say, and so on). Eighteen different accomplices participated in this part of the experiment, one in each session. Immediately afterwards the subject was administered three tasks designed to provide measures of behavior corresponding to defense mechanisms. First, he or she was requested to answer in writing two questions—one concerning his or her reaction to the experimental partner (the accomplice), the other concerning his or her opinion of the experiment as a whole. Second, the subject was presented two drawings with aggressive themes shown together with a third control drawing and asked to express an opinion about them. Third, the subject was given the Defense Mechanism Questionnaire, which consisted of seven items referring to acts violating common morality that had to be accounted for or "explained away." Each of the three measures included multiple-choice responses representing all three defenses being studied. Thus, each subject got four behavioral scores: (1) the frequency of statements reflecting the three defenses checked in response to the questions about partner and experiment; (2) the frequency of statements reflecting the three defenses checked in response to the two aggressive pictures; (3) ranking of the three defenses according to the frequency of the relevant statements checked in the Defense Mechanism Questionnaire; and (4) ranking of the three defenses according to a "weighted behavior index" representing the three preceding measures, each being assigned the equal weight of 1.

The Cognitive Orientation Questionnaire for Defensive Behavior was constructed in line with the procedure outlined in the first section of Chapter 7. The N part included 18 questions, the GB part, 11 questions, the BS part, 12 questions, and the Go part, 10 questions. Each question included two or three response alternatives, of which the subject had to check only one. Each part of the questionnaire included an equal maximum possible number of response alternatives orientative with regard to rationalization, denial, and projection. The beliefs referred to such themes as maintaining internal calm, controlling actions and emotions, optimism and pessimism, etc.

All the checks on split-half reliability were highly significant (the chi-square values of the differences between the observed and expected distributions in the number of inversions in the rankings of the three elements were, for the N part, 10.10, $p < .01$; for the GB part, 12.10, $p < .001$; for the BS part, 12.10, $p < .001$; and, for the Go part, 16.62, $p < .001$).[*] The relations among items and between items and the total score of the relevant part of the questionnaire were guaranteed by deleting any item that did not correspond to the other items in more than 25% of the cases. Table 13.5 reports the interrelations between the four CO components as well as between each of them and the CO score. An

* See footnote, p. 304.

independent check on the validity of the questionnaire showed that it discriminated as expected between the scores of aggression manifested by 45 subjects in the Buss-Durkee Inventory (Kreitler & Kreitler, 1969, Study I).

RESULTS AND CONCLUSIONS

The relation between the CO scores and the "Weighted Behavior Index" was examined by comparing the number of inversions in the ordering of the three defenses in terms of the CO scores and the index to the expected number of inversions when all 144 possible combinations of such rankings are tested.* Since the chi-square value of this comparison is significant ($\chi^2 = 8.22$, $p < .05$), it is warranted to conclude that the CO scores are correlated with the "Weighted Behavior Index," reflecting the defensive behavior of the subjects in all three behavioral measures (Kreitler & Kreitler, 1972b). This relation was perfect in 6 of the 24 subjects (Poisson Test, $p = .0004$), and reflects similarity between the two rankings across all three ranks equally (χ^2 of the differences between the three ranks $= 4.72$ $df = 2$, n.s.). More specifically, CO scores were also related significantly to each of the three behavioral measures separately (with "reactions to accomplice and experiment," Wilcoxon $z = -2.472$, $p = .0068$, one-tailed; with "opinions on drawings," Wilcoxon $z = -2.708$, $p = .0035$, one-tailed; with Defense Mechanism Questionnaire, χ^2 of number of inversions $= 7.09$, $df = 1$, $p < .01$). These findings fully support our hypothesis that CO scores are related to, and may thus predict, which defense mechanisms are adopted.

Further, the findings show that all except one of the 14 combinations of less than the four CO components were not related to behavior (the one exception was the combination of N, BS, and Go: $\chi^2 = 4.19$, $p < .05$), and that the relation to behavior increased overall with the increase in the number of CO components involved (Kreitler & Kreitler, 1972b). These findings support the conclusion that all four CO components are necessary for predicting behavior, abnormal no less than normal.

GENERAL CONCLUSIONS

The themes and studies contained in this chapter, for all their apparent disparity, are connected by an underlying purpose: to outline the core of a psychopathology based on the CO theory. The outline pre-

---

* We are grateful to Professor Ledyard R. Tucker for his help in suggesting this method for analyzing the data.

sented several major hypotheses that have to be tested, several modes of thinking that have to be pursued, several empirical studies whose implications and scope have to be examined before a firm basis for a cognitive psychopathology can be established.

Although the material presented here is highly restricted in scope, it expresses a few principles that are essential to this future cognitive psychopathology:

1. The very CO components and processes involved in eliciting and guiding normal molar behavior also form the major plausible foci of pathogeneity.

2. The same or similar abnormal behavior in the same individual or in two individuals may originate from different pathogenic CO processes or structures. Successful therapy requires, of course, a correct identification of the origin of the behavior, which may not be evident from the abnormal behavior itself.

3. A specific pathological behavior may be caused by the simultaneous or sequential cooperation of several pathogenic CO processes or structures. That is, the unraveling of a plausible origin for an observed pathological behavior in no way guarantees that no further origins have to be dealt with in order to remove the behavioral pathology.

4. Studying the effects of a process or a structure is in no way less meaningful and important than pursuing its origins.

This last point may possibly remain, for some, the most controversial. The psychoanalytically nourished attitude of looking into the genesis of symptoms and discounting an approach or therapy focusing on the here-now-and-future is still, notwithstanding the successes of behavior therapy, very much with us. In response we would like to emphasize that our approach in no way invalidates the search for origins. Quite the contrary. From a theoretical point of view, a cognitive psychopathology could not be complete without information about how deviant meaning generation was established, why the CO clustering is faulty, how the child acquired or formed spontaneously pathogenic beliefs or pathogenic behavioral programs, how the habit of shaping behavioral intents that do not predispose toward behavioral programs was formed, etc. Yet it is just as true that a cognitive psychopathology would be senseless if we did not know what the effects of deviant meaning generation, beliefs, CO clusters, behavioral intents, and behavioral programs were. More importantly, there is no justification for the claim that knowledge of causes and origins is a necessary precondition for studying effects. For once, both in theory and in practice, cause and effect are so closely interwoven that it is often difficult to identify any specific phenomenon as being exclusively cause or effect. For example, pathogenic meanings, once acquired or formed, give rise not only to acquisition and formation of further pathogenic meanings but also predispose learning, production, and preferential retrieval of pathogenic beliefs, thus leading to pathogenic belief clusters, which in turn may influence future meaning generation and belief production. In addition, there is clear evidence that despite serious gaps in information about origins, already available knowledge about effects can be applied fruitfully to predicting and changing of behavior (e.g., Chapter 7, Study VI). Indeed, research reported in Chapter 9 as well as psychotherapeutic observations discussed elsewhere (H. & S. Kreitler, 1965) make it highly probable that successful psychotherapy often requires no more than changing meaning generation and CO clustering on the here-and-now level, provided that the changes occur with regard to relevant cognitive aspects and are inclusive enough as well as sufficiently enduring to exert their effects.

The Behavioral Intent: Where From and Where To

THE CONTROVERSIAL STATUS OF BEHAVIORAL INTENTS

The functional importance of the behavioral intent seems to be most controversial. On the one hand, since information about CO clusters and available programs for action suffices for predicting behavior it could be argued that there is no need to interpose behavioral intents into the chain of processes leading to overt molar behavior. On the other hand, one could make the point that even apart from theoretical considerations urging the formation of some such concept (Chapter 6), intention is too real a phenomenon to be overlooked in any theory of behavior. Frequently CO clustering does not result in overt motor performance but merely in a disclosed or undisclosed commitment to a future action, that is, a behavioral intent, which for the time being is stored in memory. Again, ordinary introspection and observation, as well as a host of experiments, especially those by Zeigarnik (1927) and Ovsiankina (1928), clearly demonstrate the task that behavioral intents fulfill, thus emphasizing the necessity to consider them in every analysis of the evocation of molar behavior.

In opting to accord the behavioral intent a status in the CO theory, we have not ignored the requirements of economy in model construction, but rather followed them without overlooking the requirements of the data at hand. Inclusion of the behavioral intent in the theory implies the obligation to demonstrate empirically the relations between CO clusters, behavioral intents, and programs, and to prove that behavioral intents can be predicted on the basis of relevant CO clusters. The four studies reported in this chapter were designed to fulfill this task. The first and second studies deal with the relation of behavioral intents to beliefs of the four CO components. The third study deals with the meaning of behavioral intents, highlighting their links not only to beliefs but also to behavioral programs. The fourth and final study focuses on actually predicting behavioral intents on the basis of relevant CO clusters.

STUDY I
Estimating Behavioral Intents from Beliefs

PURPOSE AND HYPOTHESIS

The major purpose of this study was to investigate the relations between beliefs and behavioral intents. The particular conditions under which this was investigated involved estimating the probability of a behavioral intent from a given set of beliefs representing the four CO components. The study considered the problem whether all CO components are necessary in order to form and thus also to predict a behavioral intent. Indeed, studies reported in Chapters 7, 8, and 10 show that all four CO components are necessary for predicting molar behaviors. These repeated proofs, however, leave open the question whether all four CO components are also indispensable in order to give rise to the behavioral intent. According to the CO theory, the behavioral intent, as an essential precursor of molar action, is the result of the clustering process, which integrates in some form the four CO components. But it could also be argued that even if the behavioral intent is essential for molar action, it need not derive from all four CO components; it could perhaps reflect one or two CO components, in which case the other CO components would be added later, for example, at the programming stage preceding actual behavior.

Since this study examines the process of intent formation using the method of estimating probabilities of behavioral intents, the hypothesis was phrased in terms relevant to the experimental method. Accordingly, our hypothesis was that in estimating the probability of a behavioral intent, subjects would consider all four CO components.

METHOD

Subjects. There were 314 subjects—157 males and 157 females—ranging in age from 18 to 29 years. About 80% of the subjects were selected randomly from the population of individuals who had recently joined the army (since in Israel military service is universally obligatory, the sampled population was not biased in any form); the remaining 20% were selected randomly from the population of individuals in schools for training teachers or technicians. None of the subjects was familiar with the CO theory.

Procedure and Materials. All the subjects answered a questionnaire for estimating probabilities of behavioral intents. The questionnaire was administered in small groups varying in size from 10 to 30 individuals. No time limit was set on answering the questionnaire. An experimenter was present throughout the session and the subjects were encouraged to ask about anything not clear to them. Three different experimenters participated in the sessions. The assignment of experimenters to groups of subjects was on a completely random basis.

Each questionnaire included short descriptions of 10 different situations. Each description was presented on a separate page, and was followed by four beliefs representing the four CO components, the statement of a behavioral intent relevant to the described situation, and a horizontal scale with seven boxes labeled, on the end corresponding to the number 7, "very small chances" and, on the end corresponding to the number 1, "very high chances." The situations and accompanying behavioral intents are presented in Table 11.1. The gender of the "heroes" of the situations was varied randomly so that the same situation had a male figure in half the cases and a female figure in the other half. Each subject got five situations with a male figure and five with a female figure. It will be noted that some of the situations reflect themes dealt with in our other behavior prediction studies. This afforded us the possibility of comparing the involvement of the four CO components in determining actual behavior and in forming a behavioral intent. As Table 11.1 shows, all the behavioral intents were formulated in a positive sense. A pretest had shown that subjects have difficulty in identifying the meaning of a negatively phrased behavioral intent and much prefer the less intriguing and less disturbing positive formulation.

The four beliefs following the description of a situation represented the four CO components, each belief one of the components. The reason for using only one belief per CO component was mainly economical: with more beliefs per component, the task of controlling for the various possible combinations would have become unmanageable. Yet we also considered the fact that very often one belief may represent others as their summary statement or label (see "Beliefs," Chapter 4). Heider (1967) demonstrated empirically that such summary statements make possible meaningful study of phenomena on the cognitive level.

For those situations corresponding to behaviors predicted in former studies (Chapters 7 and 8), we selected beliefs from the most highly discriminative statements in previous questionnaires. If no behavioral parallels had been studied, the beliefs were devised particularly for this questionnaire. The relevance and the cognitive orientativeness of the latter beliefs were checked empirically by testing the meanings of the beliefs in a pretest sample.

The beliefs appended to each situation either supported or did not

TABLE 11.1
Situations and Behavioral Intents
Used in Questionnaire for Study I, Chapter 11

Situation	Behavioral Intent	Studies of Corresponding Behaviors
1. Mr. A is a technician in a screw-producing factory. One day he is requested to measure 300 items from each production series in order to establish whether the deviations in their radii don't exceed the permissible standards. No one will check his pronouncements. The checking requires high concentration and is very tiring.	Mr. A will decide to perform all necessary checkings.	Chapter 7, Study II
2. B. is a high school student who takes a bus to school every morning. One day a very old lady boards the bus. All seats are occupied. She stands near him. B. is tired because the night before he stayed up very late and he counted on having a short nap in the bus.	B. will decide to get up and offer the old lady his seat.	
3. A year ago C. applied to the department of biology at the university but failed the entrance exams and was not accepted.	C. will decide to apply again this year.	Chapter 7, Study III
4. Mr. D., a young insurance man, forgot to perform a certain transaction for an important client. Embarrassment would be great but could be avoided if Mr. D. would tell the client some lie, which would harm nobody.	Mr. D. will decide to lie in order to avoid embarrassment.	
5. An engineer got work in a big firm. When accepted for work he was told by management that they wanted him to stay on the job a long time. Management was particularly good to him and everyone was satisfied with his work. A short time later he got an offer for a better job in another firm.	The engineer will decide to go over to the other firm.	

support the stated behavioral intent ("support" here refers to the cognitive orientativeness of the belief). Thus, 16 combinations of supporting and nonsupporting beliefs were set up. If we denote support by + and nonsupport by —, then there were two ++++ combinations, three +++— combinations, six ++—— combinations, three +——— combinations, and two ———— combinations. The 10 situations were paired with each of the 16 belief combinations so that each pairing of a situation with a belief combination occurred 195 times across all subjects. Each subject got all 10 situations, which means that she or he got a

TABLE 11.1 (cont'd.)

Situation	Behavioral Intent	Studies of Corresponding Behaviors
6. Mr. F. has an appointment with Mr. X concerning a matter important to both of them on Wednesday at 11 A.M.	Mr. F will decide to come to the meeting on time.	Chapter 7, Study IV
7. In the framework of sports training, the twelfth graders are about to start a three-mile running race. The winner will get a special prize. G. does not excel in races of this kind, and knows that winning will require a special effort on his part.	G. will decide to make a special effort to win the race.	Chapter 7, Study I
8. H. and I. are friends. One day they discussed something and H. remarked on I.'s manner of speaking. I., who was irritated, answered harshly and insulted H. Next day, I. thought about this quarrel and considered the possibility of contacting H. in order to initiate a reconciliation.	I. will decide to contact H. and initiate a reconciliation.	
9. In the course of an exam a friend turned to J. and asked him to pass to him the answer to one of the questions. The proctors are very strict, and cancel on the spot the exam of anyone found copying answers from another student or passing information to another student. J. passes the answer to the friend. A week later there is another exam and the same friend again asks J. to pass him the answer to one of the questions.	J. will decide to pass the answer to his friend.	
10. Dr. K. is a busy scientist. One day he has to read a certain book important for his work. The Table of Contents indicates to him that three of the chapters though essential may perhaps be marginal to his theme.	Dr. K. will decide to read the three chapters.	

random sample of 10 of the 16 possible pairings between situations and belief combinations.

As mentioned, the sample of pairings between situations and belief combinations was specific to each questionnaire. Also, the gender of the figures in the situations and the sequence of the situations were randomized for each questionnaire. In addition, the order of the beliefs was randomized separately for each situation with regard to the sequence of supporting and nonsupporting beliefs and the representation of the four CO components. Thus, in a certain sense each subject got a unique questionnaire that formed a random sample from the finite population of questionnaires prepared for this study.

The instructions to the subject were: "Sometimes we know what a person thinks about a certain matter, but we do not know what he will decide to do. In each of the following pages you will find a description of a certain situation. The person who finds himself in that situation has to decide about how to behave. His decision derives from his opinions and beliefs about the situation. After the description of the situation you will find a sample of the opinions and thoughts of that person about the situation and a possible decision of the person. Assuming that the stated opinions and thoughts are the only basis for the person's decision, you are requested to determine, according to the given material, the chances that the person will decide to behave in the specific manner mentioned in the page." The manner of responding on the 7-point scale was explained and a detailed example was appended to the description. It was also mentioned that the various situations were unrelated and should be treated independently, each on its own merits. The subject was urged to deal with the situations in their given sequence.

The questionnaire was pretested for clarity. Its test-retest reliability over a 2-week period in a sample of 42 subjects, each of whom got the same questionnaire twice, was $r = .95$.

RESULTS AND CONCLUSIONS

The results of the study fully support our hypothesis. Table 11.2 shows that in each of the 10 situations the main effects of all four CO components were significant. The level of significance of the different CO components sometimes varied from one situation to another, but it was always high enough to indicate that the subjects considered all four components when estimating the likelihood of a behavioral intent. Analysis of the results of all 10 situations together (Table 11.3) again shows that the main effects of all four CO components are highly significant.

The findings summarized in Table 11.4 highlight the contribution of the four CO components from a somewhat different point of view. The table demonstrates that there is a perfect positive correlation between the number of CO components supporting the behavioral intent and the mean estimated probability of that intent. The estimated probability of the intent is highest when all four CO components support it. When less than three components support it, the estimated probability of the intent drops below 50%, which suggests that it may readily be replaced by another behavioral intent. These findings correspond fully to the findings concerning the importance of all four CO components in successful attempts at predicting molar behaviors (Chapters 7 and 8).

TABLE 11.2
Analysis of Variance (2 × 2 × 2 × 2) of Responses to Each Situation Separately

SOURCE OF VARIATION	df	SITUATION 1		SITUATION 2		SITUATION 3		SITUATION 4		SITUATION 5	
		MS	F	MS	F	MS	F	MS	F	MS	F
Norms (N)	1	34.93	15.51**	89.70	28.79**	76.47	25.27**	32.89	9.97**	109.07	30.01**
General beliefs (GB)	1	8.56	3.80[1]	70.15	22.51**	58.91	19.47***	53.10	16.10**	43.06	11.85***
Goals (Go)	1	45.73	20.31**	97.79	31.38***	137.31	45.38***	9.34	2.83[1]	54.36	14.96***
Beliefs about self (BS)	1	82.33	36.56**	124.57	39.97**	149.42	49.38***	68.06	20.63**	10.36	2.85[1]
Significant interactions:											
GB × BS	1										
N × BS	1					11.01	3.64[1]				
Go × BS	1										
N × GB × Go	1	11.19	4.97*	12.23	3.93*						
N × GB × BS	1	13.44	5.97*								
N × Go × BS	1										
N × GB × Go × BS	1										
Error	296	2.25		3.12		3.03		3.30		3.63	

(Table continues on following page)

TABLE 11.2 (cont'd)

	df	SITUATION 6 MS	F	SITUATION 7 MS	F	SITUATION 8 MS	F	SITUATION 9 MS	F	SITUATION 10 MS	F
Norms (N)	1	46.16	19.80**	65.73	22.42**	8.00	2.75[1]	51.54	19.70**	114.23	40.15**
General beliefs (GB)	1	85.39	36.64**	8.00	2.73[1]	20.95	7.19**	82.66	31.59***	77.24	27.15***
Goals (Go)	1	108.28	46.46***	115.82	39.51***	95.50	32.76***	66.65	25.48***	57.89	20.35***
Beliefs about self (BS)	1	129.39	55.51***	53.91	18.39***	27.79	9.53***	108.92	41.63***	120.76	42.45**
Significant interactions:											
GB × BS	1	22.68	9.73**								
N × BS	1			10.03	3.42[1]						
Go × BS	1	13.42	5.76*							14.74	5.18*
N × GB × Go	1										
N × GB × BS	1							16.86	6.44**		
N × Go × BS	1			10.32	3.52[1]						
N × GB × Go × BS	1										
Error	296	2.33		2.93		2.91		2.62		2.84	

Note. For contents of situations see Table 11.1.
[1] $p < .10$.   * $p < .05$.   ** $p < .01$.

TABLE 11.3
Analysis of Variance (2 × 2 × 2 × 2, Repeated Measures)
of Responses to All 10 Situations

Source of Variation	MS	df	Error	df	F
Norms (N)	157.20	1	3.91	791	40.20**
General beliefs (GB)	320.94	1	2.92	791	109.91**
Goals (Go)	161.00	1	3.14	791	51.27**
Beliefs about self (BS)	22.08	1	3.14	791	7.03**
Within subjects (P)	2.97	98	3.06	1470	.97
Significant interactions:					
GB × BS	19.33	1	3.30	791	5.85*
Go × BS	19.33	1	3.32	791	5.82*

* $p < .05$. ** $p < .01$.

A striking feature of the data in Tables 11.2 and 11.3 is the surprisingly low number of significant interactions among the four CO components. In all 10 situations, no more than 10 interactions of the total of 110 possible ones turned out to be significant (3 only at the .10 level). Most of these appeared only once and thus may safely be viewed as the product of the specific relations of the meaning of the situation, the behavioral intent, and the particular beliefs. More importantly, the overall low number of interactions seems to indicate the overwhelming impact of the four CO components, which far surpasses the effects of the particular nature of the situation.

This same conclusion is further strengthened by the finding that there was no significant effect of response tendencies of individuals across the

TABLE 11.4
Relation between Number of CO Components
Supporting the Behavioral Intent
and the Mean of Its
Estimated Probability

Number of CO Components Supporting Behavioral Intent	Mean of Estimated Probability[a]	SD
Four CO components	2.29	1.59
Three CO components	2.77	1.75
Two CO components	3.54	1.70
One CO component	4.38	1.96
Zero CO components	5.01	2.20

Note. Spearman rank correlation: $r_s = 1.00$, $p < .001$.
[a] The scale runs from 1 (high) to 7 (low).

10 situations (Table 11.3). Also, the table of intercorrelations between the responses to the 10 situations reveals generally low correlation values. Although 13 of the 45 correlations are significant (3 at the .01 level), the highest correlation coefficient was .18 (between situations 7 and 10), which still is low and points to only 3% of common factors in the respective variances of the two situations.

In sum, the results demonstrate that the subjects relied on all four CO components for estimating the probability of forming a specific behavioral intent. If we use the findings for drawing inferences about the processes involved in forming behavioral intents, we may conclude that a behavioral intent is invariably related to beliefs of all four CO components, each of which exerts its impact in the act of clustering that results in the formation of a behavioral intent.

STUDY II
Beliefs Underlying Behavioral Intents

PURPOSE AND HYPOTHESIS

The purpose of this study, like that of Study I, was to investigate the relation of behavioral intents to the four CO components. The two studies differ, however, in their mode of examining this relation: in Study I subjects were asked to estimate the probability of a behavioral intent from a given set of beliefs; in the present study subjects were asked to select beliefs that could underlie or lead to a given behavioral intent. In Study I, then, the subjects were required to proceed from beliefs to the behavioral intent, whereas in Study II they had to proceed in the reverse direction—from the behavioral intent back to the beliefs.

The similarity in purpose and difference in methodology of the two studies made it possible for us to examine the same hypothesis from two distinct vantage points and in two separate contexts. Accordingly, the hypothesis of the present study, formulated in terms appropriate to the method applied, was that in selecting beliefs presumed to underlie a given behavioral intent subjects would consider beliefs of all four CO components. This hypothesis is in fact identical to the hypothesis of Study I and derives from the same general considerations of CO theory as well as specific research findings of the prediction studies that have a bearing upon the role of the CO components in forming the behavioral intent. Thus, if the findings of this study tally with those of Study I, despite the difference between the two studies in method and design, our conclusions about the relations between behavioral intents and beliefs would gain greatly in validity and generality.

METHOD

Subjects. Originally 143 subjects participated in the study. Seven subjects were taken out of the sample because their responses were largely invalid (see first paragraph of "Results and Conclusions"). This reduced the effective sample to 136 subjects, 68 males and 68 females. They ranged in age from 19 to 33 years. About half the subjects were selected randomly from the population of individuals who had recently started the universally obligatory military service, and the remaining half were selected randomly from the population of students at various institutes of higher learning. None of the subjects was familiar with the CO theory.

Procedure and Materials. All the subjects were administered the standard questionnaire of this study in small groups varying in size from 3 to 15 individuals. No time limit was set on answering the questionnaire. An experimenter was present throughout the session and the subjects were encouraged to ask about anything not clear to them. Three different experimenters participated in the sessions. The assignment of experimenters to groups of subjects was on a completely random basis.

The questionnaire included a short description of a situation, the statement of a behavioral intent relevant to that situation, and a list of 144 beliefs. The situation was described as follows: "Dan and Gideon (or: Yael and Anat, if you prefer) are good friends. They have been friends for a long time and they spend much time together. One day they met and discussed some problem. Dan (or Yael) made a remark about Gideon's (or Anat's) manner of speaking. Gideon (or Anat), who was irritated, responded harshly and insulted Dan (or Yael). Then they parted. Some time later, after the meeting, Gideon (or Anat) thought a lot about what had happened and considered the possibility of contacting Dan (or Yael) in order to initiate a reconciliation with him (or her)." The statement of the behavioral intent was positive in half the cases and negative in the other half. The positive version read: "Eventually Gideon (or Anat) decided to contact Dan (or Yael) the next morning and initiate a reconciliation with him (or her)." The negative version read: "Eventually Gideon (or Anat) decided not to contact Dan (or Yael) and not to initiate a reconciliation with him (or her)."

The stated beliefs represented the four CO components, three themes, and were in principle relevant for three different behavioral intents. The three themes were "personal qualities and reconciliation," "friendship and reconciliation," and "quarreling and reconciliation." These themes were selected as the motifs most frequently occurring in the responses of 60 pretest subjects who were asked about the meaning of "reconciliation." The three behavioral intents were: initiating a reconciliation, not initiating a reconciliation, and telling a lie. The third behavioral intent was irrelevant to the described situation and the beliefs concerning it were included as a control to check the attention of the subjects and consequently the validity of their responses. The CO components, themes, and intents formed a kind of three-dimensional matrix with 36 ($4 \times 3 \times 3$) cells, each cell being defined by specific values along the CO components, themes, and intents. Each cell contained four beliefs, selected randomly from a larger pool judged as adequate by at least 85% of 30 pretest subjects. Thus, there were 36 beliefs representing each CO component, 48 beliefs representing each theme, and 48 beliefs representing each behavioral intent. Alternately, beliefs referring to the positive and negative behavioral intents may also be characterized as orientationally directed proreconciliation (48 beliefs) or antireconciliation (48 beliefs). In order to examine the relative effects of the four CO components and the three content themes on the responses of the subjects, two forms of questionnaire were used: in one the beliefs were ordered in four groups, each representing one of the CO components; in the other, the beliefs were ordered in three groups, each representing one of the themes. Each group of beliefs was typed on a separate page but was not identified as a group by any description or label. The sequence of the groups as well as the order of beliefs within each group were completely randomized. Thus, the number and nature of the beliefs remained constant across questionnaires but the order in which the beliefs were presented varied from one questionnaire to another.

The instructions to the subjects were presented both orally and in typed form. The subjects were requested to read attentively the given list of "thoughts, memories, goals, informations, etc. of Gideon (or Anat)" and to check those items in the list which "could have made Gideon (or Anat) reach the decision [not] to contact Dan (or Yael) and [not] to initiate a reconciliation with him (or her)." It was explained that the checked items should clarify why and how the decision was made. The experimenter emphasized that the subjects were free to check as many or as few items as they saw fit, that they could change their minds and revise their responses as often as necessary and that there was no time limit in answering the questionnaire. The subjects were encouraged to ask about anything unclear to them.

We settled on these instructions as the easiest and clearest for subjects to follow. The test-retest reliability of responses was found to be .95 and .98 in terms of CO components and in terms of themes, respectively, for 25 subjects over a 3-week interval.

RESULTS AND CONCLUSIONS

The validity of the responses was examined by considering the relative number of irrelevant responses checked by each subject, an irrelevant response being defined as a belief pertaining to the behavioral intent of lying (included for purposes of control). Seven subjects, whose proportion of irrelevant responses exceeded 25% of the total of beliefs they checked, were taken out of the sample.

The mean number of all beliefs checked by the subjects was 26.1 ($SD = 10.01$). When irrelevant beliefs, i.e., beliefs relating to the behavioral intent of lying, are considered as error and taken out, the mean number of relevant beliefs checked by the subjects drops to 24.3 ($SD = 9.57$), the range being 8–52. We considered the total of relevant beliefs as basic in defining the dependent variables in this study. In order to neutralize the varying number of beliefs checked by the different subjects, the responses of each subject in each of the CO components or in each of the themes were divided by the total number of relevant beliefs the subject had checked.

In order to determine whether it was justified to analyze the data of the whole sample together, we tested the effects of various factors on the subjects' responses. Table 11.5 shows that there were no significant main effects due to the form of the questionnaire, that is, the manner in which the beliefs were grouped, to the type of the behavioral intent stated in the questionnaire, to the orientativeness of the beliefs pro- or antireconciliation, or to the sex of the subjects. Thus, no differences in the subjects' responses can be attributed to any of these factors. There were, however, two significant interactions. The first demonstrates that the subjects were sensitive to the particular contents of the beliefs and tended to check predominantly proreconciliation beliefs when the behavioral intent stated in their questionnaire was "to reconcile," and alternatively, subjects checked mainly antireconcilation beliefs when the behavioral intent stated in their questionnaire was "not to reconcile." This finding lends further support to the validity of the responses. The second interaction shows that males had a slight tendency to check more beliefs when the behavioral intent was "to reconcile" than when it was "not to reconcile," whereas females checked fewer beliefs in the case of the intent "to reconcile" than in the case of the intent "not to recon-

TABLE 11.5
Four-Factor Analysis of Variance (2 × 2 × 2 × 2)
of the Choice of Belief Statements

Source of Variation	df	MS	F
Form of questionnaire (components or themes) (A)	1	.000	< 1
Type of behavioral intent (B)[a]	1	.124	2.31
Orientativeness of beliefs (C)	1	.000	< 1
Sex (D)	1	.000	< 1
Significant interactions:			
B × C[b]	1	21.001	390.21**
B × D[c]	1	.278	5.15*
Error	132	.054	

[a] The error term for this factor, which alone had repeated measures, was .000; therefore it was "added" to the overall error term.

[b] For the behavioral intent of "reconciliating," the means of beliefs pro and anti were .80 and .20, respectively; for the behavioral intent of "not reconciliating," they were .76 and .24, respectively.

[c] For the behavioral intent of "reconciliating" the means of boys and girls were .55 and .49, respectively; for the behavioral intent of "not reconciliating," they were .45 and .51, respectively.

* $p < .05.$ ** $p < .01.$

cile." The effect was, however, very moderate. Further analyses of the data showed that neither the variable of sex nor that of form of questionnaire was related to any differences in the number of checked beliefs representing the four CO components or the three themes. These results as well as those presented in Table 11.5 support the possibility of analyzing the data of the whole sample together.

Table 11.6 shows that there was no main effect due to the CO components, that is, there were no significant differences in the number of checked beliefs representing the four CO components. The means were .28 for beliefs about self, .26 for general beliefs, .24 for norms, and .24 for goals. This finding lends full support to the hypothesis. It corroborates our expectation that subjects would endorse beliefs of all four CO components when trying to account for a behavioral intent or when tracing back the considerations and processes underlying it and leading up to it.

The finding is valid not only on the group level but also on the individual level. Out of 136 subjects, 132 (95%) checked beliefs representing all four components. Only one subject did not check beliefs corresponding to general beliefs, one subject did not check any norm beliefs, and two subjects did not check any goal beliefs. These results are all the more striking when one recalls that our subjects knew nothing about the CO theory.

Another remarkable fact is the even distribution of beliefs across the four CO components. Each of the four CO components was represented by about 25% of the beliefs checked by every subject. It may be noted that in the domain of attitudes and behavior as well (Chapter 12) we found that an even distribution of belief statements across the four CO components increases the likelihood of a positive prediction of behaviors from attitudes. These two findings lend direct support to the procedure, used so far in all our prediction studies (Chapters 7 and 8), of assessing the CO components through almost equal numbers of beliefs and of assigning equal weights to the four CO components. The support is important since it derives from sources independent of the positive results of our prediction studies themselves.

The other findings of this study are of less consequence in the present framework. They reflect mainly specific effects of contents. For example, subjects checked significantly more beliefs pertaining to the third theme ($\bar{X} = .37$) than to the second ($\bar{X} = .34$) and first ($\bar{X} = .30$) themes (Table 11.6). Moreover, there were significant interactions between CO components and the themes as well as the kind of intent.

In sum, the findings of the study show that in attempting to account for a given behavioral intent, subjects have recourse to beliefs referring to all four CO components to an equal degree. Like Study I, this study shows that the four CO components are invariably involved in the deri-

TABLE 11.6
Three-Factor Analysis of Variance (4 × 3 × 2)
of the Choice of Belief Statements

Source of Variation	df	MS	F
CO components (A)	3	.003	1.37
Themes (B)	2	.040	16.53*
Behavioral intent (C)[a]	1	.005	2.47
A × B	6	.008	3.44*
A × C	3	.017	6.89*
B × C	2	.020	8.26*
A × B × C	6	.003	1.37
Within cell (Experimental Error)	3240	.002	

[a] The error term for this factor, which had repeated measures, was .000; therefore it was "added" to the overall error term.
* $p < .01$.

vation of the behavioral intent and that they exert their effect in this process regardless of the content or direction of the intent, the specific themes referred to in various belief clusters, or the particular response tendencies and sex of the subjects.

STUDY III
The Meaning of Behavioral Intents

PURPOSE AND HYPOTHESES

This study was motivated by the conceptually precarious status of the behavioral intent between beliefs on the one hand and behavioral programs on the other. The intent entertains complex relations with both. Though distinct from beliefs of the four CO components, whose clustering it manifests, in form it is similar to a belief about self, and in content it resembles a goal belief. Again, the behavioral intent is distinct from behavioral programs in content and function, yet in some sense it implies behavioral programs, directs attention to a particular class of programs, and even biases toward the choice of one program over another. The relations of the behavioral intent to beliefs and programs may be variously formulated, emphasizing their affinities and disparities, their differential functions, or their position in a continuum of increasing specification running from goals through intents to programs. All formulations, however, highlight the particular status of the behavioral intent as a bridge between beliefs and action. It is this status that gives the behavioral intent its specific role as well as its controversial standing.

It was the purpose of this study to help clarify the concept of the behavioral intent, particularly in regard to its relations with beliefs and behavioral programs. The major and special tool used for this clarification was the instrument for the assessment of meaning described in Chapter 2. This instrument made it possible to explore the similarities and differences of intents, beliefs, and programs in terms of meaning dimensions, and, alternately, to test the adequacy of these meaning dimensions for revealing nontrivial aspects of the studied relations.

The hypotheses of the study referred to the distinctive features of behavioral intents as compared to goals and behavioral programs (we focused only on goal beliefs since they bear the closest and most controversial relation to the behavioral intent). Subjects were requested to communicate the meaning of statements reflecting behavioral intents, goals, and behavioral programs. Thus, the hypotheses were formulated in terms of meaning dimensions characterizing the meaning of behavioral intents, in contrast to goals as well as to behavioral programs. The first hypothesis was based on the assumption that the central motifs in the meaning of behavioral intents would be actions designed to aid goal attainment, hence classifiable as instances of "manner of occurrence or operation," and references to the desired goal, which would be presented as instances of "function, purpose, or role" of the described actions. We expected the dimension "manner of occurrence or operation" to be dominant in the meaning of behavioral programs but not in the meaning of goals. Concerning "function, purpose, or role," we did not expect it to be dominant in the meanings of either goals or behavioral programs. Accordingly, the hypothesis: the dimension "manner of occurrence or operation" would be significantly more frequent in the meaning of behavioral intents than in the meaning of goals, but not more frequent than in the meaning of behavioral programs; and the dimension "function, purpose, or role" would be more frequent in the meaning of the behavioral intents than in the meanings of goals and of programs. The rationale for this hypothesis was that whereas the goal focuses on the desired or rejected action or state, and the behavioral program focuses on the specific "how" of performance with or without continuous awareness of the goal, the behavioral intent probably focuses on a generally outlined course of action corresponding to some envisaged goal.

The second hypothesis dealt with meaning dimensions of relatively low incidence in the meaning of behavioral intents. The hypothesis was that meaning dimensions relating to the specific details of performance, that is, mainly "time," "location," and "domain of application," would be less frequent in the meaning of the behavioral intent than in the meaning of the behavioral program. The rationale for this hypothesis was that the behavioral intent implies only one or more general courses of action appropriate for attaining the goal, whereas the selection, outlining, and coordination of the specifics are left to the behavioral program.

METHOD

Subjects. The subjects of the study were 55 individuals (25 males and 30 females) ranging in age from 16 to 46 years. Fifteen were students in high schools, 13 were students in teachers' seminars and universities, and 27 were clerks or secretaries in various firms. None was acquainted with the system of meaning dimensions used in the study. (The same subjects were used in Chapter 10, Study II.)

Procedure and Materials. Each subject was interviewed individually by one of three experimenters. The experimenter explained to the subject that his or her task would be to communicate to some other person, an imagined partner, the meaning of a few statements. The subject was encouraged to communicate the meaning of the statements using any medium of expression—talking, writing, drawing, pantomiming, describing drawing or bodily expression, and so on. If the subject asked whether to explain the meaning of individual words, the experimenter emphasized that in principle there was no need to do that, unless the subject thought the word itself or the communication of its meaning was particularly important. For the sake of general clarification the experimenter explained that the subject should supplement the given statement with any additions or explications that might conceivably help the listener to understand the statement adequately, in the same way the subject understood it.

The statements were presented in typed form, each on a separate card placed in front of the subject. Some of the statements were complete, whereas others were to be completed by the subject before their meaning could be conveyed. The reason for presenting incomplete statements was the expectation that responses would be more valid and revealing if the subjects participated in the formulation of the stimuli than if they got ready-made stimuli. However, in order to make it possible to compare responses of different subjects, we sometimes delineated the range of possible completions of a statement by presenting a few alternatives as examples, without, however, suggesting the need to select one of them.

The six statements relevant to this study were interspersed randomly with eight other statements. The order of presentation was random. The subject's task in regard to all 14 statements was alike. The six relevant statements were:

"My goal is . . . (to study, to succeed, to avoid tension, to . . .)";
"I want . . . (to live an orderly life, to live an adventurous life, to . . .)";
"I intend . . . (to buy a car, to . . .)";
"I made up my mind . . .";
"My plan(s) is (are) . . .";
"My plan(s) for tomorrow . . .".

The first two statements were designed to reflect goal beliefs; the third and fourth, behavioral intents; and the fifth and sixth, behavioral programs.

The responses of the subjects to the statements were analyzed, in terms of the meaning dimensions presented in Chapter 2, by two independent judges, who first designated the response units (i.e., meaning values) in each communication of meaning and then classified each as exemplifying one—and only one—of the meaning dimensions. The interjudge reliability was perfect in 100% of the cases with regard to definition of units and in 98% of the cases with regard to classifying these units into meaning dimensions. Here are some examples of responses to the behavioral intent "I intend to take a vacation" and their classification: "It means, to get up very late, talk with my friend on the phone for an hour, swim in the sea, drink my morning coffee very slowly . . ." —manner (action); "I have to take a vacation because I am too tense and overtired"—antecedents; "I think I will take the vacation next week"—time; "It will serve to make me fit again"—function.

RESULTS AND CONCLUSIONS

Table 11.7 presents the distribution of patterns in the subjects' responses to the six statements reflecting goals, behavioral intents, and behavioral programs. Each pattern consists in the specification of one or more meaning dimensions referred to in the response, regardless of the number of meaning values used in referring to the dimension. The range of different dimensions per pattern is 1 to 5. On the average each subject referred in each response to 2.87 different meaning dimensions (see Table 11.8). It is to be noted that this mean is very near to the mean of 2.80 meaning dimensions per term based on the responses of hundreds of subjects to various single-word stimuli (Kreitler & Kreitler, 1968). Nevertheless, there are differences in the mean number of dimensions used in response to the various statements. Following an overall significant F ($F = 3.20$, $df = 2/108$, $p < .05$) in a single-factor repeated-measures analysis of variance, a test of the differences between the individual means revealed significant differences in the mean numbers of dimensions between intents and goals ($q_r = 3.01$, $p < .05$), as well as between intents and programs ($q_r = 2.84$, $p < .05$). As a post hoc explanation we might suggest that the number of meaning dimensions is highest for behavioral intents because the meaning communication has to refer both to some of the aspects of goals and to some of the characteristics of behavioral programs.

Tables 11.9 and 11.10 present the findings relevant to the first and second hypotheses. Since in some cases the differences in findings concerning two statements exemplifying the same concept were significant, and since averaging would not have been a reasonable procedure under these circumstances, the significance of the differences among goals, intents, and programs in the frequency of the meaning dimensions was tested separately for each of the eight combinations (i.e., 2 goals × 2 intents × 2 programs) of data (see Table 11.10). Only results confirmed across the eight separate tests were considered stable enough to qualify as findings in this study.

Concerning the first hypothesis, Tables 11.9 and 11.10 show that the dimension "manner of occurrence or operation" as manifested in actions

TABLE 11.7

Frequencies of Meaning Dimension Patterns in the Meaning
of Goals, Behavioral Intents, and Behavioral Programs

Goals	% of Ss	Behavioral Intents	% of Ss	Behavioral Programs	% of Ss
Goal 1		**Behavioral Intent 1**		**Program 1**	
Action	9.09	Manner (action),		Manner (action),	
Action, function	7.27	function, time	21.82	location, domain	
Action, manner		Antecedents, function	1.82	of application	7.27
(action)[a]	7.27	Manner (action),		Manner (action), time	34.55
Action, antecedents	14.55	function, time	10.91	Manner (action),	
Action, location	3.64	Manner (action),		time, location, domain	
Action, domain of		function, consequences	27.27	of application	25.51
application	9.09	Manner (action),		Manner (action),	
Action, emotion	5.45	function, emotion	5.45	time, location	14.55
Action, manner		Manner (action), func-		Manner (action),	
(action), antecedents	10.92	tion, domain of appli-		time, judgment	9.09
Action, function, ante-		cation, consequences	1.82	Manner (action), time,	
cedents, consequences	9.09	Manner (action), func-		function, antecedents	9.09
State	7.27	tion, time, antecedents	14.55	**Program 2**	
State, antecedents	7.27	Manner (action), func-		Manner (action),	
State, manner (action),		tion, time, location,		location, domain of	
antecedents	9.59	antecedents	9.09	application	20.02
Goal 2		Manner (action),		Manner (action),	
Action	5.45	function, antecedents,		time, location	30.91
Action, function	5.45	emotion	3.64	Manner (action),	
Action, manner (action)	7.27	Manner (action),		time, antecedents	38.22
Action, consequences	7.27	function, antecedents,		Manner (action),	
Action, antecedents	10.91	emotion	1.82	function	1.82
Action, emotion	3.64	Manner (action),		Manner (action), time,	
Action, manner		location	1.82	location, domain of	
(action), antecedents	7.27	**Behavioral Intent 2**		application	3.64
Action, function,		Manner (action),		Manner (action), time,	
antecedents	7.27	function	21.82	antecedents, function	3.64
Action, function,		Manner (action),		Manner (action),	
consequences	12.73	function, antecedents	25.45	antecedents, time,	
Action, manner		Manner (action),		emotion	1.82
(action), judgment	3.64	function, time	21.82		
Action, function,		Manner (action),			
judgment	9.09	function, antecedents	16.36		
Action, inclusion,		Manner, (action),			
domain of application	3.64	location, time	3.64		
Action, inclusion,		Manner (action),			
judgment	5.45	antecedents, location	3.64		
State, time	1.82	Manner (action),			
State, time	1.82	function, antecedents,			
State, time, inclusion	3.64	emotion, location	5.45		
		Manner (action),			
		consequences, location	1.82		

[a] Stands for "manner of occurrence or operation" manifested in the form of actions.

TABLE 11.8
Means and *SDs* of Distributions of Meaning
Patterns Presented in Table 11.7

Distributions	$\overline{X}$	SD
Goal 1	2.31	.85
Goal 2	2.42	.68
Behavioral intent 1	2.89	.65
Behavioral intent 2	3.51	.76
Behavioral program 1	3.00	.83
Behavioral program 2	3.07	.32
Total	2.87	.68

was used, as expected, more frequently in responses to behavioral intents than in responses to goals. In contrast, it was used, again in line with the hypothesis, with an almost identical frequency in the responses to intents and programs. The overall differences in the frequencies of this dimension were highly significant. Yet this finding reflects only the significant differences in the frequency of this dimension between the meanings of intents and goals (χ^2 values in the range 40.08–58.19, $p < .001$) as well as between programs and goals (χ^2 values in the range 40.28–56.64, $p < .001$), but not between intents and programs.

The second aspect of the first hypothesis deals with the dimension "function, purpose, or role." Again, the findings show that, concerning the meaning communications of the three types of statements, the differences in the frequency of this dimension are highly significant. As expected, this dimension is more frequent in response to behavioral intents than in response to goals (χ^2 values in the range 25.32–58.46, $p < .001$) or in response to behavioral programs (χ^2 values in the range 66.94–70.48, $p < .001$). The chi-square values are high enough to compensate even for the nonindependence of the tests between intents and goals and between intents and programs.

When testing both aspects of the first hypothesis together we readily find that approximately 90% of the subjects used both "manner of occurrence or operation" and "function, purpose, or role" in communicating the meaning of behavioral intents (see fifth line from bottom in Tables 11.9 and 11.10). This high percentage contrasts markedly with the 3–9% of subjects who used this pattern of dimensions in communicating the meaning of programs, and with the absence of even a single subject using this pattern to communicate the meaning of goals. Thus, the findings fully confirm the first hypothesis in showing the intimate relation of behavioral intents to programming a course of action and to the functional value of the planned actions with regard to some goal.

The findings also confirm our second hypothesis. They show, as expected, that subjects use the following dimensions less frequently to convey the meaning of behavioral intents than to convey the meaning of programs: "location" (χ^2 values in the range 17.36–26.02, $p < .001$), "domain of application" (χ^2 values in the range 18.72–32.78, $p < .001$), and "time" (χ^2 values ranging from 3.60, between intent 1 and program 2, which is nonsignificant; through 8.89, $p < .01$, between intent 1 and program 1; and 26.86, $p < .001$, between intent 2 and program 2; to 38.34, $p < .001$, between intent 2 and program 1). Thus, the dimensions reflecting the specifics of programming a course of action are, as expected, much more dominant in the meaning communications

TABLE 11.9
Frequency of Meaning Dimensions in the Meaning of
Goals, Behavioral Intents, and Behavioral Programs

Meaning Dimensions	Goals[a]		Behavioral Intents[b]		Behavioral Programs	
	1	2	1	2	1	2
Action	76.36	89.08	—	—	—	—
State	23.63	10.91	—	—	—	—
Manner (action)	27.27	18.18	98.19	100	100	100
Function	16.36	34.54	98.19	90.90	9.09	5.46
Antecedents	50.91	25.45	30.92	50.90	9.09	43.68
Location	3.64	—	12.73	14.55	47.33	54.57
Domain of application	9.09	3.64	1.82	—	32.78	23.66
Emotion	5.45	3.64	10.91	5.45	—	1.82
Time	—	3.64	56.37	25.46	92.79	78.23
Consequences	9.09	20.00	29.09	1.82	—	—
Range of inclusion	—	9.09	—	—	—	—
Beliefs and judgments	—	12.73	—	—	9.09	—
Manner (action) and function	—	—	87.28	90.90	9.09	3.64
Manner (action) and time	—	—	56.37	25.46	92.79	78.23
Manner (action) and location	—	—	12.73	14.55	47.33	54.57
Manner (action) and domain of application	—	—	1.82	—	32.78	23.66
Manner (action) and/or time and/or location and/or domain of application	—	—	60.01	36.37	100	100

Note. For the significance of differences in frequency see Table 11.10.
[a] These findings do not differ significantly from findings about the meaning of goals obtained in another group of subjects (Chapter 10, Study II and Table 10.4).
[b] The same data are presented in Table 10.5.

TABLE 11.10

Significance of Differences (x^2) in the Frequency of Meaning Dimensions among Goals, Behavioral Intents, and Behavioral Programs

Meaning Dimensions	Goal 1, Intent 1, Program 1	Goal 1, Intent 1, Program 2	Goal 1, Intent 2, Program 1	Goal 1, Intent 2, Program 2	Goal 2, Intent 2, Program 1	Goal 2, Intent 2, Program 2	Goal 2, Intent 1, Program 1	Goal 2, Intent 1, Program 2
Action	152.74†	152.74†	152.74†	152.74†	178.18†	178.18†	178.18†	178.18†
State	47.24†	47.24†	47.24†	47.24†	21.80†	21.80†	21.80†	21.80†
Manner (action)	45.79†	45.79†	46.56†	46.56†	61.35†	61.35†	54.31†	54.31†
Function	15.62†	5.63*	16.35†	6.22*	35.18†	23.00†	36.56†	22.98†
Antecedents	23.87†	4.90	31.53†	.72	83.39†	32.16†	11.83**	5.25
Location	50.07†	62.39†	47.35†	59.31†	56.98†	69.32†	59.92†	72.68†
Domain of application	35.91**	21.43**	40.96†	26.18†	53.11†	35.65†	47.26†	30.22†
Emotion	10.91**	6.91*	5.45	2.08	3.98	1.80	12.72**	6.35*
Time	87.92†	72.62†	116.62†	92.14†	106.30†	82.21†	78.90†	63.82†
Consequences	34.80†	34.80†	12.73**	12.73**	33.65†	33.65†	30.10†	30.10†
Range of inclusion	.00	.00	.00	.00	18.18†	18.18†	18.18†	18.18†
Beliefs and judgments	18.18†	.00	18.18†	.00	11.83**	25.48†	11.83**	25.48†
Manner (action) and function	94.73†	160.82†	150.40†	159.40†	94.73†	160.82†	150.40†	159.40†
Manner (action) and time	87.88†	72.62†	116.62†	92.14†	87.88†	72.62†	116.62†	92.14†
Manner (action) and location	59.92†	72.68†	56.98†	69.32†	59.92†	72.68†	56.98†	69.32†
Manner (action) and domain of application	58.87†	40.84†	65.54†	47.30†	58.87†	40.84†	65.54†	47.30†
Manner (action) and/or time and/or location and/or domain of application	94.99†	94.99†	112.71†	112.71†	94.99†	94.99†	112.71†	112.71†

Note. For the data see Table 11.9.
* $p < .05$.   ** $p < .01$.   † $p < .001$.

329

of behavioral programs than in those of behavioral intents, or for that matter, of goals. If we examine the frequency of patterns consisting of more than one meaning dimension, it turns out that the combination of "manner of occurrence or operation" with "time" is the most frequent in the subjects' responses, and that it is followed by the combination of "manner of occurrence or operation" with "location," or "domain of application," in that order. These patterns are significantly more frequent in the responses to programs than in the responses to behavioral intents (the χ^2 values are the same as those mentioned above with regard to differences in the incidence of the single relevant dimensions). Most important, however, is the finding that the pattern of "manner of occurrence or operation" coupled with any one or more of the three mentioned dimensions "time," "location," and "domain of application" occurs in the responses to programs of 100% of the subjects (χ^2 values with regard to the data of the behavioral intents range from 10, $p < .01$, to 29.70, $p < .001$).

Yet to characterize the findings fully we should also mention that in responses to intents and programs there is a difference in the specificity of the meaning values subsumed under the dimension "manner of occurrence or operation." The meaning values referring to intents are more general than those referring to programs. "Generality" and "specificity" here signify the relative range of different actions that may be envisaged as implementing or manifesting the action mentioned in the subject's response. Thus, "earning money" is a relatively more general meaning value than "earning money by working as a lawyer in a law firm," and "taking care" is more general than "driving cautiously" or "not walking in side streets at night." When the meaning values of the dimension "manner of occurrence or operation" were classified by two independent judges as manifesting one of two levels of generality, it was found that 81% of the meaning values in responses to programs were specific, whereas only 23% of meaning values were specific in responses to behavioral intents ($\chi^2 = 32.35$, $p < .001$). This finding corresponds to the former findings, which revealed the focusing of the programs' meaning on the details of performance.

In sum, the findings show that the meanings of goals, behavioral intents, and behavioral programs are each characterized by a different focal pattern of meaning dimensions. The meaning of goals characteristically consists of the specification of an action or state desired as an end, accompanied by fringe statements about the reasons for preferring this action or state, or the envisaged consequences of having attained it, or the evaluation of this goal, and sometimes even indications of possible actions that may help in attaining it. In the meaning communications of behavioral intents we usually find general descriptions of types of actions to be undertaken and their relation to the envisaged goal, plus secondary statements referring to other meaning dimensions. In the meaning communications of behavioral programs we usually find highly specific descriptions of actions to be undertaken, including their "when," "where," "by which means," and "how."

Concerning the behavioral intent, this study confirmed the assumption that it forms a real bridge between beliefs, specifically goal beliefs, and behavioral programs. Its meaning reveals as much concern with the envisaged end, as in goals, as with the practical actions to be undertaken for its implementation, as in behavioral programs. Yet, unlike goals, in whose meaning the desired action or state figures centrally, in the meaning of the behavioral intent the desired action or state merely explains the reason(s) for the actions one has decided to undertake. Again, in contrast to behavioral programs, which deal with the specifics of particular actions and with the "when," "where," and "how" of performance, the behavioral intent is focused on more generally outlined actions that stand in need of further determination before the stage of performance. More importantly, the study shows that a behavioral intent implies programs of action that must be subjected to detailed "programming"; however, it should be noted that under normal circumstances a renewed process of CO clustering is not required in order to outline acceptable or possible courses of action.

STUDY IV
Predicting Commitments to Action

PURPOSE AND HYPOTHESES

The purpose of this study was to examine the predictive power of the CO cluster with regard to behavioral intents. Since we view behavioral intents as direct products of CO clusters, it is only natural to expect that behavioral intents will be related positively to CO scores.

In this study behavioral intents were operationalized as commitments to action on the part of the subjects. The term "commitment" is used here in a sense similar to the one it has in the studies of DeFleur and Westie (1958) and of Kiesler (1968), with the difference that theoretically we view commitments to action as behavioral intents and not as actual behavior or as a moderator variable. Of course, the process of forming a behavioral intent with regard to a future action differs psychologically from announcing this intent in the form of a binding commitment. But the commitment reflects more of the underlying intent than does actual performance of the intended behavior.

Accordingly, our general hypothesis was that commitments to action would be related to CO scores based on beliefs relevant to the domain of the studied commitments. More specifically, since all the commitments in this study referred to achievement, we expected individuals with higher CO scores of achievement (see Chapter 7, Study I) to commit themselves to the more achievement-oriented alternatives rather than to the less achievement-oriented ones among those presented. In the case of two of the studied commitments the more achievement-oriented alternatives involved committing oneself to tasks requiring an effort and offering chances for success and the gaining of prestige, whereas the non-achievement-oriented alternatives involved committing oneself to tasks requiring no special effort and offering no chances for subjective or objective success. The third commitment studied was different in that it required committing oneself to a more or less achievement-oriented alternative under conditions of risk. The situation was so defined that the greater the effort and the chances for success the higher the chances for failure. In the case of this latter commitment no clear prediction was possible. Insofar as studies within the framework of general achievement theory about choices under risk are relevant, the contradictory findings to date make it difficult to set up a clear hypothesis. On the one hand, there are studies that support Atkinson's (1964, pp. 240–268) theoretical deduction that achievement-oriented individuals, in whom the striving for success is stronger than the striving for avoidance of failure, tend to select tasks intermediate in difficulty, whereas those low in achievement motivation, in whom the tendency to avoid failure is stronger than the striving for success, prefer either very easy or very difficult tasks (e.g., Atkinson & Litwin, 1960; Isaacson, 1964; McClelland, 1958). On the other hand, many studies show that these predictions do not hold at all (e.g., DeCharms & Davé, 1965), or only under very particular conditions (e.g., Brody, 1963; Hancock & Teevan, 1964; Kukla, 1970; Littig, 1963; Raynor & Smith, 1965). Indeed, these contradictory findings were what induced us to use, for predicting the third commitment, not only the CO of achievement (Chapter 7, Study I) but also the COs of postsuccess and postfailure behavior (Chapter 7, Study III). Thus, with regard to the third commitment, the study was exploratory.

METHOD

Subjects. The subjects were 50 high school students ranging in age from 16 to 18 years, selected randomly from three schools in Israel. The group included 27 boys and 23 girls. (The subjects were the same as those in Chapter 8, Study I.)

Procedure and Materials. Each subject was invited to two sessions. One was a group session in which the CO questionnaires of achievement (Chapter 7, Study I) and of postsuccess and postfailure behavior (Chapter 7, Study III) were administered, together with other questionnaires dealing with attitudes, mostly political. The other session was an individual session. For half the subjects it took place about 7–12 days before the group session and for the other half 7–12 days after the group session. In the individual session the subject had to perform the following three tasks: proofreading, copying letters, and simple calculations. These were sham tasks and their results were not evaluated. At the end of the session the subject was asked orally, and in random order, three questions designed to assess commitments to action. The experimenter noted down the responses in a visible and emphatic manner. The experimenter told the subject that since she or he would be invited to participate in further experiments, it was desirable to know which types of tasks were preferred so that she or he could be invited to participate in the appropriate experiments. Thus, the responses would count as commitments on the part of the subject to participate in the kind of experiment indicated. In one commitment the subject was asked to commit himself to performing (a) tasks that required some creative effort, intellectual (e.g., clear thinking) or imaginative (e.g., artistic production, empathic understanding) with the chance that successful performance would be made known to his classmates; or (b) tasks that required no special effort but would be administered anonymously merely for the sake of establishing age-relevant "norms" for these tasks. In another commitment the subject was asked to commit himself to participating in (a) a study to be performed in a slum area requiring special efforts for making the necessary observations, with the possibility of being interviewed by the press when the study is completed; or (b) an equally time-consuming study requiring no special efforts but merely attendance with free tickets at movies (for girls) or football matches (for boys). Finally, in the third commitment the subject was asked to commit himself to performing tasks in which 10%, or 50%, or 90% of the people usually succeeded. The experimenter emphasized that the most challenging tasks were those with the lowest chances of success.

The subject was asked to sign at the bottom of the series of his or her responses to the three questions. The order of presenting the three commitments was randomized. After the end of the experiment all subjects were debriefed.

RESULTS AND CONCLUSIONS

Table 11.11 shows that in the case of two commitments CO scores of achievement were related in the predicted manner to the commitments of the subjects. Subjects with higher CO scores of achievement committed themselves in each case to the more achievement-oriented alternative.

With regard to the commitment involving risk, Table 11.12 shows

TABLE 11.11
Relation of CO Scores of Achievement
to Commitments to Action (Behavioral Intents)

COMMITMENTS TO ACTION[a]	NO. OF SUBJECTS WITH CO SCORES OF:			χ^2 [b]	$\overline{X}$	SD	t
	4 & 3	2	1 & 0				
Commitment 1							
Tasks requiring creative effort	11	8	7		2.12	1.12	
Tasks for establishing norms	2	6	16	6.42*	1.04	1.10	3.38**
Commitment 2							
Study in slums	12	4	6		2.18	1.27	
Study with visits to movies/football	1	9	18	5.36*	1.14	.95	3.25**

[a] For each commitment the first line represents the alternative hypothesized to be positively correlated with CO scores; the second line represents the alternative hypothesized to be negatively correlated with CO scores.
[b] Owing to the small number of cases, χ^2 analyses were performed on grouped data: CO 4, 3, & 2 vs. CO 1 & 0.
* $p < .05$.   ** $p < .01$.

that CO scores of achievement are related to the actual commitments of the subjects in a linear and positive manner, so that the higher the CO scores, the higher the difficulty of the task to which the subjects committed themselves, or, alternately, the lower the chances of success at this task.

Incidentally, it is noteworthy that the mean level of difficulty selected by our subjects is approximately 35%, corresponding to the similar value of 34% found by DeCharms and Davé (1965).

TABLE 11.12
CO Scores of Achievement and Risky Choices
in Commitment to Action

CO Score	n[a]	$\overline{X}$[b]	SD
4 & 3	12	16.67	14.91
2	13	31.54	25.37
1	12	33.33	30.37
0	9	54.44	22.66

$F = 3.74$, $df = 3/42$, $p < .05$.
[a] Four subjects said "It does not matter which task" and made no choice.
[b] The numbers represent means of the selected probabilities weighted through the frequency of subjects, e.g., if tasks of probabilities 10%, 50%, and 90% were each selected by one subject, the mean would be 50.

Table 11.13 presents the results of applying the CO scores of postsuccess and of postfailure behavior to the commitment involving risk. Since the two COs are unrelated ($r = .05$ n.s.), an analysis of variance was performed. The results (Table 11.13) show that joint consideration of the two COs is necessary in order to account for the actual commitments of the subjects. As Table 11.14 shows, subjects with either a high postsuccess CO and a low postfailure CO or a low postsuccess CO and a high postfailure CO committed themselves most often to the most difficult tasks. These would be the subjects mainly interested in attaining success for its own sake or in avoiding failure (see Chapter 7, Study III, "Results and Conclusions"). In contrast, subjects low in both COs committed themselves to the easiest tasks, whereas those high in both COs committed themselves to tasks intermediate between the two extremes.

TABLE 11.13
Analysis of Variance of Risky Choices in Commitment to Action

Source of Variation	SS	df	MS	F
Postfailure CO (A)	467.74	1	467.74	< 1
Postsuccess CO (B)	299.68	1	299.68	< 1
A × B	2525.97	1	2525.97	4.08*
Within cell	25383.33	41	619.11	

*$p < .05$.

The findings demonstrate that all three commitments were predicted by CO scores, thus lending full support to our hypothesis about the relation of behavioral intents to CO clusters. The same CO scores of achievement predicted all three commitments. In addition, the CO scores of postsuccess and postfailure predicted commitments to alternatives involving risk.

TABLE 11.14
CO Scores of Postsuccess and Postfailure Behavior
and Risky Choices in Commitment to Action

CO Scores[a]	n	$\overline{X}$	SD
High postsuccess CO, high postfailure CO	10	38	31.24
High postsuccess CO, low postfailure CO	12	30	25.82
Low postsuccess CO, high postfailure CO	15	28.67	28.72
Low postsuccess CO, high postfailure CO	9	50	28.28

[a] Subjects were classified as high in a CO if they got a CO of 4, 3 or 2; and as low if they got a CO of 1 or 0.

The study also leads to further though less important conclusions. The findings bear implications for the general achievement theory insofar as they show that subjects high in achievement or concerned about attaining success or avoiding failure commit themselves to the most difficult tasks and not to those intermediate in difficulty.* From the viewpoint of the CO theory, the findings imply that in some situations two different sets of CO scores may show orientative equivalence (e.g., the CO score of achievement and the CO scores of postsuccess and postfailure behavior), whereas in other situations the interaction of two different CO scores (e.g., the CO of postsuccess behavior and the CO of postfailure behavior) may be required for predicting one single act (see Chapter 8, Study I, "Results and Conclusions").

GENERAL CONCLUSIONS

The four studies reported in this chapter deal with various aspects of the concept of behavioral intent. Whereas the first two studies focus on the relation of the intent to the four CO components, the third deals with its relation both to goal beliefs and to behavioral programs, and the fourth is devoted to clarifying its relation to the CO cluster. The studies also differ greatly in methodology. Studies I and II involve a projective element in the procedure; Study III is based purely on an analysis of communications of meaning; and Study IV is an instance of the experimental paradigm, involving the CO score as an independent variable, used in all predictive studies (Chapters 7, 8, and 10).

This variety of purposes and methodologies reinforces the major conclusions to which the findings give rise. The studies show that the behavioral intent derives from all four CO components; that it may be predicted on the basis of CO clusters; and that it implies a course of action outlined sufficiently clearly to obviate the need for a separate phase of CO clustering especially designed for determining action possibilities, yet not sufficiently detailed to obviate the need for a separate stage of "programming."

These findings lend full support to our theoretical conception of the behavioral intent as a bridge between beliefs and behavioral programs,

---

* Since scores of n Ach and the TAQ were available for the subjects of this study, the distribution of subjects choosing each of the commitments was examined for these two variables singly and in combination. Only in one case were the findings significant: the mean n Ach score of those who chose to participate in the "slums" choice was 12.94 ($SD = 8.73$) as compared to a mean of 8.42 ($SD = 5.39$) for those who chose the "movies/football" alternative ($t = 2.09$, $p < .05$).

or between clustering and programming. It forms a focal point at which, following clustering, the actional implications of a goal undergo specification into a course of action essentially ready for performance immediately or at some later time. In this sense, the intent harks both backward and forward, bringing together the potential of what is to be with the actuality of what has preceded it. It is these properties of the intent that express its major role in the transformation of meanings into action. This role is evident in our findings although they do not refer specifically to the three functions of the behavioral intent in regard to behavior: triggering programming, regulating action, and completing action. Nevertheless, the findings of the four studies contribute toward establishing the status of the behavioral intent not only as a hypothetical construct, but as an intervening variable tapping a dynamically real psychological phenomenon.

CHAPTER 12

CO Theory and the Attitude-Behavior Gap

STUDY
CO Components in Attitude Scales

PURPOSE AND HYPOTHESES

The major purpose of this study was to shed light on the notorious problem of the inconsistency between attitudes and behavior. The failure to demonstrate the relation of attitudes to behavior has been documented in so many varied domains (e.g., Athanasiou, 1969, p. 95; Thomas, 1971; Wicker, 1969; Vroom, 1964, chap. 6) that the inconsistency cannot be dismissed as due to chance. Nor can it be overlooked as unimportant, since its existence defies scientific and common-sense expectations. How deeply it must disturb the conceptual comfort of psychologists can be judged from the persistent attempts to account for the common absence of correlations between attitude and behavior. Since Wicker (1969) has summarized many of the major explanations, it should suffice to point out in general terms that most attempts consist in suggesting factors other than attitudes that might help to wipe out the inconsistency. In recent years this trend has greatly gained in popularity (e.g., Ajzen & Fishbein, 1970; Kelman, 1974; McArthur, Kiesler, & Cook, 1969; Rotter, 1972; Warner & DeFleur, 1969), so much so that the additional variables threaten to fill up the gap to its very brim and thus hide the problem rather than solve it. Laying the burden on additional variables seems to us essentially uneconomical and inadequate, particularly since there is an alternative hypothesis based on more economical assumptions. This hypothesis derives directly from the CO theory, and especially from the positive results of our studies dealing with predicting behavior through CO clusters (Chapters 7, 8, and 10). According to this hypothesis, an attitude scale can predict behavior only if its statements adequately represent the CO components.

The general tenor of this hypothesis belies the twofold source of our concern with the attitude-behavior gap. On the one hand, we were definitely tempted to test the possible utility of the CO theory in resolving common problems in psychology by interpreting in a new light already available findings of studies carried out in different conceptual frameworks and practical contexts. On the other hand, we were concerned about the discrepancy between the attitude-behavior gap and the persistently positive findings we got when studying relations between cognitive contents and behavior. Conceptually the problem should not have been worrisome, because the theoretical differences between beliefs or CO clusters and attitudes are so clear and dominant (see Chapter 4) that no comparison between the empirical findings to which they lead had to be undertaken. Yet practically there is a remarkable similarity between beliefs and the verbal statements most commonly used for assessing subjects' attitudes. This similarity is great enough to demand a comparison between the empirical findings attained by means of beliefs structured in the form of CO scores and verbal statements of attitude scales summed up in the form of attitude scores. Indeed, the similarity makes such a comparison not only desirable but also easy.

The connecting link between the two motives of our concern with the attitude-behavior gap was formed precisely by the affinity between beliefs and actual verbal expressions of attitudes. This affinity enabled the operational translation of attitude statements into beliefs of the four CO components. Highlighting a common denominator between CO theory and attitudes made possible a comparison between these two domains of research, a comparison that may help clarify their interrelations as well as their sharp distinctions.

Accordingly, our hypothesis referred to the population of studies dealing with the relations between attitudes and behavior. The hypothesis was that attitude scales of studies demonstrating positive relations between attitudes and behavior would include statements representing CO components more adequately than the attitude scales of studies demonstrating no relations or even negative relations between attitudes and behavior. More specifically, in line with the findings in our studies (Chapters 7, 8, and 10), we expected, first, that the majority of attitude scales of "positive" studies would include statements representing three or four CO components whereas the majority of attitude scales of "no or negative" studies would include statements representing only one or two CO components; and second, that the attitude scales of "positive" studies would include statements representing the CO components more homogeneously than the attitude scales of "no or negative" studies. With regard to attitude scales yielding inconsistent findings—if such scales are identified—our hypothesis was that they would include statements representing CO components in a number and degree of homogeneity intermediate between the two extremes of scales yielding positive findings and scales yielding no or negative findings.

THE SAMPLE

When first approaching the domain of attitude-behavior studies we were naive victims of the illusion that attitude-behavior studies dealt with actual attitudes and actual behaviors. We soon encountered many cases that did not accord with our expectations. The discrepancies consisted mostly in confounding attitudes with behaviors and behavior with self-reports of behavior. Whereas confounding attitudes with behavior could perhaps be justified by reference to the common conception of attitudes as including a behavioral component in addition to the evaluative and conative ones, confounding behavior with self-reports of behavior seems to be a case of succumbing to an experimentally comfortable arrangement based on a fiction. Not only are there enough studies showing that equating self-reports and behavior is unwarranted (e.g., Parry & Crossley, 1950; Stricker, Messick, & Jackson, 1967), but also common psychological reasoning shows that even if there is no clear motive for dissembling, people cannot be assumed to be sufficiently aware of what they do and how they behave to make their self-reports valid. Nevertheless, it is comforting to observe that the frequent expulsion of behavior from this research domain has not improved the chances of demonstrating a relation between attitudes and behavior. Obviously "behavior" does not behave—nor do self-reports of behavior. In fact, this conforms well to what may be deduced from CO theory. Self-reports of behavior correspond to beliefs about self. Attitudes as commonly assessed (see "Results and Conclusions" below) correspond to beliefs in the various CO components. Yet, as often noted, beliefs of the different CO components mostly do not correlate and thus are poor predictors for the beliefs about self constituting self-reports of behavior.

In view of the frequent confounding of attitudes with behavior and behavior with self-reports of behavior, we settled on the following relatively stringent criteria in selecting the studies for the testing of our hypothesis. First, the behavior had to be an actual overt behavior, that is, observed behavior, behavior obtained from records or otherwise verifiable, and not merely the subject's verbal report of his or her own behavior. As stated above, we reasoned that a self-report of behavior is a "belief about self." As such it in no way represents behavior but rather leads to a blurring of the distinctions between the cognitive and behavioral levels in whose interrelation we are mainly interested in this context. Thus, if a study dealt with several behavioral variables only one or more of which reflected actual behavior, we considered only those results referring to the real behavioral variables. Decisions about whether a behavioral variable reflected behavior or not were difficult only when the variable referred to the act of belonging to some criterion group. In such cases we counted the belonging as behavior only if joining the group was voluntary and if belonging to the group involved some clear and specified act(s) of behavior. For example, while being "a housewife" or "a Chilean" was not considered a behavioral variable, belonging to a pro- or anti-Japanese organization was counted as behavior since joining was voluntary and belonging meant doing specified things for or against the Japanese. In general, we were stringent in applying our standards to a given variable.

Second, the attitude had to be assessed directly and verbally, for example through the subject's answers to some questionnaire or to questions in an oral or written form, and not indirectly, through observing the subject's behavior or inferring his attitudes in some other way. Here we reasoned that attitude is first and foremost a cognitive and conscious variable. By emphasizing this common aspect of attitude and disregarding other definitions sometimes offered for this term, we could pose the question of the relation between attitudes and behavior in most trenchant and unambiguous terms. Any other definition or method of assessment of attitudes that emphasizes its behavioral aspect introduces operational ambiguities and thus is likely to blur the issue theoretically and empirically.

Third, we selected only studies whose design made it reasonably plausible that the relation or lack of relation between attitudes and behavior was not a result of some artifact or inadmissible experimental or statistical procedure, such as assessing attitudes and behavior jointly, suggesting to the subjects the experimenter's goal, or focusing on some group of subjects in whom both attitudes and behavior were predetermined or restricted in a particular manner.

Fourth, we attempted to select studies that used attitude scales reflecting only or mainly beliefs rather than personality traits. The distinction between scales of attitudes and of personality traits is admittedly difficult, the latter being based on beliefs no less than the former. In practice we have followed convention and the focusing or nonfocusing of the scale on some attitudinal theme as rough guidelines in our selection. Thus, the MMPI, the CPI, Bass's Orientation Inventory—to give only a few examples—were not regarded as attitude scales, whereas the F scale, the E scale, and an ambiguity scale were counted in.

In addition, we strove to include mainly studies whose unit of analysis was the individual. As Table 12.1 shows, only three studies were based on analyzing group data. Moreover, in order to control for the possibly different effects of different degrees of change on the relation between attitudes and behavior, no studies dealing with the change of attitudes or behavior, or both, were included.

In our search for relevant studies meeting the above criteria we were guided by *Psychological Abstracts* (1940 onward), by handbooks and manuals including attitude scales (mainly those by Lake, Miles, & Earle, 1973; Miller, 1970; Robinson, Rusk, & Head, 1968; Robinson & Shaver, 1969; and Shaw & Wright, 1967), by special bibliographies about the attitude-behavior domain (such as those prepared by Deutscher, 1966; and Suarez & Miller, 1970), and by reviews dealing with attitude-behavior relations in general (e.g., Wicker, 1969) or in specific domains (e.g., Lefcourt, 1966; Vroom, 1964).

The major problem encountered in our search was the unavailability of the attitude scales used in the various studies. Our study necessitated analysis of these scales in their full form, as they were actually administered. We would like to mention at this point our gratitude to all the individual investigators, organizations, and institutes who cooperated by making available to us attitude scales used by them or by others.

Our final selection includes 117 studies: 34 demonstrating positive relations between attitudes and behavior, 68 demonstrating no or negative relations, and 15 demonstrating mixed relations, that is, both positive and no or negative relations in the same study or in their replications. This list includes all the studies out of those originally scanned whose text and attitude scales could be located—given library limitations and other restrictions on availability—and which met the above-stated criteria. The list may not present a complete coverage of all existing studies. We want to emphasize, however, that its loopholes reflect limitations of availability and possibly of information on our part but not personal biases and willful overlooking of evidence.

Table 12.1 presents a summary of all the studies used in the present review. Each pairing of an attitude scale and one or more types of behavior is counted as one item. Thus, if one study or several studies deal with correlating one attitude scale with several different behaviors the study or studies constitute only one item in our list. If, however, one study deals with analyzing the relations of several different attitude scales to one particular behavior it provides several items to our count, the number of items reflecting the number of different attitude scales involved. Depending on the kind of demonstrated relations between these scales and the behavior, the same study may be mentioned in any one or more of the three category types of studies in Table 12.1.

TABLE 12.1
Summary of Studies Demonstrating Positive, No or Negative, and Mixed Relations between Attitudes and Behavior

Investigators	Attitude Scale or Attitude Object	% of Items in Attitude Scale Representing:				Type of Attitude Questionnaire	Overt Behavior
		N	GB	BS	Go		
Positive Relation between Attitudes and Behavior							
1. Allport & Kramer (1946)[a]	Jews & Negroes	6.60	42.45	45.28	5.66	Forced-choice, self-expressed answers	Identifying the ethnic identity of Jews according to photographs
2. Berger (1952)	Accepting self & others	7.03	5.47	82.81	4.69	Modified Likert	Stuttering
3. Carey (1958)	Problem-solving	5.56		77.78	16.67	Likert	Problem-solving behavior under experimental conditions
4. Chapman (1960)	Attitude toward police	7.69	88.46		3.85	Likert	Delinquency
5. Christie & Geis (1970)	Machiavellianism	30	70			Likert	Persuasion of others, self-persuasion, etc.
6. Clum & Nathan (1971)	Marine Corps Opinion Survey I	12.50	31.25	43.75	12.50	Likert	Combat effectiveness ratings by superior (after recruit training)
7. Clum & Nathan (1971)	Marine Corps Opinion Survey II		76.92	7.69	15.38	Likert	Combat effectiveness ratings by superior (after two years of active duty)
8. Dean (1958)[b]	Union, political & social processes		62.50	25	12.50	Forced choice	Attending local labor union meetings
9. Dudycha (1941)	Dependability (Dudycha, 1937)	22.22	77.78			Thurstone	Coming markedly early or late to classes

TABLE 12.1 (cont'd.)

Investigators	Attitude Scale or Attitude Object	% of Items in Attitude Scale Representing:				Type of Attitude Questionnaire	Overt Behavior
		N	GB	BS	Go		
	Positive Relation between Attitudes and Behavior						
10. Fendrich (1967)	Negroes	7.81	54.69	18.75	18.75	Likert	Participation in group discussion on race relations and signing commitment for further actions
11. Frieders, Warner, & Albrecht (1970)	Marijuana	6.25	53.13	15.53	25	Likert	Committing themselves by voting or signing a ballot to act for the legalization of the use of marijuana
12. Friesen (1952)	Working situation, work, self, & leisure		47.53	45.06	8.64	Incomplete sentences	Employment stability
13. Hand (1953)	Attitudes toward college courses	15.56	66.67	17.78		Modified Thurstone	Effort in a course (achievement score minus an ability score)
14. Katz & Benjamin (1960)	Authoritarianism (Webster, Sanford, & Freedman, 1955; shortened)	7.30	30.66	57.66	4.38	Forced choice of T or F	Communication while performing tasks, asking for advice and getting advice from nonauthoritarian subjects
15. Khanna, Pratt, & Gardiner (1962)	Attitudes toward "criminally insane" patients	15.79	61.84	22.37		Four-point forced choice	Performance ratings
16. Kimbraugh & Cofer (1958)	Attitude toward the law	15	85			Checking items if agrees or disagrees; Thurstone & Guttman	Content of free associations to verbal stimuli

17. Kogan & Downey (1956)	Social situations questionnaire about Negroes	11.67		11.67	76.67	Guttman	Youth club participation
18. Nettler & Golding (1946)	Japanese	12.50	58.33	25	4.17	Checking items if agrees or disagrees; Thurstone	Belonging officially to a pro-Japanese or anti-Japanese organization
19. Patchen (1965)	Identification with the company where one works	22.22	55.56	22.22		Forced choice	Use of the company's sticker on one's car
20. Pulos & Spilka (1961)	Anti-Semitism scale (Levinson & Sanford, 1944)	32.69	65.38	21.15		Modified Likert	Accuracy in identifying Jewish (or non-Jewish) photographs and in remembering Jewish (or non-Jewish) photographs
Weatherley (1961)	"	"	"	"		"	Displacing experimentally aroused aggression selectively onto Jews or avoiding the expression of aroused aggression against Jews
Bray (1950)	"	"	"	"		"	Conforming to Jew's autokinetic movement judgments—correlation nonsignificant but interaction significant (i.e., high scorers conform more to Jew's judgments)
21. Shepps & Shepps (1971)	Study habits (Brown & Holzman, 1967)	0.5	38.5	59	2	Forced choice	Math and reading achievements in boys and girls
22. Smith (1946)	The Soviet Union	58.33	33.33	8.33		Likert	Membership in pro-Soviet organizations

TABLE 12.1 (cont'd.)

Investigators	Attitude Scale or Attitude Object	% of Items in Attitude Scale Representing:				Type of Attitude Questionnaire	Overt Behavior
		N	GB	BS	Go		
Positive Relation between Attitudes and Behavior							
23. Stagner, Flebbe, & Wood (1952)[b]	Job satisfaction		63.33	30	6.67	Forced choice	Accident rates in work
24. Streuning & Efron (1965)	Work	4.05	51.80	41.44	2.70	Partly Likert, partly checking T or F	Working or not working while being a patient
25. Tittle & Hill (1967)	Student politics	20	6.67	60	13.33	Likert, summated rating scales (15 items)	Voting in student elections
26. "	Student politics	10		80	10	Likert, summated rating scales (10 items)	Voting in student elections
27. Thurstone (1931)	Attitude toward Sunday observance	61.91	31.82	2.27		Thurstone	Belonging to the Seventh Day Adventists and other denominational groups
28. Tydlaska & Mengel (1953)	View of oneself		13.51	83.78	2.70	Checking T or F	Being a good worker (by merit ratings) or a bad worker (i.e., malingering, obedience problems, etc.)
29. Van Zelst & Kerr (1953)	Merit rating	15.38	19.23	61.54	3.85	Forced choice	Absences from work and tardiness
30. Uphoff & Dunnette (1956)	Unions	23.38	63.64	12.99		Forced choice	Being a union member, number of union meetings attended, being an officer of a union

	Attitude					Method	Behavior
31. Warner & DeFleur (1969)	Negroes	6.25	46.88	28.13	18.75	Likert	Returning signed agreement or disagreement to a request to engage in behavior involving Negroes
32. Weaver (1959)	Studying, schools and teachers	14.29	61.43	24.29		Modified Thurstone	Achievement scores of students
33. Wesley (1953)	Rigidity	2.44	14.63	78.05	4.88	Forced choice of T or F	Time needed to shift sets in concept formation, amount of perseverance
34. Wicker (1971)	Attitude toward the church (Thurstone & Chave, 1929)		66.67	29.17	4.17	Thurstone	Church attendance, contributions, holding responsible positions in church

No or Negative Relation between Attitudes and Behavior

	Attitude					Method	Behavior
1. Bar-Gal, Kreitler, & Kreitler (1960)	Cheating on exams	20	80			Partly sentence completion, partly forced choice	Cheating on Hartshorne & May's Test of Accurate Perception
2. Bernberg (1952)	Group morale	100				Judging correctness of statements	Absences from work, coming late, short-term absences from work, going to infirmary
3. ”	Supervisor	100				Rating on a 100-point rating scale	”
4. ”	Morale	100				Rating	”
5. Brannon et al. (1973)[e]	Open housing	100				Forced choice	Willingness to sign and have published a petition concerning open housing or owner's rights

TABLE 12.1 (cont'd.)

Investigators	Attitude Scale or Attitude Object	% of Items in Attitude Scale Representing:				Type of Attitude Questionnaire	Overt Behavior
		N	GB	BS	Go		
No or Negative Relation between Attitudes and Behavior							
6. Bray (1950)	Attitude toward the Negro (Likert, 1932)	56.67	16.67	26.67		Likert, forced choice, rating, free answers	Judging autokinetic movement in the presence of a Negro
7. Bellows, cited in Brayfield & Crockett (1955)	Index of job satisfaction (Brayfield & Rothe, 1951)	19.44	80.56			Thurstone, answers in form of Likert	Ratings of skill
Brayfield, cited in Brayfield & Crockett (1955)[a]	"	"	"			"	Ratings of productivity
Brayfield & Mangelsdorf (1950), cited in Brayfield & Crockett (1955)	"	"	"			"	Ratings of productivity
Brayfield & Marsh (1953), cited in Brayfield & Crockett (1955)	"	"	"			"	Ratings of productivity
8. Carr & Roberts (1965)	Civil rights activities		100			Semantic Differential	Participation in civil rights activities
9. "	"			100		Bogardus' Social Distance	Participation in civil rights activities

No. Author (year)	Variable			Method	Description
10. Cattell, Heist, Heist, & Stewart (1950)	Activities such as football, movies, social games, sleep, etc.	100		Checking T or F (false belief)	Daily log of money and/or time spent on activities such as football, movies, sleep, etc.
11.	"	100		Preference statement	"
12.	"	100		Forced choice (information)	"
13. Cattell, Maxwell, Light, & Unger (1949–50)	"	100		Preference	"
14. Crawford (1968)	Driving	77.50	22.50	Likert, forced choice	Having accidents in driving
15. DeCharms, Morrison, Reitman, & McClelland (1955)	Achievement	33.33	66.67	Checking agreement on graphic scale	Memory for content, performance and learning, holding offices
16. Freeman & Aataöv (1960)	Cheating	100		Guttman	Cheating on self-graded exam
17.	"	100		Guttman	"
18.	"	100		Guttman	"
19.	"		100	Conversation completion	"
20. Gadel & Kreidt (1952)	Satisfaction from job	45	65	Forced choice	Ratings of effectiveness in work
21. Gorham & Lasky (1962)	Medication	13.33	86.67	Forced choice	Treatment outcome in chronic apathetic schizophrenics
Gorham & Sherman (1961)	"	"	"	"	"

TABLE 12.1 (cont'd.)

Investigators	Attitude Scale or Attitude Object	% of Items in Attitude Scale Representing: N	GB	BS	Go	Type of Attitude Questionnaire	Overt Behavior
		No or Negative Relation between Attitudes and Behavior					
22. Hofman (1973)	Education: autonomy factor	25	75			Likert, summated ratings	Teacher's behavior in classroom in categories such as competence, humanism, self-control, etc.
23. "	Education: conservatism factor	20	80			"	"
24. "	Education: egalitarianism factor	100				"	"
25. "	Education: liberalism factor	50	50			"	"
26. Katz & Kahn (1952)	Satisfaction with job, company, supervision, and work group	40	60			Likert	Absenteeism from work
27. "	Company and work group	83.33	16.67			Likert	Productivity in work
28. Kobelman, Kreitler, & Kreitler (1967)	Cooperation	100					Observation of social behavior in youth camp, e.g., initiative, helping others, giving advice, etc. (seven aspects)
29. "		100					"

No.	Study	Sample/Instrument	%	%	%	Method	Behavioral criterion
30.			100			"	"
31.				100		"	"
32.				100		"	"
33.			50	50		"	"
34.			62.50	37.50		"	"
35.	Krasner, Knowles, & Ullman (1965)	Medical Science Information Survey		100		Checking extent of agreement	Strength of grip on dynamometer (in control group)
36.	Kutner, Wilkins, & Yarrow (1952)	Negroes		100		Answers to questions on the phone	Providing service to a Negro
37.	"	"		100		"	"
38.	LaPiere (1934–35)	Chinese			100	Answers to questions on the phone	Providing service to Chinese
39.	Lent (1960)	Ambiguity (Hamilton, 1957?)	10	70	20	Likert	Identifying ethnic identity and shade of color of photographed faces
40.	Linn (1965)	Negroes (Scale I)			100	Checking degree of agreement	Willingness to have photographs with a Negro of opposite sex taken and distributed (signing)
41.	"	Negroes (Scale II)			100	Checking degree of agreement	Willingness to have photograph with a Negro of opposite sex taken and distributed, and actually coming for the photograph
42.	Maher, Watt, & Campbell (1960)	Attitudes toward law & justice (Watt & Maher, 1958)		100		Forced choice	Type of crime

TABLE 12.1 (cont'd.)

Investigators	Attitude Scale or Attitude Object	% of Items in Attitude Scale Representing:				Type of Attitude Questionnaire	Overt Behavior
		N	GB	BS	Go		
	No or Negative Relation between Attitudes and Behavior						
43. Medinnus (1966)	Morality	100				Open ended questions	Cheating on results of a shooting game
44. Metzner & Mann (1953)[a]	One's job		45	55		Forced choice	Frequency of absences from work
45. Mossin (1949)	One's job	100				Forced choice	Ratings of productivity
46. Null & Smead (1971)	Florida Scale of Civic Beliefs (Kimbrough & Hines, 1963)	31.82	76.67			Likert	Behavior as a superintendent
47. Porier & Lott (1967)	Opinionation Scale: American version (Rokeach, 1960)		100			Checking degree of agreement	GSR reactivity to the presence of an assistant
48. Rokeach & Mezei (1966)	Anti-Negro Scale (Adorno et al., 1950)	8.33	91.67			Likert	Choice of group members with whom to have coffee
49. Rosen & Komorita (1971)	Federal support for the poverty program		100			Semantic Differential (Evaluation)	Signing commitment to participate in a discussion on war against poverty
50.	"		100			Semantic Differential (Extremity)	"
51.	Internal-external control (Rotter)	82.61	17.39			Forced choice between pairs	"

Author	Measure	Values	Method	Criterion
Seeman (1963)	"		"	Learning of material concerning parole
52. Saenger & Gilbert (1950)	Negroes	100	Oral interview	Buying from a Negro salesman
53. Taylor & Hilton (1960)	Sales attitude checklist (Taylor, 1960)	.81 .81 96.76 1.62	Forced choice	Average number of orders written monthly or average monthly sales
54. Tittle & Hill (1967)	Student politics	5 40 55	Guttman	Voting in student elections
55. "	"	100 100	Self-rating	"
56. "	"	100	Semantic Differential	"
57. "	"	13.33 80 6.67	Thurstone	"
58. Vroom (1962)	Ego-involvement	100	Forced choice	Absences from work
59. "	Job satisfaction	100	"	"
60. "	Self-express on	100	Ratings	"
61. "	Work-related tension	100	Forced choice	"
62. "	Satisfaction with self	100	"	"
63. "	Satisfaction with health	100	"	"
64. Walters & Roach (1971)	Pay (Smith, 1967)	100	Modified checklist	Termination of work and frequency of absences
65. "	Promotions (Smith, 1957)	100	"	"
66. "	Supervision (Smith, 1957)	100	"	"
67. Wicker (1971)	The church	100	Semantic Differential	Worship service attendance, contributions to church, holding responsible positions in church

353

TABLE 12.1 (cont'd.)

Investigators	Attitude Scale or Attitude Object	% of Items in Attitude Scale Representing: N	GB	BS	Go	Type of Attitude Questionnaire	Overt Behavior
		No or Negative Relation between Attitudes and Behavior					
68. Yaffe, Shiler, Kreitler, & Kreitler (1966)	Ethnic communities in Israel	9.52	90.48			Forced choice, Likert	Readiness to rent a room to members of certain ethnic communities
		Mixed (Positive and Negative) Relations between Attitudes and Behavior					
1. Aiken & Dreger (1961)	Mathematics		5	95		Likert	Related positively to final course grades of females but not of males
2. Berg (1966)	Ethnocentrism Scale (Adorno et al., 1950)	11.11	83.33	5.56		Likert	Judging autokinetic movement in the presence of a Negro or white partner (no relation)
Lent (1960)	"	"	"	"		"	Identifying ethnic identity and shade of color of photographed faces (no relation)
Malof & Lott (1962)	"	"	"	"		"	In Asch-type situation, subjects with higher scores showed more conformity than subjects with lower scores *but* accepted support from Negro as readily as from white
Porier & Lott (1967)	"	"	"	"		"	GSR reactivity to Negro assistant (positive relation)

Author	Instrument				Scale	
3. Berg (1966)	F Scale (modified)	22.5	77.5		Likert	Judging autokinetic movement in the presence of a Negro or white partner (no relation)
4. Izett (1971)	F Scale (Form 45–40)	32.22	67.78		Likert	Presence in lectures on the moratorium day for Vietnam (positive relation)
5. McGee (1955)	F Scale (Form 30)	26.67	70	3.33	Likert	Behavior of teachers in classroom e.g., aloof, inflexible, etc. (positive relation)
6. Brody	Parental Attitude Research Instrument (Schaeffer & Bell, 1958)	36.52	63.48		Likert	Observed interaction of mother with child, e.g., directing, helping, etc. (only 13% of comparisons significant)
Zunich (1971)	"	"	"		"	Observed interaction of mother with child (only 2.14% of correlations significant)
7. Cook, Leeds & Callis (1951)	Minnesota Teacher Attitude Inventory	35.33	64.67		Likert	Ratings of effectiveness by pupils, principal, and an expert (positive relations in two studies)
Fuller (1951)	"	"	"		"	Rating of effectiveness (negative relation)
Oelke (1956)	"	"	"		"	"
8. Crandall, Katkovsky, & Preston (1962)	Intellectual Achievement Responsibility Questionnaire (IARQ) (I+)	50	50	50	Forced choice	Inconsistent relations in boys and girls of various grades with achievement tests

TABLE 12.1 (cont'd.)

Investigators	Attitude Scale or Attitude Object	% of Items in Attitude Scale Representing:				Type of Attitude Questionnaire	Overt Behavior
		N	GB	BS	Go		
	Mixed (Positive and Negative) Relations between Attitudes and Behavior						
9. "	IARQ (I−)		50	50		"	"
"	IARQ (I)		50	50		"	"
Crandall, Katkovsky, & Crandall (1965)	IARQ (I+)		"	"		"	Time spent in intellectual activities and intensity of striving for it (positive relation only in boys)
"	IARQ (I−)		"	. "		"	"
"	IARQ (I)		"	"		"	"
Powell (1971)	IARQ (I+)		"	"		"	Grade point averages (no relations in boys or girls)
"	IARQ (I−)		"	"		"	"
"	IARQ (I)		"	"		"	"
10. Hulin	Job satisfaction		100			Checking T or F	Turnover in work (positive in experimental group, no relation in follow-up group)
11. Lent	Desegregation Scale (Kelly, Ferson, & Holtzman, 1958)	8.33	58.33	30	3.33	Likert	Identifying ethnic identity of photographed faces (no relation); identifying their shade of color (positive)

Study	Attitude topic				Method	Behavior
12. Lutzker (1960)	Internationalism	61.11	38.89		Likert	Cooperative and competitiveness in Prisoner's Dilemma (no relation for high scorers, positive for low scorers)
McClintock, Harrison, Strand, & Gullo (1963)	"	"			"	Number of cooperative choices (positive relation)
13. Raz, Kreitler, & Kreitler (1975)	Social behavior	85.71	7.14	7.14	Forced choice	Ten aspects of social behavior (observed experimentally and reported by marriage partner) e.g., starting conversation, keeping up relations (positive relation in four aspects)
14. Smith & Kendall (1963)	Job satisfaction (Smith, 1967)	100			Modified checklist	Termination of work (90% positive relation for men, 61% for women)
Walters & Roach (1971)	"	"			"	Termination of work and absences (positive relations in only one out of five scales)
15. Wirt, Navon, Kreitler, & Kreitler	Honesty in sports	6.67	86.67	6.67	Forced choice and open-ended	Honest and fair behavior of soccer players, observed during matches (positive relation with dishonest but not honest behavior in center forward players but not in fullback and halfback players or others)

[a] The numbers denote sequential pairings of attitude scale with particular behaviors.
[b] Based on group data.
[c] The item positively related to behavior reflects in our terms a behavioral intent.
[d] The single group out of six that showed positive relations to attitudes involved unexperienced and unskilled female office employees.

Table 12.1 demonstrates the wide coverage of the selected studies from the viewpoint of the theme or object of the attitude scales, the formal structure of the scales and the response mode required from the subject, as well as the variety of behavioral variables whose relation to the scales was analyzed.

In addition, for the purposes of a control comparison we analyzed, from the viewpoint of their CO componential structure, the contents of a representative sample of attitude scales. This sample consisted of 413 scales. It included all the attitude scales presented in the handbooks of Robinson, Athanasiou, and Head (1969), Robinson, Rusk, and Head (1968), and Robinson and Shaver (1969), as well as random samples of the scales presented by Miller (1970) and Shaw and Wright (1967), representing the scales in these sources that did not overlap with scales presented in the three mentioned handbooks. Missing are only those scales which are not fully reproduced in these sources and which we were unable to obtain complete copies of. The composition of the sample reflects the rationale that the handbooks and other works we have listed—the major sources in this domain—include all the most common, best-known, thematically varied, and psychometrically screened attitude scales and thus present a sample most fit in its form, content, coverage, and absence of bias to serve as a representative sample of the population of attitude scales.

PROCEDURE

All the selected scales were subjected to a content analysis. The analysis consisted in identifying which CO component(s) was represented by each statement or item in the attitude scales. The counting was done so that each statement in the scale retained its unitary character; that is, if a statement represented one CO component it was assigned a score of 1 on that component, but if it represented two CO components it was assigned two scores, each of 0.5, on the two relevant CO components. The analysis was done separately by two judges who were acquainted with the CO components but not with the purpose of the present study. They were given the attitude scales with no indication of authors and purpose of the scale, as well as of the study in which the scale was used and how it was related to behavior. The interscorer reliability was .98, that is, agreement between the two judges was complete in 96% of the scorings.

For the purpose of testing our hypothesis, the studies were divided, as mentioned, into three types: studies demonstrating positive relations with behavior, those demonstrating no or negative relations, and those demonstrating mixed relations. Since the studies differ greatly in the kind of data reported and the statistical analysis used, no finer distinctions reflecting the degree of association between attitudes and behavior could be adopted.

The attitude scales of the three types of study were compared to each other with regard to three interrelated variables: the number of CO components represented by the statements included in the scales, the nature of the CO components represented by the statements included in the scales, and an index of dispersion reflecting the degree of homogeneity in the distribution of statements across the four CO components. The index was constructed by establishing the percentage of statements representing each of the four CO components, determining the absolute difference in these percentages for each of the six possible pairs of the four CO components, summing these differences, and then dividing by six. Percentages were used instead of the actual numbers of statements in order to neutralize the effect of differences in the number of items in the various attitude scales. The dispersion index has the minimum value of zero when the number of items in each CO component is equal, that is, 25% of the total, and has the maximum value of 50 when all items of the scale are concentrated in only one of the CO components. Thus, the index of dispersion depends on the number of CO components represented by the statements of an attitude scale as well as on the number of statements representing each CO component.

RESULTS AND CONCLUSIONS

The findings summarized in Tables 12.2, 12.3, and 12.4 lend full support to our hypothesis. They show, as expected, that there are remarkable differences between the attitude scales of the three types of study. The attitude scales of studies demonstrating a positive relation between attitudes and behavior include statements that represent on the average 3.29 CO components, whereas the attitude scales of studies demonstrat-

TABLE 12.2
Analyses of Variance of Index of Dispersion and Number of CO
Components in the Attitude Scales of Studies with Positive,
No or Negative, and Mixed Attitude-Behavior Relations

Variable	Source of Variation	df	MS	F
Index of Dispersion	Type of Study	2	1887.75	58.79*
	Error	114	32.11	
Number of CO	Type of Study	2	39.84	86.31*
components	Error	114	.46	

* $p < .001$.

TABLE 12.3
Means and Standard Deviations of Index of Dispersion
and Number of CO Components in the Attitude Scales
of the Three Types of Study

TYPE OF STUDY		INDEX OF DISPERSION		NO. OF CO COMPONENTS IN ATTITUDE SCALE	
	n	$\overline{X}$	SD	$\overline{X}$	SD
Positive relation	34	34.06	6.66	3.29	.62
No or negative relation	68	46.88	5.50	1.43	.69
Mixed relation	15	40.61	5.67	2.27	.75

ing no or a negative relation between attitudes and behavior include statements that, represent on the average 1.43 CO components. In fact, 91.18% of the scales of "positive" studies represent three or four CO components, whereas only 7.35% of the "no or negative" studies do so. The attitude scales of "mixed" studies represent, as expected, an intermediate number of CO components ($\overline{X} = 2.27$). The differences among the three types of attitude scales in the number of CO components they represent are highly significant (Tables 12.2 and 12.3). So are the differences in the index of dispersion (Tables 12.2 and 12.3). The attitude scales of "positive" studies have the lowest mean value of the index, those of the "no or negative" studies the highest, indeed near to the maximum level of the index, and those of the "mixed" studies an intermediate mean value of the index.

Again, a comparison of the frequencies of the four CO components in the attitude scales of the "positive," "no or negative" and "mixed" types

TABLE 12.4
Distribution of Number of CO Components in the
Attitude Scales of the Three Types of Study

NO. OF CO COMPONENTS	TYPE OF STUDY		
	Positive Relations	No or Negative Relations	Mixed Relations
1	0	45	2
2	3	18	8
3	18	4	4
4	13	1	1

$\chi^2_{(1 + 2 \text{ vs. } 3 + 4)} = 70.03, p < .001$

of study shows that the four components are represented about equally in the scales of the "positive" studies, but highly unequally in those of the "no or negative" and "mixed" studies (Table 12.5).

Table 12.5 also shows that the relatively greatest differences in the scales of the three types of studies occur in the component of goals, and the smallest differences in the component of general beliefs. Indeed, goals appears to be the component least represented in the beliefs of the scales in the "no or negative" studies.

There were five attitude scales that included statements representing three or four CO components but did not correlate with behavior. A closer examination of these scales revealed that in three of them at least one CO component is represented by only 5% or less of the statements in the scale. Such a degree of representation may be too low for demonstrating a relation between attitudes and behavior. Conversely, an examination of the three scales that yielded positive relations despite their referring to only two CO components revealed that at least their index of dispersion reflected a more homogeneous distribution of the statements than the scales referring to one or two CO components that yielded no or negative findings ($\overline{X}$ of "positive" $= 42.53$, $SD = 2.50$; $\overline{X}$ of "no or negative" $= 47.40$, $SD = 4.81$; $t = 3.12$, $df = 64$, $p < .001$).

In sum, the findings show that two conditions are necessary for demonstrating positive relations between attitudes and behavior: the attitude scales must include statements representing three or four CO components, and the number of statements representing the four components must not differ too much. Otherwise formulated, the chances of demonstrating a positive relation between attitudes and behavior increase with the number of CO components represented in the attitude

TABLE 12.5
Percentage of the Different CO Components
in the Attitude Scales of the Three Types of Study

Type of Study	N	GB	BS	Go	χ^2
Positive relation	76%	91%	88%	74%	2.65
No or negative relation	28	66	41	7	60.69**
Mixed relation	60	100	40	27	53.46**
$\chi^{2}{}^{a}$	21.85**	7.25*	26.71**	65.72**	

[a] Computed section-wise owing to the nonindependence of the data in the different cells.
* $p < .05$.
** $p < .001$.

TABLE 12.6
Mean and Standard Deviation of Number
of CO Components in Attitude Scales

Domain	No. of Scales	Mean No. of CO Components	SD of CO Components
Political Attitudes[a]			
(Robinson, Rusk, & Head, 1968)			
Liberalism-conservatism	17	2.24	.83
Democratic principles	6	1.83	.75
Domestic government policies	3	2.00	1.00
Racial & ethnic attitudes	12	1.75	.87
International affairs	11	1.82	.40
Hostility-related international			
attitudes	11	1.55	.69
Community-based political attitudes	5	1.40	.55
Political information	4	1.50	1.00
Political participation	10	1.50	.71
Attitudes toward the			
political process	14	2.57	.94
Total	93	1.90	.84
Social Psychological Attitudes[b]			
(Robinson & Shaver, 1969)			
Life satisfaction and happiness	4	1.25	.50
Self-esteem and related constructs	20	2	.73
Alienation and anomie	15	2	.53
Authoritarianism, dogmatism and			
related measures	26	2.27	.92
Other sociopolitical attitudes	7	2	1.00
Values	9	1.56	.73
General attitudes toward people	8	2	.93
Religious attitudes	18	2.17	.99
Total	107	2.03	.83
Occupational Attitudes[c]			
(Robinson, Athanasiou, & Head, 1969)			
General job satisfaction scales	11	2.27	.90

scale and with the degree of homogeneity in the representation of the four CO components.

We might venture to suggest that if in the "positive" studies a sort of scoring or computation preserving to some degree the autonomy of the CO components—as in the CO score—had been used, the demonstrated relation with behavior would have been higher. But there was no way for us to check this suggestion. Also, the form of computation, unlike

TABLE 12.6 (cont'd.)

Domain	No. of Scales	Mean No. of CO Components	SD of CO Components
Job satisfaction and particular occupations	4	3.25	.50
Satisfaction with specific job features	7	2.29	1.11
Concepts related to job satisfaction	8	2.13	.64
Occupational values	7	2.57	1.40
Leadership styles	5	1.40	.55
Other work-related attitudes	10	2.30	1.34
Total	52	2.29	1.04
Diverse Attitude Scales[d] (Shaw & Wright, 1967)	142	2.23	.79
Diverse Attitude Scales[e] (Miller, 1970)			
Satisfaction with job	4	2.75	.96
Community	4	1.50	1.00
Social participation	4	1.25	.50
Attitudes, values and norms	5	1.80	.45
Family and marriage	2	3	.00
Total	19	1.95	.88
Grand total	413	2.10	.85

[a] Does not include survey questions of election studies (Robinson, Rusk, & Head, ch. 13), since they are not strictly attitude scales.
[b] Does not include methodological scales (Robinson & Shaver, 1969, ch. 10).
[c] Does not include measures and indices of occupational status and situs, social mobility and occupational similarity (Robinson, Athanasiou, & Head, 1969, chaps. 14–18), since they are not attitude scales.
[d] Out of the total of 176 scales in Shaw and Wright (1967) we examined a sample of 142; most of the remainder occurred also in Robinson, Rusk, & Head (1968), Robinson, Athanasiou, & Head (1968) or in Robinson & Shaver (1969), and are included in this table under the headings of these handbooks.
[e] A sample of attitude scales presented in Sections C, D, E, G, H and not repeated in the sources sampled above.

the number of CO components and the homogeneity of representation, is evidently not crucial for demonstrating the relation.

If—with these conclusions in mind—we now scan the componential structure of a representative sample of the most common and psychometrically best attitude scales in various domains (Table 12.6), it becomes immediately evident that the majority of studies using these scales would inevitably show no or at best "mixed" relations between attitudes and behavior. It should be noted that the mean number of CO components represented in the scales (mean $= 2.10$, $SD = .85$), regardless of their relations to behavior, lies between the values characterizing scales used in the studies yielding no relations and the scales used in the studies yielding mixed results (Table 12.4). Hence, the majority of attitude scales apt to be picked up by an investigator in the domain of attitudes and behavior do not have the characteristics necessary for demonstrating a positive relation between attitudes and behavior.

Thus, our answer to the familiar question "Are attitudes necessary?" is twofold. If verbally expressed attitudes are conceived as behavior or as surrogates of behavior, then they are unnecessary. If they are conceived as cognitive units that may help to predict behavior, then their usefulness depends on whether they represent an adequate sample of the four CO components.

More importantly, the study lends further support to our insistence on a fuller representation of beliefs from the four CO components in the instruments used for predicting behavior and highlights the utility of the CO theory in shedding new light on an old problem.

Beliefs and CO Components: Methodological Considerations

INTRODUCTORY REMARKS: THE PROBLEMS

It is a truism of science that content and method are closely interrelated. One practical implication, however, is that a new domain of contents often requires devising new methods or adapting old ones. As the theory of cognitive orientation has led to the use of new or partly new methods of data collection, it is desirable to examine these methods.

In this chapter we bring together several summaries of data and specific studies dealing with methodological questions of particular importance for future research: (1) the adequate formulation of beliefs in a CO questionnaire, (2) the interrelations between the four CO components, and (3) the role of each CO component in predicting behavior. All three problems also have theoretical aspects and implications, partly discussed in Chapters 4 and 5. Here, however, we will deal almost exclusively with methodological aspects, in particular as they refer to the construction and use of CO questionnaires.

The second and third of these problems are highly complex, their solution requiring studies in many different behavioral contexts and the consideration of diverse variables. Their treatment in the present context, therefore, must be preliminary and incomplete.

STUDIES I AND II
The Belief Unit—Nucleus and Specifying Extensions

PURPOSE AND QUESTIONS (STUDIES I AND II)

Since the validity of CO measures and their power to predict various psychological phenomena depend on the interest and sincerity of the

We wish to thank Mr. Shimon Abramovici and Mrs. Sophia Oron-Grossman for their devoted help in carrying out Study II.

subjects in answering the questionnaire, it is of great importance to formulate the beliefs in such a way that they will appear to the subjects as meaningful and adequately expressed, being neither too general nor too detailed in form. Studies I and II dealt in methodologically different ways with the problem of formulating beliefs in a questionnaire designed to provide CO measures.

We started from the assumption that each belief consists of a nucleus or core to which various specifying extensions can be added if necessary (Chapter 4). If the nucleus is, for example, "I like ice cream," then the specifying extensions could be "only in summer," "particularly strawberry-flavored," "but not too much of it," etc. The extensions are called "specifying" since they specify the outlines of the potential range of meaning of the nucleus belief, usually by imposing limitations on it. The distinction between the nucleus and the extensions underlies the questions that guided Studies I and II:

1. Do subjects consider the statement of the nucleus belief to be sufficient and satisfactory or do they regard the addition of specifying extensions as necessary?

2. If the addition of specifying extensions is regarded as necessary, which extensions are added most often?

3. Are there differences in the number and kind of added specifying extensions between beliefs of the four CO components?

4. Are there differences in the number and kind of added specifying extensions between beliefs the subject accepts and beliefs he or she does not accept?

5. Are there differences in the number and kind of added specifying extensions between beliefs considered by the subject as important and those considered by him or her as unimportant (Study II only)?

6. Are there differences in the number and kind of added specifying extensions between beliefs the subject had thought about and those he or she had not thought about (Study II only)?

The variables referred to in questions 3, 4, and 5 are relevant for all experimental situations where a CO questionnaire is used. The variable "having (not) thought about the theme" (question 6) was introduced in order to test the effect of experimental manipulations that might make subjects fully aware of certain domains or themes of their cognitive orientation. Since questions 1 through 4 were tested in two parallel studies, once in the form of an open-ended interview (Study I), and once in the form of a closed written questionnaire (Study II), the generality of the answers to these questions across the two experimental situations will be tested.

METHOD (STUDY I)

The subjects were 181 individuals (90 males and 91 females), ranging in age from 18 to 52 years, of various professions and various ethnic and socioeconomic backgrounds. They were selected randomly in schools, industrial plants, government and municipality offices, police, and so on. Each subject was interviewed separately by one of 15 different experimenters. At the outset the interviewer explained to the subject that the study dealt with means for reducing possible misunderstandings between people. Hence, it would be the subject's task to state what additions, if any, should be made to four presented statements so that they would be accurate, and the "hearer will understand the statement properly, without error, in the same way you understand it." It was emphasized that if the subject considered the statement sufficiently clear, he or she should add nothing to it. The statements were presented each on a separate page, the subject being free to write the answers or communicate them orally. Each statement was typed on the page in two forms, one positive (e.g., "people should read newspapers") and one negative (e.g., "people must not read newspapers"). The subject was requested to respond only to that one of the two statements he or she considered true or correct. Each subject got four statements referring to the CO components, one to each component. The statements did not necessarily reflect the same domain of contents. Thirty different domains of contents, derived from psychological, sociological, anthropological, and literary texts, were sampled in this study (e.g., believing in God, having friends, visiting art exhibitions, daydreaming, etc.). Since each domain of contents was phrased in accordance with the four CO components, there were 120 statements, from which the individual questionnaires were formed by random sampling.

The extensions added by the subjects were classified by two independent judges in accordance with the meaning dimensions described in Chapter 2 or subsections of these dimensions (e.g., "duration" and "frequency" are subsections of the dimension "temporal qualities"). Interjudge reliability in analyzing the data was complete in 97% of the cases.

METHOD (STUDY II)

The subjects were 220 individuals (105 males and 115 females), ranging in age from 17 to 56, of various professions and various ethnic and socioeconomic backgrounds, sampled randomly from the populations of schools, military units, industrial plants, and municipal offices. The subjects got a typed questionnaire in groups varying in size from 3 to 30 people, in the presence of 1 of 5 experimenters. None of the subjects participated in Study I.

The questionnaire included four statements phrased in a positive and negative form, each referring to a different CO component. The four statements in a questionnaire referred to one or more domains of contents, and represented a sample out of 120 statements (i.e., 30 domains of contents formulated in terms of the four CO components). The domains of contents were derived from psychological and other sources as in Study I. Only 12 domains of contents were identical in Studies I and II.

Each statement in the questionnaire was followed by a randomly ordered list of 10 pairs of specifying extensions. The pairs exemplified the extension usually through contrasting statements (e.g., "in their vicinity," "not in their vicinity") and were designed merely to illustrate a particular extension, not to be considered factually. The extensions referred to meaning dimensions and their subsections (see list in Table 13.3 or 13.4) pointed out by five judges as most relevant for specifying the meaning of statements. The subject's task concerning each of the four statements was (1) to indicate which of the two formulations she or he considered true or correct (if the subject indicated the positive formulation it was scored as "acceptance" of the belief, and if the negative, as "rejection"); (2) to mark two, if any, of the extensions presented that she or he considered important for adequately understanding the statement, as well as two that she or he considered unimportant; and (3) to check on one 6-point scale (defined by "very important" vs. "not at all important") the importance of the statement and on another 6-point scale (defined by "a lot" vs. "very little") how much she or he had thought about the statement before answering the questionnaire. The scale markings were dichotomized at the median.

RESULTS AND CONCLUSIONS (STUDIES I AND II)

In Study I, 71.82% of the subjects and, in Study II, 72.27% of the subjects added at least one extension to one or more of the four statements. On the average each subject of Study I mentioned 2.90 extensions, and each subject of Study II added 3.35 extensions. The percentage of statements to which extensions were added was 48% in Study I and 43% in Study II (Table 13.1). Otherwise expressed, in Studies I and II respectively, the mean number of extensions added per statement was .75 and .84 if all statements are included, but 1.55 and 1.94 if only those statements to which extensions were added are considered. Thus, the answer to question 1 is that around 70% of the subjects in the interview and questionnaire studies consider addition of extensions

TABLE 13.1
Percentages of Accepted and Nonaccepted Beliefs
to Which Extensions Were Added (Study I and Study II)

CO COMPONENTS	ACCEPTED BELIEFS[a]		NONACCEPTED BELIEFS[a]		χ^2		TOTAL OF ACCEPTED AND NONACCEPTED	
	Study I	*Study II*	*Study I*	*Study II*	*Study I*	*Study II*	*Study I*	*Study II*
Norms	50.62%	50.12%	34.65%	45.34%	2.98	.14	45.93%	47.73%
General beliefs	59.29	43.13	55.10	42.33	.16	.01	58.29	42.73
Beliefs about self	48.90	44.61	37.01	40.85	1.64	.16	44.63	42.73
Goals	45.14	43.02	42.11	35.16	.10	.79	44.32	39.09
Total	50.99	45.22	42.22	40.92			48.29	43.07

[a] None of the differences between Study I and Study II is significant; none of the differences between the four CO components in Study I or in Study II was significant.

as important with regard to approximately 45% of the statements. The addition of about one extension per statement seems to suffice.

Concerning question 2, Tables 13.2 and 13.3 show that in both studies the most frequently added extensions referred to the dimensions "causes," "domain of application," and "function" with regard to what was stated in the nucleus belief. Indeed, the frequencies of the added extensions are so low that only these extensions (plus extensions referring to "quantity" in Study I) have frequencies higher than 10%. There are no significant differences between the two studies in any of the extensions but one ("location," $p < .05$). The Spearman rank correlation between the lists for the two studies was .81 ($p < .01$). Concerning the content of the added extensions (Study I) it should be noted that extensions referring to "domain of application" and "frequency" are often more general and unspecific than extensions referring to "cause," "function," and "consequences." Whereas the latter are expressed in 90% of the cases through definite references to specific contents, the former are expressed in at least 60% of the cases through phrases such as "in certain cases," "mostly," "depends who," "not everybody," and the like. Again, Study I showed that the overwhelming majority of the added extensions (98.48%) served to tone down, delimit, or otherwise reduce the generalization of the nucleus belief, and only 1.52% expressed clearly no restrictions on the generalization (e.g., "in every case," "absolutely everybody," "at all times").

Question 3 referred to differences between beliefs of the four CO components. There are no differences in the number of beliefs of the

TABLE 13.2

Frequency of Subjects Mentioning Extensions as
Important for Beliefs of the Four CO Components (Study I)

EXTENSIONS	NO. OF SUBJECTS MENTIONING EXTENSION AS IMPORTANT[a]					TOTAL NO.	%
	Go	GB	N	BS	x^2		
Cause	39	39	28	30	3.01	136	25.90
Consequences	12	6	16	5	8.28*	39	7.73
Domain of application							
Subject	0	43	8	1	95.23**		
Object	7	7	9	14	3.55		
Total	7	50	17	15	48.07**	89	16.95
Quantity	13	12	15	17	.97	57	10.86
Manner	7	7	8	6	.28	28	5.33
Function	16	19	17	15	.51	67	12.76
Time	6	6	5	14	6.82	31	5.90
Frequency	9	14	4	15	7.33	42	8.00
Duration	0	1	0	0	4.50	1	.19
Location	0	1	2	0	3.66	3	.57
Feeling	5	0	0	3	9.00*	8	1.52
Action	2	0	1	0	3.66	3	.57
Evaluation	5	3	10	4	5.28	22	4.19
Total	121	158	123	124	7.18	525	

[a] The only significant differences in number of extensions between accepted and nonaccepted beliefs were: "manner" (BS), 6–0*; "frequency" (Go), 8–1*; "frequency" (BS), 12–3*; "time" (Go), 6–0*; "time" (GB), 6–0*; "domain of application" (GB), 29–14*; "domain of application" (N), 9–0**. Totals: goals, 83–38*; general beliefs, 105–53**; norms, 88–35**; beliefs about self, 81–43**; total 357–169**. (The first number denotes the frequency in regard to accepted beliefs, the second nonaccepted beliefs.)
* $p < .05$.
** $p < .001$.

four components to which extensions were added (Table 13.1, column 5). There are also no differences in the number of extensions added to beliefs of the four components (Tables 13.2 and 13.3, last rows). Moreover, there are no differences in Study I and almost none in Study II in the number of beliefs of the four CO components to which extensions are added (Table 13.1) and in the number of extensions added when comparisons are made for beliefs grouped according to importance, acceptance, and previous thinking about (Table 13.4). Again, on the whole, there are no differences in the kinds of extensions added to beliefs of the four types. In Study II there were no differences (Table

13.3), whereas in Study I there were differences in regard to "domain of application" (used more frequently concerning general beliefs), "consequences" (this difference occurred in Study II as well when the data were analyzed in terms of the variables "acceptance" and "thought about," Table 13.4), and the infrequently used dimension of "feeling." In sum, beliefs of the four CO components do not differ with regard to the number and kind of extensions added.

Question 4 deals with the effects of acceptance or rejection of beliefs. In the two studies there were no differences between accepted and rejected beliefs in the number of beliefs to which extensions were added (Table 13.1) and in the kinds of extension that were added (Tables 13.2 and 13.4) but there were differences between them in the number of extensions added (for details see Tables 13.2 and 13.4). In general, more extensions were added to accepted beliefs than to rejected ones, particularly extensions such as "cause" (Study II) and "'domain of application" (Study I), which were frequently used with regard to all beliefs. These conclusions hold for accepted and nonaccepted beliefs across all four CO components.

With regard to the variable of the judged importance of beliefs (question 5), beliefs considered as important did not differ from beliefs considered as unimportant in the number and kind of extensions added (Table 13.4).

TABLE 13.3
Frequency of Subjects Mentioning Extensions as Important
for Beliefs of the Four CO Components (Study II)

EXTENSIONS	NO. OF SUBJECTS MENTIONING EXTENSIONS AS IMPORTANT					TOTAL NO.	
	Go	GB	N	BS	x^2		%
Cause	38	56	46	48	3.78	188	23.50
Consequences	11	14	24	21	6.22	70	8.75
Domain of application	15	20	25	11	6.72	72	9.00
Quantity	15	10	18	22	4.72	65	8.13
Manner	12	12	17	13	1.27	54	6.75
Function	32	25	34	24	2.60	115	14.38
Time	12	12	14	8	1.65	46	5.75
Frequency	11	13	11	10	.43	45	5.63
Duration	9	8	4	8	2.04	29	3.63
Location	9	13	12	19	3.98	53	6.63
x^2	46.26*	41.39*	52.15*	55.49*			
Total	164	184	205	184	4.56	737	

* $p < .001$.

TABLE 13.4
Significant Differences in Extensions within and between CO Components, between Beliefs Evaluated as Important and Unimportant, Accepted and Nonaccepted, Thought About and Not Thought About

RESTRICTIVE EXTENSIONS	DIFFERENTIATING VARIABLES	SIGNIFICANT DIFFERENCES WITHIN CO COMPONENTS				SIG. DIFF. (χ^2) BETWEEN CO COMPONENTS	
		G_O	GB	N	BS	Positive[a]	Negative
Cause	Important–unimportant					4.39	2.40
	Accepted–nonaccepted	30–8**	47–9***	33–13**	34–14**	5.61	2.36
	Thought about–not thought about	26–11**	42–11***	34–11***	35–12***	3.76	.08
Consequences	Important–unimportant					6.00	1.13
	Accepted–nonaccepted		11–2*	23–1**		10.62*	8.18*
	Thought about–not thought about			18–4***		8.78*	2.90
Domain of application	Important–unimportant					2.94	3.40
	Accepted–nonaccepted					3.92	2.69
	Thought about–not thought about					2.96	5.28
Quantity	Important–unimportant					3.14	1.55
	Accepted–nonaccepted	13–2**	9–1*	14–4*	17–5**	2.47	3.32
	Thought about–not thought about					1.79	3.66
Manner	Important–unimportant					1.79	1.12
	Accepted–nonaccepted	11–1**	10–2*		11–2*	.18	3.60
	Thought about–not thought about	10–2*	10–2*	13–2**		.85	1.20

Function						
Important–unimportant	23–9*	22–3**	29–5****	19–4**	2.24	3.95
Accepted–nonaccepted		22–3**	26–7**	17–6*	2.01	6.00
Thought about–not thought about					1.41	2.01
Time						
Important–unimportant	11–1**		13–1**		2.38	2.05
Accepted–nonaccepted			12–2**		2.74	1.57
Thought about–not thought about					5.26	.26
Frequency						
Important–unimportant					2.00	1.50
Accepted–nonaccepted					.76	2.07
Thought about–not thought about					.39	2.34
Duration						
Important–unimportant					7.50	2.45
Accepted–nonaccepted					2.99	6.66
Thought about–not thought about					2.90	.34
Location						
Important–unimportant					.40	5.39
Accepted–nonaccepted					1.00	4.55
Thought about–not thought about					2.75	1.42
Total						
Important–unimportant	125–39***	142–42***	162–43***	129–56***	2.13	3.64
Accepted–nonaccepted	107–52***	136–42***	149–50***	120–55***	5.97	3.78
Thought about–not thought about					7.90*	1.86

[a] The terms "positive" and "negative" refer to positive or negative responses to questions concerning the "differentiating variables." Thus, "positive" denotes items evaluated as important, items the subject accepts, or items the subject has thought about.
* $p < .05$.
** $p < .01$.
*** $p < .001$.

Finally, beliefs that have been thought about differ from beliefs that have not been thought about (question 6) in the number of extensions added to them, particularly in the rather frequently used extensions of "cause," "function," and "consequences" (Table 13.4). There are no differences in the kinds of extensions added.

In sum, the two studies indicate that there is a moderate tendency to specify the potential meaning range of a nucleus belief by adding to it approximately one specifying extension, particularly if the nucleus belief is an accepted belief or a belief one has thought about. There are no differences in this respect between beliefs of the four CO components. The extensions most often added refer to "cause," "domain of application," "function," "consequences," and "quantity." Practically, these findings suggest that the investigator constructing a CO questionnaire would be well advised to add to about half the beliefs in all CO components one or two specifying extensions, mostly delimiting, referring to "causes," "domain of application," "function," "consequences," or "quantity" (degree) of the stated content.

INTERRELATIONS BETWEEN CO COMPONENTS

THE PROBLEM

When we speak of interrelations between the four CO components we refer only to the orientative directions overtly or covertly implied by beliefs belonging to the different CO components (see "The Cognitive Orientativeness of Beliefs," Chapter 4). For instance, the beliefs "I want to buy at least three dresses" and "A person should fight inflation by minimizing consumption" point in contrasting orientative directions since they imply different actions, or, alternatively, they do not support the same action. Thus, measuring the interrelations between the four CO components depends on our definition of the concept of orientativeness of beliefs and on the possibility of identifying the action implied overtly or covertly by the relevant beliefs. If each CO component is represented only by a single belief, the measure of interrelation between any two CO components takes the form of correspondence or noncorrespondence between the orientativeness of the two respective beliefs (see Study III, this chapter). If each CO component is represented by several beliefs, as is the rule in CO questionnaires, the measure of interrelation between any two CO components takes the form of a regular correlation coefficient or any analogous substitute in line with the properties of the data.

The problem of interrelations between the CO components is of theoretical and methodological importance. The theoretical aspects, mainly the implications with regard to the autonomic status of the four CO components, were discussed in Chapter 4. In the present context we will focus on the methodological aspects of the problem.

SUMMARY OF FINDINGS CONCERNING CO QUESTIONNAIRES

The problem of interrelations between the four CO components arises most often in constructing and testing CO questionnaires. Therefore it is of particular importance to analyze these interrelations by examining the correlations between all answers to the 11 different CO questionnaires used in all the studies reported in this book. The results are presented in Table 13.5. (The table includes 13 rather than 11 rows since it also lists, in row 7, results for a combined questionnaire and, in row 9, results for a repeated questionnaire, neither of which can be considered as an independent questionnaire.)

Table 13.5 shows that, of the 66 correlations between all possible pairs of the four CO components, 30 (45.45%) are positive and significant. These 30 correlations are distributed equally across the pairs of CO components: 4–6 positive significant correlations out of the 11 correlations listed for each pair of components. The differences between the various pairs of CO components with regard to the numbers of significant correlations are nonsignificant ($\chi^2 = .80$, n.s.). This might suggest that the distribution of significant correlations in this sample is completely random. Two observations impose restrictions on such a conclusion. First, most correlations in this sample (88.88%) are positive—though not significant—the difference between the positive and negative correlations being highly significant ($z = 6.03$, $p < .001$). Second, if we consider the distribution of positive significant correlations from the point of view of questionnaires rather than of pairs of CO components, we find a U-shaped distribution: there are five questionnaires that yielded zero or one positive significant correlation between components, there are four questionnaires that yielded five or six positive significant correlations, and there are only two questionnaires that yielded two, three, or four positive significant correlations. Thus, there seem to be two types of questionnaire: those yielding consistently noncorrelated measures of components and those yielding consistently correlated measures of components. There is no difference between the two types in the extent to which they are correlated with behaviors. Both types predict behaviors equally successfully (see Chapters 7, 8, and 10). Moreover, there are no consistent differences in structure, psychometric characteristics, and content between the two types of questionnaire that might account for the

TABLE 13.5
Interrelations between the Four CO Components and CO Scores in Various Domains

Domain	No. of Ss	N–GB	N–BS	N–Go	GB–BS	GB–Go	BS–Go	N–CO	GB–CO	BS–CO	Go–CO
Achievement (Chapter 7, Study I)	50	−.09	.31*	.34*	.08	.05	.24	.59**	.33**	.58**	.59**
Accuracy (Chapter 7, Study II)	50	−.02	−.13	.21	−.18	.27	−.28*	.41**	.48**	.41**	.54**
Postsuccess (Chapter 7, Study III)	49	−.16	−.20	−.21	.23	.16	.08	.45**	.58**	.46**	.41**
Postfailure (Chapter 7, Study III)	50	.27	.47**	.50**	.40**	.12	.47**	.71**	.56**	.65**	.70**
In favor of coming on time (Chapter 7, Study IV)	70	.36**	.56**	.54**	.54**	.41**	.49**	.73**	.77**	.88**	.72**
Opposed to being late (Chapter 7, Study IV)	70	.44**	.47**	.64**	.41**	.37**	.51**	.79**	.69**	.76**	.84**
In favor of coming on time and opposed to being late combined (Chapter 7, Study IV)	70	.50**	.58**	.63**	.60**	.58**	.61**	.78**	.80**	.88**	.85**

Tolerance of pain (premanipulations) (Chapter 7, Study V)	112	.37**	.29**	.43**	.26**	.39**	.06	.63**	.71**	.49**	.61**
Tolerance of pain (postmanipulations) (Chapter 7, Study V)	112	.49**	.38**	.45**	.46**	.26**	.18	.68**	.72**	.60**	.56**
Quitting smoking (Chapter 7, Study VI)	32	.05	.08	.17	.25	.11	.53**	.45**	.49**	.72**	.73**
High achievement and underachievement at school (Chapter 8, Study II)	92	−.05	.18	.18	.15	.18	.08	.48**	.50**	.59**	.59**
Curiosity (Chapter 8, Study III)	64	.70**	.66**	.81**	.73**	.74**	.76**	.89**	.88**	.87**	.93**
Defense mechanisms[a] (Chapter 10, Study IV)	24	.24	1.91	1.02	2.83	.50	.17	16.62****	19.14****	24.74****	8.29*

[a] The numbers represent chi-square values of the differences between two distributions: that of the observed number of inversions between the ordering of the three studied defense mechanisms in terms of the variables mentioned in the heading of the column, and the expected number of inversions computed on the basis of the distribution of the number of inversions in all 144 possible combinations of rankings $(df = 1)$.

* $p < .05$.   ** $p < .01$.   *** $p < .001$.

difference in the interrelation between their measures of CO components. For example, one of the "correlated" questionnaires (CO of curiosity) differs in form from the other questionnaires in that beliefs of all CO components are presented in it together in relation to specific themes. But, as mentioned, this is not true of any other of the "correlated" questionnaires. Again, it could be claimed that one of the "correlated" questionnaires was administered to children, whose level of differentiation may be low (Table 13.5, row 12), and that another of the "correlated" questionnaires (Table 13.5, row 8), as well as an almost "correlated" questionnaire (Table 13.5, row 4) dealt with emotion-laden themes like pain and failure that could have temporarily reduced the differentiation capability of the subjects. Yet no similar arguments could be sensibly raised with regard to the other "correlated" questionnaires, which dealt with coming late or being on time.

In sum, correlations between the orientativeness of beliefs belonging to different CO components tend to be positive, and in about half the cases positive and significant. CO questionnaires may yield measures of CO components that are either consistently correlated or consistently uncorrelated, both types being equally well predictive of behaviors.

STUDY III
Correspondence of CO Components
Represented by Single Beliefs

PURPOSE AND HYPOTHESIS

The purpose of this study was to examine the impact of the number of beliefs presented to the subject on the interrelations between the four CO components. Proponents of consistency theories could claim that the relatively low consistency between CO components, at least in some domains, is due to the subject's confusion, resulting from the great number of beliefs used for representing each CO component in a regular CO questionnaire. If this argument if valid, then presenting the subject with only four beliefs, each representing one of the four CO components, would make it easier for him or her to deal with the implications of the beliefs, and should therefore lead to a higher degree of consistency between the CO components. Hence, the hypothesis was that the degree of correspondence between the four CO components would be higher when subjects are presented with only four beliefs at a time than when they answer questionnaires with many beliefs representing each CO component. Since in questionnaires somewhat less than 50% of the correlations between CO components were positive and significant (see "Summary of Findings Concerning CO Questionnaires") we tested the hypothesis that in the case of single beliefs representing the CO components, more than 50% of the pairings between CO components, at the very least, would manifest correspondence in the orientative directions of the respective beliefs.

METHOD

The subjects were 110 individuals (59 males and 51 females), ranging in age from 22 to 45 years, who were selected randomly from the population of industrial plants, educational institutions, and business offices.

In a short interview each subject was presented with four pairs of beliefs reflecting the four CO components. Each pair consisted of a positive and negative formulation of the same content, e.g., "People should try new foods" and "People should not try new foods." All four pairs referred to the same content. There were 35 content areas (e.g., concerning health, appearance, entertainment, work, study, family, children, interpersonal relations, and so on), sampled randomly in the interviews. The beliefs were read aloud and also shown in typed form. The order of the beliefs was random. The subject's task was to point out which of the beliefs in each presented pair of beliefs he or she accepted or approved of.

The subject was not pressed if he or she claimed difficulty in making a decision on any item. Hence the slight differences in the number of subjects listed for each pairing of two CO components in Table 13.6 (the range was 100–110 subjects). There were 95 subjects who responded to all four beliefs (Table 13.7).

RESULTS AND CONCLUSIONS

Identity in the orientative directions of any two beliefs was scored as correspondence and nonidentity as noncorrespondence. Table 13.6 shows that in almost three out of the six pairings between any two CO components the distribution of corresponding and noncorresponding beliefs deviates from chance, in a direction that indicates identity in the orientative directions of the beliefs. A similar conclusion is supported by considering the data from the point of view of subjects. Table 13.7 shows that a third of the subjects (32) responded highly consistently to the four beliefs (see rows 1, 2, 6, and 7 in Table 13.7); a third (31) responded fairly consistently (see rows 3 and 5 in Table 13.7); and a third (32) responded inconsistently (see row 4 in Table 13.7). The

TABLE 13.6
Distribution of Beliefs Corresponding
and Noncorresponding in Orientativeness

| CO COMPONENTS | NO. OF BELIEFS[a] | | z-VALUES |
	Corresponding	Noncorresponding	
Norms–general beliefs	49	58	.77
Norms–beliefs about self	70.5	36.5	3.19**
Norms–goals	66	44	2.00*
General beliefs–beliefs about self	63	45	1.63
General beliefs–goals	58.5	43.5	1.38
Beliefs about self–goals	59.5	40.5	1.80[1]

[a] Beliefs intermediate in correspondence were scored as .5 with respect to correspondence and as .5 with respect to noncorrespondence.
[1] $p < .10$.
* $p < .05$.
** $p < .01$.

TABLE 13.7
Distribution of Response Patterns of Correspondence (+)
and Noncorrespondence (−) between Beliefs of the Four CO Components

| PATTERNS OF INTERRELATION OF CO COMPONENTS | | OBSERVED NO. OF SUBJECTS | EXPECTED NO. OF SUBJECTS (NORMAL DISTRIBUTION) |
No. of +	No. of −		
6	0		
5	1	22	10.23
4	2	13	24.75
3	3	32	35.03
2	4	18	24.75
1	5		
0	6	10	10.23

$\chi^2 = 21.23, p < .01$.

whole distribution of subjects deviates from that expected on the basis of the normal distribution owing to the tendency of subjects to approve of positive beliefs in a consistent manner to a higher degree than expected by chance.

In sum, the degree of correspondence between single beliefs of the four CO components is not higher than that obtained in regular CO questionnaires in which each CO component is represented by several beliefs. Regardless of whether the number of beliefs in each CO component is one or more than one, the orientative directions of beliefs of the four CO components are correlated in somewhat less than 50% of the cases of possible pairings between CO components. This finding disconfirms the hypothesis derived from consistency theory and shows that confusion or difficulty in coping with the orientative directions of many diverse beliefs could not be the cause for the moderate degree of consistency between the four CO components.

STUDY IV
The Effects of Content Areas, Personality Trait, and Life Styles on Correspondence between CO Components

PURPOSE AND HYPOTHESES

This study was designed to explore factors determining correspondence between CO components. It was not meant to provide a conclusive answer but to demonstrate how the problem can be studied. We examined the effect of three factors on the degree of correspondence of CO components: (1) content areas, that is, general sociopolitical themes versus themes relevant to women's status; (2) a personality trait, that is, the dimension of extroversion-introversion; and (3) life styles, specifically, working regularly outside the home as a paid employee, working occasionally as a voluntary worker in various women's organizations, or being a housewife without working outside the home.

These three factors were chosen because they allow for testing the general hypothesis that correspondence between beliefs depends at least to some extent on acquired conventional approaches to specific themes and on pressures toward consistency that may be more pronounced in some social contexts than in others. Triandis (1964b) substantiated the latter point with regard to cultural pressures. We assumed that such conventions and pressures existed in Israel at the time of the study (1967) with regard to general sociopolitical themes but not (or not yet) with regard to women's lib themes. Further, we expected that extrovert women and working women would have more incentive and more opportunity to be exposed to these conventions and pressures and to yield to them than introvert women and housewives, whose contacts with public opinions and pressures are more restricted (in 1967 TV was not yet instituted in Israel).

This study was carried out with Mrs. Irit Zeltzer. It formed a part of a larger study on the factor of conservatism-liberalism in three groups of women.

Hence our hypotheses were that correspondence between CO components would be higher (1) with regard to general sociopolitical themes than with regard to themes relevant to women's status, (2) in extrovert women than in introvert women, and (3) in working women than in housewives, with voluntary workers occupying a middle position.

METHOD

The subjects were 42 women ranging in age from 31 to 55 years; 16 were women who worked regularly outside the home as paid employees in offices, hospitals, plants, etc.; 11 were women who worked as registered volunteers in women's organizations and hospitals; and 15 were housewives who never worked regularly outside the home. The women of the three groups were similar in their sociocultural and educational background. Fourteen of the working women, 9 of the voluntary workers, and all the housewives were married at the time of the study.

Each subject was interviewed individually and could give the answers orally or in writing. The interview consisted in administering Eysenck's Extroversion-Introversion Scale and a conservatism-liberalism questionnaire. The questionnaire consisted of four parts, each referring to one of the four CO components. In each part there were 11 clusters of statements: five clusters referred to general sociopolitical themes (authoritarianism, religion, criminality, ethnic discrimination, and government functions), five clusters referred to themes relevant for women's status (work of women, the home, family life, women's legal rights, rearing and education of children) and one cluster included repeat statements for the sake of testing reliability. Two of the statements in each cluster pointed in the direction of conservatism and two in the direction of liberalism. The themes of the clusters and many of the specific statements were selected out of existing questionnaires in this domain. They were rechecked for relevance and directionality by judges. Themes of clusters and statements within clusters were presented to the subjects in random order.

In scoring the responses one point was assigned to the checking of a conservative statement and one point was subtracted for the checking of a liberal statement. Reliability of the responses, as tested by comparing twice-repeated responses to the same statements, was perfect in 88.3% of the cases (range with regard to the four CO components separately: 76.2%–88.1%). The probabilities of obtaining such high numbers of identical responses upon repeat are in all cases lower than 1:1000.

Correspondence in the directionality of the checked statements was examined for each pairing of any two CO components in each of the two content areas of themes separately. Thus, each subject got 12 scores of correspondence (i.e., 6 pairings of CO components $\times$ 2 content areas). The correspondence score reflected the signed result of subtracting the content area score in one CO component from that in another CO component.

RESULTS AND CONCLUSIONS

The importance of distinguishing between the two content areas is supported by the finding that in all three subgroups of women responses to the two content areas are uncorrelated in each of the four CO components, with the exception of one correlation in the group of working women (Table 13.8). In the sample as a whole the two content areas are correlated with regard to norms and beliefs about self but not with regard to goals and general beliefs.

Table 13.9 shows the dependence of correlations between CO components on life style. Whereas in the group of housewives only one correlation is significant but negative (!), and in the group of voluntary workers none is significant, in the group of working women seven correlations between CO components are positive and significant. It may also be noted that whereas some correlations in the first two groups are even negative (three in housewives, and six in volunteers), only one is so in the working women's group.

The two-factor analyses of variance summarized in Table 13.10 show that in five cases there was a significant main effect due to type of work, working women being always highest in correspondence and housewives always lowest in correspondence. Three of these cases were in regard to general themes and two in regard to women's themes. Only in one case was there a main effect due to extroversion-introversion, and in another an interaction effect.

TABLE 13.8
Rank Correlations between Two Content Areas
in Three Groups of Women

CO COMPONENT	RANK CORRELATIONS BETWEEN GENERAL AND WOMEN'S AREAS OF CONTENT			
	Housewives	*Voluntary Workers*	*Working Women*	*Whole Sample*
Norms	.13	−.18	.39	.27*
Beliefs about self	.15	.13	.28	.45**
General beliefs	−.30	.19	−.21	.13
Goals	.20	.28	.55*	.17

* $p < .05$.   ** $p < .01$.

TABLE 13.9
Rank Correlations between CO Components
in Three Groups of Women in Two Content Areas

| CO Components | Rank Correlations (r_s) | | | | | |
| | HOUSEWIVES | | VOLUNTARY WORKERS | | WORKING WOMEN | |
	General	Women's	General	Women's	General	Women's
Norms–beliefs about self	.02	.18	−.43	−.37	72**	.71**
Norms–general beliefs	.13	.19	−.12	.14	.39	.24
Norms–goals	.31	.08	.51[1]	−.06	.52*	.48*
General beliefs– beliefs about self	−.50*	.34	−.26	.37	.29	.18
Beliefs about self–goals	−.22	.10	−.37	.02	.59*	.68**
General beliefs—goals	.21	−.04	.18	.21	.65*	−.38

[1] $p < .10$.   * $p < .05$.   ** $p < .01$.

In sum, the findings support mainly the second hypothesis concerning the dependence of correspondence between CO components on life style. They also suggest that content areas play a role, but that extroversion-introversion has practically no impact at all. It may be mentioned that in a study reported earlier (Chapter 8, Study II; see especially Table 8.5) it was shown that another personality feature, that is, high achievement versus underachievement at school, also had no impact whatsoever on the degree of correspondence between CO components.

GENERAL CONCLUSIONS

The summary of interrelations between measures of CO components yielded by 11 CO questionnaires, as well as Studies III and IV, show that the orientative directions of beliefs of the four CO components with regard to specific themes tend to be correlated only to a moderate degree, that is, in less than 50% of the cases; or, conversely expressed, they are mostly uncorrelated. This finding suggests that the four CO components are essentially distinct factors, each of which potentially makes a unique contribution to predicting and understanding behavior. This conclusion is reinforced in particular by our repeated findings that all four CO components are necessary for predicting behavior (Chapters 7–10, 11).

The summary in Table 13.5 and Study IV suggest that the extent of correspondence between CO components varies from one area of con-

TABLE 13.10
Two-Factor Analyses of Variance of Correspondence Scores
between Beliefs in Different Pairs of CO Components

CO Components: Content:		N-BS				N-GB				N-Go			
		GENERAL		WOMEN'S		GENERAL		WOMEN'S		GENERAL		WOMEN'S	
	df	MS	F	MS	F	MS	F	MS	F	MS	F	MS	F
Extrovert-introvert (A)	1	6	<1	14.96	1.93	18.47	2.74	25.56	4.33*	3.91	<1	5.39	<1
Type of work (B)	2	35.45	4.90*	15.60	2.01	3.50	<1	3.17	<1	18.84	3.65*	36.36	5.35**
A × B	2	2.02	<1	27.33	3.52*	9.07	1.34	8.39	1.42	6.13	1.19	10.48	1.54
Within cell	36	7.23		7.76		6.75		5.90		5.16		6.80	

CO Components: Content:		GB-BS				BS-Go				GB-Go			
		GENERAL		WOMEN'S		GENERAL		WOMEN'S		GENERAL		WOMEN'S	
	df	MS	F	MS	F	MS	F	MS	F	MS	F	MS	F
Extrovert-introvert (A)	1	9.17	<1	12.74	1.45	9.09	1.84	5.53	1.39	21.03	2.84	26.69	2.46
Type of work (B)	2	5.50	<1	9.71	1.10	42.02	8.52**	22.41	5.64**	15.50	2.09	14.53	1.34
A × B	2	1.58	<1	.84	<1	5.19	1.05	7.82	1.97	7.65	1.03	1.89	<1
Within cell	36	10.39		8.80		4.93		3.97		7.41		10.86	

*$p < .05$.
**$p < .01$.

385

tent to another and that it is affected by life style or exposure to sociocultural pressures for consistency. In contrast, it is not affected by a general personality feature like extroversion-introversion or a personality feature specific to the domain of study (e.g., high achievement and underachievement). These conclusions seem to us only tentative. They merely
chart the outlines of a future domain of research that will deal with
dependence of correspondence between CO components on content
areas, situational factors, and personality features, perhaps even a personality trait like striving for consistency between beliefs.

What are the implications with regard to constructing CO questionnaires? Both questionnaires with intercorrelations between CO components and those without such intercorrelations predict behaviors successfully. We would nevertheless suggest, even though tentatively, that questionnaires with low intercorrelations between CO components would in
general be preferable mainly because they would better guarantee wider
sampling of beliefs in each CO component and thus enable the unique
contribution of each component to become operative. Reduction of
redundancy is preferable also on statistical grounds.

THE FOUR CO COMPONENTS IN PREDICTING BEHAVIOR

In the studies reported in this book we have not dwelt on the problem
of the specific contribution of each CO component to predicting behavior. We have not done so because this problem requires a special large-
scale investigation planned to yield statistically the adequate information. Such a study is being carried out now at Tel Aviv University by
Mrs. Talma Lobel. Until this study is completed, the problem can be
approached only on the basis of evidence accumulated up to now.

Table 13.11 summarizes the data of the correlations of each CO component separately with the behavioral variables in the various studies
reported in this book. Of the 232 cited correlations, only 22 (9.48%)
are significant. All of these are positive. The percentage is so low that it
lies near the chance level. These findings confirm our repeated claim
that the CO components separately do not in general predict behavior.
As we have often shown, in order to predict behavior not even two or
three of the CO components will usually suffice; all four are needed.

The data in Table 13.11 may also be considered from another point of
view. If we rank order the correlations in each row from highest to
lowest, regardless of significance, and then classify the resulting rank
orderings, we find that the 58 rank orderings are distributed in the following manner: 13 patterns start with norm beliefs (e.g., N–BS–Go–
GB, 5; N–Go–BS–GB, 4); 12 patterns start with general beliefs; 22 pat-

TABLE 13.11
Correlations between Behavior Variables
and Each of the Four CO Components Separately

Behavior Variables	CO Questionnaire	No. of Cases	N	GB	BS	Go
Achievement (Ch. 7, Study I)	Achievement	50				
Task I: Neutral						
No. solved			.16	—.09	.15	—.04
No. right			.23	—.24	.03	—.04
Index			.21	—.17	.09	—.04
Task II: Postsuccess		50				
No. solved			.14	.14	.06	.13
No. right			.18	—.04	.16	.17
Index			.17	—.08	.11	.16
Task III: Postfailure		50				
No. solved			.09	.10	.19	—.02
No. right			.01	—.01	.31*	—.06
Index			.05	.05	.25	—.04
Accuracy (Ch. 7, Study II)	Accuracy	50	.01	.13	—.01	.26
Postsuccess (Index) (Ch. 7, Study III)	Postsuccess	49	—.03	.08	.12	.08
Postfailure (Index)	Postfailure	50	.15	.01	.29*	.39**
Being late (Ch. 7, Study IV)	In favor of coming on time	70	—.24	—.13	—.39**	—.14
	Opposed to being late	70	.28*	.13	.35**	.29*
	Combined CO	70	.31**	.18	.42**	.29*
Tolerance of pain (Ch. 7, Study V)	Pain tolerance	112				
Threshold of sensitivity			.13	.16	.28**	.10
Threshold of pain			—.00	.16	.35**	—.08
Threshold of pain intolerance			.06	.21*	.34**	.01
Evaluation of pain			.01	.04	—.07	.11
Quitting smoking (Ch. 7, Study VI)	Quitting smoking	32				
Relative to estimate:						
End of treatment			.17	.13	.19	.05
Follow-up 1			.14	.13	.25	.00
Follow-up 2			.10	.17	.42*	.08
Follow-up 3			.07	.20	.35*	.03
Relative to recorded no.:						
End of treatment			.10	.14	.10	—.03
Follow-up 1			.11	.14	.21	—.03
Follow-up 2			.08	.22	.39*	.05
Follow-up 3			.05	.25	.32	—.01

TABLE 13.11 (Cont'd.)

Behavior Variables	CO Questionnaire	No. of Cases	N	GB	BS	Go
Grade Point Average (Ch. 8, Study I)		50				
	Achievement		.02	−.15	.13	−.17
	Postsuccess		−.22	−.07	.09	.06
	Postfailure		.24	−.002	.10	.12
Achievement & underachievement at school[a] (Ch. 8, Study II)	Underachievement	92	.05	.19	1.06**	.28
Curiosity (Ch. 8, Study III)	Curiosity					
1. Simple stimuli—observ. time		58	−.11	.02	−.00	.08
2. Complex stimuli—observ. time		58	−.13	.15	.13	.16
3. Mean time difference between complex & simple stimuli		58	−.03	.19	.19	.10
4. Switching glance— total no.		58	−.12	.06	.03	.03
5. No. of pairs whose complex stimulus was viewed longer		58	.14	.06	.10	.08
6. No. of complex stimuli preferred		64	.07	.15	.21	.13
7. Switching preference— total no.		64	−.13	.19	.15	.17
8. Choosing the unknown— total no.		64	−.07	.31	.14	.05
9. Switching choice— total no.		64	−.05	−.04	−.03	.00
10. No. of meaning values		64	.09	−.17	−.11	−.10
11. No. of meaning dimensions		64	.18	.05	.02	−.01
12. Time interval of choice		64	−.24	−.10	−.21	−.09
13. No. of inspecting manipulations		64	.05	.37**	.30**	.36**
14. No. of customary use manipulations		64	−.02	.09	.07	.04
15. No. of exploratory manipulations		64	.16	.26*	.18	.13
16. No. of exploratory manipulations		64	.14	.35**	.25	.23
17. Total time of manipulations		64	.00	.23	.17	.19

TABLE 13.11 (cont'd.)

Behavior Variables	CO Questionnaire	No. of Cases	N	GB	BS	Go
18. Weighted index of questions		64	−.04	.05	.09	.05
19. Teacher's rating of curiosity		64	.11	−.24	−.15	−.22
Choice of new or familiar objects for play		64	.20	.34	.27*	.25
Probability learning (Ch. 8, Study IV)	Curiosity	64				
Maximizing			.05	−.01	−.05	−.10
Minimizing			−.18	−.15	−.33**	−.17
Index of Stereotypy C_1			.09	−.09	−.04	−.07
Index of Stereotypy C_2			.12	.06	.04	.07
Index of Stereotype C_3			.02	.08	.05	.12
Preoccupation with pattern & hypothesis testing			.01	.06	−.00	.07
Defense mechanisms[b] (Ch. 10, Study IV)	Defense mechanism	24	.66	.66	.16	1.50

[a] Since the behavioral variable was dichotomized, the coefficients represent point-biserial correlations.

[b] The numbers represent chi-square values of the differences between two distributions: that of the observed number of inversions between the ordering of the three studied defense mechanisms in terms of CO scores and in terms of a Weighted Behavior Index, and the expected number of inversions computed on the basis of the distribution of the number of inversions in all 144 possible combinations of rankings. None of the chi-square values is significant ($df = 1$).

* $p < .05$.
** $p < .01$.

terns start with beliefs about self; and 11 start with goal beliefs. The difference is not significant ($\chi^2 = 5.31$, $df = 3$, n.s.). Thus, any CO component was equally often most intimately related to the behavioral variable relative to the other components. Again, each CO component was also equally often least intimately related to the behavioral variable relative to the other components (N in 19 patterns, BS in 6, GB in 15, and Go in 18; $\chi^2 = 6.39$, $df = 3$, n.s.). Moreover, it is important to note that of the 24 theoretically possible different arrangements of the four CO components, 20 actually occur in our data. This again indicates that no one of the four CO components can at this stage be pointed out unreservedly as most or more or least crucial than any other for predicting behavior. In this context it may also be worth mentioning that in estimating the probability of behavioral intents subjects assign equal weight to beliefs of the four components (Chapter 11, Study I) and in attempting to account for given behavioral intents they select comparable numbers of beliefs of the four CO components. To our mind, all the cited evidence supports the view that, until firm information exists about the variation of weights of the CO components in line with behavioral domains or perhaps also personality structures, the procedure of assigning equal weights to the four components is methodologically not only the most conservative but also the safest.

CONCLUDING REMARKS: PRACTICAL IMPLICATIONS

This chapter has dealt with three separate problems: the formulation of beliefs, the interrelations between CO components, and the role of each CO component in predicting behavior. All three problems have direct implications for the further development of CO questionnaires.

With regard to formulating beliefs for questionnaires designed to yield CO measures, meaning responses, and so on, we found that it is most adequate to complement at least some of the core beliefs of any of the CO components by the addition of one to a maximum of two specifying extensions. The most appropriate extensions are those that refer to the causes, domain of application, function, consequences, and quantity or degree of the stated content. The extensions should preferably be restrictive of the content. In the case of domain of application and quantity the extensions may be of a most general nature, recalling the applicability of the relevant restriction rather than a specific delimiting factor.

As to the interrelations between CO components, our results are less conclusive. We found indications for the dependence of interrelations upon life styles or sociocultural factors and also upon content areas. More importantly, the existing evidence warrants the conclusion that the number of correlations between the measures of separate CO components in a CO questionnaire is unrelated to the success of the CO questionnaire in predicting behavior. Yet, in the interests of wider sampling of relevant contents and the avoidance of unnecessary redundancies, we would suggest striving for CO questionnaires that yield largely uncorrelated measures of the separate CO components, at least insofar as this fits the nature of the content area and the particular subjects of the study.

With regard to the separate contribution of each CO component to predicting behavior our findings are least conclusive. So far there exists no empirical evidence urging the assignment of a greater or lesser weight to any one of the CO components. There are, however, several theoretical considerations in favor of deviating from the assumption of the equal weight of all four CO components. Some are grounded specifically in the CO theory (Chapter 5), and some are of a more general nature, reflecting the expectation for individual and situational differences. These possibilities are being explored at present in a large-scale study.

Of course the three problems dealt with in this chapter form only a sample of a number of other problems of similar nature that have yet to be resolved. For example: Should beliefs of the four CO components be presented separately as different parts of a questionnaire, or could they be intermingled randomly? Which type of scoring of the orientative direction of a CO component is most adequate: in terms of separate beliefs or in terms of clusters of beliefs within the component? Regardless of the problem of weights of the separate CO components, which form of combination of CO components is preferable: algebraic addition of dichotomized scores reflecting each CO component, vectorial addition in terms of belief clusters within each CO component, or any other combination in accordance with some formula? It is this type of methodological question we are attempting at present to answer empirically.

CHAPTER 14

Answers and Questions

The most important answer given in this book responds to a question that has not been asked explicitly before: Does the human tendency to establish, widen, and deepen cognitive orientation fulfill such important functions that it can serve as the core of a theory of human behavior, a theory that gives at least some of the many explanations missing in other psychological theories? We hope that the CO theory and the research presented in this book constitute an affirmative answer to this question, notwithstanding their shortcomings and gaps, which provide for us and our coworkers a welcome challenge for further theoretical and empirical inquiry.

Of course, those readers—perhaps very few, perhaps a great many— who regard our description of the evocation of human molar behavior as relatively adequate, and who are even inclined to accept our empirical findings as supporting the CO theory and as indicating its psychological usefulness, may still wonder whether further experiments will yield less positive results. Methodological considerations and in particular Popper's theory of science show convincingly that we can never predict with sufficient certainty the scientific findings of tomorrow. Thus we are left with our more or less reasonable and probable expectation. If a theory is logically consistent, professionally convincing, and empirically falsifiable yet has hitherto withstood the repeated test of experimental confirmation, we are entitled to a modicum of optimism. We may expect the theory to hold at least in those areas in which it has already been shown to hold, while the likelihood of its success in other areas can merely be estimated by considering the comprehensiveness and quality of the theory and the methods derived from it.

At this point the thoughtful reader might hesitate, worried by the following argument: Since CO clusters need not be conscious they may contain repressed and hence completely unconscious beliefs that, on the one hand, may exert their orientative impact on intent formation and output behavior but, on the other hand, might elude the psychologist who has to take them into account in order to predict behavior successfully. The argument sounds cogent, but whether it is sound and pertinent to our method of information gathering can only be decided after a further qualification is made. It must first be stated univocally whether a repressed belief is assumed to be unconscious under all situational conditions and in every context, or only if activated in particular situations or in conjunction with certain other beliefs. As is well known, psychoanalytic theory distinguishes between preconscious and unconscious entities. The former can be lifted to the level of consciousness, even if they never are, whereas the latter—owing to repression—are barred from entering consciousness unless symbolically disguised or otherwise distorted. Thus, only elimination or considerable relaxation of the repressing process would make it possible for a person to become aware of his unconscious beliefs, to recognize them as his own and to express them in their original form as he is free to do with preconscious contents.

This extreme position of psychoanalytic theory is amazingly inconsistent with techniques and results of psychoanalytic practice, which are more in line with the less radical idea of restricting the impact of repressions to particular external situations and internal constellations. Even before Freud developed methods specific to the psychoanalytic treatment he succeeded in making repressed content conscious by means of hypnotic induction. Later he used for the same purpose and with even greater success the method of free associations and thus became acquainted with repressed content long before developing the techniques of symbol interpretation and management of transference for combating repression. In other words, accepting the extreme position we would be forced to conclude that the method of free associations cannot induce a patient to produce repressed content. Thus Freud could not have gotten any evidence of unconscious contents and, in the first place, would not even have known that they exist.

Left with the more restricted position, we are completely at ease because it does not constitute a challenge to CO techniques. If previously repressed beliefs remain unconscious only in particular situations or in conjunction with certain other beliefs, then the CO questionnaires are preferable to the method of free associations, especially when the latter is applied in the course of psychoanalytic treatment. However free free associations may be, the associated beliefs are more meaning-related to each other than are the beliefs mixed together randomly in our CO questionnaires. Therefore evocation of a belief conjunction that activates repression is more likely in the course of free associations than it is in response to a CO questionnaire. Moreover, however little a patient may know about the intentions of his therapist, his unconscious expectations and the emotion-laden psychoanalytic situation are more repression-activating than the circumstances under which a CO questionnaire is administered. Indeed, beliefs of a particular CO cluster may not only be preconscious but fully unconscious in the psychoanalytic sense. Yet when they are separated from each other by other relatively irrelevant beliefs and presented in a neutral manner, in a context that does not suggest a general or specific type of behavior, the probability of activating repression appears to be low. Obviously our regrettable inability to observe the CO cluster directly and the consequent necessity of presenting beliefs out of their CO context also have their merits.

Though the risk is small that a subject will fail to check a particular belief because of repression, it does exist, and might not only frustrate behavior prediction but even interfere with our attempt to modify a particular behavior. Therefore we welcome the attempt of educational and therapeutic methods, psychoanalytic and others, to make unconscious content conscious and thus render it accessible to rational reevaluation. But we are likewise convinced that the necessary search for repressed beliefs would be greatly facilitated by using the CO theory as a guide.

The answer to a less demanding query has already been indicated, we hope, by the presentation of our experimental research. The reader interested in the CO theory may question the practicality of applying in his or her own research this theory and its techniques, which are of very recent origin and do not offer the comfort of prefabricated questionnaires. Our answer to this is twofold: A theory whose experimental application has yielded many successful studies and, for that matter, not a single one that failed, can be considered well beyond the pioneering stage. As for the lack of questionnaires that can be automatically applied to the analysis, prediction, and modification of human behavior, this is not a transient shortcoming but rather the price to be paid for remaining faithful to the intricacies of individual differences and the complexities of human nature. Certainly many meanings, beliefs, and perhaps even CO clusters are shared by the members of culturally homogeneous groups, and thus could be tapped by a ready-made questionnaire. Yet more meaning values and beliefs pertinent to guiding behavior vary from individual to individual, for people tend to change even commonly shared meanings and beliefs in the course of their personal growth, with or without reference to the changes resulting from the cultural development of the whole community. Therefore, as long as individuals and groups preserve their unique ability to develop intellectually and their productive inclination to create ever new problems, ready-made questionnaires will remain only narrowly valid, and they will be completely useless for the psychological effort to understand and predict the behavior of individuals and groups. What is needed are instruments with wide margins of adaptability to different problem areas and to the differing characteristics of the persons being studied, or, should even these wide margins prove too narrow, a method for developing a particular instrument whenever needed. We have outlined the method of adapting already existing CO questionnaires to the requirements of individual meanings and to different subject matters as well as of developing completely new questionnaires. Beyond some understanding of the meaning system, the method does not require special skills. What it does require is the readiness to perform pretests and the openmindedness to learn from their results. We have reasons for expecting that future studies in generation and perception of meaning as well as in acquisition and production of beliefs will help to refine these methods, but they will certainly not produce a standard questionnaire that can be administered without first pretesting whether the prospective subjects construe the situation in terms of the same aspects of meaning and understand the questions in the same sense in which they are asked.

Notwithstanding our efforts, the questions left open outnumber the questions answered in this book. Little is known about the process of meaning generation and even less about the way in which the meaning attributed to an input gives rise to a pertinent CO cluster. Thus far we cannot specify the conditions under which a belief of this or that CO component is the first to be evoked and serves as core of the CO cluster. With regard to belief substitution our studies have not progressed beyond goal hierarchies and their contribution to this process. The study of interrelations between CO processes and thinking is still in its first exploratory stage. The same holds for our inquiry into the dynamics of production, acquisition, and adaptation of behavioral programs. More advanced but still uncompleted are studies about the relation of personality theories and the CO theory, the processes of clustering, conflict resolution, and others more. We are still far from knowing which adjustments are needed in order to apply the CO theory to different domains of behavior. Finally, we have not thus far dared to approach in a scientific manner the two questions closest to our hearts: In emphasizing the cognitive nature of man, does the theory of cognitive orientation contribute to making humans more humane? What problems must be raised and solved and what methods developed in order to come closer to achieving this goal?

Indeed, the list of unanswered questions could be continued. But the fact that the CO theory gave rise to these questions, provides an adequate framework for their systematic study, and may be helpful in answering some of them gives us the courage to characterize the present stage of our work by adopting a famous remark of Sir Winston Churchill: "It is not the end. It is not even the beginning of the end. But it is perhaps the end of the beginning."*

* Speech at the Mansion House, "Of the Battle of Egypt," November 10, 1942.

References

Abelson, R. P. Modes of resolution of belief dilemmas. *Journal of Conflict Resolution*, 1959, 3, 343–352.

Abelson, R. P., Aronson, E., McGuire, W. J., Newcomb, T. M., Rosenberg, M. J., & Tannenbaum, P. H. *Theories of cognitive consistency: a sourcebook*. Chicago: Rand McNally, 1968.

Abelson, R. P., & Carroll, J. D. Computer simulation of belief systems. *American Behavioral Scientist*, 1965, 8, 24–30.

Abelson, R. P., & Rosenberg, M. J. Symbolic psycho-logic: a model of attitudinal cognition. *Behavioral Science*, 1958, 3, 1–8.

Abramovici, S. Laws of combination in psychology: a review of literature. Unpublished manuscript, Department of Psychology, Tel Aviv University, 1972.

Abramovici, S. Why can't "Colorless green ideas sleep furiously"? A study on the laws of combination of meanings. Unpublished Master's thesis, Department of Psychology, Tel Aviv University, 1973.

Ach, N. *Über die Willenstätigkeit und das Denken*. Göttingen: Vandenhöck u. Ruprecht, 1905.

Ach, N. *Analyse des Willens*. Berlin & Vienna: J. Springer, 1935.

Achenbach, T., & Zigler, E. Cue-learning and problem-learning strategies in normal and retarded children. *Child Development*, 1968, 39, 827–848.

Ackoff, R. L. Systems, organizations, and interdisciplinary research. *General Systems Yearbook*, 1960, Society for General Systems Research, 1–8.

Ackoff, R. L., & Emery, F. E. *On purposeful systems*. London: Tavistock Publications, 1972.

Adams, J. A. Response feedback and learning. *Psychological Bulletin*, 1968, 70, 486–504.

Adorno, T., Frenkel-Brunswik, E., Levinson, D., & Sanford, R. N. *The authoritarian personality*. New York: Harper, 1950.

Aiken, L. R., Jr., & Dreger, R. M. The effect of attitudes on performance in mathematics. *Journal of Educational Psychology*, 1961, 52, 19–24.

Ajzen, I., & Fishbein, M. The prediction of behavioral intentions in a choice situation. *Journal of Experimental Social Psychology*, 1969, 5, 400–416.

Ajzen, I., & Fishbein, M. The prediction of behavior from attitudinal and normative variables. *Journal of Experimental Social Psychology*, 1970, *6*, 466–487.

Ajzen, I., & Fishbein, M. Attitudes and normative beliefs as factors influencing behavioral intentions. *Journal of Personality and Social Psychology*, 1972, *21*, 1–9.

Ajzen, I., & Fishbein, M. Attitudinal and normative variables as predictors of specific behaviors. *Journal of Personality and Social Psychology*, 1973, *27*, 41–57.

Allport, G. W. *Personality: a psychological interpretation*. New York: Holt, 1937.

Allport, G. W. Scientific models and human morals. *Psychological Review*, 1947, *54*, 182–192.

Allport, G. W. The historical background of modern social psychology. In G. Lindzey (Ed.), *Handbook of social psychology*. Vol. 1. Reading, Mass.: Addison Wesley, 1954.

Allport, G. W. *Pattern and growth in personality*. New York: Holt, Rinehart & Winston, 1961.

Allport, G. W., & Kramer, B. M. Some roots of prejudice. *Journal of Psychology*, 1946, *22*, 9–39.

Alper, T. G. Achievement motivation in college women: a now-you-see-it-now-you don't phenomenon. *American Psychologist*, 1974, *29*, 194–203.

Alschuler, A. S., Tabor, D., & McIntyre, J. *Teaching achievement motivation: theory and practice in psychological education*. Middletown, Conn.: Education Ventures Inc.; and Cambridge, Mass.: Behavioral Science Center of the Sterling Institute, 1970.

Anderson, L. R., & Fishbein, M. Prediction of attitude from the number, strength, and evaluative aspect of beliefs about the attitude object: a comparison of summation and congruity theories. *Journal of Personality and Social Psychology*, 1965, *2*, 437–443.

Angyal, A. *Foundations for a science of personality*. New York: The Commonwealth Fund, 1941.

Annett, J. *Feedback and human behaviour*. Harmondsworth, England: Penguin Books, 1969.

Anokhin, P. K. The role of the orienting-exploratory reaction in the formation of the conditioned reflex. In L. G. Voronin, A. N. Leontiev, A. R. Luria, E. N. Sokolov & O. S. Vinogradova (Eds.), *Orienting reflex and exploratory behavior*. Moscow: Publishing House of the Academy of Pedagogical Sciences of RSFSR, 1958.

Appelbaum, M. H. Special guidance program for gifted underachievers of the tenth grade. In J. French (Ed.), *Educating the gifted*. New York: Holt, Rinehart & Winston, 1964.

Arbib, M. A. *The metaphorical brain*. New York: Wiley, 1972.

Argyle, M., & Robinson, T. Two origins of achievement motivation. *British Journal of Social and Clinical Psychology*, 1962, *1*, 107–120.

Armstrong, D. M. *A materialistic theory of mind*. London: Routledge and Kegan Paul, 1968.

Arnold, M. B. *Emotion and personality*. New York: Columbia University Press, 1960.

Asch, S. E. *Social psychology*. New York: Prentice-Hall, 1952.

Ashby, W. R. *Introduction to cybernetics*. New York: Wiley, 1956.

Athanasiou, R. Job attitudes and occupational performance: a review of some important literature. In J. P. Robinson, R. Athanasiou, & K. B. Head (Ed.), *Measures of occupational attitudes and occupational characteristics*. Ann Arbor: Institute for Social Research, University of Michigan, 1969.

Atkinson, J. W. Motivational determinants of risk-taking behavior. *Psychological Review*, 1957, *64*, 359–372.

Atkinson, J. W. *An introduction to motivation*. Princeton, N.J.: Van Nostrand, 1964.

Atkinson, J. W., & Birch, D. *The dynamics of action*. New York: Wiley, 1970.

Atkinson, J. W., & Feather, N. T. (Eds.), *A theory of achievement motivation*. New York: Wiley, 1966.

Atkinson, J. W., & Litwin, G. H. Achievement motive and test anxiety conceived as motive to approach success and motive to avoid failure. *Journal of Abnormal and Social Psychology*, 1960, *60*, 52–63.

Attneave, F. *Applications of information theory to psychology*. New York: Holt, 1959.

Ax, A. F. The physiological differentiation between fear and anger in humans. *Psychosomatic Medicine*, 1953, *15*, 433-442.

Bandler, R. J., Mandaros, G. R., & Bem, D. J. Self-observation as a source of pain perception. *Journal of Personality and Social Psychology*, 1971, *17*, 154–157.

Bandura, A. *Principles of behavior modification*. New York: Holt, Rinehart & Winston, 1969.

Banta, J. J. Tests for the evaluation of early childhood education: The Cincinnati Autonomy Test (CATB). In J. Hellmuth (Ed.), *Cognitive studies*. Vol. 1. New York: Brunner/Mazel, 1970.

Banuazizi, A., & Movahedi, S. Interpersonal dynamics in a simulated prison: a methodological analysis. *American Psychologist*, 1975, *30*, 152–160.

Barber, T. X. Experimental analyses of hypnotic behavior: a review of recent empirical findings. *Journal of Abnormal Psychology*, 1965, *70*, 132–154.

Bar-Gal, D., Kreitler, H., & Kreitler, S. The relation between attitudes toward cheating and actual cheating. Unpublished manuscript, Tel Aviv University, 1966.

Bar-Hillel, Y. An examination of information theory. *Philosophical Science*, 1955, *22*, 86–105.

Bartlett, F. C. *Remembering*. Cambridge, England: Cambridge University Press, 1932.

Baumeister, A. A. Analysis of errors in the discrimination learning of normal and retarded children. *Psychonomic Science*, 1966, *6*, 515–516.

Bem, D. J. Self-perception: an alternative interpretation of cognitive dissonance phenomena. *Psychological Review*, 1967, *74*, 183–200.

Bem, D. J. Self-perception theory. In L. Berkowitz (Ed.), *Advances in experimental social psychology*. Vol. 6. New York: Academic Press, 1972.

Bending, A. W. Manifested anxiety and projective and objective measures of need achievement. *Journal of Consulting Psychology*, 1957, *21*, 354.

Bending, A. W. Predictive and postdictive validity of need achievement measures. *Journal of Educational Research*, 1958, *52*, 119–120.

Berg, K. Ethnic attitudes and agreement with a Negro person. *Journal of Personality and Social Psychology*, 1966, *4*, 215–220.

Berger, E. The relation between expressed acceptance of self and expressed acceptance of others. *Journal of Abnormal and Social Psychology*, 1952, *47*, 778–782.

Berger, S. M. Conditioning through vicarious instigation. *Psychological Review*, 1962, *69*, 450–466.

Berkowitz, L. Social norms, feelings, and other factors affecting helping and altruism. In L. Berkowitz (Ed.), *Advances in experimental social psychology.* Vol. 6. New York: Academic Press, 1972.

Berlyne, D. E. Conflict and information theory variables as determinants of human perceptual curiosity. *Journal of Experimental Psychology,* 1957, *53,* 395–404.

Berlyne, D. E. The influence of the albedo and complexity stimuli on visual fixation in the human infant. *British Journal of Psychology,* 1958, *49,* 315–318. (a)

Berlyne, D. E. The influence of complexity and novelty in visual figures on orienting responses. *Journal of Experimental Psychology,* 1958, *55,* 289–296. (b)

Berlyne, D. E. *Conflict, arousal, and curiosity.* New York: McGraw-Hill, 1960.

Berlyne, D. E. *Structure and direction in thinking.* New York: Wiley, 1965.

Bernberg, R. E. Socio-psychological factors in industrial morale.: I. The prediction of specific indicators. *Journal of Social Psychology,* 1952, *36,* 73–82.

Bertalanffy, L. v. *Problems of life: an evaluation of modern biological thought.* New York: Wiley, 1952.

Bever, T. G., & Rosenbaum, P. S. Some lexical structures and their empirical validity. In R. A. Jacobs & P. S. Rosenbaum (Eds.), *Readings in English transformational grammar.* Waltham, Mass.: Ginn, 1970.

Binet, A. *L'etude experimentale de l'intelligence.* Paris: Schleicher, 1903.

Bingham, W. E. A study of the relations which the galvanic skin response and sensory reference bear to judgments of the meaningfulness, significance, and importance of 72 words. *Journal of Psychology,* 1943, *16,* 21–34.

Biriulov, D. A. On the nature of the orienting reaction. In L. G. Voronin, A. N. Leontiev, A. R. Luria, E. N. Sokolov, & O. S. Vinogradova (Eds.), *Orienting reflex and exploratory behavior.* Moscow: Publishing House of the Academy of Pedagogical Sciences of RSFSR, 1958.

Birney, R. C., Burdick, H., & Teevan, R. C. *Fear of failure.* New York: Van Nostrand-Reinhold, 1969.

Blitz, B., & Dinnerstein, A. J. Effects of different types of instruction on pain parameters. *Journal of Abnormal Psychology,* 1968, *73,* 276–280.

Blitz, B., & Dinnerstein, A. J. Role of attentional focus in pain perception: manipulation of response to noxious stimulation by instructions. *Journal of Abnormal Psychology,* 1971, *77,* 42–45.

Bogardus, E. S. Measuring social distance. *Journal of Applied Sociology,* 1925, *9,* 299–308.

Boiko, E. I. On the double role of positioning reflexes in complex system reactions. In L. G. Voronin, A. N. Leontiev, A. R. Luria, E. N. Sokolov, & O. S. Vinogradova (Eds.), *Orienting reflex and exploratory behavior.* Moscow: Publishing House of the Academy of Pedagogical Sciences of RSFSR, 1958.

Bollinger, D. The atomization of meaning. *Language,* 1965, *41,* 553–573.

Borgatta, E. F. An analysis of three levels of response: an approach to some relationships among dimensions of personality. *Sociometry Monographs,* 1952, No. 26.

Bourne, L. E., Jr. *Human conceptual behavior.* Boston: Allyn & Bacon, 1966.

Bower, G. A multicomponent theory of memory trace. In K. W. Spence & J. T. Spence (Eds.), *The psychology of learning and motivation.* New York: Academic Press, 1967. (a)

Bower, G. H. A descriptive theory of memory. In D. P. Kimble (Ed.), *The organization of recall.* New York: The New York Academy of Science, 1967. (b)

Brackbill, Y., Kappy, M. S., & Starr, R. H. Magnitude of reward and probability learning. *Journal of Experimental Psychology,* 1962, *63,* 32–35.

Brannon, R., Cyphers, G., Hesse, S., Hesselbart, S., Keane, R., Schuman, H., Viccaro, T., & Wright, D. Attitude and action: a field experiment joined to a general population survey. *American Sociological Review,* 1973, *38,* 625–636.

Bray, D. W. The prediction of behavior from two attitude scales. *Journal of Abnormal and Social Psychology,* 1950, *45,* 64–84.

Brayfield, A. H., & Crockett, W. H. Employee attitudes and employee performance. *Psychological Bulletin,* 1955, *52,* 396–424.

Brayfield, A. H., & Rothe, H. F. An index of job satisfaction. *Journal of Applied Psychology,* 1951, *35,* 307–311.

Brehm, J. W. *A theory of psychological reactance.* New York: Academic Press, 1966.

Brehm, J. W., & Cohen, A. R. *Explorations in cognitive dissonance.* New York: Wiley, 1962.

Bridgeman, P. W. *The logic of modern physics.* New York: Macmillan, 1927.

Broadbent, D. E. *Perception and communication.* New York: Pergamon, 1958.

Broadbent, D. E. *Decision and stress.* New York: Academic Press. 1971.

Brody, G. F. Relationship between maternal attitudes and behavior. *Journal of Personality and Social Psychology,* 1965, *2,* 317–323.

Brody, N. *n* achievement, test anxiety and subjective probability of success in risk taking behavior. *Journal of Abnormal and Social Psychology,* 1963, *66,* 413–418.

Brown, D. R. Stimulus similarity and the anchoring of subjective scales. *American Journal of Psychology,* 1953, *66,* 199–214.

Brown, R. *Words and things.* Glencoe, Ill.: Free Press, 1958.

Brown, W. F., & Holzman, W. II. *Survey of study habits and attitudes.* New York: The Psychological Corporation, 1967.

Bruner, J. S., Goodnow, J. J., & Austin, G. A. *A study of thinking.* New York: Wiley, 1956.

Bruner, J. S. The growth of mind. *American Psychologist,* 1965, *20,* 1007–1017.

Burgess, E. Personality factors in over and underachievers in engineering. *Journal of Educational Psychology,* 1956, *47,* 89–99.

Burghardt, G. M. Instinct and innate behavior: toward an ethological psychology. In J. A. Nevin & G. S. Reynolds (Eds.), *The study of behavior.* Glenview, Ill.: Scott, Foresman, 1973.

Buytendijk, F. J. J. *Pain: its modes and functions.* Chicago, Ill.: University of Chicago Press, 1961.

Bykov, V. D. On the dynamics of the orienting-exploratory reaction during the formation of positive and inhibitory conditioned reflexes and their alterations. In L. G. Voronin, A. N. Leontiev, A. R. Luria, E. N. Sokolov, & O. S. Vinogradova (Eds.), *Orienting reflex and exploratory behavior.* Moscow: Publishing House of the Academy of Pedagogical Sciences of RSFSR, 1958.

Byrne, D. Repression-sensitization as a dimension of personality. In B. A. Maher (Ed.), *Progress in experimental personality research.* Vol. 1. New York: Academic Press, 1964.

Campbell, D. T. The indirect assessment of social attitudes. *Psychological Bulletin,* 1950, *47,* 15–38.

Campbell, D. T. Social attitudes and other acquired behavioral dispositions. In S. Koch (Ed.), *Psychology: a study of a science.* Vol. 6. New York: McGraw-Hill, 1963.

Cannon, W. B. *The wisdom of the body.* New York: W. W. Norton, 1932.

Cannon, W. B. The James-Lange theory of emotions; a critical examination and an alternative theory. *American Journal of Psychology,* 1927, *39,* 106–124.

Carey, G. L. Sex differences in problem-solving performance as a function of attitude discrepancies. *Journal of Abnormal and Social Psychology,* 1958, *56,* 256–260.

Carlson, A. R. The relationships between a behavioral intention, attitude toward the behavior and normative beliefs about behavior. Unpublished doctoral dissertation, University of Illinois, 1968.

Caron, A. J. Curiosity, achievement, and avoidant motivation as determinants of epistemic behavior. *Journal of Abnormal and Social Psychology,* 1963, *67,* 535–549.

Carr, L., & Roberts, S. O. Correlates of civil-rights participation. *Journal of Social Psychology,* 1965, *67,* 259–267.

Castellan, J. On the partitioning of contingency tables. *Psychological Bulletin,* 1965, *64,* 330–338.

Cattell, R. B., Heist, A. B., Heist, P. A., & Stewart, R. G. The objective measurement of dynamic traits. *Educational and Psychological Measurement,* 1950, *10,* 224–248.

Cattell, R. B., Maxwell, E. F., Light, B. H., & Unger, M. P. The objective measurement of attitudes. *British Journal of Psychology,* 1949/50, *40,* 81–90.

Chapman, A. W. Attitude toward legal agencies of authority for juveniles: a comparative study of 133 delinquent and 133 nondelinquent boys in Dayton, Ohio. *Dissertation Abstracts,* 1960, *20,* No. 7.

Cherry, C. *On human communication.* New York: Wiley, 1957.

Christie, R., & Geis, F. L. *Studies in Machiavellism.* New York: Academic Press, 1970.

Clarke, H. M. Conscious attitudes. *American Journal of Psychology,* 1911, *22,* 214–249.

Clum, G. A., & Nathan, J. L. Attitudes predictive of Marine combat effectiveness. *Journal of Social Psychology,* 1971, *83,* 55–62.

Cohen, A. R. Attitudinal consequences of induced discrepancies between cognitions and behavior. *Public Opinion Quarterly,* 1960, *24,* 297–318.

Cohen, A. R. *Attitude change and social influence.* New York: Basic Books, 1964.

Cohen, M., & Nagel, E. *An introduction to logic and scientific method.* New York: Harcourt, 1934.

Colby, K. M. A programmable theory of cognition and affect in individual personal belief systems. In R. P. Abelson et al., *Theories of cognitive consistency: a sourcebook.* Chicago, Ill.: Rand McNally, 1968.

Colby, K. M., & Gilbert, J. P. Programming a computer model of neurosis. *Journal of Mathematical Psychology,* 1964, *1,* 405–417.

Cole, D., Jacobs, S., Zubok, B., Fagot, B., & Hunter, I. The relation of achievement imagery scores to academic performance. *Journal of Abnormal and Social Psychology,* 1962, *65,* 208–211.

Collins, A. M., & Quillian, M. R. How to make a language user. In E. Tulving & W. Donaldson (Eds.), *Organization of memory.* New York: Academic Press, 1972. (a).

Collins, A. M., & Quillian, M. R. Experiments on semantic memory and language comprehension. In L. W. Gregg (Ed.), *Cognition in learning and memory.* New York: Wiley, 1972. (b)

Cook, S. W., & Selltiz, C. A. A multiple-indicator approach to attitude measurement. *Psychological Bulletin,* 1964, *62,* 36–55.

Cook, W. W., Leeds, C. H., & Callis, R. *Minnesota teacher attitude inventory: manual.* New York: Psychological Corporation, 1951.

Cooper, J. B., & McGaugh, J. L. Attitude and related concepts. In M. Jahoda & N. Warren (Eds.), *Attitudes: selected readings*. Harmondsworth, England: Penguin, 1966.

Corcoran, D. W. J. *Pattern recognition*. Harmondsworth, England: Penguin, 1971.

Crandall, V., Good, S., & Crandall, V. J. Reinforcement effects of adult reactions and nonreactions on children's achievement expectations: a replication study. *Child Development*, 1964, 35, 485–497.

Crandall, V. C., Katkovsky, W., & Crandall, V. J. Children's beliefs in their own control of reinforcements in intellectual-academic achievement situations. *Child Development*, 1965, 36, 90–109.

Crandall, V., Katkovsky, W., & Preston, A. Motivational and ability determinants of young children's intellectual achievement behaviors. *Child Development*, 1962, 33, 643–661.

Crawford, P. L. Reliability and validity of the Siebrecht attitude scale. *Educational and Psychological Measurement*, 1968, 28, 609–613.

Crockett, W. H. Cognitive complexity and impression formation. In B. A. Maher (Ed.), *Progress in experimental personality research*. Vol. 2. New York: Academic Press, 1965.

Darroch, R. K., & Steiner, I. D. Role playing: an alternative to laboratory research? *Journal of Personality Research*, 1970, 38, 302–311.

Day, H. Role of specific curiosity in school achievement. *Journal of Educational Psychology*, 1968, 59, 37–43.

Dean, L. R. Interaction reported and observed: the case of one local union. *Human Organization*, 1958, 17, 36–44.

DeCharms, R., & Davé, P. N. Hope of success, fear of failure, subjective probability, and risk-taking behavior. *Journal of Personality and Social Psychology*, 1965, 1, 558–568.

DeCharms, R., Morrison, H. W., Reitman, W., & McClelland, D. C. Behavioral correlates of directly and indirectly measured achievement motivation. In D. C. McClelland (Ed.), *Studies in motivation*. New York: Appleton-Century-Crofts, 1955.

Deese, J. On the structure of associative meaning. *Psychological Review*. 1962, 69, 161–175.

Deese, J. *The structure of associations in language and thought*. Baltimore: Johns Hopkins Press, 1965.

DeFleur, M. L., & Westie, F. R. Verbal attitudes and overt acts. *American Sociological Review*, 1958, 23, 667–673.

Dembo, T. A theoretical and experimental inquiry into concrete values and value systems. In S. Wapner & B. Kaplan (Eds.), *Perspectives in psychological theory*. New York: New International Universities Press, 1960.

De Nike, L. D., & Tiber, N. Neurotic behavior. In P. London & D. Rosenhan (Eds.), *Foundations of abnormal psychology*. New York: Holt, Rinehart & Winston, 1968.

Desoille, R. *Théorie et pratique du rêve éveillé dirigée*. Génève, Switzerland: Editions du Mont-Blanc SA (Collection Action et Pensée), 1961.

Deutsch, J. A., & Deutsch, D. Attention: some theoretical considerations. *Psychological Review*, 1963, 70, 80–90.

Deutscher, I. Bibliography on the relation between sentiments and acts. Syracuse, N.Y.: Syracuse University Youth Development Center, 1966.

Dillehay, R. C., Bruvold, W. H., & Siegel, J. P. Attitude, object label, and stimulus factors in response to an attitude object. *Journal of Personality and Social Psychology*, 1969, *11*, 220–223.

Dodd, C., & Lewis, M. The magnitude of the orienting response in children as a function of changes in color and contour. *Journal of Experimental Child Psychology*, 1969, *8*, 296–305.

Dolin, A. O., Zborovskaya, I. I., & Zamakhovev, S. M. On the role of the orienting-exploratory reflex in conditioned reflex activity. In L. G. Voronin, A. N. Leontiev, A. R. Luria, E. N. Sokolov & O. S. Vinogradova (Eds.), *Orienting reflex and exploratory behavior*. Moscow: Publishing House of the Academy of Pedagogical Sciences of RSFSR, 1958.

Dollard, J., & Miller, N. E. *Personality and psychotherapy*. New York: McGraw-Hill, 1950.

Douglas R. J., & Pribram, K. H. Learning and limbic lesions. *Neuropsychology*, 1966, *4*, 197–220.

Düker, H. Über ein Verfahren zur Untersuchung der psychischen Leistungsfähigkeit. *Psychologische Forschung*, 1949, *23*, 10–24.

Dudycha, G. J. A scale for measuring attitude toward dependability. *Journal of Social Psychology*, 1937, *8*, 3–16.

Dudycha, G. J. A scale for measuring attitudes toward dependability. *Journal of Social Psychology*, 1941, *13*, 59–69.

Duffy, E. *Activation and behavior*. New York: Wiley, 1962.

Dulany, D. E. Awareness, rules, and propositional control: A confrontation with S-R behavior theory. In T. R. Dixon & D. L. Horton (Eds.), *Verbal behavior and general behavior theory*. Englewood Cliffs, N.J.: Prentice-Hall, 1968.

Duncan, D. B. Multiple range and multiple F tests. *Biometrics*, 1955, *11*, 1–42.

Dunlap, R. L. Changes in children's preferences for goal objects as a function of differences in expected social reinforcement. Unpublished doctoral dissertation, Ohio State University, 1953.

Dykman, R. A. Toward a theory of classical conditioning: cognitive, emotional, and motor components of the conditioned reflex. In B. A. Maher (Ed.), *Progress in experimental personality research*. Vol. 2. New York: Academic Press, 1965.

Eccles, J. C. Conscious experience and memory. In J. C. Eccles (Ed.), *Brain and conscious experience*. Berlin: Springer, 1966.

Eiser, J. R., & Stroebe, W. *Categorization and social judgement*. London & New York: Academic Press, 1972.

Eldow, D. W., & Kiesler, C. A. Ease of denial and defensive projection. *Journal of Experimental Social Psychology*, 1966, *2*, 56–59.

Elms, A. (Ed.), *Role playing, reward and attitude change: an enduring problem in psychology*. New York: Van Nostrand-Reinhold, 1969.

Epstein, S. The self-concept revisited or a theory of a theory. *American Psychologist*, 1973, *28*, 404–416.

Eriksen, C. W. (Ed.), *Behavior and awareness*. Durham, N.C.: Duke University Press, 1962.

Estes, W. K. Probability learning. In A. W. Melton (Ed.), *Categories of human learning*. New York: Academic Press, 1964.

Evarts, E. V. Pyramidal tract activity associated with a conditioned hand movement in the monkey. *Journal of Neurophysiology*, 1966, *29*, 1011–1027.

Evarts, E. V. Relation of pyramidal tract activity to force exerted during voluntary movement. *Journal of Neurophysiology*, 1968, *31*, 14–27.

Eysenck, H. J. The effects of psychotherapy. In H. J. Eysenck (Ed.), *Handbook of abnormal psychology*. New York: Basic Books, 1961.

Feather, N. T. The relationship of persistence at a task to expectation of success and achievement-related motives. *Journal of Abnormal and Social Psychology*, 1961, *63*, 552–561.

Feather, N. T. Effects of prior success and failure on expectations of success and subsequent performance. *Journal of Personality and Social Psychology*, 1966, *3*, 287–298.

Fendrich, J. M. A study of the association among verbal attitudes, commitment and overt behavior in different experimental situations. *Social Forces*, 1967, *45*, 347–355.

Fenz, W. D., & Epstein, S. Gradients of physiological arousal in parachutists. *Psychosomatic Medicine*, 1967, *29*, 33–51.

Festinger, L. Behavioral support for opinion change. *Public Opinion Quarterly*, 1964, *28*, 404–417.

Festinger, L., et al. *Conflict, decision, and dissonance*. Stanford, California: Stanford University Press, 1964.

Fillenbaum, S., & Rapaport, A. *Structure in the subjective lexicon*. New York: Academic Press, 1971.

Fishbein, M. An investigation of the relationships between beliefs about an object and the attitude towards that object. Technical Report No. 6. Los Angeles, Calif.: University of California, 1961.

Fishbein, M. Attitude and the prediction of behavior. In M. Fishbein (Ed.), *Readings in attitude theory and measurement*. New York: Wiley, 1967. (a)

Fishbein, M. A consideration of beliefs, and their role in attitude measurement. In M. Fishbein (Ed.), *Readings in attitude theory and measurement*. New York: Wiley, 1967. (b)

Fitts, P. M. Factors in complex skill training. In R. Glaser (Ed.), *Training research and education*. New York: Wiley, 1965 (originally published by University of Pittsburgh Press, 1962).

Flavell, J. H. *The developmental psychology of Jean Piaget*. Princeton, N.J.: Van Nostrand, 1963.

Flavell, J. H., & Draguns, J. A microgenetic approach to perception and thought. *Psychological Bulletin*, 1957, *54*, 197–217.

Fothergill, J. E. Do attitudes change before behavior? *Proceedings of ESOMAR (European Society for Opinion and Marketing Research) Congress*, 1968.

Fowler, H. *Curiosity and exploratory behavior*. New York: Macmillan, 1965.

Fowler, H. Satiation and curiosity. In K. W. Spence & J. T. Spence (Eds.), *The psychology of learning and motivation*. Vol. 1. New York: Academic Press, 1967.

Frankena, W. K. "Cognitive" and "noncognitive." In P. Henle (Ed.), *Language, thought and culture*. Ann Arbor, Mich.: University of Michigan Press, 1965.

Frankl, V. E. *Psychotherapy and existentialism: selected papers on logotherapy*. Harmondsworth, England: Penguin Books, 1973.

Freeman, L. C., & Aataöv, T. Invalidity of indirect and direct measures of attitude toward cheating. *Journal of Personality*, 1960, *28*, 443–447.

Frenkel, E. A comparative study of achieving and underachieving high school boys of high intellectual ability. *Journal of Educational Research*, 1960, *53*, 172–180.

Freud, A. *The ego and the id*. London: Institute for Psycho-Analysis and Hogarth Press, 1927.

Freud, S. *New introductory lectures on psychoanalysis*. New York: W. W. Norton, 1933.

Freud, S. The unconscious. (1915). *Collected Papers*, Vol. IV. London: Hogarth Press & The Institute of Psycho-Analysis, 1934.

Freud, S. *The ego and the mechanisms of defense*. New York: International Universities Press, 1946.

Freud, S. Inhibitions, symptoms and anxiety. In *Standard edition of the writings of* . . . , Vol. 20. London: Hogarth Press, 1959.

Freud, S. Formulation on the two principles of mental functioning. (1911). In J. Strachey (Ed.), *The standard edition of the complete psychological works of* . . . , Vol. 12. London: Hogarth Press, 1962.

Frick, F. C. Information theory. In S. Koch (Ed.), *Psychology: a study of a science*. Vol. 2. New York: McGraw-Hill, 1959.

Frieders, J. S., Warner, L. G., & Albrecht, S. L. The impact of social constraints on the relationship between attitudes and behavior. *Social Forces*, 1970, *50*, 102–112.

Friesen, E. P. The incomplete sentences technique as a measure of employee attitudes. *Personnel Psychology*, 1952, *5*, 329–345.

Fromm, E. *The forgotten language*. New York: Grove Press, 1951.

Fuller, E. M. The use of teacher-pupil attitudes, self-rating and general measures of general ability in the pre-service selection of nursery–school–kindergarten–primary teachers. *Journal of Educational Research*, 1951, *44*, 675–686.

Furth, H. G. *Piaget and knowledge*. Englewood Cliffs, N.J.: Prentice-Hall, 1966.

Gadel, M. S., & Kriedt, P. H. Relationship of aptitude, interest, performance and job satisfaction of IBM operators. *Personnel Psychology*, 1952, *5*, 207–212.

Gagné, R. *The conditions of learning*. 2nd ed. New York: Holt, Rinehart & Winston, 1970.

Gardner, R. W. The development of cognitive structures. In C. Scheerer (Ed.), *Cognition: theory, research, promise*. New York: Harper, 1964.

Gardner, R. W., Holzman, P. S., Klein, G. S., Linton. H., & Spence, D. P. Cognitive control. *Psychological Issues*, 1959, *1*, No. 4.

Garner, W. R. *Uncertainty and structure as psychological concepts*. New York: Wiley, 1962.

Gastaut, H. The role of the reticular formation in establishing conditioned reactions. In W. H. Jaspar (Ed.), *Reticular formation of the brain*. Boston: Little, Brown, 1957.

Gebhart, G. G., & Hoyt, D. P. Personality needs of under- and overachieving freshmen. *Journal of Applied Psychology*, 1958, *42*, 125–128.

Gelfand, S. The relationship of experimental pain tolerance to pain threshold. *Canadian Journal of Psychology*, 1964, *18*, 36–42.

Gibson, J. J. *The senses considered as perceptual systems*. Boston: Houghton Mifflin, 1966.

Glaze, J. A. The association value of nonsense syllables. *Journal of Genetic Psychology*, 1928, *35*, 255–267.

Goldstein, K., & Scheerer, M. Abstract and concrete behavior: an experimental study with special tests. *Psychological Monographs*, 1941, *53*, No. 2.

Goodwin, K. Changes in probability learning as a function of age, number of choices, and information procedure. Unpublished Master's thesis, West Virginia University, 1969.

Gorham, D. R., & Lasky, J. J. Do the attitudes depressed patients have towards chemotherapy affect their treatment response? *American Psychologist*, 1962, 17, 323.

Gorham, D. R., & Sherman, L. J. The relation of attitude toward medication to treatment outcomes in chemotherapy. *American Journal of Psychiatry*, 1961, 117, 830–832.

Graham, F. K., & Jackson, J. C. Arousal systems and infant heart rate responses. In H. W. Reese & L. P. Lipsitt (Eds.), *Advances in child development and behavior*. Vol. 5. New York: Academic Press, 1970.

Grant, D. A. Adding communication to the signalling property of the CS in classical conditioning. *Journal of General Psychology*, 1968, 79, 147–175.

Greenberg, J. H. *Language universals*. The Hague: Mouton, 1966.

Greenberg, M. S. Role playing: an alternative to deception? *Journal of Personality and Social Psychology*, 1967, 7, 152–157.

Grice, G. R. Do responses evoke responses? *American Psychologist*, 1965, 20, 282–294.

Griffiths, A. P. (Ed.) *Knowledge and belief*. London: Oxford University Press, 1967.

Gruen, G., & Zigler, E. Expectancy of success and the probability-learning of middle-class, lower-class, and retarded children. *Journal of Abnormal Psychology*, 1968, 73, 343–352.

Goulet, L. R., & Goodwin, K. S. Development and choice behavior in probabilistic and problem-solving tasks. In H. W. Reese & L. P. Lipsitt (Eds.), *Advances in child development and behavior*. Vol. 5. New York: Academic Press, 1970.

Gowan, J. M. The underachieving gifted child: a problem for everyone. *Journal of Exceptional Children*, 1955, 21, 247–249.

Hackett, T. P., & Weisman, A. D. Reactions to the imminence of death. In G. H. Grosser, H. Wechsler, & M. Greenblatt (Eds.), *The threat of impending disaster*. Cambridge, Mass.: M.I.T. Press, 1964.

Hamilton, V. Perceptual and personality dynamics in reactions to ambiguity. *British Journal of Psychology*, 1957, 48, 200–215.

Hammond, K. R. Probabilistic functioning and the clinical method. *Psychological Review*, 1955, 62, 255–262.

Hancock, J. G., & Teevan, R. C. Fear of failure and risk-taking behavior. *Journal of Personality*, 1964, 32, 200–209.

Hand, J. A method of weighing attitude scale items from subject responses. *Journal of Clinical Psychology*, 1953, 9, 37–39.

Harvey, O. J. (Ed.), *Motivation and social interaction: cognitive determinants*. New York: Ronald, 1963.

Head, H. *Studies in neurology*. Vol. 2. London: Hodder & Stoughton and Oxford University Press, 1920.

Hebb, D. O. Drives and the C.N.S. (Conceptual Nervous System). *Psychological Review*, 1955, 62, 243–254.

Hebb, D. O. The semi-autonomous process: its nature and nurture. *American Psychologist*, 1963, 18, 16–27.

Hebb, D. O. Concerning imagery. *Psychological Review*, 1968, 75, 466–477.

Heckhausen, H. *Hoffnung und Furcht in der Leistungsmotivation*. Meisenheim/Glan: Hain, 1963.

Heckhausen, H. *The anatomy of achievement motivation.* New York: Academic Press, 1967.

Heider, F. On social cognition. *American Psychologist,* 1967, 22, 25–31.

Held, R. Exposure history as a factor in maintaining stability of perception and coordination. *Journal of Nervous and Mental Diseases,* 1961, 132, 26–32.

Helson, H. Adaptation level theory. In S. Koch (Ed.), *Psychology: a study of a science.* Vol. 1. New York: McGraw-Hill, 1959.

Hintikka, J. *Models for modalities.* Dodrecht, Holland: Reidel, 1969.

Hochberg, J. E. In the mind's eye. In R. N. Haber (Ed.), *Contemporary theory and research in visual perception.* New York: Holt, Rinehart & Winston, 1968.

Hoffman, P. J. The paramorphic representation of clinical judgment. *Psychological Bulletin,* 1960, 57, 116–131.

Hofman, J. E. Teachers' attitudes and classroom behavior. Unpublished manuscript, Haifa University, 1973.

Holmes, D. S., & Tyler, J. D. Direct versus projective measurement of achievement motivation. *Journal of Consulting and Clinical Psychology,* 1968, 32, 712–717.

Holt, R. R. (Ed.), Motives and thought: psycho-analytic essays in honor of David Rapaport. *Psychological Issues,* Monogr. 18/19, 1967.

Horowitz, E. L. The development of attitude toward the Negro. *Archives of Psychology,* 1936, No. 194.

Horowitz, I. A., & Rothschild, B. H. Conformity as a function of deception and role playing. *Journal of Personality and Social Psychology,* 1970, 14, 224–226.

Hovland, C. I., Janis, I. L., & Kelley, H. H. *Communication and persuasion.* New Haven: Yale University Press, 1953.

Hull, C. L. The meaningfulness of 320 selected nonsense syllables. *American Journal of Psychology,* 1933, 45, 730–734.

Hulin, C. L. Job satisfaction and turnover in a female clerical population. *Journal of Applied Psychology,* 1966, 50, 280–285.

Humphrey, G. *Thinking.* New York: Wiley, 1963.

Hunt, D. E. Changes in goal-object preference as a function of expectancy for social reinforcement. *Journal of Abnormal and Social Psychology,* 1955, 50, 372–377.

Hunt, J. McV. Intrinsic motivation and psychological development. In H. M. Schroder & P. Suedfeld (Eds.), *Personality theory and information processing.* New York: Ronald, 1971.

Inhelder, B., & Piaget, J. *The growth of logical thinking.* New York: Basic Books, 1958.

Insko, C. A., & Schopler, J. Triadic consistency: a restatement of affective-cognitive-conative consistency. *Psychological Review,* 1967, 74, 361–376.

Isaacson, R. L. Relations between n achievement, test anxiety, and curricular choices. *Journal of Abnormal and Social Psychology,* 1964, 68, 447–452.

Izett, R. R. Authoritarianism and attitudes toward the Vietnam war as reflected in behavioral and self-report measures. *Journal of Personality and Social Psychology,* 1971, 17, 145–148.

Jacobson, E. Meaning and understanding of letters, words and sentences. *American Journal of Psychology,* 1911, 22, 553–577.

Jacobson, E. Electrophysiology of mental activities. *American Journal of Physiology,* 1931, 97, 200–209.

Jacobson, E. Electrophysiology of mental activities. *American Journal of Psychology,* 1932, 44, 677–694.

James, W. *Principles of behavior.* New York: Holt, 1890.

Jasper, H., Ricci, G. F., & Doane, B. Patterns of cortical neuronal discharge during conditioned responses in the monkey. In G. E. W. Wolstenholme & C. M. O'Conner (Eds.), *Neurological basis of behavior.* London: Churchill, 1958.

Jeffrey, W. E. The orienting reflex and attention in cognitive development. *Psychological Review,* 1968, 75, 323–334.

Johnson, L. C. State conditions and the OR. Paper presented at the meeting of the American Psychological Association, symposium "The orienting reflex," San Francisco, 1968.

Johnson, L. C., & Lubin, A. The orienting reflex during waking and sleeping. *Encephalography and Clinical Neurophysiology,* 1967, 22, 11–21.

Johnson, N. F. Sequential verbal behavior. In T. R. Dixon & D. L. Horton (Eds.), *Verbal behavior and general behavior theory.* Englewood Cliffs, N.J.: Prentice-Hall, 1968.

Jones, A. Information deprivation in humans. In B. A. Maher (Ed.), *Progress in experimental personality research.* Vol. 3. New York: Academic Press, 1966.

Jones, A., Bentler, P.M., & Petry, G. The reduction of uncertainty concerning future pain. *Journal of Abnormal Psychology,* 1966, 71, 87–94.

Jones, H. E., & Wechsler, D. Galvanometric technique in studies of association. *American Journal of Psychology,* 1928, 40, 607–612.

Jung, J. Experimental studies of factors affecting word associations. *Psychological Bulletin,* 1966, 66, 125–133.

Kagan, J., & Kogan, N. Individual variation in cognitive processes. In P. H. Mussen (Ed.), *Carmichael's manual of child psychology* (3rd ed.). Vol. 1. New York: Wiley, 1970.

Kagan, J., Sontag, L. W., Baker, C. T., & Nelson, V. T. Personality and IQ change. *Journal of Abnormal and Social Psychology,* 1958, 56, 261–266.

Kahaneman, E. Smoking habits and trends of changes. *Survey of the Institute for Applied Social Research and the Institute for Communication at the Hebrew University,* 1970.

Kanfer, F. H. Verbal conditioning: a review of its current status. In T. R. Dixon & D. L. Horton (Eds.), *Verbal behavior and general behavior theory.* Englewood Cliffs, N.J.: Prentice-Hall, 1968.

Kanfer, S. H., & Goldfoot, D. A. Self-control and tolerance of noxious stimulation. *Psychological Reports,* 1966, 18, 79–85.

Kaplan, E. An experimental study on inner speech as contrasted with external speech. Unpublished Master's thesis, Clark University, 1952.

Katz, I., & Benjamin, L. Effects of white authoritarianism in biracial work groups. *Journal of Abnormal and Social Psychology,* 1960, 60, 448–456.

Katz, J. J., & Fodor, J. A. The structure of a semantic theory. *Language,* 1963, 39, 170–210.

Katz, D., & Kahn, R. L. Some recent findings in human relations research in industry. In G. E. Swanson, T. M. Newcomb & E. L. Hartley (Eds.), *Readings in social psychology* (rev. ed.). New York: Holt, 1952.

Kelley, J. G., Ferson, J. E., & Holtzman, W. H. The measurement of attitudes toward the Negro in the South. *Journal of Social Psychology,* 1958, *48,* 305–317.

Kelly, G. A. *The psychology of personal constructs.* New York: Norton, 1955.

Kelman, H. C. Attitudes are alive and well and gainfully employed in the sphere of action. *American Psychologist,* 1974, *29,* 310–324.

Kendler, T. S., Kendler, H. H., & Wells, D. Reversal and nonreversal shifts in nursery school children. *Journal of Comparative and Physiological Psychology,* 1960, *53,* 83–88.

Kerlinger, F. N. Social attitudes and their criterial referents: a structural theory. *Psychological Review,* 1967, *74,* 110–122.

Khanna, J. L., Pratt, S., & Gardiner, G. Attitudes of psychiatric aides toward "criminally insane" patients. *Journal of Criminal Law, Criminology and Police Science,* 1962, *53,* 55–60.

Kimble, G. A. Attitudinal factors in eyelid conditioning. In G. A. Kimble (Ed.), *Foundations of conditioning and learning.* New York: Appleton-Century-Crofts, 1967.

Kimbrough, R. B., & Hines, V. A. *The Florida scale of civic beliefs.* Gainesville, Fla.: College of Education, University of Florida, 1963.

Kimbrough, W. W., & Cofer, C. N. Attitudes and stimuli as determiners of response. *Psychological Reports,* 1954, *4,* 61.

King, J. B. Curiosity in young children. *Dissertation Abstracts,* 1969, *29,* 9–13, 3468.

Kintsch, W. Memory and decision aspects of recognition learning. *Psychological Review,* 1967, *74,* 496–504.

Kintsch, W. Models for free recall and recognition. In D. A. Norman (Ed.), *Models of human memory.* New York: Academic Press, 1970.

Kintsch, W. Notes on the structure of semantic memory. In E. Tulving & W. Donaldson (Eds.), *Organization of memory.* New York: Academic Press, 1972.

Klein, G. S. *Perception, motives and personality.* New York: Knopf, 1970.

Klinger, E. Fantasy need achievement as a motivational construct. *Psychological Bulletin,* 1966, *66,* 291–308.

Klinger, E. *Structure and functions of fantasy.* New York: Wiley-Interscience, 1971.

Kluckhohn, C. Values and value-orientations in the theory of action: an exploration in definition and classification. In T. Parsons & E. A. Shils (Eds.), *Toward a general theory of action.* Cambridge, Mass.: Harvard University Press, 1951.

Köhler, W. *Gestalt psychology.* New York: Liveright, 1929.

Kogan, N., & Downey, J. F. Scaling norm conflicts in the area of prejudice and discrimination. *Journal of Abnormal and Social Psychology,* 1956, *53,* 292–295.

Kogan, N., & Wallach, M. A. *Risk-taking: study in cognition and personality.* New York: Holt, Rinehart & Winston, 1964.

Kolb, D. Achievement motivation training for underachieved high-school boys. *Journal of Personality and Social Psychology,* 1965, *2,* 783–792.

Krasner, L., Knowles, J. B., & Ullman, L. P. Effects of verbal conditioning of attitudes on subsequent motor performance. *Journal of Personality and Social Psychology,* 1965, *1,* 407–412.

Kreitler, H., & Bornstein, S. Some aspects of the interaction of psychodrama and group psychotherapy. *Group Psychotherapy,* 1958, *11,* 332–337.

Kreitler, H., & Elblinger, S. Individual psychotherapy, group psychotherapy, psychodrama. In J. H. Masserman & J. L. Moreno (Eds.), *Progress in psychotherapy.* Vol. 5. New York: Grune and Stratton, 1960.

Kreitler, H., & Kreitler, S. Modes of action in the psychodramatic role test. *International Journal of Sociometry and Sociatry*, 1964, *4*, 10–15.

Kreitler, H. & S. *Die weltanschauliche Orientierung der Schizophrenen.* Basel & Munich: Reinhardt, 1965.

Kreitler, H., & Kreitler, S. *Die Kognitive Orientierung des Kindes.* Basel & Munich: Reinhardt, 1967. (a)

Kreitler, H., & Kreitler, S. Crucial dimensions of the attitude towards national and supra-national ideals: a study on Israeli youth. *Journal of Peace Research*, 1967, *4*, 107–124. (b)

Kreitler, H., & Kreitler, S. Unhappy memories of the happy past: studies in cognitive dissonance. *British Journal of Psychology*, 1968, *59*, 157–166. (a)

Kreitler, H., & Kreitler, S. The validation of psychodramatic behavior against behavior in life. *British Journal of Medical Psychology*, 1968, *41*, 185–192. (b)

Kreitler, H., & Kreitler, S. Cognitive orientation and defense mechanisms. RB-69-23. Princeton, N.J.: Educational Testing Service, 1969.

Kreitler, H., & Kreitler, S. The cognitive antecedents of the orienting reflex. *Schweizerische Zeitschrift für Psychologie*, 1970, Meili Festschrift, 94–105.

Kreitler, H., & Kreitler, S. The model of cognitive orientation: towards a theory of human behaviour. *British Journal of Psychology*, 1972, *63*, 9–30. (a)

Kreitler, H., & Kreitler, S. The cognitive determinants of defensive behavior. *British Journal of Social and Clinical Psychology*, 1972, *11*, 359–372. (b)

Kreitler, H., & Kreitler, S. *Psychology of the arts.* Durham, N.C.: Duke University Press, 1972. (c)

Kreitler, H., & Kreitler, S. *Meaning in thinking and action.* Academic Press, 1977 (in press).

Kreitler, S. *Symbolschoepfung und Symbolerfassung: eine experimentalpsychologische Studie.* Basel-Munich: Reinhardt, 1965.

Kreitler, S., Ensenberg, M., and Kreitler, H. The effects of meaning training on sorting, creativity, and curiosity behaviors. In preparation, 1976.

Kreitler, S., & Kreitler, H. Dimensions of meaning and their measurement. *Psychological Reports*, 1968, *23*, 1307–1329.

Kreitler, S., Kreitler, H., & Zigler, E. Cognitive orientation and curiosity. *British Journal of Psychology*, 1974, *65*, 43–52.

Kreitler, S., Kreitler, H., & Zigler, E. Probability learning and curiosity. Unpublished manuscript, Tel Aviv University, 1975.

Kreitler, S., Maguen, T., & Kreitler, H. The three faces of intolerance of ambiguity. *Archiv für die Gesamte Psychologie*, 1976 (in press).

Kreitler, S., Zigler, E., & Kreitler, H. The nature of curiosity in children. *Journal of School Psychology*, 1975, *13*, 185–200.

Kreitler, S., Shahar, A., & Kreitler, H. Cognitive orientation, type of smoker and behavior therapy of smoking. *British Journal of Medical Psychology*, 1976 (in press).

Kobelman, R., Kreitler, H., & Kreitler, S. The relation between attitudes toward cooperative behavior and actual behavior. Unpublished manuscript, Tel Aviv University, 1967.

Kuenne, K. Experimental investigation of the relation of language to transposition behavior in young children. *Journal of Experimental Psychology*, 1946, *36*, 471–490.

Kukla, A. *Cognitive determinants of achieving behavior.* Unpublished doctoral dissertation, University of California, Los Angeles, 1970.

Kutner, B., Wilkins, C., & Yarrow, P. Verbal attitudes and overt behavior involving race prejudice. *Journal of Abnormal and Social Psychology,* 1952, *47,* 649–652.

Kvasov, D. G., & Korovina, M. V. The reflex organization of perception and the proiomuscular apparatus of the analysers (of the sense organs). In L. G. Voronin, A. N. Leontiev, A. R. Luria, E. N. Sokolov, & O. S. Vinogradova (Eds.), *Orienting reflex and exploratory behavior.* Moscow: Publishing House of the Academy of Pedagogical Sciences of RSFSR, 1958.

Kyburg, H. E., Jr., & Smokler, H. E. (Eds.), *Studies in subjective probability.* New York: Wiley, 1964.

Lagutina, N. I. On the question of structure of orienting reflexes. In L. G. Voronin, A. N. Leontiev, A. R. Luria, E. N. Sokolov, & O. S. Vinogradova (Eds.), *Orienting reflex and exploratory behavior.* Moscow: Publishing House of the Academy of Pedagogical Sciences of RSFSR, 1958.

Lake, D. G., Miles, M. B., & Earle, R. B. (Eds.), *Measuring human motivation.* New York: Teachers College Press, 1973.

Lakoff, G. Presupposition and relative well-formedness. In D. D. Steinberg & L. A. Jakobovits (Eds.), *Semantics.* Cambridge, England: Cambridge University Press, 1971.

LaPiere, R. T. Attitudes versus actions. *Social Forces,* 1934–5, *13,* 230–237.

Lashley, K. S. The problem of serial order in behavior. In L. A. Jeffress (Ed.), *Cerebral mechanisms in behavior, the Hixon symposium.* New York: Wiley, 1951.

Lashley, K. S. In F. A. Beach, D. O. Hebb, C. T. Morgan & H. W. Nissen (Eds.), *The neuropsychology of Lashley.* New York: McGraw-Hill, 1960.

Lazarus, R. S. *Psychological stress and the coping process.* New York: McGraw-Hill, 1966.

Lazarus, R. S. Emotions and adaptation: conceptual and empirical relations. In W. J. Arnold (Ed.), *Nebraska symposium on motivation.* Lincoln: University of Nebraska Press, 1968.

Leech, G. N. *Towards a semantic description of English.* Bloomington: Indiana University Press, 1970.

Lefcourt, H. M. Internal versus external control of reinforcement: a review. *Psychological Bulletin,* 1966, *65,* 206–220.

Lent, R. H. Prejudice and the perception of race. Unpublished doctoral dissertation, Harvard University, 1960.

Levinson, D. J., & Sanford, R. N. A scale for the measurement of anti-Semitism. *Journal of Psychology,* 1944, *17,* 339–370.

Lewin, K. *A dynamic theory of personality: selected papers.* New York: McGraw-Hill, 1935.

Lewin, K. The conceptual representation and measurement of psychological forces. *Contributions to Psychological Theory,* 1, no. 4. Durham, N.C.: Duke University Press, 1938.

Lewin, K. Intention, will and need. In D. Rapaport, *Organization and pathology of thought.* New York: Columbia University Press, 1951.

Lewis, M. Individual differences in the measurement of early cognitive growth. In J. Hellmuth (Ed.), *Exceptional infant.* Vol. 2. Bainbridge Island, Wash.: Brunner-Mazel, 1970.

Likert, R. A technique for the measurement of attitudes. *Archives of Psychology,* 1932, *22,* 5–55.

Lindsay, P. H., & Norman, D. A. *Human information processing: an introduction to psychology.* New York: Academic Press, 1972.

Lindsley, D. B. Emotion. In S. S. Stevens (Ed.), *Handbook of experimental psychology.* New York: Wiley, 1951.

Linn, L. S. Verbal attitudes and overt behavior: a study of racial discrimination. *Social Forces,* 1965, *43,* 353–364.

Lisak, M. Patterns of stratification and mobility aspirations. *Megamot,* 1967, *15,* 67–82 (Hebrew).

Littig, L. W. Effects of motivation on probability preferences. *Journal of Personality,* 1963, *31,* 417–427.

Locke, E. A., Cartledge, N., & Koeppel, J. Knowledge of results: a goalsetting phenomenon? *Psychological Bulletin,* 1968, *6,* 474–485.

Longstreth, L. E. A cognitive interpretation of secondary reinforcement. In J. K. Cole (Ed.), *Nebraska Symposium on Motivation.* Vol. 19. Lincoln: Nebraska University Press, 1971.

Lorenz, K. Innate bases of learning. In K. Pribram (Ed.), *On the biology of learning.* New York: Harcourt Brace Jovanovich, 1969.

Luce, R. D., & Raiffa, H. *Games and decisions.* New York: Wiley, 1957.

Lunzer, E. A. *The regulation of behavior.* London: Staples, 1968.

Luria, A. R. The directive function of speech in development and dissolution. *Word,* 1959, *15,* 341–352.

Luria, A. R. *The role of speech in the regulation of normal and abnormal behavior.* New York: Pergamon, 1961.

Luria, A. R. *The mentally retarded child.* Oxford: Pergamon, 1963.

Luria, A. R., & Homskaya, E. D. Disturbance in the regulative role of speech with frontal lobe lesions. In J. M. Warren & K. Akert (Eds.), *The frontal granular cortex and behavior.* New York: McGraw-Hill, 1964.

Luria, A. R., & Vinogradova, O. S. An objective investigation of the dynamics of semantic systems. *British Journal of Psychology,* 1959, *50,* 89–105.

Lutzker, D. R. Internationalism as a predictor of cooperative behavior. *Journal of Conflict Resolution,* 1960, *4,* 426–430.

Lynn, R. Russian theory and research on schizophrenia. *Psychological Bulletin,* 1963, *60,* 486–498.

Lynn, R. *Attention, arousal and the orientation reaction.* London: Pergamon, 1966.

McArthur, L. A., Kiesler, C. A., & Cook, B. P. Acting on an attitude as a function of self-percept and inequity. *Journal of Personality and Social Psychology,* 1969, *12,* 295–302.

McCawley, J. D. The role of semantics in a grammar. In E. Back & R. Harms (Eds.), *Universals in linguistic theory.* New York: Holt, Rinehart & Winston, 1968.

McClelland, D. C. *Personality.* New York: Dryden, 1951.

McClelland, D. C. The psychology of mental content reconsidered. *Psychological Review,* 1955, *62,* 297–302.

McClelland, D. C. Risk-taking in children with high and low need for achievement. In J. W. Atkinson (Ed.), *Motives in fantasy, action and society.* Princeton, N.J.: Van Nostrand, 1958.

McClelland, D. C. Toward a theory of motive acquisition. *American Psychologist,* 1965, *20,* 321–333.

McClelland, D. C., Atkinson, J. W., Clark, R. A., & Lowell, E. L. *The achievement motive.* New York: Appleton-Century-Crofts, 1953.

McClelland, D. C., & Winter, D. G. *Motivating economic achievement.* New York: Free Press, 1969.

McClintock, C. G. , Harrison, A., Strand, S., & Gullo, P. Internationalism–isolationism, strategy of the other player and two person game behavior. *Journal of Abnormal and Social Psychology*, 1963, 67, 631–635.

McFarland, J. W., Gimbel, H. W., Donald, W. A. J., & Folkenberg, E. J. The five-day program to help individuals stop smoking. *Connecticut Medicine*, 1964, 28, 885–891.

McGee, H. M. Measurement of authoritarianism and its relation to teachers' classroom behavior. *Genetic Psychology Monographs*, 1955, 52, 89–146.

McGuire, W. J. A syllogistic analysis of cognitive relationships. In C. Hovland & M. Rosenberg (Eds.), *Attitude organization and change*. New Haven: Yale University Press, 1960.

McGuire, W. J. Suspiciousness of experimenter's intent. In R. Rosenthal & R. L. Rosnow (Eds.), *Artifact in behavioral research*. New York: Academic Press, 1969.

MacKay, D. M. The informational analysis of questions and commands. In W. Buckley (Ed.), *Modern system research for the behavioral scientist*. Chicago: Aldine, 1968.

McKeachie, W. J. Motivation, teaching methods, and college learning. In M. R. Jones (Ed.), *Nebraska symposium on motivation*. Vol. 9. Lincoln: University of Nebraska Press, 1961.

McKellar, P. Imagery from the standpoint of introspection. In P. E. Sheehan (Ed.), *The function and nature of imagery*. New York: Academic Press, 1972.

McNeill, D. A. A study of word association. *Journal of Verbal Learning and Verbal Behavior*, 1966, 5, 548–557.

McNeill, D. *The acquisition of language*. New York: Harper & Row, 1970.

McKennel, A. C. Smoking motivation factors. *British Journal of Social and Clinical Psychology*, 1970, 9, 8–22.

McReynolds, P., Acker, M., & Pietila, C. Relation of object curiosity to psychological adjustment in children. *Child Development*, 1961, 32, 393–400.

Mackworth, J. F. *Vigilance and habituation: a neuropsychological approach*. Harmondsworth, England: Penguin Books, 1969.

Maher, R. A., Watt, N., & Campbell, D. T. Comparative validity of two projective and two structured attitude tests in a prison population. *Journal of Applied Psychology*, 1960, 44, 284–288.

Malof, M., & Lott, A. J. Ethnocentrism and the acceptance of Negro support in a group pressure situation. *Journal of Abnormal and Social Psychology*, 1962, 65, 254–258.

Maltzman, I., & Mandell, M. P. The orienting reflex as a predictor of learning and performance. *Journal of Experimental Research in Personality*, 1968, 3, 99–106.

Maltzman, I., & Raskin, D. C. Effects of individual differences in the orienting reflex on conditioning and complex processes. *Journal of Experimental Research in Personality*, 1965, 1, 1–16.

Mandler, G. Response factors in human learning. *Psychological Review*, 1954, 61, 235–244.

Mandler, G. From association to structure. *Psychological Review*, 1962, 69, 415–427.

Mandler, G. The interruption of behavior. In D. Levine (Ed.), *Nebraska Symposium on motivation*. Lincoln: University of Nebraska Press, 1964.

Mandler, G. Organization and memory. In K. W. Spence & J. T. Spence (Eds.), *The psychology of learning and motivation*. Vol. 1. New York: Academic Press, 1967.

Mandler, G. Association and organization: facts, fancies and theories. In T. R. Dixon & D. C. Horton (Eds.), *Verbal behavior and general behavior theory*. Englewood Cliffs, N.J.: Prentice-Hall, 1968.

Mandler, G. Anxiety and the interruption of behavior. In C. D. Spielberger (Ed.), *Anxiety and behavior*. New York: Academic Press, 1966.

Mandler, G., & Sarason, S. B. A study of anxiety and learning. *Journal of Abnormal and Social Psychology*, 1952, 47, 166–173.

Marshall, G. R., & Cofer, C. N. Associative indices as measures of word-relatedness —a summary and comparison of ten methods. *Journal of Verbal Learning and Verbal Behavior*, 1963, 1, 408–421.

Marston, A. R., & McFall, R. M. Comparison of behavior modification approaches to smoking reduction. *Journal of Consulting and Clinical Psychology*, 1971, 36, 153–162.

Martin, R. M. On connotation and attribute. *Journal of Philosophy*, 1964, 61, 711–724.

Mason, M. Changes in the galvanic skin response accompanying reports of changes in meaning during oral repetition. *Journal of General Psychology*, 1941, 25, 353–401.

Maw, W. H., & Maw, E. W. An exploratory investigation into the measurement of curiosity in elementary school children. CRP 801. Washington, D.C.: U.S. Office of Education, 1964.

Maw, W. H., & Maw, E. W. Personal and social variables differentiating children with high and low curiosity. CRP 1511. Washington, D.C.; U.S. Office of Education, 1965.

Max, L. W. Experimental study of the motor theory of consciousness: IV. Action current responses in the deaf during awakening, kinesthetic imagery and abstract thinking. *Journal of Comparative Psychology*, 1937, 24, 301–344.

Medinnus, G. R. Behavioral and cognitive measures of conscience development. *Journal of Genetic Psychology*, 1966, 109, 147–150.

Mehrabian, A. Male and female scales of the tendency to achieve. *Educational and Psychological Measurement*, 1968, 28, 493–502.

Meili, R. *Analytischer Intelligenztest (AIT)*. Bern & Stuttgart: Huber, 1966.

Melzack, R., & Wall, P. D. Pain mechanisms: new theory. *Science*, 1965, 150, 971–979.

Metzner, H., & Mann, F. Employee attitudes and absences. *Personnel Psychology*, 1953, 6, 467–485.

Miller, A. G. Role playing: An alternative to deception? A review of the evidence. *American Psychologist*, 1972, 27, 623–636.

Miller, D. C. *Handbook of research design and social measurement* (2nd ed.). New York: David McKay, 1970.

Miller, G. A. What is information measurement? *American Psychologist*, 1953, 8, 3–11.

Miller, G. A. A psychological method to investigate verbal concepts. *Journal of Mathematical Psychology*, 1969, 6, 161–191.

Miller, G. A. English verbs of motion: a case study in semantics and lexical memory. In A. W. Melton & E. Martin (Eds.), *Coding processes in human memory*. Washington, D.C.: V. H. Winston & Sons, 1972.

Miller, G. A., Galanter, E., & Pribram, K. H. *Plans and the structure of behavior*. New York: Holt, Rinehart & Winston, 1960.

Miller, G. A., & Frick, F. C. Statistical behavioristics and sequences of responses. *Psychological Review*, 1949, 56, 311–324.

Miller, J. The rate of conditioning of human subjects to single and multiple conditioned stimuli. *Journal of General Psychology*, 1939, 20, 399–408.

Miller, J. G. Living systems: basic concepts. *Behavioral Science*, 1965, 10, 193–237. (a)

Miller, J. G. Living systems: cross-level hypotheses. *Behavioral Science*, 1965, 10, 380–411. (b)

Miller, R. B. Handbook of training and equipment design. *WADC Technical Report*, 1953, 53–136.

Milner, B. Some effects of frontal lobectomy in man. In J. M. Warren & K. Akert (Eds.), *The frontal granular cortex and behavior*. New York: McGraw-Hill, 1964.

Milner, P. M. *Physiological psychology*. New York: Holt, Rinehart & Winston, 1970.

Minuchin, P. Correlates of curiosity and exploratory behavior in preschool disadvantaged children. *Child Development*, 1971, 42, 939–950.

Mischel, W., & Staub, E. Effects of expectancy on working and waiting for larger rewards. *Journal of Personality and Social Psychology*, 1965, 2, 625–633.

Mitchell, J. V. An analysis of the factorial dimensions of the achievement motivation construct. *Journal of Educational Psychology*, 1961, 52, 179–182.

Montague, J. D., & Coles, E. M. Mechanism and measurement of the galvanic skin response. *Psychological Bulletin*, 1966, 65, 261–279.

Moray, N. *Attention: selective processes in vision and hearing*. London: Hutchinson Educational, 1969. (a)

Moray, N. *Listening and attention*. Harmondsworth, England: Penguin, 1969. (b)

Moreno, J. L. *Psychodrama*. Vols. 1 & 2. New York: Beacon House, 1946, 1959.

Mossin, A. C. *Selling performance and contentment in relation to school background*. New York: Columbia University Teachers' College, Bureau of Publications, 1949.

Moulton, R. W. Effects of success and failure on level of aspiration as related to achievement motives. *Journal of Personality and Social Psychology*, 1965, 1, 339–406.

Natsoulas, T. Concerning introspective "knowledge." *Psychological Bulletin*, 1970, 73, 89–111.

Neisser, U. *Cognitive psychology*. New York: Appleton-Century-Crofts, 1967.

Nettler, G., & Golding, E. H. The measurement of attitudes toward the Japanese in America. *American Journal of Sociology*, 1946, 52, 31–40.

Newcomb, T. M. Individual systems of orientation. In S. Koch (Ed.), *Psychology: a study of a science*. Vol. 3. New York: McGraw-Hill, 1959.

Newell, A., & Simon, H. A. *Human problem solving*. Englewood Cliffs, N.J.: Prentice-Hall, 1972.

Nisbett, R. E., & Schachter, S. The cognitive manipulation of pain. *Journal of Experimental Social Psychology*, 1966, 2, 227–236.

Nisbett, R. E., & Valins, S. *Perceiving the causes of one's own behavior*. New York: General Learning Press, 1971.

Noble, C. E. An analysis of meaning. *Psychological Review*, 1952, 59, 421–430.

Norman, D. A. *Memory and attention: an introduction to human information processing*. New York: Wiley, 1969.

Norman, D. A. (Ed.), *Models of human memory*. New York: Academic Press, 1970.

Null, E. J., & Smead, W. H. Relationships between the political orientation of superintendents and their leader behavior as perceived by superordinates and their leader behavior as perceived by subordinates. *Journal of Educational Research*, 1971, 65, 103–106.

Oelke, M. C. A study of teachers' attitudes towards children. *Journal of Educational Psychology*, 1956, 47, 193–196.

Ogden, R. M. Imageless thought: résumé and critique. *Psychological Bulletin*, 1911, 8, 183–197.

Ogden, R. M., & Richards, I. A. *The meaning of meaning*. London: Routledge and Kegan Paul, 1949.

Öhman, S. Theories of the linguistic field. *Word*, 1953, 9, 123–134.

Okabe, T. An experimental study of disbelief. *American Journal of Psychology*, 1910, 21, 563–596.

Osgood, C. E. *Interpersonal verbs and interpersonal behavior*. Technical Report No. 64 (68–9). Urbana, Ill.: Group Effectiveness Research Laboratory, 1968.

Osgood, C. E., Saporta, S., & Nunnally, J. C. Evaluative assertion analysis. *Litera*, 1956, 3, 47–102.

Osgood, C. E., Suci, G. J., & Tannenbaum, P. H. *The measurement of meaning*. Urbana, Ill.: Illinois University Press, 1958.

Osgood, C., & Tannenbaum, P. The principle of congruity in the prediction of attitude change. *Psychological Review*, 1955, 62, 42–55.

Ovsiankina, M. Die Wiederaufnahme von unterbrochenen Handlungen. *Psychologische Forschung*, 1928, 11, 302–389.

Paivio, A. A theoretical analysis of the role of imagery in learning and memory. In P. E. Sheehan (Ed.), *The function and nature of imagery*. New York: Academic Press, 1972.

Palmer, R. D. Patterns of defensive response to threatening stimuli: antecedents and consistency. *Journal of Abnormal Psychology*, 1968, 73, 30–36.

Paramanova, I. P. Influence of extinction and recovery of the orienting reflex on development of conditioned connections. In L. G. Voronin, A. N. Leontiev, A. R. Luria, E. N. Sokolov, & O. S. Vinogradova (Eds.), *Orienting reflex and exploratory behavior*. Moscow: Publishing House of the Academy of Pedagogical Sciences of RSFSR, 1958.

Parry, H. J., & Crossley, H. M. Validity of responses to survey questions. *Public Opinion Quarterly*, 1950, 14, 61–80.

Parsons, T., Shils, E. A., & Olds, J. Values, motives and systems of action. In T. Parsons & E. A. Shils (Eds.), *Toward a general theory of action*. Cambridge, Mass.: Harvard University Press, 1951.

Patchen, M. Some questionnaire measures of employee motivation and morale: A report on their reliability and validity. Monograph 41. Ann Arbor: Michigan Institute for Social Research, 1965.

Pavlov, I. P. *Conditioned reflexes*. Oxford: Clarendon, 1927.

Peirce, C. S. *The collected papers of . . .* (Vols. 1–6 edited by C. Hartshorne and P. Weiss, Vols. 7–8 edited by A. W. Burks). Cambridge, Mass.: Harvard University Press, 1931–35; 1958.

Penfield, W. The cerebral cortex in man. *Archives of Neurology and Psychiatry*, 1938, 40, 417–442.

Penney, R. K. Reactive curiosity and manifest anxiety in children. *Child Development*, 1965, 36, 697–702.

Perfetti, C. A. A study of denotative similarity with restricted word associations. *Journal of Verbal Learning and Verbal Behavior*, 1967, 6, 778–795.

Petrie, A. *Individuality in pain and suffering*. Chicago: University of Chicago Press, 1967.

Piaget, J. *Language and thought of the child*. London: Routledge and Kegan Paul, 1948.

Piaget, J. *Traité de logique*. Paris: Colin, 1949.

Piaget, J., & Inhelder, B. *The child's conception of space*. London: Routledge and Kegan Paul, 1956.

Pillsbury, W. B. Meaning and image. *Psychological Review*, 1908, *15*, 150–158.

Polanyi, M. *The tacit dimension*. Garden City, N.Y.: Doubleday, 1966.

Pollack, I. Action selection and the Yntema-Torgerson "Worth" function. Paper read at the meetings of the Eastern Psychological Association, 1962.

Porier, G., & Lott, A. J. Galvanic skin responses and prejudice. *Journal of Personality and Social Psychology*, 1967, *5*, 253–259.

Powell, A. Alternative measures of locus of control and the prediction of academic performance. *Psychological Reports*, 1971, *29*, 47–50.

Pribram, K. H. A review of theory in physiological psychology. *Annual Review of Psychology*, 1960, *11*, 1–40.

Pribram, K. H. The limbic systems, efferent control of neural inhibition and behavior. In W. R. Adey & T. Tokizane (Eds.), *Progress in Brain Research*. Vol. 27. Amsterdam: Elsevier, 1967.

Pribram, K. H. The four R's of remembering. In K. H. Pribram (Ed.), *On the biology of learning*. New York: Harcourt, Brace & World, 1969.

Pribram, K. H. *Languages of the brain: experimental paradoxes and principles in neuropsychology*. Englewood Cliffs, N.J.: Prentice-Hall, 1971.

Pribram, K. H., Spinelli, D. N., & Kamback, M. C. Electrocortical correlates of stimulus response and reinforcement. *Science*, 1967, *157*, 94–96.

Price, H. H. *Belief*. London: George Allen & Unwin, 1969.

Pulos, L., & Spilka, B. Perceptual selectivity, memory, and anti-Semitism. *Journal of Abnormal and Social Psychology*, 1961, *62*, 690–692.

Pyle, W. H. An experimental study of expectation. *American Journal of Psychology*, 1909, *20*, 530–569.

Quillian, M. R. Word concepts: a theory and simulation of some basic semantic capabilities. *Behavioral Science*, 1967, *12*, 410–430.

Quillian, M. R. Semantic memory. In M. Minsky (Ed.), *Semantic information processing*. Cambridge, Mass.: M.I.T. Press, 1968.

Rapaport, D. *Diagnostic psychological testing*. Vol. 1. Chicago, Ill.: Yearbook Publications, 1945.

Rapaport, D. *Collected papers*. New York: Basic Books, 1967.

Raynor, J. O. Relationships between achievement-related motives, future orientation, and academic performance. *Journal of Personality and Social Psychology*, 1970, *15*, 28–33.

Raynor, J. O., & Smith, C. P. Achievement-related motives and risk taking in games of skill and chance. Princeton University, 1965 (mimeographed paper).

Raz, A., Kreitler, H., & Kreitler, S. Actual behavior, role-playing behavior and paper and pencil behavior. Unpublished manuscript, Tel Aviv University, 1976.

Razran, G. Conditioned responses: an experimental study and a theoretical analysis. *Archives of Psychology*, 1935, *28* (Whole No. 190).

Razran, G. Evolutionary psychology: levels of learning—and perception and thinking. In B. Wolman (Ed.), *Scientific psychology: principles and approaches*. New York: Basic Books, 1965.

Razran, G. *Mind in evolution: an East-West synthesis of learned behavior and cognition*. Boston: Houghton Mifflin, 1971.

Reitman, W. R. *Cognition and thought.* New York: Wiley, 1965.

Robinson, J. P., Athanasiou, R., & Head, K. B. (Eds.), *Measures of occupational attitudes and occupational characteristics.* (Appendix A to Measures of political attitudes). Ann Arbor: Institute for Social Research, University of Michigan, 1969.

Robinson, J. P., Rusk, J. G., & Head, K. B. (Eds.), *Measures of political attitudes.* Ann Arbor: Institute for Social Research, University of Michigan, 1968.

Robinson, J. P., & Shaver, P. B. (Eds.), *Measures of social psychological attitudes.* Ann Arbor: Institute for Social Research, University of Michigan, 1969.

Robinson, J. S., Brown, L. T., & Hayes, W. H. Test of effects of past experience on perception. *Perceptual and Motor Skills,* 1964, *18,* 953–956.

Robinson, W. P. The achievement motive, academic success, and intelligence test score. *British Journal of Social and Clinical Psychology,* 1964, *4,* 98–103.

Rogers, C. R. A theory of therapy, personality and interpersonal relationships, as developed in the client-centered framework. In S. Koch (Ed.), *Psychology: a study of a science.* Vol. 3. New York: McGraw-Hill, 1959.

Rokeach, M. *Beliefs, attitudes and values: a theory of organization and change.* San Francisco: Jossey-Bass, 1968.

Rokeach, M. *The nature of human values.* New York: Free Press, 1973.

Rokeach, M., & Mezei, L. Race and shared belief as factors in social choice. *Science,* 1966, *151,* 167–172.

Rokeach, M., & Rothman, G. The principle of belief congruence and the congruity principle as models of cognitive interaction. *Psychological Review,* 1965, *72,* 128–172.

Rosen, B., & Komorita, S. S. Attitudes and action: the effects of behavioral intent and perceived effectiveness of acts. *Journal of Personality,* 1971, *39,* 189–203.

Rosen, B. C. The achievement syndrome: A psychocultural dimension of social stratification. *American Sociological Review,* 1956, *21,* 203–211.

Rosenberg, M. J. Cognitive structure and attitudinal affect. *Journal of Abnormal and Social Psychology,* 1956, *53,* 367–372.

Rosenberg, M. J. An analysis of affective-cognitive consistency. In M. J. Rosenberg et al. *Attitude organization and change.* New Haven: Yale University Press, 1960.

Rosenberg, M. J., & Hovland, C. I. An analysis of cognitive balance. In M. J. Rosenberg et al. *Attitude organization and change.* New Haven: Yale University Press, 1960.

Rosenberg, M. J., Hovland, C. I., McGuire, W. J., Abelson, R. P., & Brehm J. W. *Attitude organization and change.* New Haven: Yale University Press, 1960.

Rotter, J. B., & Wickens, D. W. The consistency and generality of ratings of social aggressiveness made from observation of role-playing situations. *Journal of Consulting Psychology,* 1948, *12,* 234–239.

Rotter, J. B., Chance, J. E., & Phares, E. J. *Applications of a social learning theory of personality.* New York: Holt, Rinehart & Winston, 1972.

Rotter, J. B. Beliefs, social attitudes and behavior: a social learning analysis. In Rotter, J. B., Chance, J. E., & Phares, E. J. *Applications of a social learning theory to personality.* New York: Holt, Rinehart & Winston, 1972.

Rumelhart, D. E., Lindsay, P. H., & Norman, D. A. A process model for long-term memory. In E. Tulving & W. Donaldson (Eds.), *Organization of memory.* New York: Academic Press, 1972.

Ryan, T. A. *International behavior: an approach to human motivation.* New York: Ronald Press, 1970.

Saenger, G., & Gilbert, E. Customer reactions to the integration of negro sales personnel. *International Journal of Opinion and Attitude Research*, 1950, *4*, 57–76.

Sarason, I. G. Empirical findings and theoretical problems in the use of anxiety scales. *Psychological Bulletin*, 1960, *57*, 403–517.

Sarason, S. B. The measurement of anxiety in children: some questions and problems. In C. D. Spielberger (Ed.), *Anxiety and behavior*. New York: Academic Press, 1966.

Sarbin, T. R. A contribution to the study of actuarial and individual methods of prediction. *American Journal of Sociology*, 1942, *48*, 593–602.

Sarbin, T. R. Imagining as muted role-taking: a historical-linguistic analysis. In P. E. Sheehan (Ed.), *The function and nature of imagery*. New York: Academic Press, 1972.

Sarbin, T. R., Taft, R., & Bailey, D. E. *Clinical inference and cognitive theory*. New York: Holt, Rinehart & Winston, 1960.

Scandura, J. M. Role of rules in behavior: toward an operational definition of what (rule) is learned. *Psychological Review*, 1970, *77*, 516–533.

Schachter, S. The interaction of cognitive and physiological determinants of emotional state. In L. Berkowitz (Ed.), *Advances in experimental social psychology*. Vol. 1. New York: Academic Press, 1964.

Schachter, S. Cognitive effects on bodily functioning: studies of obesity and eating. In D. C. Glass (Ed.), *Neurophysiology and emotion*. New York: Rockefeller University Press & Russell Sage Foundation, 1967.

Schachter, S., & Singer, J. E. Cognitive, social and physiological determinants of emotional state. *Psychological Review*, 1962, *69*, 379–399.

Schaefer, E. S., & Bell, R. Q. Development of a parental attitude research instrument. *Child Development*, 1958, *29*, 339–361.

Scheibe, K. E. *Beliefs and values*. New York: Holt, Rinehart & Winston, 1970.

Schermann, A. Cognitive goals in the nursery school. *Child Study*, 1966, *28*, 109.

Schmidt, S. J. *Texttheorie*. Munich: Wilhelm Fink, 1973.

Schoeffler, M. S. Probability of responses to compounds of discriminated stimuli. *Journal of Experimental Psychology*, 1954, *48*, 323–329.

Schroder, H. M., Driver, M. J., & Streufert, S. *Human information processing*. New York: Holt, Rinehart, & Winston, 1967.

Schwartz, S. H. Moral decision making and behavior. In J. R. Macaulay & L. Berkowitz (Eds.), *Altruism and helping behavior*. New York: Academic Press, 1970.

Sears, R. R., Maccoby, E. E., & Levin, H. *Patterns of child rearing*. New York: Harper & Row, 1957.

Seeman, N. Alienation and social learning in a reformatory. *American Journal of Sociology*, 1963, *69*, 270–284.

Selfridge, O. G. Pandemonium: a paradigm for learning. In *Symposium on the mechanisation of thought processes*. London: HM Stationery Office, 1959.

Shallice, T. Dual functions of consciousness. *Psychological Review*, 1972, *79*, 383–393.

Sharpless, S., & Jasper, H. Habituation of the arousal reaction. *Brain*, 1956, *79*, 655–680.

Shaw, M. C. Need achievement scales as predictors of academic success. *Journal of Educational Psychology*, 1961, *52*, 282–285.

Shaw, M. C. Definitions and identification of academic underachievers. In J. L. French (Ed.), *Educating the gifted*. New York: Holt, Rinehart & Winston, 1964.

Shaw, M. C., & McOwen, J. T. The onset of underachievement in bright children. *Journal of Educational Psychology*, 1960, *51*, 103–108.

Shaw, M. E., & Wright, J. M. *Scales for the measurement of attitudes.* New York: McGraw-Hill, 1967.

Sheehan, P. E. (Ed.), *The function and nature of imagery.* New York: Academic Press, 1972.

Sheffield, F. D., Wulff, J. S., & Backer, R. Reward value of copulation without sex drive reduction. *Journal of Comparative and Physiological Psychology*, 1951, *44*, 3–8.

Shepard, R. N. On subjectively optimum selections among multi-attribute alternatives. In M. W. Shelley & G. L. Bryan (Eds.), *Human judgments and optimality.* New York: Wiley, 1964.

Shepps, F. P., & Shepps, R. R. Relationship of study habits and school attitudes to achievement in mathematics and reading. *Journal of Educational Research*, 1971, *65*, 71–73.

Sherif, C. W., & Sherif, M. *Attitude change: the social judgment-involvement approach.* Philadelphia: Saunders, 1965.

Sherif, C., Sherif, M., & Nebergall, R. *Attitude and attitude change.* Philadelphia: Saunders, 1965.

Sherif, M., & Hovland, C. I. *Social judgment: assimilation and contrast effects in communication and attitude change.* New Haven: Yale University Press, 1961.

Sherif, M., & Sherif, C. W. Attitude as the individual's own categories: the social judgment-involvement approach to attitude and attitude change. In C. W. Sherif & M. Sherif (Eds.), *Attitude, ego-involvement, and change.* New York: Wiley, 1967.

Sherrington, C. *The integrative action of the nervous system.* New Haven: Yale University Press, 1947.

Sherwood, J. Self-report and projective measures of achievement and affiliation. *Journal of Consulting Psychology*, 1966, *30*, 329–337.

Shiffrin, R. M. Memory search. In D. A. Norman (Ed.), *Models of human memory.* New York: Academic Press, 1970.

Shimberg, M. The role of kinesthesis in meaning. *American Journal of Psychology*, 1924, *35*, 167–184.

Silverstone, J. T., & Solomon, T. The long-term management of obesity in general practice. *British Journal of Clinical Practice*, 1965, *19*, 395–398.

Simon, H. A. Rational choice and the structure of the environment. *Psychological Review*, 1956, *63*, 129–138.

Simon, H. A. Motivational and emotional controls of cognition. *Psychological Review*, 1967, *74*, 29–39.

Singer, J. L. *Daydreaming.* New York: Random House, 1966.

Singer, J. L. Drives, affects, and daydreams: the adaptive role of spontaneous imagery or stimulus-independent mentation. In J. S. Antrobus (Ed.), *Cognition and affect.* Boston: Little, Brown, 1970.

Singer, J. L., & Antrobus, J. S. Daydreaming, imaginal processes, and personality: a normative study. In P. E. Sheehan (Ed.), *The function and nature of imagery.* New York: Academic Press, 1972.

Skinner, B. *Verbal behavior.* New York: Appleton-Century-Crofts, 1957.

Smith, G. H. Attitude toward Soviet Russia: I. The standardization of a scale and some distributions of scores. *Journal of Social Psychology*, 1946, *23*, 3–16.

Smith, P. C. The development of a method of measuring job satisfaction: the Cornell studies. In E. Fleishman (Ed.), *Studies in personnel and industrial psychology* (rev. ed.). Homewood, Ill.: Dorsey Press, 1967.

Smith, P. C., & Kendall, L. M. Cornell studies of job satisfaction: VI. Implications for the future. Unpublished manuscript, 1963.

Smith, W. W. *The measurement of emotion.* New York: Harcourt & Brace, 1922.

Snider, J. G., & Osgood, C. E. (Eds.), *Semantic differential technique.* Chicago, Ill.: Aldine, 1969.

Snygg, D., & Combs, A. W. *Individual behavior.* New York: Harper, 1949.

Sokolov, E. N. The orienting reflex, its structure and mechanisms. In L. G. Voronin, A. N. Leontiev, A. R. Luria, E. N. Sokolov, & O. S. Vinogradova (Eds.), *Orienting reflex and exploratory behavior.* Moscow: Publishing House of the Academy of Pedagogical Sciences of RSFSR, 1958.

Sokolov, E. N. *Perception and the conditioned reflex.* New York: Macmillan, 1963.

Sokolov, E. N. The modeling properties of the nervous system. In M. Cole & I. Maltzman (Eds.), *A handbook of contemporary Soviet psychology.* New York: Basic Books, 1969.

Sommerhoff, G. The abstract characteristics of living systems. In F. E. Emery (Ed.), *Systems thinking.* Harmondsworth, England: Penguin, 1969.

Spence, J. T. Preface. In K. W. Spence & J. T. Spence (Eds.), *The psychology of learning and motivation.* New York: Academic Press, 1967.

Spence, K. W. Cognitive factors in the extinction of conditioned eyelid response in humans. *Science,* 1963, *140,* 1224–1225.

Spiegel, R. Specific problems of communication in psychiatric conditions. In S. Arieti (Ed.), *American handbook of psychiatry.* Vol. 2. New York: Basic Books, 1959.

Spielberger, C. D., & Katzenmeyer, W. C. Manifest anxiety, intelligence, and college grades. *Journal of Consulting Psychology,* 1959, *23,* 278.

Staats, A. W. Verbal habit families, concepts, and the operant conditioning of word classes. *Psychological Review,* 1961, *68,* 190–204.

Stagner, R., Flebbe, D. R., & Wood, E. F. Working on the railroad: a study of job satisfaction. *Personnel Psychology,* 1952, *5,* 293–306.

Stanton, H., Kurt, W. B., & Litwak, E. Role-playing in survey research. *American Journal of Sociology,* 1956, *62,* 172–176.

Sternbach, R. A. *Pain.* New York: Academic Press, 1968.

Sternbach, R. A., & Tursky, B. Ethnic differences among housewives in psychophysical and skin potential responses to electric shock. *Psychophysiology,* 1965, *1,* 241–246.

Stevenson, H. W., & Zigler, E. F. Probability learning in children. *Journal of Experimental Psychology,* 1958, *56,* 185–192.

Stone, P. J., Dexter, C. D., Marshall, S. S., & Ogilvie, D. M. *The General Inquirer: a computer approach to content analysis.* Cambridge, Mass.: M.I.T. Press, 1966.

Stotland, E., & Cannon, L. K. *Social psychology: a cognitive approach.* Philadelphia: W. B. Saunders, 1972.

Streuning, E. L., & Efron, H. Y. The dimensional structure of opinions about work and the social content. *Journal of Counseling Psychology,* 1965, *12,* 316–321.

Stricker, L. J., Messick, S., & Jackson, D. N. Desirability judgments and self-reports as predictors of social behavior. *Research Bulletin 67-58.* Princeton, N.J.: Educational Testing Service, 1967.

Suarez, F., & Miller, D. C. A comprehensive inventory of sociometric and attitude scales: an inventory of measures utilized in the *American Sociological Review* 1965–1968. In D. C. Miller (Ed.), *Handbook of research design and social measurement* (2nd ed.). New York: David McKay, 1970.

Suchman, J. R. Inquiry training: building skills for autonomous discovery. *Merrill Palmer Quarterly*, 1961, 7, 147–169.

Sullivan, H. S. *Conceptions of modern psychiatry*. Washington, D.C.: William Alanson White Psychiatric Foundation, 1947.

Suppes, P. *Introduction to logic*. Princeton: Van Nostrand, 1957.

Susskind, E. C. Questioning and curiosity in the elementary school classroom. *Dissertation Abstracts*, 1970, 30, 8-B, 3879.

Sutherland, N. S. Outlines of a theory of visual pattern recognition in animals and man. In R. M. Gilbert & N. S. Sutherland (Eds.), *Animal discrimination learning*. New York: Academic Press, 1969.

Sweeney, D. R., & Fine, B. H. Pain reactivity and field dependence. *Perceptual and Motor Skills*, 1965, 21, 757–758.

Taub, E., & Berman, A. J. Movement and learning. In S. J. Freedman (Ed.), *The neuropsychology of spatially oriented behavior*. Homewood, Ill.: Dorsey, 1968.

Taylor, E. K. Manual for sales attitudes check list. Chicago, Ill.: *Science Research Associates*, 1960.

Taylor, E. K., & Hilton, A. Sales Personnel Description Form: summary of validities. *Personnel Psychology*, 1960, 13, 173–179.

Terwilliger, R. F. *Meaning and mind: a study in the psychology of language*. New York: Oxford University Press, 1968.

Thomas, K. Introduction. In K. Thomas (Ed.), *Attitudes and behavior: selected readings*. Harmondsworth, England: Penguin Books, 1971.

Thorpe, W. H. *Learning and instinct in animals*. London: Methuen, 1956.

Thorson, A. M. The relation of tongue movements to internal speech. *Journal of Experimental Psychology*, 1925, 8, 1–32.

Thurstone, L. L. (Ed.), *The measurement of social attitudes*. Chicago: University of Chicago Press, 1931.

Thurstone, L. L., & Chave, E. J. *The measurement of attitude*. Chicago: University of Chicago Press, 1929.

Tinbergen, N. The hierarchical organization of nervous mechanisms underlying instinctive behavior. *Symposium of the Society for Experimental Biology*, 1950, 4. Cambridge: Cambridge University Press.

Tinbergen, N. *The study of instinct*. Oxford: Clarendon, 1951.

Titchener, E. B. *Experimental psychology of the thought processes*. New York: Macmillan, 1909.

Tittle, C. R., & Hill, R. J. Attitude measurement and prediction of behavior: an evaluation of conditions and measurement of techniques. *Sociometry*, 1967, 30, 199–213.

Tolman, E. C. A behavioristic theory of ideas. *Psychological Review*, 1926, 33, 352–369.

Tolman, E. C. Psychology vs. immediate experience. *Philosophy of Science*, 1935, 2, 356–380.

Tomkins, S. S. Psychological model for smoking behavior. *American Journal of Public Health*, 1966, 56, 17–20.

Treisman, A. Strategies and models of selective attention. *Psychological Review*, 1969, 76, 282–299.

Triandis, H. C. Exploratory factor analyses of the behavioral component of social attitudes. *Journal of Abnormal and Social Psychology*, 1964, 68, 420–430. (a)

Triandis, H. C. Cultural influences upon cognitive processes. In L. Berkowitz (Ed.), *Advances in experimental social psychology*. Vol. 1. New York: Academic Press, 1964. (b)

Triandis, H. C., & Triandis, L. M. Some studies of social distance. In I. D. Steiner & M. Fishbein (Eds.), *Recent studies in social psychology*. New York: Holt, Rinehart & Winston, 1965.

Trier, J. *Der deutsche Wortschatz in Sinnbezirk des Verstandes*. Vol. 1. Heidelberg: C. Winter, 1931.

Tulving, E. Subjective organization in free recall of "unrelated" words. *Psychological Review*, 1962, *69*, 344–354.

Tulving, E. Episodic and semantic memory. In E. Tulving & W. Donaldson (Eds.), *Organization of memory*. New York: Academic Press, 1972.

Tulving, E., & Thomson, D. M. Encoding specificity and retrieval processes in episodic memory. *Psychological Review*, 1973, *80*, 352–373.

Tversky, A. Additivity, utility, and subjective probability. *Journal of Mathematical Psychology*, 1967, *4*, 175–201.

Tversky, A., & Krantz, D. H. Similarity of schematic faces: a test of interdimensional additivity. *Perception and Psychophysics*, 1969, *5*, 124–128.

Tydlaska, M., & Mengel, R. A scale for measuring work attitude for the MMPI. *Journal of Applied Psychology*, 1953, *37*, 474–477.

Uhlinger, C. A., & Stephens, M. W. Relation of achievement and motivation to the academic achievement of students of superior ability. *Journal of Educational Psychology*, 1960, *51*, 259–266.

Unger, S. M. Habituation of the vasoconstrictive orienting reaction. *Journal of Experimental Psychology*, 1964, *67*, 11–18.

Uphoff, W. H., & Dunnette, M. D. *Understanding the union member*. Minneapolis: University of Minnesota Press, 1956.

Valins, S. The perception and labelling of bodily changes as determinants of emotional behavior. In P. Black (Ed.), *Physiological correlates of emotion*. New York: Academic Press, 1970.

Valins, S., & Nisbett, R. E. *Attribution processes in the development and treatment of emotional disorders*. Morristown, N.J.: General Learning Press, 1971.

Van Zelst, R. H., & Kerr, W. A. Workers' attitudes towards merit rating. *Personnel Psychology*, 1953, *6*, 159–172.

Vinogradova, O. S. On the dynamics of the orienting reflex in the course of closure of a conditioned connection. In L. G. Voronin, A. N. Leontiev, A. R. Luria, E. N. Sokolov, & O. S. Vinogradova (Eds.), *Orienting reflex and exploratory behavior*. Moscow: Publishing House of the Academy of Pedagogical Sciences of RSFSR, 1958.

Vinogradova, O. S. *The orientation reaction and its neurophysiological mechanisms*. Moscow: Academy of Pedagogical Sciences of RSFSR, 1961.

Voronin, L. G., Leontiev, A. N., Luria, A. R., Sokolov, E. N., & Vinogradova, O. S. (Eds.), *Orienting reflex and exploratory behavior*. Moscow: Publishing House of the Academy of Pedagogical Sciences of RSFSR, 1958.

Vroom, V. H. Ego-involvement, job satisfaction, and job performance. *Personnel Psychology*, 1962, *15*, 159–177.

Vroom, V. H. *Work and motivation*. New York: Wiley, 1964.

Walcher, D. N., & Peters, D. L. (Eds.), *Early childhood: the development of self-regulatory mechanisms*. New York: Academic Press, 1971.

Walters, L. K., & Roach, D. Relationship between job attitudes and two forms of withdrawal from the work situation. *Journal of Applied Psychology*, 1971, *55*, 92–94.

Wanounou, V., Kreitler, S., & Kreitler, H. The effect of content and structure of meaning on thought disturbances in schizophrenics. Unpublished manuscript, Tel Aviv University, 1975.

Warner, L. G., & DeFleur, M. L. Attitude as an interactional concept: social constraint and social distance as intervening variables between attitudes and action. *American Sociological Review*, 1969, 34, 153–169.

Watson, J. B. *Psychology from the standpoint of a behaviorist.* Philadelphia: Lippincott, 1919.

Watt, N., & Maher, B. A. Prisoners' attitudes toward home and the judicial system. *Journal of Criminal Law, Criminology and Police Science*, 1958, 49, 327–330.

Weatherley, D. Anti-Semitism and the expression of fantasy aggression. *Journal of Abnormal and Social Psychology*, 1961, 62, 454–457.

Weaver, C. H. Semantic distance between students and teachers and its effect upon learning. *Speech Monographs*, 1959, 26, 273–281.

Webster, H., Sanford, N., & Freedman, M. A new instrument for studying authoritarianism in personality. *Journal of Personality*, 1955, 40, 73–84.

Weick, K. E. Processes of ramification among cognitive links. In R. P. Abelson et al. (Eds.), *Theories of cognitive consistency: a sourcebook.* Chicago: Rand McNally, 1968.

Weiner, B. The effects of unsatisfied achievement motivation on persistence and subsequent performance. *Journal of Personality*, 1969, 33, 428–442.

Weiner, B. New conceptions in the study of achievement motivation. In B. A. Maher (Ed.), *Progress in experimental personality research.* Vol. 5. New York: Academic Press, 1970.

Weiner, B. *Theories of motivation: from mechanism to cognition.* Chicago: Merkham, 1972.

Weiner, B., Frieze, I., Kukla, A., Reed, L., Rest, S., & Rosenbaum R. M. *Perceiving the causes of success and failure.* New York: General Learning Press, 1971.

Weiner, B., & Kukla, A. An attributional analysis of achievement motivation. *Journal of Personality and Social Psychology*, 1970, 15, 1–20.

Weinstock, A. R. Family environment and the development of defense and coping mechanisms. *Journal of Personality and Social Psychology*, 1967, 5, 67–75.

Weiss, P. Central versus peripheral factors in the development of coordination. *Research Publications of the Association for Research in Nervous and Mental Diseases*, 1952, 30, 3–23.

Weiss, P., Wertheimer, M., & Groesbeck, B. Achievement motivation, academic aptitude, and college grades. *Educational and Psychological Measurement*, 1959, 19, 663–666.

Wesley, E. Perseverative behavior, manifest anxiety, and rigidity. *Journal of Abnormal and Social Psychology*, 1953, 48, 129–134.

Wicker, A. W. Attitudes versus actions: the relationship of verbal and overt behavioral responses to attitude objects. *Journal of Social Issues*, 1969, 25, 41–78.

Wicker, A. W. An examination of the "other variable" explanation of attitude-behavior inconsistency. *Journal of Personality and Social Psychology*, 1971, 19, 18–30.

Wier, M. W. Developmental changes in problem-solving strategies. *Psychological Review*, 1964, 71, 473–490.

Willis, R. H., & Willis, Y. A. Role playing versus deception: An experimental comparison. *Journal of Personality and Social Psychology*, 1970, 16, 472–477.

Winer, B. J. *Statistical principles in experimental design.* New York: McGraw-Hill, 1962.

Wirt, S., Navon, S., Kreitler, H., & Kreitler, S. The relation between attitudes toward honesty in sports and actual honesty in two football teams. Unpublished manuscript, Tel Aviv University, 1966.

Wolff, B. B., Krasnegor, N. A., & Farr, R. S. Effect of suggestion upon experimental pain response parameters. *Perceptual and Motor Skills*, 1965, *21*, 675–683.

Wood, G. Organizational processes and free recall. In E. Tulving & W. Donaldson (Eds.), *Organization of memory*. New York: Academic Press, 1972.

Woodworth, R. S., & Schlosberg, H. *Experimental psychology*. London: Methuen, 1954.

Yaffe, O., Shiler, E., Kreitler, H., & Kreitler, S. The relation between attitudes and behavior with regard to renting rooms. Unpublished manuscript, Tel Aviv University, 1966.

Young, P. T. *Motivation and emotion*. New York: Wiley, 1961.

Zakay, D. Decision by meaning: a decision making model based on the cognitive orientation theory. Ph.D. dissertation submitted to Tel Aviv University, 1976.

Zaporozhets, A. V. The role of the orienting activity and of the image in the formation and performance of voluntary movements. In L. G. Voronin, A. N. Leontiev, A. R. Luria, E. N. Sokolov, & O. S. Vinogradova (Eds.), *Orienting reflex and exploratory behavior*. Moscow: Publishing House of the Academy of Pedagogical Sciences of RSFSR, 1958.

Zajonc, R. B. The process of cognitive tuning in communication. *Journal of Abnormal and Social Psychology*, 1960, *61*, 159–164.

Zborowski, M. *People in pain*. San Francisco: Jossey-Bass, 1969.

Zeigarnik, B. Über das Behalten von erledigten und unerledigten Handlungen. *Psychologische Forschung*, 1927, *9*, 1–85.

Zimbardo, P. G. *The cognitive control of motivation: the consequences of choice and dissonance*. Glenview, Ill.: Scott, Foresman, 1969.

Zimbardo, P. G., Cohen, A., Weisenberg, M., Dworkin, L. I., & Firestone, I. The control of experimental pain. In P. G. Zimbardo (Ed.), *The cognitive control of motivation*. Glenview, Ill.: Scott, Foresman, 1969.

Zimbardo, P. G., & Montgomery, K. C. The relative strengths of consummatory response in hunger, thirst and exploratory behavior. *Journal of Comparative and Physiological Psychology*, 1957, *50*, 504–508.

Zunich, M. Lower-class mothers' behavior and attitudes toward child rearing. *Psychological Reports*, 1971, *29*, 1051–1058.

Name Index

427

Subject Index

433